Keeping Christmas

KEEPING

Yuletide Traditions
in Norway and the New Land

CHRISTMAS

Kathleen Stokker

Minnesota Historical Society Press · St. Paul

©2000 by the Minnesota Historical Society. All rights reserved. No part of this book may be reproduced in any manner whatsoever without written permission, except in the case of brief quotations embodied in critical articles and reviews. For information, write to the Minnesota Historical Society Press, 345 Kellogg Boulevard West, St. Paul, MN 55102-1906.

www.mhspress.org

Manufactured in the United States of America

10 9 8 7 6 5 4 3

International Standard Book Number
ISBN 13: 978-0-87351-390-6
ISBN 10: 0-87351-390-8

♾ The paper used in this publication meets the minimum requirements of the American National Standard for Information Sciences Permanence for Printed Library materials, ANSI Z39.48-1984.

The following materials are used with the permission of their publishers or authors: recipes on page 30 from *The Norwegian Kitchen*, ed. Kjell E. Innli (Kristiansund: KOM, 1993); recipes on pages 78, 255, 257, and 259 from *Eat the Norway: Traditional Dishes and Specialties from Norwegian Cooking* by Aase Strømstad, translated by Mary Lee Nielsen (Oslo: Aschehoug, 1984); quotation on page 250 from "Lutefisk Lament," ©1978 by Don Freeburg; quotation on page 254 from "Just a Little Lefse Will Go a Long Way" by Stan Boreson and Doug Setterberg.

Library of Congress Cataloging-in-Publication Data

Stokker, Kathleen, 1946–
Keeping Christmas : Yuletide traditions in Norway and the new land / Kathleen Stokker.
p. cm.
Includes bibliographical references and index.
ISBN 0-87351-389-4 (cloth : alk. paper) —
ISBN 0-87351-390-8 (pbk. : alk. paper)
 1. Christmas — Norway — History.
 2. Norway — Social life and customs.
 3. Christmas — United States — History.
 4. Norwegian Americans — Social life and customs.
 I. Title.

GT4987.59 .S76 2000
263'.915'09481 — dc21

00-056085

Dedicated to all those who so generously shared
their yuletide stories, and to the memory of my parents,
Emily Valborg Fretheim Stokker (1908–1958)
and *George Oluf Stokker* (1906–1957),
who first taught me to keep Christmas

Preface

Thousand-year-old customs reside like a force of nature upon a peo-
ple of strong traditions even when they live under new conditions.
D. G. Ristad, "Slik holder vi jul," 1923

As modern as tomorrow, Norway is a prosperous, industrialized country increasingly attracting international attention for its admirable leadership in areas as diverse as commerce, diplomacy, and social legislation. These commendable accomplishments notwithstanding, at the core of Norway's unique identity lie centuries of folklore. To forget this distinctive heritage in the midst of its modern achievements would be to miss the country's soul.

Norway's rich folkloric heritage undergirds the country's celebration of Christmas, to which Norwegians devote unexcelled spirit and sparkle. My own curiosity about the background of their yuletide practices, along with queries from students and the general public, have prompted this book.

In truth, though, the journey that led to this book began many years before, in the 1950s Christmases of my childhood. But who knew? The Norwegian pedigree of the cone-shaped baskets loaded with hard candies hanging on our St. Paul, Minnesota, Christmas tree and even the lutefisk that accompanied the Christmas turkey received little comment, easily overshadowed by the ubiquitous wax figures of Santa, his sleigh, and caroling angels manufactured by my father's employer, Socony Mobil Oil Company.

Though my parents revered their Norwegian heritage—their various grandparents having emigrated in the 1860s and 1870s from Sogn (Flåm, Undredal, and Leikanger), Agder (Halsa), Ringerike (Ådalen), and Romerike (Skedsmo)—the two children they brought up almost a hundred years later ostensibly emerged from the American melting pot. My parents' own use of Norwegian (the language in which both had been confirmed around 1920) was by then confined to keeping exciting secrets from my brother, older by eight years, and me, especially during the time leading up to Christmas.

When both parents died in my tenth year (and their fiftieth), it seemed more likely than not that my Norwegian heritage would remain a closed book. Yet somehow their own love for the country (which neither they nor their parents had ever seen) had transplanted itself into the far recesses of my mind. For despite my initial objections to "all that Norwegian stuff" at St. Olaf College, I found myself, upon completing a chemistry degree there in 1968, planning a summer vacation to Norway before beginning graduate work in chemistry.

Going to Norway and attending the Oslo International Summer School changed all that. That short, intense summer revealed a country too compelling to leave. Fall, winter, spring, and then another summer and fall would pass before I finally returned to the States in January 1970 with all plans of graduate work in chemistry permanently replaced by thoughts of (and eventually a doctorate in) Scandinavian studies. While teaching Norwegian language and literature at Moorhead State University, St. Olaf College, the University of California at Berkeley, and Luther College, my research interest gradually turned to Norwegian folklore.

If you, like me, are drawn to the insights that folklore provides into a country's cultural identity, you will find the Norwegian Christmas particularly rewarding. Not surprisingly, a number of fine books have already appeared in Norway describing yuletide traditions: Olav Bø's *Vår norske jul* (Our Norwegian Christmas); *Jul i norsk og utenlandsk tradisjon* (Christmas traditions in Norway and abroad), by Knut Anders Berg, Liv Berit Tessem, and Kjetil Wiedswang; Anne-Lise Mellbye's *Den store juleboken for hele familien* (The big Christmas book for the entire family) and *Julen i Norge* (Christmas in Norway); and *Glædelig jul! Glimt fra julefeiringens historie* (Merry Christmas: Glimpses from the history of Christmas) by Bjarne Hodne and Anna-Marie Wiersholm. No one has previously, however, combined the study of Norwegian Christmas customs with an examination of Christmas as it developed among the Norwegian Americans.

Though the evolution of Christmas in America has received attention in two recent books (Penne Restad, *Christmas in America: A History,* and Stephen Nissenbaum, *The Battle for Christmas*), these exemplary histories deal largely with Christmas in East Coast and urban settings. The volume you hold in your hands, by contrast, focuses on settlers in the Upper Midwest. It considers a single ethnic group, whose Christmas customs it traces from the very beginnings, paying particular attention to the folk beliefs underlying the Christmas traditions practiced in both countries, past and present.

In addition to the books mentioned above, Dorothy Skårdal's *The Divided Heart* and the publications of the various *bygdelag* (organizations representing immigrants from individual regions of Norway), notably *Valdres Samband, Nord-Norge,* and *Hallingen,* have informed this work, as have the family histories and memoirs collected by the Norwegian-American Historical Association.

Supplementing these printed sources, unpublished sources of enormous value came to me by way of Liv Dahl, who kindly suggested including a questionnaire in the Sons of Norway newsletter. The questions published there and in the Norwegian newspaper *Verdens Gang* garnered insightful responses from Norwegian Americans and Norwegians alike. My profound gratitude for these replies goes as much to letter writers not specifically identified in the text as to those individually quoted and attributed there; all have helped shape the present volume.

The esteem in which many of these respondents held the Christmas annual *Jul i Vesterheimen,* for example, prompted me to read cover to cover every one of its forty-six-year issues; the result is a chapter surveying the key immigration issues addressed in its fiction. The respondents' colorful reminiscences of *julebukking* expanded my previously published research on the subject, and their enthusiastic descriptions of Christmas meals simply demanded the inclusion of a chapter on Norwegian American foodways, a treatment reinforced by Aase Strømstad's *Eat the Norway;* Astrid Karlsen Scott's *Authentic Norwegian Cooking; The Norwegian Kitchen,* edited by Kjell Innli; *The Minnesota Ethnic Food Book,* edited by Anne Kaplan, Marjorie Hoover, and Willard Moore; Marjorie Kreidberg's *Food on the Frontier;* the classic 1845 *Lærebog i de forskjellige Grene af Husholdningen* (Textbook in the various aspects of housekeeping) by Hanna Winsnes; *Minneapolis Tidende's norsk-amerikansk kogebog* (*Minneapolis Times'* Norwegian American cookbook); and other vintage Norwegian and Norwegian American cookbooks.

In addition to those printed and human resources, several other individuals deserve thanks for their help in producing this book. First, the parents of my St. Olaf classmate Unni Petersen, of Levanger, Norway, who in 1968 shared the unique pleasures of a *norsk jul* with this first-time participant. Little did I realize the seeds of later interests then being sown.

In more recent years, Midge Kjome, Darla Thorland, and Professor John Christianson, all of Decorah, Iowa, have generously provided information from their own research and observations about Christmas in Norway and in Norwegian America, as did Aud Ross Solberg, curator at the Sogn Folk Museum, Sogndal, Norway.

I am also grateful to Professors Todd Nichol of Luther Seminary (St. Paul, Minnesota), Lloyd Hustvedt of the Norwegian-American Historical Association, and James Leary of the University of Wisconsin Folklore Program for their insightful suggestions on various aspects of the manuscript. And once again I owe a tremendous debt of gratitude to the indispensable Jane Jakoubek, dean of Hanover College (Indiana), who provided (as with *Folklore Fights the Nazis*) careful readings of the manuscript in two of its earlier versions.

Finally, I acknowledge with deep gratitude the Minnesota Historical Society, which provided a research grant permitting uninterrupted work on this project during the summer of 1996, in its commodious archives and well-equipped Knight Research Suite, along with the consistently helpful guidance of its research supervisor, Debbie Miller, and the enduring support and sensitive editing skills of Ann Regan and Anne Running.

All have enriched the book you are about to begin. May it stimulate your own further engagement in the folklore of a Norwegian American Christmas.

A NOTE ABOUT NORWEGIAN ORTHOGRAPHY

As you read this book you will note that the spellings of some words vary from those you have seen elsewhere; they even vary, in differing contexts, within this book. You may encounter both *rømmegrøt* and *raummegraut*, *fattigmann* and *fattigmand*, or *brød* and *brod*. These discrepencies occur for three reasons:

A There are differences in the spoken dialects of various regions, for example *raummegraut* and *rømmegrøt*, or *helligtrekongerslys* and *heilagtrekongarsljos*, or *kumle*, *komle*, and *krumne*.

B Spelling reforms in the early twentieth century reflected the Norwegianization of the Dano-Norwegian that since the Reformation had been Norway's official written language. Thus the pastry now spelled *fattigmann* was known by the nineteenth-century immigrants as *fattigmand*, *fattigmandbakkelse*, *fattigmandbakkels*, or *fattig mands bakelse*; *vortekage* would now be spelled *vortekake*; *grød* has become *grøt*; *sødsuppe*, *søtsuppe*; and *pebberkager*, *pepperkaker*.

C Since most Norwegian Americans do not use Norwegian on a daily basis and because English orthography lacks the characters æ, ø, and å, one often sees spellings such as *brod* for *brød*, along with a variety of phonetic transcriptions of "julebukk" and other Norwegian words.

Introduction

The Norwegian Jul
Meets the American Christmas

Dear Mary,

So you would like to know what Christmas was like in my young days: It was beautiful! On Christmas Eve, with the house all scrubbed clean, we dressed up in our very best and sat down to lefse and lutefisk, rice pudding, fruit cake and all, just like they had in Norway.

Christmas Day we went to church.

On the second day of Christmas we had our "Christmas Tree" program at the church. Then I dressed up in my new Christmas dress and said my piece in the program.

For two weeks we celebrated, eating up all the cookies and Christmas goodies we had baked.

So Christmas came and went.

Love, Grandmother

Dorothy Nelson Helmke, born 1892

Preserving the Old World Christmas

During the second half of the nineteenth century, emigrating Norwegians brought to America a Christmas that had evolved through the centuries into a "splendid celebration of home and church that made a deep impression upon the hearts of [the] people."[1] Once in America, the Norwegian immigrants encountered new Christmas "traditions" that had, in fact, only recently begun. Pressed by rapidly expanding immigration and growing commercialism, America had needed its own Christmas ritual, one that could bind together the increasingly varied ethnic groups housed within the borders of the new nation. Characterized by Santa Claus, the Christmas tree, and gift giving, this uniquely American celebration evolved about the same time as the heaviest waves of Norwegian immigrants were arriving on American shores.

Because of the way these two different celebrations met, Christmas reveals better than any other aspect of Norwegian American culture the forces of evolution, preservation, and assimilation that faced the Norwegians as they made their new home on American soil. Certain Norwegian Christmas traditions remain not only the most stable of the folkways Norwegians brought to America, but also the ones through which the immigrants revealed their deepest feelings about adjusting to American culture.

Christmas helped or forced the immigrants to confront their roots. An examination of *Amerikabrev* (letters the immigrants wrote home to Norway) reveal that many immigrants communicated only at Christmastime. Even newcomers who left in the spring tended to wait until Christmas came before writing their first letter. Lloyd Hustvedt, an astute scholar of Norwegian American history, goes so far as to assert "But for Christmas, I fear that letters home [an extremely valuable source of our knowledge about the pioneers] might have been a total neglect." Regular letter writers, of course, always included a Christmas letter in their correspondence.[2]

Feeling especially nostalgic at Christmastime, the early Norwegian immigrants consciously modeled their celebration on Old World ways.[3] So much else in the New Land differed from their native Norway, but Christmas, they determined, would be celebrated in America just as they had known it at home. With great piety they set out to follow established traditions, both as a bond with their ancestors and as a heritage to pass on to their children.[4] But how could they continue these customs if they also wanted to fit into their new surroundings?

Before focusing on the intermingling of Norwegian and American Christmas traditions in the nineteenth century, I will examine in Part One the way present-day Norwegians celebrate Christmas from Advent through Epiphany, taking special note of the traditional folk beliefs and practices that underlie their modern ways. Turning attention to the Christmas that the Norwegian immigrants brought to America, I then explore in Part Two how this long-evolved Norwegian celebration confronted the newly invented American Christmas during the nineteenth and early twentieth centuries. I pay special attention to three Old Country customs that most vigorously survived in the New Land: publishing Christmas annuals (notably *Jul i Vesterheimen* [Christmas in the western home]), *julebukking* (Christmas masquerading), and enjoying traditional Norwegian holiday foods. Throughout, these chapters address the question of what the Norwegian Americans' Christmas reveals about their response to the competing pressures of preserving Old World ways and of becoming American.

The final chapter surveys the Norwegian American Christmas observances alive today, noting that far from dying out—as once seemed inevitable—the Norwegian American Christmas appears to be growing increasingly vital. The current reviving interest in family history reveals ethnicity as a dynamic process that is constantly being renegotiated.[5] In the case of Norwegian American ethnicity, I contend, its process and progress may be clearly viewed through the lens of Christmas.

Before exploring either the Norwegian or the Norwegian American Christmas, however, we must set the stage by noticing the evolution that was also taking place within the American Christmas, since this was the stage onto which the immigrants stepped as they adapted their customs to fit new circumstances.

Inventing the American Christmas

While the Norwegian Christmas had roots firmly anchored in centuries past, the American Christmas—the customs practiced by the majority culture surrounding the Norwegian immigrants—had barely begun. As late as 1832 the English actress Fanny Kemble noted in her diary: "Comparatively no observances of 'tides and times' punctuated the American year. Christmas Day is no religious day and hardly a holiday with them. New-year's day is perhaps a little more, but only a little more so. As for Twelfth-day, it is unknown."[6]

To understand the absence of Christmas observances noted by Fanny Kemble, we must go back to the nation's earliest days, when the colonial Americans, Puritans, Presbyterians, Quakers, and Baptists tried to suppress the celebration of Christmas. Finding no biblical evidence for the date of Jesus' birth, they found no reason to celebrate the day as a holiday, let alone observe it in church. Their disdain for Christmas only grew as peasant-class settlers from other European countries began arriving, bringing their Old World Christmas customs along.[7]

Characterized by prolonged and raucous festivity, these customs had arisen at the one time of the year that offered both a reduced workload and an abundance of food. For hard-laboring peasants, Christmas provided a welcome occasion to let off steam and to gorge themselves. The carnival mood that resulted permitted—even encouraged—the participants to violate the usual rules of conduct. Celebrants blackened their faces or disguised themselves as animals and members of the opposite sex; thus cloaked in anonymity, they begged for money from the prosperous. From house to house they marched while (as one contemporary described it) "shouting, singing, blowing penny-trumpets and long tin horns, beating on kettles, firing crackers, hurling missiles, etc."[8] Barging into the homes of the well-to-do, they also demanded gifts of food and drink. The upper classes participated in hopes that the workers, with this spree behind them, would put more effort into their labors the rest of the year.

Such a celebration could function in confined neighborhoods, but as the working class expanded, the wealthy felt increasingly threatened by the marauding masses. The growth of cities deepened the social inequity between rich and poor, and the revelry became the occasion for expressing class and ethnic hatred. Pressure against the chaos of the Christmas revels began to mount, as the growing middle class also felt the need of an alternative to "these disgraceful saturnalia" which, according to the observer just quoted, had only gotten worse.[9]

While the seventeenth- and eighteenth-century Puritans and Presbyterians had given up on Christmas, seeing repression as the best path of reform, Anglicans commended both the religious observance and the festive hospitality that Christmas could provide. Though they, too, viewed with alarm the holiday's "current riot and excess," they thought they should avail themselves of the festival and sought a way to "hallow the occasion" and "redeem the exultation," to perpetuate an "innocent and laudable festivity" by which people were made "more generous, virtuous and religious."[10]

Toward that end a group of wealthy, conservative New Yorkers known as the Knickerbockers met during the 1810s and 1820s. A group of High Church Episcopalians, they aimed to devise a Christmas holiday that would be celebrated at home and allow each family's children—rather than the unknown poor—to benefit from its bounty.[11] Clement Clark Moore belonged to the group, and his familiar 1822 poem "A Visit from St. Nicholas," popularly known by its first line " 'Twas the night before Christmas," played an instrumental role in transforming the American Christmas, replacing the rowdy roaming bands demanding gifts from homeowners with a benevolent man who comes to bestow them.

The St. Nick thus invented by Moore differed substantially from the one known to Europeans as the stern bishop who brought presents to the virtuous and punishment to the wicked.[12] The American creation was a jolly old elf who bore only gifts; the saint had lost his religious nature and emerged as a nondenominational folk hero.

Directly addressing the Christmas revelry to which the Knickerbockers objected, Moore's St. Nick comes like a potential reveler to the narrator's upper-class home, dressed in a fur-lined suit worthy of a street masquerade. Making a lot of "clatter," he may even intend to barge inside. Instead of posing a threat, however, he displays good cheer and changes the narrator's mood from fear to amusement, causing him to "laugh out loud in spite of [him]self." Possessing neither the power of the bishop nor the animosity of the poor, the plebeian visitor in Moore's poem engages the patrician narrator in a scene of shared festivity, showing that a celebration that satisfied both classes could be devised.[13]

Together with Santa, the Christmas tree came to characterize the American Christmas, and like Santa, the tree is a relatively recent addition. Apocryphal accounts of Martin Luther inventing it notwithstanding, the Christmas tree had existed only in rather isolated areas (notably in Strasbourg) before the late 1700s. It began spreading to the rest of Germany only after Goethe, who visited Strasbourg in 1774, described the custom in his subsequent novel, *The Sorrows of Young Werther*.[14] The first American Christmas trees appeared in Pennsylvania German settlements sometime between 1810 and 1820. Even more time passed before the Christmas tree came into general use, not until the 1830s in Germany and still later in America.

A well-known account describes the introduction of the first urban American Christmas tree during the 1830s by Charles Follen (1797–1840). A Hessian and the first professor of German at Harvard College, Follen was also an active member of the New England Anti-Slavery Society, an involvement that soon ended his academic career. Putting up a tree in his home in Cambridge in 1835, he decorated it with "seven dozen wax tapers, gilded egg cups, paper cornucopiae filled with comfits, lozenges and barley sugar."[15] Outspoken in matters of child rearing as well, Follen strongly opposed corporal punishment. He advocated the tree as a benign, nondenominational Christian icon and claimed its pedigree in a post-Reformation German tradition that portrayed the Christ child (in German, *Christkindlein;* in Pennsylvania Dutch, *Christkindl;* and later corrupted to "Kriss Kringle") personally bringing the tree into family homes.

Follen was one of many in both Europe and America who during the early 1800s began promoting new views of childhood. Recent declines in the birthrate among middle-class women caused childbirth to be regarded as a more momentous occasion and childhood as a unique period in human development. The trend toward treasuring children also brought narratives of Jesus' birth into the forefront of the Christmas celebration. Moore's St. Nick as a bringer of gifts rather than switches suited this movement well and received Follen's hearty endorsement.

Through selective reworking of older practices, nineteenth-century Americans recast Christmas to fit American culture.[16] The new holiday took hold remarkably quickly; within forty years the majority of states had declared the day a legal holiday. Between 1840 and 1870, it acquired a unified set of rituals and symbols, along with the indispensable underlying concept that all members of the increasingly heterogeneous American society could participate in it equally.

During the 1850s and 1860s magazines such as *Godey's* and *Harper's* played a vital role in familiarizing urban Americans with the new Christmas by publishing both Moore's poem and a series of drawings by the famous political cartoonist Thomas Nast (creator of such indelible national icons as the Republican elephant, the Democratic donkey, and Uncle Sam). Nast's drawings portrayed a Santa with a humorous, witty, and naively optimistic persona, which quickly became part of the emerging national folklore. Magazines also helped make the Christmas tree a visual magnet of the holiday by showing handsomely decorated evergreens surrounded by happy families.[17] These images became further standardized through the medium of Christmas cards, which came into their own among the affluent during the 1870s and 1880s, and were popular among all classes by 1910.

Shopkeepers saw the advantage of the newly invented Christmas: keeping the downtown clear of revelry brought in more customers. Encouraging the rapid adoption of the holiday, these merchants also helped determine the nature of the presents exchanged, as the increasing American focus on consumerism made the homemade gifts of the past seem inadequate.

Perhaps more than any other element, the rise of consumerism as a central feature of the American economy defined the custom of Christmas gift giving.[18] The exchange of presents at this time of year had actually begun with New Year's gifts, an ancient Roman custom that provided a solid foundation for the new practice. These New Year's gifts increasingly yielded after 1820 to Christmas presents, which by the middle decades of the nineteenth century had completely taken over. Noticing the growing role of Christmas gifts, merchants had begun as early as the 1820s, '30s, and '40s laying in additional wares to be sold during the winter season. After the Civil War, they redoubled these efforts in magnitude and intensity; what formerly had been individual initiative became the undertaking of commerce and industry.

Indeed it may have been commerce and industry that prompted the changeover from New Year's to Christmas gifts.[19] For the sake of capitalist growth, industrial efficiency, and urban order, many felt that the drawn-out Christmas season brought to America by the Europeans needed to shrink. This could be accomplished by placing the focus of the revelry earlier—on Christmas rather than New Year's.[20]

Magazine stories and their advertising promoted Christmas gift giving,[21] and so did an increasing variety of stores and services tailored to holiday shopping. The Santa image only added to the merchants' cachet—a peddler with an inexhaustible supply of gifts and the mission to transform ordinary stockings into cornucopias. This peddler Santa was a merchant just like them, all the while that his magical travel over rooftops made giving presents seem fantastic, even mystical.[22]

As commerce became more and more dependent on Christmas sales, merchants increasingly became more organized, competitive, and aggressive in their bid for the Christmas dollar.[23] And their modern methods soon brought modern-sounding complaints, such as these from the December 23, 1894, *New York Tribune:*

> The modern expansion of the custom of giving Christmas presents has done more than anything else to rob Christmas of its traditional joyousness. . . . Most people nowadays are so fagged out, physically and mentally, by the time Christmas Day arrives that they are in no condition to enjoy it. . . . As soon as the Thanksgiving turkey is eaten, the great question of buying Christmas presents begins to take the terrifying shape it has come to assume in recent years.[24]

How Fares the Norwegian Christmas?

In rural areas Norwegian Americans succeeded better at retaining their Old Country customs than did immigrants living in towns and cities. Though the hardship-plagued first years of settlement often limited their celebration to nothing more than the ritual housecleaning or a humble serving of rice porridge, improving finances eventually enabled the immigrants to slaughter, bake, and brew in the Norwegian style.[25]

Even as their attempt succeeded, however, it failed. In nineteenth-century Norway, Christmas customs varied considerably from place to place, but in America the mixture of settlers from different areas evened out the distinctions and produced a generic Norwegian celebration.[26] Even so, the resulting celebration brought enormous satisfaction. The problem was that vastly different values and practices prevailed in the surrounding majority culture. In Norway individual families were intertwined in a complicated network necessitated by preindustrial farming and fishing methods. Their close cooperation knitted the peasants into strong, strictly defined neighborhoods and created an equally interdependent social web.[27] In the new environment, where customs once shared by the entire community became a private matter, the purely Norwegian Christmas disintegrated.[28] American mobility exacerbated the breakdown. What had once been exclusively Norwegian settlements became less homogeneous, and the full complexity of the Norwegian Christmas could not be maintained. Eventually only bits and pieces remained.

The fear of appearing foolish by practicing Old World ways in public and the faster pace of American society also led to the demise of Norwegian traditions among the immigrants. They lamented the drastic reduction in the time Americans allotted to socializing during the Christmas season and made bitter and unbelieving complaints about having to work full time and even overtime on the very eve or day of Christmas. Harsh weather conditions and long distances also kept Norwegian Americans from visiting back and forth among relatives and friends, a practice still an integral part of the Norwegian Christmas.

The different attitudes and practices of the dominant Yankee culture transformed and ultimately destroyed the intricately woven tapestry of home, church, and neighborhood that had characterized the deeply meaningful holidays back home.[29] Writers of Christmas articles warned their fellow Norwegian Americans to protect their Christmas customs as "precious heirlooms" and to maintain them carefully as a "sacred trust."[30] Yet the dominant impression left by Norwegian American memoirs is the delight each family took in making its own mixture of preserved Norwegian traditions and adopted American ones, assisted by the twin goals of perpetuating the Christmas of their forefathers while quickly and seamlessly fitting into the New Land. Santa Claus, putting up a Christmas tree, and buying presents could go quite well, they found, with a lutefisk dinner preceded by the Norwegian table prayer and followed by *sandbakkels, fattigmann,* and dancing around the tree in the parlor.

PART ONE
Christmas in Norway

Everyone has had a bath and changed into clean clothes. The men and children have gone to bed. When they wake up or are awakenend, the floor is washed and strewn with sand and eine *(juniper), everyday clothes are put away, holiday clothes laid out, on the open shelf on the free-standing cupboard stand the beer tankard and* brennevin *(brandy) bottle, on the table a three-armed Christmas candle, fish (lutefisk or fresh), butter, cheese, flatbread, and yeast-raised ryebread. When we have eaten, it is midnight, and we sing the Christmas song, "Et lidet barn så lystelig" (A little child so joyously), because it is the hour of Christ's birth. We sing it three times, then we shake hands with each other—Father and Mother first, and joyous are we all, though neither Christmas tree nor Christmas gifts are present.*

Kristen, born 1860, recalling Christmas Eve in Hafslo

Roman and Viking Roots
How the Norwegian Christmas Began

There are old customs and many matters wherein care must be taken; each thing must be begun on its proper day, with due regard to all upon and under the earth. There are so many forces at work around Christmas time.

Trygve Gulbranssen, *Beyond Sing the Woods*

The midwinter celebration that has come down to us as Christmas has been reinvented innumerable times through the ages. We begin our survey of these previous incarnations by looking to ancient Rome, where the early Christian church was struggling to gain a foothold. The present-day image of Christmas as a time of supreme peace and tranquillity obscures the holiday's origins in violent religious and political strife.[1]

The Roman emperor Diocletian, like his predecessors, believed that the fate of Rome depended on its alliance with the gods. Unlike his predecessors, Diocletian initially showed tolerance toward the Christians, but he ultimately became convinced that their refusal to make sacrifices to the gods was rupturing Rome's all-important covenant with them. Beginning in 303, therefore, he rapidly issued a series of edicts to destroy churches, confiscate sacred books, imprison the Christian clergy, and compel all Christians to make animal sacrifices. Widespread suffering and death followed. Diocletian retired from office in the year 305. During the power struggle that ensued, another emperor, Galerius—who during his reign had been ruthlessly in-

tolerant of Christianity—signed on his deathbed in 311 an edict of tolera-
tion, affirming that "Christians may again exist."

Eventually Constantine became ruler of the western realm of the Roman
Empire. He firmly opposed the Christian persecution that had preceded his
rule, but continued to promote the popular custom of worshiping the Sun
God. Then, on the eve of an important battle, Constantine had a dream in
which he saw the initial letters of Christ's name (the Greek *chi* and *rho*) together with the words "By this sign you will conquer." His success in the
battle persuaded him to cast his lot with the minority cause of the Christians,
and he henceforth regarded the Christian God as the protector of the empire.
Publicly cautious, however, he continued to use the pagan title of Pontifex
Maximus and to employ the emblem of the Sun God on his coins.

Although Licinius, the ruler of the eastern realm of the Roman Empire,
took a more punitive stance toward the Christians, the two rulers met in
Milan in 313 and reached an agreement that accorded to Christianity full legal
equality with other cults and ordered the restoration of all church property
confiscated during the persecution. After this agreement, however, tensions
between the two rulers grew, and in 324 Constantine invaded Licinius's ter-
ritories and prevailed over him. Now Constantine alone ruled the empire,
and the Christian church suddenly found that the Roman emperor openly
espoused the cause of Christ.

In the peaceful period that followed, the Christian church grew rapidly
and urgently needed a systematic way to instruct scores of new converts.
Church leaders found that feast days that highlighted essential items of doctrine were an effective way to teach the tenets of the Christian religion.

Most acutely the church needed a festival to celebrate God's incarnation
as a human being. Though an Epiphany celebration (January 6) already existed to commemorate Christ's birth, that holiday lacked focus, for it also
celebrated Christ's baptism and his miraculous conversion of water to wine
at the feast of Cana. It would require a festival devoted solely to the birth
of the Christian God to provide the appeal necessary to convert the multi-
tudes still anchored in the competing religions that dramatically ritualized
the birth of their deities.

Roman Solstice Celebrations

The emerging Christian church lacked sufficient strength to suppress these competing religions, but came instead to employ an effective alternative. It adopted a policy of co-opting established Roman traditions and making them Christian.[2] During the first half of the fourth century, the bishop of Rome instituted December 25 as the day on which to celebrate Christ's birth. The day chosen was the winter solstice according to the Julian calendar then in use, which had firmly established itself among Rome's greatest festival days. Marking the change in the course of the sun, which henceforth would ascend and restore the growing season, the celebration was known as *dies natalis solis invicti* (the day of the birth of the unconquered sun). It featured torchlight processions and numerous other sun-related symbols.

Since the Roman emperor by tradition identified himself with the Sun God to underline his supremacy, the Christian church's choice of the solstice for its own celebration effectively challenged two competing religions at once: emperor worship and solar monotheism. In the solstice, moreover, church leaders found a symbol that complemented their own message of Christ as the "light of the world."[3]

The solstice itself concluded week-long revelries, known as Saturnalia, that honored Saturn, the god of agriculture. Originally a harvest festival dating back to 200 B.C., Saturnalia glorified abundance, peace, and intoxication. Its celebration inverted established patterns of behavior: masters served the choicest delicacies to their slaves, who in turn could ridicule their superiors with impunity. Saturnalia's reversal of established order, along with its celebration of abundance, peace, and intoxication, became prominent features of the Christmas celebration and remain so to this day. Placing Christmas at the time of long-ensconced celebrations helped make the Christian observance a dominant part of the culture; Christmas rapidly gained popularity as it spread, and the festival eventually reached Norway.

The Viking Jól

By the time of Norway's official conversion to Christianity (around the year 1000), Christmas had elsewhere gained a firm footing among the observances of the church. As the Christian Christmas entered Norway, however, it once again faced stiff competition from other well-established beliefs and practices. Now the major opposition came from the Vikings' rousing midwinter feast known as *jól*. Only a rough idea of this celebration can be obtained, as scholars present quite divergent pictures of the timing, purpose, and content of the Viking jól. Some emphasize its elements of ancestor worship and believe it was a celebration held for the dead, who were commonly believed to return to their former homes during the darkest nights of winter. Others believe it was a festive conclusion to the autumn slaughter and beer brewing, and they underscore the feast's symbolic practices aimed at increasing the yield of the coming year's crops. Still others believe it was a solstice celebration like those found in many cultures around the world.

What most researchers do agree upon is that ritual beer drinking figured prominently in the Viking jól. They find evidence in the writing of historian Snorri Sturluson (1179–1241), who chronicled the lives of Norway's early kings in his epic *Heimskringla*. Centuries-old oral poetry provided a principal source for his work; an example is the ninth-century "Haraldskvadet," quoted in his *Saga of Harald Fairhair* (the king who first united Norway into a single realm, around the year 900). "Haraldskvadet" recounts how this adventurous king intended to "drikke jól" out on the sea or in foreign lands. The scholars argue that the verse's use of the verb "drink" to stand for "celebrate" shows the central role beer played in the overall festival. Some believe that the celebrants who ritually passed the drinking horn from mouth to mouth sought an ecstatic connection with each other and with the gods.

Snorri further chronicles how the Viking feast was Christianized in his *Saga of Haakon the Good,* Harald Fairhair's son. He lived around 920–60 and was the first of three Norwegian kings to work for Norway's Christian conversion. According to the saga's thirteenth chapter,

> he had it established in the laws that the Yule celebration was to take place at the same time as is the custom with the Christians. And at that time everyone was to make ale for the celebration from a measure of grain, or else pay fines, and to keep the holidays while the ale lasted. Before that, Yule was celebrated on midwinter night, and for the duration of three nights.[4]

King Haakon the Good had been raised in the court of the English king Athelstan and had grown up as a Christian. Despite his upbringing and the initiatives he had taken to introduce Christian reform—such as moving the Viking jól to the date of the Christian Christmas—he reverted to paganism on his deathbed, and more than thirty years passed before Norway had another Christian king. Nevertheless, by this time, many individual Norwegians had converted. Stone crosses from the tenth century, along with other early archaeological finds, bear witness to the adoption of Christianity well before the country's official conversion.

Still, fierce opposition to Christianity met the next two missionary kings, Olav Tryggvasson and Olav Haraldsson. Both employed more violent means than Haakon, threatening those who resisted conversion with property destruction, exclusion from the kingdom, and even paralysis or death. These methods proved successful. Olav Tryggvasson, reigning from 995 to 1000, managed to convert large areas of the coast. Conversion of the inland areas followed during Olav Haraldsson's reign (from 1015 to 1028), which also saw the country's official conversion and the assembly at Moster in 1024, when the rudiments of church organization were established.

Assemblies that brought together representatives of local and regional areas to make or change laws had been held in Norway since the tenth century.[5] It was these bodies that passed the ecclesiastical laws that furthered Christianity—and not least the Christian way of celebrating Christmas—in Norway. Scholars have theorized about the nature of the Viking jól by working backward from the oldest of these Christian laws, known as the Law of Gulating (the Gulatingslov), devised at the assembly at Gula in West Norway.[6]

Not surprisingly, the Gulatingslov forbade the *blaut,* or animal sacrifice, the central cult activity of the pre-Christian religion: "Blaut is forbidden to us. We shall not make animal sacrifices to heathen gods or to grave mounds or altars. Those found guilty of doing so will forfeit every penny of their property and must go to confession and do penance. Those who refuse must leave the kingdom."[7]

Given the central position of the blaut and the Gulatingslov's ban of it, scholars have theorized that the Viking jól probably featured animal sacrifices resembling those described in Snorri's *Saga of Haakon the Good* (chapter 14): "It was ancient custom that when sacrifice was made all farmers were to come to the temple and bring along with them the food they needed while the feast lasted. At this feast all were to take part in the drinking of ale. Also all kinds of livestock were killed in connection with it."

The text of the Gulating law states: "Yet another amount of ale we have promised to make, husband and wife, with equal malt to each, according to weight, and consecrate it on Christmas night with gratitude to Christ and Saint Mary, for a good harvest and peace." ("Enda en ølgjerd har vi lovet å gjøre, husbonde og husfrue like mye malt hver, etter vekt, og signe det julenatten som takk til Kristus og Sankta Maria, til godt år og fred.")

Quoted in Andersen, Samlingen av Norge, *194*

The Gulatingslov additionally required that beer be brewed by each peasant and drunk on Christmas night in honor of Christ and the Virgin Mary while uttering the toast "Til árs ok friðar" (for good harvest and fertility and peace). The formulation "til árs ok friðar" is so intricately bound up with the Old Norse way of thinking that scholars theorize that the Viking jól featured similar toasts to the gods Frey, Odin, and Thor—toasts that the identical, attested ones to Christ and Mary merely replaced. Once again we see the Christian church following the strategy of Christianizing established practice, both to avoid resistance and to benefit from the strength of existing observances.[8]

Early Norwegian Celebrations of Christmas: Religious and Popular

Norway's conversion to Christianity occurred in three phases—individual adoption preceding the country's official adoption of the new religion and eventually the change in people's actual practices and beliefs. Crucial to the latter phase was the death of Olav Haraldsson at the Battle of Stiklestad in the year 1030. Two years earlier, Olav's subjects had expelled him from Norway and sworn allegiance to his rival, the absentee king Knut of Denmark. In one last bid to rule a united, Christian Norway, Olav returned on July 29, 1030. Confronted by an army several times the size of his own, he soon fell in battle.

Olav's story doesn't end with the Battle of Stiklestad, however. Almost immediately rumors began to circulate about miraculous occurrences at his grave. Only one year and five days after his death, Olav's body was exhumed. Bishop Grimkjell, who had instrumentally assisted Olav in converting Norway to Christianity, declared the fallen king a saint. Pilgrim throngs began streaming to Norway from all over the Christian world, giving the country greater international significance.[9] These pilgrimages also helped further Norway's Christian conversion by bringing innumerable practitioners and role models of the new religion to Norway from countries with well-established Christian traditions.

In these countries Christmas, too, had developed a well-defined character with fixed forms—some imposed by the church and some devised by the people. The religious and folk customs coexisted peacefully, with the clergy largely ignoring the folk customs as long as they didn't interfere with church attendance and financial support. The church observance encompassed a period of preparation (Advent) with extended fasting to underscore the festival's significance, a custom also adopted in Norway.

The folk Christmas celebration that accompanied Christianity to Norway had by now adopted elements of yet another Roman festival. The New Year's observance known as the Calends of January included a gift exchange, omen reading, and prognostication, all of which have remained part of Christmas festivities to this very day. Celebrants of the Calends also kept the dinner table set with food throughout the night as a way to magically increase prosperity in the coming year. This custom came to be widely practiced in Norway's preindustrial agrarian society and continues to underlie the modern practices of the pre-Christmas buffet (*julebord*) and the Christmas morning brunch (*koldtbord*).

The Gulatingslov and other medieval sources suggest that the eleventh-century Norwegian Christian Christmas consisted of a days-long family celebration. This was followed by larger *drikkelag* (drinking parties) held during a protracted period when most outside work could rest, food abounded, and family members enjoyed an unusual level of comfort. Christmas Eve and Christmas Day were probably spent quietly at home, interrupted only by attending church. Many held a vigil at midnight on Christmas Eve, said to be the hour of Christ's birth.

To maximize the potential of Christmas in teaching Christian doctrine, the church instituted three separate worship services for December 25. An Old Norse homily relates these three masses to three stages of human existence. The midnight mass signified the era before the Law when the grace that accompanied Christ's birth remained unknown to the patriarchs; it is therefore sung in darkness. The second mass, sung at the meeting of night and day, stands for the era of Law, for though Christ had not yet come, the prophets had foretold (shed light upon) his coming. The daytime mass signifies the era of grace when Christ's birth had expelled the darkness and brought eternal light.[10]

Though the customs of the Christian celebration caught on quickly in Norway, the church achieved no success in attaching the name of these masses—Kristmesse—to the observance. In fact, only in Scandinavia does the pre-Christian name of the winter solstice festival persist as the name of the Christian festival. The Old Norse word *jól,* which in later Norwegian became *jul,* occurs in Old English sources as early as the eighth century, but is probably even older; it survives in the modern English "yuletide" and "yule log." Its origin remains uncertain; some relate it to "sacrifice"; others to "wheel," alluding to the "turning of the sun," as people formerly conceived the solstice. Thus, while the Christian tradition of Christmas replaced the Viking celebration, the name itself—along with a surprising portion of its practices—remained unchanged.

In addition to the prefestival fasting (Advent) and the new worship services, the church also introduced the concept of Christmas peace, or *jule-fred.* Spelling out its conditions, another of the medieval Christian laws, the Frostatingslov (circa 1260), details a number of constraints on behavior and work designed to assure yuletide serenity. It decrees, for example, that "the Christmas holy day shall be protected from intrusion for four days and four nights," but "fodder may be collected on the fifth and sixth and seventh days, and on those mornings manure may be cleared." No marriages could be performed during Advent or the thirteen days of Christmas, and no legal business could be transacted or court cases brought; Christmas was reckoned as lasting from December 24 to either January 6 or 13 (sources disagree). King Magnus Lagabøtter's 1274 Landslov (law of the land) lengthened the peace with a decree that during the three weeks following December 4, double fines would be exacted against anyone who subjected a fellow human being to "*fiendskap* [hostility] in word or deed." Together, these restrictions altered Norway's established social routine and resulted in the unusually long abstinence from official business that still gives the Norwegian Christmas its characteristic tranquillity.

The Lutheran Reformation

Just as the Christian jul retained many features from the Viking jól when the country converted to Christianity, so, too, the celebration of Christmas remained more constant than changed when Norway abandoned Roman Catholicism to adopt Lutheranism. The official reform took place in 1537. In that year King Christian III of Denmark signed an ordinance creating the Lutheran Church in Denmark. Since he had just the year before decreed Norway a Danish province, the 1537 Danish church ordinance applied to Norway as well. (Realizing that Norwegian conditions differed from those in Denmark, the king modified the ordinance in 1539 to allow Catholic priests to retain their parishes until retirement; eventually Norway got its own ordinance in 1607.) The Lutheran church ordinances called for much of the Catholic ritual in the worship service to be abolished and replaced with an emphasis on the Word of the Bible. As a result, such recently encouraged practices as pilgrimages and vigils, the use of holy water and incense, and the veneration of saints suddenly became unlawful. (Roman Catholicism remained illegal in Norway until 1843.) The service was no longer to be in Latin, but in the language of the people, and its focus was to be on the sermon rather than the sacrificial mass.

Replacing the Catholic mass with the Lutheran service presented unique challenges in Norway.[11] Certainly the congregations—in Norway as elsewhere—must have missed the impressive ceremony of the service they had known. Celebrated by a priest in rich vestments who performed the mysterious but familiar and deeply meaningful sacrament of the Last Supper, the Latin-language Catholic mass had been accompanied by flickering candles, choral music, incense, and bell ringing. The Lutheran service, by contrast, featured a minister in a black robe whose austerity was broken only by a white ruff. In Norway, however, the goal of presenting the service in the language of the people could not be realized, for the Bible readings and sermon were in Danish, which during the 1400s had become Norway's official written language. Held in a building increasingly in need of repair (the church's former wealth having been taken over by the Crown), the early Lutheran service featured hymn singing by an untrained and largely illiterate congregation, and a sermon read by an unpracticed minister from a Danish *postill* (printed book of sermons).

The situation improved dramatically during the 1600s, when new churches were built and old ones renovated. Several elements of these churches' interiors reflected the change in worship form, especially the Lutheran emphasis on the biblical Word. Pews and a pulpit accommodated the lengthy Lutheran sermons, whose Scripture explications could fill an hour and more. (During the relatively short Catholic service, the congregation had stood.) The altarpiece no longer depicted saints; the most conservative ones displayed no figures at all, but only the painted or carved words of the Bible. Others depicted the four writers of the Gospels. Windows expanded in size and number to provide light for reading the Bible, sermons, and hymns.[12]

Just as the minister's plainer vestments symbolized his status as one among the community of worshipers, so, too, did a wider opening between the altar and nave reflect the Lutheran concept of increased equality between the pastor and his congregation.

As perceived by the Norwegian congregation of the time, however, the movement seemed to be going in the opposite direction, for it seemed to remove the minister from their realm and make him an outsider, a foreigner. For one thing the post-Reformation church sharpened its requirements concerning pastoral education. While priests in training had formerly served a period of apprenticeship in their home parish, a 1629 church ordinance required ministers to obtain a university degree before they could be ordained.[13]

Since Norway lacked a university until 1811, this requirement meant a period of study in either Denmark or Germany. The returning minister, even if originally from the local milieu, often seemed like an alien. Far superior in education to his parishioners, he had frequently adopted urban patterns of behavior and speech. The resultant perceived gulf between the minister and the congregation became the subject of legends and folktales portraying certain pastors as having superhuman powers (being capable of using the esoteric Black Book) and others as lacking the humanitarian qualities appropriate to their calling.[14]

Christmas in the Wake of the Reformation

Adding to an already difficult situation, the number of ministers in Norway did not equal the number of churches. This forced individual ministers to assume responsibility for more than one parish. That circumstance still affects how Norwegians celebrate Christmas, explaining the mystery of why Norway has not one but two Christmas Days.

The minister, serving several parishes that might lie as much as sixty miles apart, could not possibly reach all his congregations on December 25, and the deeply ingrained Norwegian sense of equality demanded institution of a no less sacred Second Christmas Day (*annen juledag*). While the necessity that mothered this invention disappeared long ago, Norwegians continue to observe December 26 as a full holiday.

Though the reluctance of the people to accept the arrival of the Reformation in Norway delayed the implementation of its teachings, by the middle of the 1600s well-trained Lutheran pastors stood in Norwegian pulpits. These clergymen mounted a concerted effort to eliminate all remnants of pre-Christian and Catholic practices from the Lutheran worship service. This cleansing included customs surrounding Christmas, whose Christian content they vigorously revived, even as they opposed (far more outspokenly than their predecessors) the holiday's "heathen" folk traditions.

It was during this period (1650–1750) that professional weavers in the Gudbrandsdal Valley area produced Norway's characteristic *billedvev,* or pictorial tapestries. Most often based on the New Testament parable of the five wise and five foolish virgins and on the Three Kings' adoration of the Christ child, these tapestries, displayed in affluent homes during the Christmas season, could almost be called the "woven Word," embodying as they did the Lutheran focus on the Bible.

Achieving the second aim of the Lutheran clergy—to combat established folk custom—proved considerably more vexing. As late as 1735, for example, the Lutheran Church had yet to eradicate the *julestuer* (home celebrations of Christmas featuring party games and festive eating and drinking), despite several decades of declaring them "absolutely forbidden." (Parlor games descended from these customs continue to be a beloved part of a modern Norwegian Christmas; family Christmas books and now Internet Web sites routinely contain numerous suggestions for them.)[15]

Another problematic custom was the peasant habit of leaving porridge for the household elf known as the *nisse* (plural *nisser*). According to long-standing popular belief, a farm's prosperity derived from this elf's hard work. To ensure the continuation of good fortune, the farmer had to reward the nisse appropriately at Christmastime by providing him with a generous portion of porridge. A. A. Flor wrote about the custom in 1688, managing simultaneously to deplore the practice and yet to reveal his own firmly held conviction of the nisse's existence:

A tapestry of the wise and foolish virgins, probably dating to the mid-1600s, purchased in Norway in the 1870s (wool on linen, 141 cm. by 195.5 cm.).

People have fallen into deep delusion when seeing the rich abundance brought to them by the hand of God; they cannot believe that such sweet profusion will persist unless they put out a bowl of porridge or other delicacy for the nisse. Especially during the holidays, they are certain that all will go awry if they should deviate in the slightest from this practice, even though it is quite clear that such nisser take the proffered goods not to enjoy them, but all the more to seduce naive persons into venerating them.[16]

Even strenuous clerical protests did little to end the folk custom, however. Veneration of the nisse not only lasted far into the nineteenth century, it remains a theme and image (though no longer accompanied by belief) deeply woven into the fabric of the Norwegian Christmas.

Though the Reformation had little success in changing these folk customs, it did succeed in altering the way the church observed Christmas, a modification that probably gave rise to the profoundly haunting legend known as "The Midnight Mass of the Dead." When Lutheran clergy banned the Catholic practice of holding vigil, they put an end to the midnight worship service on Christmas Eve. The clergy's condemnation of the midnight mass and its eventual unfamiliarity caused people to view the practice with awe and foreboding. The legend capturing this anxious mood is familiar in numerous variants all over Norway.

An apprehensive atmosphere accompanied the Norwegian Christmas up through the nineteenth century. Beliefs that ghosts and other normally hidden beings returned at Christmas caused many Norwegians to seek comfort in each other's company on Christmas Eve, when they shared a bed of straw on the farmhouse floor.[17] It was these fears that the Christian Christmas sought to soothe and mediate. But even as the real fear subsided, the telling of ghost stories—including the legend of the Midnight Mass of the Dead—remained a favored custom of Christmas, not only in Norway but in other parts of the Christian world as well, including colonial and frontier America. Charles Dickens's *Christmas Carol,* one of the most famous and beloved Christmas stories of all, is, of course, also a ghost story.

The considerable efforts of the Lutheran reformers, not withstanding, Norway's Christmas celebration remained essentially unaltered from the Viking and early Christian period until industrialization. Far greater change came with the conversion from self-sustaining agriculture to cash crops

The Midnight Mass of the Dead

It was Christmas Eve . . . and the widow, faithful as always to her church, prepared to attend the next morning's service, putting out coffee so she would have something warm to drink and avoid going to church on an empty stomach.

When she awoke, moonlight shone on the floor, but the clock had stopped; its hands showed half past eleven. Uncertain what time of the night it might be, she went over to the window and when she looked out, saw light shining from inside the church. Immediately she aroused the maid to make the coffee, then hurried to dress herself; at last she took her hymnal in hand and set out for church.

The streets were silent and she saw not a soul along the way. Arriving at the church, she sat in her usual pew, but glancing around at the congregation, she found them deathly pale and strange. Nor did she know them. Several she may have seen before, though she could not say where or when.

When the minister climbed the stairs to the pulpit, she saw that he was not one of the town's clergy, but a tall, pale man who somehow seemed familiar, too. He preached quite movingly and there was none of the shuffling and coughing and clearing of throats one usually hears at the Christmas morning service. It was so quiet that she could have heard a pin drop; in fact, it was so quiet she grew quite alarmed.

When they started to sing again, the woman sitting next to her leaned over and whispered in her ear: "Put your coat loosely on your shoulders and go. If you stay until the service is over, they'll put an end to you; it is the dead who are holding service here."

Now the widow knew terror, for hearing the voice and seeing the woman's face, she recognized her neighbor, long since deceased. Glancing around the church again, she recognized both the minister and many in the congregation, and realized that they, too, had died long ago. Stiff with fright, she draped the coat loosely over her shoulders, as the woman had instructed, and stood to leave.

Now they all seemed to turn and grab for her, and her legs trembled so, she only barely kept from falling. When she reached the church steps, she could feel them take hold of her coat. She let it go, and ran for home as fast as she could. The clock struck one as she reached her door, and by the time she got inside, her fright had nearly killed her.

This version of the midnight mass legend is retold by Norway's famous collector of folktales, P. C. Asbjørnsen. Other variations of the story conclude with congregants arriving at the Christmas Day service and finding on the church steps the widow's coat, torn to shreds.

Asbjørnsen and Moe, Samlede eventyr, *1:23–36*

and machine-based manufacturing that occurred during the second half of the nineteenth century (1881–95), which in Norway is known as *det store hamskifte* (the great metamorphosis).[18] The cultural and material changes wrought by this revolution—now joined by those brought about by the international information age—continue to transform the nature of Norwegian society, including Christmas. Yet despite these changes, the Norwegian Christmas of today includes innumerable elements of the holiday's past. It seems that just as modern Norway tries to free itself from old customs and beliefs, the need persists to retain and renew vital ties with well-established tradition.[19]

The contemporary Norwegian Christmas represents a rich mixture of ancient heritage and modern impulses, merging elements of pre-Christian solstice celebrations, Viking jól, and early Christian practices with more recent folklore. As ancient rituals lost their original function, new customs arose to fit new social realities. Yet a surprising number of today's yuletide practices have their roots in the distant past.

Advent
Preparing the Way

Nå tenner vi det første lys
alene må det stå.
Vi venter på det lille barn
som i en krybbe lå.

The first candle we light tonight
but it must stand alone,
as we await the little child
who was in a stable born.

T. Sigurd Muir

Long before the Norwegian Christmas reaches its climax on December 24, colorful Christmas customs engage young and old alike during the period popularly known as *julestria* (the Christmas rush) but more formally designated "Advent" (from Latin *Adventus Domini*, "the coming of the Lord"). By the end of the fourth century, the patriarchs had set aside this period of waiting for Christ's birth. Few Norwegians outside the clergy observed Advent before World War II, but now Advent decorations and calendars abound. Many families light one of the violet or white candles on their Advent wreaths on each of the four Sundays before Christmas.[1] In school, children learn verses, like the one in the epigraph to this chapter, to recite during the ceremony.

Few probably give a thought to the long pedigree of the Advent wreath, which harks back to the festive green garlands that decorated celebrations during the Middle Ages. Their present form as four-candled wreaths originated in Germany and came to Norway by way of Denmark. Though the church originally banned them, their popularity won out, and eventually the clergy adopted and promoted them.

Advent calendars, too, add much to the anticipation of Christmas in contemporary Norwegian homes but have only recently become widespread in Norway, despite having arrived there as early as the 1930s. A German mother created the first known Advent calendar about one hundred years ago in an effort to ease her son's wait for Christmas. The idea caught on, and German factories began mass-producing the calendars to keep up with demand.

In Norway they became customary only after World War II. The five-year occupation of Norway by Hitler's forces and its accompanying Nazi control of public space gave Norwegians a new appreciation of family life and prompted the embrace of new family customs. In addition to the store-bought, internationally produced calendars, many Norwegian families use homemade ones, with pockets or rings that hold a daily surprise.

Though candles have a special place in a Norwegian Christmas, two recent decorations rely on electricity. The Advent *stjerne,* a five-pointed hollow paper star illuminated by an internal electric lightbulb, is always hung in a prominent window. In addition, many now keep a seven-armed candlestick burning on the windowsill around the clock from the first Sunday in Advent through the thirteenth day of Christmas (January 6). Though somewhat resembling the Jewish menorah, this distinctive electric candleholder constitutes a strictly secular celebration of light in a time of darkness, when the length of the day (as far south as Oslo) has shortened from twenty-two and a half hours at midsummer to seven and a half on Christmas Day.

Advent calendars and wreaths serve as reminders that the period of preparation for Christmas passes all too quickly. Capturing this universal perception of time's fleet-footedness—for adults, if not children—the Norwegians have the expression *det kom som julekvelden på kjerringa* ("it came as suddenly as Christmas Eve to the housewife"), used year-round to refer to things that catch up with them before they know it.

Fasting and Lutefisk

As new customs arise, older ones disappear. Such has been the fate of Advent fasting. Instituted by the patriarchs around the year 480 to underscore the significance of Christ's birth and to ensure celebrants' spiritual preparedness, the custom of fasting came to Norway with Christianity. Long after Norway had adopted Lutheranism as its state religion in 1537, Norwegian peasants continued to reduce their food intake during Advent, the better to appreciate the rich yuletide fare to come.[2]

Though fasting itself has disappeared from today's Norway, a significant feature of this centuries-old practice remains: the pre-Christmas lutefisk dinner. Few Norwegians may associate this dish with their country's pre-Reformation Catholic past, but during the weeks before Christmas, Norwegian restaurants report record consumption of the gelatinous white cod. They encourage this phenomenon by sponsoring special lutefisk nights.[3]

In the period of Norwegian history known as the Catholic Middle Ages (about 1000–1537), lutefisk figured prominently as a fasting food, and Scandinavia's last Catholic archbishop, Olaus Magnus, described its preparation as a well-established practice in his *History of the Nordic People* (1555). Prescribing a two-day lye soaking for the toughened cod that had dried for weeks outdoors on wooden racks, the archbishop recommended following the soaking by a fresh water rinse the day before the fish was to be boiled and served with butter. The lye or *lute* (potassium carbonate), from which the dish gets its name, was most commonly obtained by boiling the ash of deciduous trees in water for fifteen to thirty minutes.

Why lye? Legend attributes this to the Vikings. What is no doubt an apocryphal account reports that while raiding a certain fishing village, the Vikings burned down some wooden racks on which cod was drying. When one of the inhabitants poured water over the fire to douse it, the fish was left soaking in a solution of ashes and water—that is, lye. Poking through the ashes days later, villagers noticed that the once dried and hardened fish now appeared fresh. Rinsing and boiling it, they discovered that—at least by some accounts—it was edible.[4]

Actually the method did not come out of nowhere. The Norwegian ethnologist and food chemist Astrid Riddervold, who has written most knowledgeably about the delicacy, points out that seventeenth-century cookbooks in Poland, the Netherlands, Spain, and Germany cite soaking fish in lye as a well-known preparation method. She also notes how little modern preparation methods for lutefisk differ from the description Olaus Magnus wrote down in the Middle Ages: The cod—still air-dried on the distinctive wooden frames seen in Norway's Lofoten Islands—is first soaked in fresh water for several days to restore its original consistency, then treated for three days with the lye solution (said to be "strong enough to strip paint").[5] A thorough three-to-four-day rinsing with either running or frequently changed fresh water follows. Finally the cook poaches the fish for fifteen to twenty minutes in salt water and serves it steaming hot, drizzled with melted butter and accompanied by crisp *flatbrød* (an unleavened crisp bread).

Chemically, the process of soaking the fish in lye breaks down the protein to amino acids; this gives the fish its jellylike consistency and produces a readily digestible food of high nutritional value. The process also results in controversy: people either love lutefisk or they hate it. There is no middle ground.

Norwegian Americans have a long tradition of proudly and painstakingly preparing lutefisk for Christmas and other special occasions while simultaneously cultivating entire joke cycles that resoundingly disparage the dish. In Norway, however, the lutefisk tradition had made little stir, being faithfully kept by some and simply ignored by others. Then toward the end of the 1980s, broadcast and print media began bombarding the public each autumn with brochures, interviews, advertisements, and programs highlighting both the cultural-historical background and the nutritional value of lutefisk. Occasionally this media blitz even revealed the whimsical humor characteristic of the way Norwegian Americans view lutefisk. This resemblance was by no means coincidental, for the Norwegian lutefisk campaign had followed American marketing methods.[6] The ads aimed to confer upon those who ate the fish a group identity as "lutefisk lovers," a status which also implied enhanced sexual prowess. Norwegian sales of lutefisk soared, and lutefisk became in Norway, as it long had been in America, a cherished badge of Nordic identity—and a great source of fun.[7]

Though today's Norwegian lutefisk lovers eat from a plate with a knife and fork and usually accompany the fish with flatbread, boiled potatoes, mashed peas, and perhaps a tangy mustard or bacon sauce, their ancestors

Norway's Fish Information Board produced this promotional sign, which was in use in the 1990s. Made to hang in a window, about 19 inches by 13 inches, and printed in orange and black, it proclaims (loosely translated), "Lutefisk lovers last longer!"

placed the fish right on the flatbread, which they ate with their hands. Plates and forks did not arrive in rural Norway until the twentieth century.[8] Even after these urban amenities had spread to the countryside, the custom of placing lutefisk on the handheld flatbread persisted, being replaced in some areas (notably Gudbrandsdal) by wrapping it in lefse (a rolled thin, tortilla-like soft bread). Adherents of the latter method placed the lutefisk on the lefse with some butter and salt, then rolled the lefse around the fish, securing the flaps in a usually vain attempt to keep the butter from running out. The resulting roll—looking not unlike a burrito—they then ate with their hands.

I include these historical facts to end rife speculation among Norwegian Americans that the lefse-wrapped method of consuming lutefisk arose among their misguided relatives in the United States; history establishes the custom's pedigree as originally Norwegian. Norwegian Americans may also be reassured to know that, just as in this country, controversy about which is the "right" way to eat lutefisk (including "not at all") characterizes these Norwegian meals. Meanwhile a growing export market for the dried, unsalted fish from which lutefisk is made provides the basis for increasingly numerous gourmet dishes in Italy, a country suffering no lack of good things to eat.

Christmas Preparations

Alongside the Norwegians' lutefisk dinners and Advent wreaths, elaborate Christmas preparations take place. The roots of these preparations reach far back into Norway's past, to a time quite unlike our own, characterized by a radically different lifestyle and worldview.

After the industrial revolution, the once joint spheres of work and family life diverged. In more recent decades women's employment outside the home has surged. (While in the 1950s few of married Norwegian women had outside employment, by the 1970s only about half of all adult Norwegian women were full-time housewives; by the 1990s most women worked outside the home.) Though some in our stressful era may find it difficult to spend the enormous amounts of time required by traditional Christmas preparations, others find them comforting. For these individuals the old customs hold deep meaning, and they willingly perpetuate latter day versions of the painstaking yuletide chores that Norway's preindustrial agrarian society required.

Each self-sustaining farm family of that pre-1900 era was guided by strong folk traditions that strictly enforced the holiday's proper celebration. Some of these customs are consciously followed to this day; other customs—even more numerous and enchanting, but often unknown to present-day Norwegians—underlie modern practices. Though two-career marriages have transformed Norwegian lifestyles in recent years, heroic amounts of time and effort still go into making the Norwegian Christmas special.

THE SLAUGHTER

Among the myriad Christmas preparations in the preindustrial peasant society, butchering occupied a pivotal position. Each year the farm family faced the difficult task of choosing which animals to keep through the winter and which to slaughter. They carefully calculated the quantity of fodder on hand against the amount of meat needed during the coming year. They had to maintain as large a herd as possible while neither starving the livestock nor running out of meat. Either alternative would bring not only hardship but also social stigma upon the family.

The family paid close attention to the timing of the slaughter. Naturally they waited until the cold had set in, when the meat could best be preserved, but other considerations played an equally important role, such as butchering during the waxing moon. Why the waxing moon? Long established folk belief promised a favorable outcome for tasks performed under its light; in the case of slaughter, firmer and fattier meat was said to result. Folk belief also held that slaughtering during the early morning hours and at flood tide would assure the freer flow of the animal's blood and easier removal of its hide. It would also make the meat last longer.

Preparing for the slaughter was an enormous job in itself. The *husmor* (housewife) had to assemble the great variety of wooden buckets and basins needed and make sure they were clean and watertight. She first soaked the leaky ones in water to make the wood swell, then she scrubbed them all

---

Anne-Lise Mellbye describes the slaughter at the Mellbye farm during the 1950s:

The slaughter was a bloody and intense affair, and I can still see the scene by the farmhands' quarters in the evening darkness, the big sow lying on the slaughtering bench ready for scalding, lit by oil lamps, steam rising from water troughs all around, and strange, steamy shadows undulating across the outbuilding walls. It could be a cold job in the winter, and the butchers occasionally needed to be thawed out and cheered on with blistering hot coffee and a dram. Dividing up of the carcass and its further treatment came later, in the cellar and farm kitchen, where strong-armed women saw to those jobs. The intestines were scrubbed out and rinsed in the cellar. Water had to be carried there. Two workers had the job of grinding the meat. No electrical grinders or mixers existed then! Standing with a freshly honed broad ax in each hand, they slashed back and forth until the womenfolk approved of the ground meat that resulted. Any roasting and cooking of the meat took place at the large kitchen stove, but most of the beef and pork was not prepared fresh. Instead it was cut in pieces and salted down in enormous brine tubs in the stabbur.

Mellbye, Jul i Norge, *18–19*

---

with hot water infused with juniper. (Familiar today as the flavoring in gin, the readily available juniper functioned as an all-purpose cleaner, disinfectant, air freshener, flavoring agent, and preservative on Norway's self-sufficient farms.) Her husband sharpened the knives and axes, and together they arranged the equipment so that once begun, the butchering could proceed smoothly.

The day of slaughter began at dawn. Once the carcass had been split, they removed and thoroughly washed the intestines, stomach, and organs, a process that might take the entire first day. The next day, when the carcass had cooled, they cut up the meat and salted it down as soon as possible. Very little of the meat would be eaten fresh; most they would cure by salting, drying, or smoking. This they believed would make the meat last longer; when it was less tasty and harder to digest, the meat encouraged consumption based on hunger rather than appetite, a vital consideration in times of scarcity.[9]

Running out of meat before the next slaughter reflected badly on a farm. There should be enough left over to allow the new slaughter to get well salted and dried before they needed to use it. The husmor therefore kept a careful eye on the supply, portioning out the meat to each person along with some flatbread.[10] No wonder Christmas stood out as such a special time. It provided the only occasion when people could freely eat fresh meat in the quantity they desired.

Always resourceful, the preindustrial Norwegians used every part of the slaughtered animal. The horns alone had many uses, among them as a tool to stuff sausage. Threading the intestine through the horn, they folded it back to make a lip, then stuffed the casing with chopped meat and fat. Young and old alike enjoyed this part of the slaughter best; the hardest work lay behind them, and they could soon savor the results.

Among the most anticipated treats, *sylte* (head cheese) was made by alternating layers of meat and fat from the head of a cow, sheep, or pig. Cured in its own juices and a salty brine, the resulting mold made attractive cold cuts when sliced.[11]

Fundamental to the yuletide feast was the *julegris* (Christmas pig), fattened until the last waxing moon before Christmas. In addition to sylte, it provided *blodpudding* (blood pudding), *blodpølse* (blood sausage), *blodklubb* (blood dumplings),[12] and *griselabber* (pickled pigs' feet).[13] These pork delicacies could keep quite a few days in the chilly *stabbur,* or storehouse, where barrels and pails lined the walls and sausages, hams, and other dried meat hung in rows under the rafters. They constituted a welcome addition to the seasonal food supply. Though they may not have much appeal for modern readers, these dishes reflect the honored principle of Norway's preindustrial, self-sufficient farms that discarding anything that could be eaten or used was both *synd og skam* (a sin and shameful).[14] Some even used the animal's bladder to make a hot water bottle, highly prized as an effective cure for rheumatism.[15]

Another much anticipated slaughter-time treat, *rullepølse* (rolled sausage, now known as *rull*), was made by seasoning, rolling, and tying or sewing a suitably sized (eight to twelve inches long) rectangular flank of lamb or veal. Like sylte, rullepølse was sliced for cold cuts after being cooked and cured.[16]

These days even Norwegians living on farms rarely participate in the slaughter except for bringing the livestock to a professional meat processor and receiving the meat wrapped in convenient sizes for storing in the freezer. Still, the butcher cuts the meat in traditional ways for home preparation of the time-honored Christmas Eve favorites *ribbe* (pork rib roast) and *pinne-kjøtt* (steamed mutton), and specialty shops still produce sylte, rull, and *griselabber.* While fresh meat could formerly be had only in season and was otherwise eaten salted, smoked, or dried, now the opposite is true. Fresh meat is available on a daily basis, while cured meats such as *spekeskinke* (dried ham) and *fenelår* (dried mutton) provide a welcome variation in the Norwegian diet on special occasions.[17]

BAKING

One of the delights of Christmas is its seemingly endless variety of special pastries. Norwegians serve them to guests with a glass of wine at midday or with after-dinner coffee—a daily must in most homes. Far more than a piece of furniture, the Norwegian coffee table is an institution. Taller than its American counterpart and set at a moment's notice with tablecloth, candles, and fancy china if guests arrive unannounced, it also serves as a primary focus of family life.

Though two-career marriages have reduced the amount of time devoted to pre-Christmas baking, most Norwegian housewives still immerse them-

The Norwegian quality of being instantly ready for company has long roots. In preindustrial times the *husmor* always had a basket hanging under the stabbur roof. It contained folded flatbread, a butter box, and cured meat and sausage, and was covered by a white table-cloth—just in case someone dropped by.

Ambjørnrud et al., eds. Norsk mat, 24

selves in the flurry of producing the traditional *sju slags* (seven kinds [of cookies]). In former times as many as nine or eleven kinds were made, the number (always uneven) being a kind of status symbol that indicated the family's wealth. Exactly which kinds appear varies from place to place and from family to family, but a 1992 poll in *Aftenposten* (Norway's largest daily paper) identified the seven kinds as most likely to be the following: *smultringer* (doughnuts) or, tying for first place, *hjortetakk* (crullers made with hartshorn salt, that is, ammonium carbonate, also known as baker's ammonia); *sandkaker* (almond cookies baked in fluted tins, more familiar to Norwegian Americans as *sandbakelse* or *sandbakkels*);[18] *sirupssnipper* (similar to gingersnaps, but diamond-shaped and decorated with a blanched almond); *Berlinerkranser* ("Berlin wreaths," made from a rich egg-yolk dough and sprinkled with large-grained sugar); *goro* (a rectangular cookie made with an intricately imprinted iron); *krumkaker* (a thin, cone-shaped cookie also baked on a decorative iron); and *fattigmann* (dough twisted into a fancy shape and fried in deep fat).

The oldest of these, krumkake and goro, along with *vafler,* a waffle-like pastry, go back to at least the 1700s, as attested by the existence of irons that old for making them. These irons, once produced by local blacksmiths who often included their initials in the pattern, might weigh as much as fifteen pounds and had long handles for holding them over open cooking fires. When the *komfyr* (wood-burning cookstove) came into use in the mid to late 1800s, irons that could be seated in the round burner holes replaced the long-handled ones. They were so much easier to use that people called them *maskiner* (machines).

Most of the cookies mentioned in *Aftenposten*'s 1992 list appeared in the pioneering Norwegian cookbook written by a pastor's wife, Hanna Winsnes, in 1845.[19] They will also seem familiar to Norwegian Americans. Tremendously popular in Norway, Winsnes's book also found its way west in immigrant trunks, helping to account for these cookies' transplantation to America. Oral tradition probably played an even greater role, though, judging from these comments by Shirley Olson Sorensen, born in 1928, who grew up in Eau Claire, Wisconsin. There her maternal grandmother, an 1893 emigrant from Skjåk in Gudbrandsdal, passed along much of her Norwegian heritage:

> I can remember as a child sitting in the kitchen with grandma and my mother and aunts, pushing the dough for sandbakkels into the little pans. There was always fattigmann, rosettes, home made doughnuts (fry cakes), home baked bread, baked beans, strong coffee with sugar lumps and thick cream, open faced sandwiches, rømmegrøt—tons of good food, all made on a wood burning stove.[20]

The rosettes Sorensen mentions also appear in Winsnes's cookbook, though they never attained the popularity in Norway that they did in Norwegian America. Winsnes describes the special iron for *roset-bakkelse,* as she calls them, and the method for frying them in deep fat. "These cookies are very inexpensive," she notes, "and look pretty. They also keep well, but they don't have much taste all by themselves. I have therefore tried to fill them with cream, which looks lovely and gives them a good taste."[21]

Baked cookies like sandbakkels and Berlinerkranser, though now regarded as traditional, actually entered the Norwegian kitchen fairly recently, reaching the *kondisjonerte,* the professional, cultured class, around the time of Winsnes's cookbook, but not known among *almuen* (the common folk, or peasants) until much later in the nineteenth century. Most Norwegians lacked the fine flour to make any cookies or pastries that needed to rise, and as Winsnes says, "If it [fine flour] can't be gotten, it is wiser to choose other kinds of pastries." Further indicating the challenge of keeping usable flour, even among the kondisjonerte class for which she is writing, she counsels that if the flour is the least bit lumpy or damp it must be dried on plates on top of the stove or in the oven, then cooled and rolled out before it can be used.[22] As flour, along with sugar and spices, became more available, pastry baking grew in popularity, also influenced by the greater popularity of coffee, which by the end of the 1800s had become the drink of choice.

Though known in Norway since 1840, coffee wasn't much drunk until the 1860s or 1870s, and then only on festive occasions; in most parts of Norway the daily drink was *blande,* a thirst-quenching mixture of sour milk and water. As coffee began to replace this drink, Norwegians extended their coffee supply for everyday use with *knupp,* bits of potato dough roasted like regular coffee over the open fire in a *kaffebrenner* (coffee roaster), consisting of a long handle with a flat box at one end.

Having a far longer tradition than coffee or any of the baked cookies are *peppernøtter* (pepper nuts) and cookies fried in deep fat. Ever-popular peppernøtter (though they are perhaps not among the obligatory "sju slags") date as far back as the Middle Ages and are actually Europe's oldest and best-known Christmas treat. Originally made on a griddle from rye flour mixed with honey, wormwood (*malurt,* or *artemisia absinthium*) and other strong spices, they tasted very different from foods in the daily diet, a vital attribute of Christmas fare. Today's peppernøtter are baked in the oven and made from a flour, butter, and baking powder dough sweetened with corn syrup and sugar and spiced with anise. Then and now, the active role children could take in rolling the balls of the less precisely formed peppernøtter has added to their popularity. The similarly spiced *pepperkaker* (ginger snaps), cut from thinly rolled dough with plastic cookie cutters, have grown increasingly popular as a cookie that children can make, and some families even construct elaborate *pepperkakehus* (gingerbread houses) from this dough.

Cookies fried in unsalted fat have medieval origins, too. This method of food preparation was often employed by those of lesser means, as perhaps attested by the name *fattigmann* (poor man), one of the most popular cookies among Norwegians on both sides of the Atlantic.[23] Modern fattigmann recipes abound in Norwegian America,[24] but I quote the directions for *Fattig mands bakelse* that H. K. Daniels includes in his 1911 book, *Home Life in Norway.* There he identifies them as "a pastry which one ought to know something about, seeing that it is as popular in towns among every class as it is in the country." Daniels's recipe reflects the large families of his time—and the less precise measurements also characteristic of that period's recipes:

18 eggs, 2 lbs. of flour, 1 lb. butter, a couple of small wine glasses of cognac, some cinnamon finely ground, 2 lbs. sugar and some baking-powder.

Mix all the ingredients thoroughly, roll out very thinly, cut into little circular cakes and fry in a deep pan of pork drippings or lard until of a light golden brown.

❖ ❖

Peppernøtter

1 cup light corn syrup
1 scant cup sugar
4 Tbsp. butter
3 Tbsp. whipping cream
1 tsp. ground star anise
$\frac{1}{2}$ tsp. pepper
$\frac{3}{4}$ tsp. baking soda
about $3\frac{1}{2}$ cups flour

Bring syrup, sugar, butter, and cream to a boil. Combine the dry ingredients and add, mixing well. Refrigerate overnight. Preheat the oven to 400° F. Make small round nuts and place on a greased baking sheet. Bake 8 minutes. Makes about 10 dozen cookies.

Hjortetakk

3 eggs
$\frac{3}{4}$ cup sugar
$\frac{2}{3}$ cup whipping cream
$\frac{2}{3}$ cup 35% fat sour cream
3 cups flour
2 tsp. hartshorn salt (or 2 Tbsp. baking powder)
1 tsp. cardamom
2 Tbsp. melted butter, shortening or oil.

Beat eggs and sugar until light and lemon-colored. Whip cream and sour cream lightly together. Stir the dry ingredients. Add alternatingly with melted butter and both creams to the egg mixture. Mix lightly together. Refrigerate overnight.

Roll the dough to $\frac{1}{3}$-inch sausages. Cut into 5-inch lengths. Form into a wreath. Make 2 notches along the edges. Heat the shortening or oil to 350° F. Deep fry a few at a time until golden, 3–4 minutes.

Hanna Winsnes's daughter, Maren Winsnes, who updated her mother's classic cookbook in 1876, advised adding a "knife's edge" of *hjortesalt* (hartshorn salt) to help the dough rise.

Innli, ed., Norwegian Kitchen, *219, 208; Winsnes,* Lærebog, *264*

❖ ❖

"You will find them everywhere, especially during Christmas and Easter," Daniels concludes.

Even today, many Norwegians say it isn't really Christmas unless the house smells of deep-fat frying. Often competing with fattigmann in Norway these days is another deep–fried cookie, *hjortetakk* (deer antlers). This recipe calls for hartshorn salt, the secret ingredient that lends Scandinavian baking its special crispness and which the Norwegian immigrants also brought along to America.

Flatbrød and *lefse,* with an even longer history than any of the cookies I've described, remain popular in today's Norway. Dry, crisp flatbread constituted the Norwegians' daily bread at least as long ago as the Viking age (about 800–1000). (Yeast bread as we know it remained rare in Norway until the 1700s and was eaten only among the *kondisjonerte* until around the end of the 1800s.)[25] Variety and profusion characterized both flatbread and lefse. The flour might consist of ground barley or oats, but peas and later potatoes often supplemented the grain, as did bark from trees in times of famine. The recipes used varied widely from place to place, not only in the kind of flour used, but also the method of baking, the thickness, and the liquid used (water, whey, milk, or buttermilk). How the flatbread was named also varied, such that identical recipes often went by differing names in different locations.

Baking flatbread served an essential function in a country whose cold, wet summers often kept the grain crop from fully ripening. Sure to spoil if stored, the still–green grain was instead ground and immediately used for making flatbread.[26] Itinerant baking women would stay several days on each farm to complete half–year supplies at midsummer and Christmas. Carefully monitoring the flatbread supply throughout the year, the husmor tried to have some flatbread in reserve from the previous baking when the next round of baking began, as one never knew how the current grain crop would turn out.

Baking the semiannual flatbread supply was hard work, but it also brought enjoyment. Both children and adults would drop by the *eldhus,* the cookhouse, to check on the bakers' progress. Maybe the husmor had some newly churned butter and they could get a taste? When the baking was finished, tall stacks of several hundred *leiver* (large, round sheets) stood in the stabbur. No wrapping covered them, nor container enclosed them.

Standing in the open air of the stabbur, the flatbread could keep for years; it had to last at least six months. In more recent times, families kept their flatbread in a drawer in the kitchen table, always close at hand.

While flatbread is crisp and dry, lefse is soft, and is usually eaten with butter and sugar or cheese. Even more than flatbread, lefse varies greatly from region to region. *Havrelefse* (oat lefse) and other types of everyday lefse were made of coarser flour, rolled out thick, and baked with sufficiently high heat to crispen. Baked with the semiannual flatbread supply, crisp lefse was softened before use by sprinkling with lukewarm water and wrapping in a dry cloth.

Special occasions called for more finely milled and sifted flours and more thinly rolled dough. The preindustrial peasants gratefully exchanged the everyday flatbread, *ertebrød* (a coarse, unleavened pea–flour bread), and *havrelefse* for *kling,* a tastier rye and wheat lefse baked during the week before Christmas.[27] Kling was spread while still warm with butter and sour cream, ingredients done without throughout the year to increase their supply at Christmas. Rooted in this tradition, modern Norwegian still has the phrase "striskjorte [a coarsely woven, scratchy shirt] og havrelefse" to describe going "back to the old grind."

While havrelefse is rolled thick and baked crisp, potato lefse (the type best known among Norwegian Americans) remains soft. It is rolled out thin and quickly baked on a medium warm *takke* (griddle). Light yellow in color with evenly distributed brown spots, the round sheets are placed in a cloth to let off steam. Most lefse is served as a sweet with coffee, but potato lefse also accompanies lutefisk.

Decorated breads as a part of Christmas carried over from the Roman Saturnalia celebration. Festive baking during the pre-Christian period had ritual overtones and featured painstaking decorations, often achieved by pressing dough into intricately patterned forms, not unlike the process still used to produce goro and krumkake. Bakers also shaped and baked dough in the form of pigs, goats and chickens. Christianity added crosses and other religious symbols to the baker's design repertoire, but did not otherwise change the ritualized function of Christmas baking.

Decorated breads and pastries—lefse and flatbread, goro and krumkake—remain common, even expected parts of a household's Christmas. The "obligatory" seven kinds of Christmas cookies still popular in Norway arose in a society with tastes different from those of present-day Norwegians. Prepared with different preparation methods, technology, and ingredients than those normally employed today, these pastries nevertheless unmistakably belong to and even help define the modern Norwegian and Norwegian American Christmas.

CANDLES

Candles came to Norway with the introduction of Christianity, and burning them has now replaced the once necessary pre-Christmas chore of making them. Still they constitute an essential part of Christmas, when Norway's four million people manage to burn some seventeen million candles.[28]

In rural areas candle making naturally followed the fall slaughter, which provided the necessary tallow. Older family members oversaw the procedure as younger ones joined in melting the tallow and twisting hemp strands into wicks. Suspending them in groups of five from thin wooden sticks, they repeatedly dipped the wicks into the tallow, then waited for the tallow to stiffen before dipping them again—many, many times—until the candles attained the desired thickness.

Molded candles had even higher status. Originally using the throats of newly slaughtered deer as forms, preindustrial Norwegians subsequently developed a loose-legged table bored through with many round holes, each of which held a metal candle form, open on top and tapering to a narrow end with a small hole. Pulling wicks through the holes, they fastened them to small sticks over the top opening, then poured melted tallow into the forms. When hardened, the finished candles were pulled from the forms by means of the wooden sticks.

This annual, grand-scale candle making produced an intense, rank odor that permeated clothes, hair, walls, floor, and everything else in the room, which had to be kept tightly closed to prevent drafts. Drafts would blister the candles or make them crooked, causing them to burn unevenly or with a flickering flame instead of the steady, clear light needed for doing close work. Saving the best tallow for these *arbeidslys* (work candles), the peasants used tallow that was less pure for candles employed while cooking or to light their way outdoors.[29]

The supply of candles had to last throughout the year, and the husmor carefully supervised their use. As a rule only one candle burned at a time in the main room of the *våningshus* (dwelling house). Everyone had to gather around, moving their work as close to the light as possible. During *kveldseta,* as this evening work period was called, the spinning wheel hummed as the women spun yarn or wove, men fashioned tools or mended fishing nets, young boys carved, and young girls knitted or embroidered. Legends and folktales punctuated the conversation, and traditions passed from one generation to the next.

Folk belief decreed that candles be made during the new moon, lest they too quickly melt away. From the year's painstakingly made supply, the peasants selected only the whitest, longest, and straightest candles for Christmas Eve. Keeping a watchful eye on how each one burned that night, they anxiously sought clues to their fate in the coming year. A brightly burning taper augured well, while one that suddenly went out portended untimely death.

After Christmas the remnants of these candles were not discarded, but put away for use throughout the year. The farmer might rub his plow and harrow with the wax to increase his yield while his wife added the scraps to salves and medicines to make them especially effective. Both believed the candles had acquired special power by their presence on Christmas Eve.

During the 1800s, paraffin greatly improved the quality of candles, but their use soon declined with the introduction of electricity. Edison's invention notwithstanding, Norwegians now burn more candles than ever before. Their softening light adds much to the highly valued *kos* (coziness) and *hygge* (comfort) of the Norwegian home, especially at Christmastime.

BEER BREWING

Norwegians drink approximately ten million liters of beer during December, a quantity surpassed only during the hottest July. *Juleøl* (Christmas beer)—commercially brewed since 1936—accounts for over half of this amount.[30]

Much of what is known about the celebration of the pre–nineteenth-century Norwegian Christmas comes from brewing lore. Beer drinking held an honored place in Norway's preindustrial peasant society, which used the drink to commemorate all special occasions. The names of events such as *barnsøl* (child—that is, baptismal—beer), *festerøl* (engagement beer), and *gravøl* (funeral beer) reflect beer's prominence in marking these rites of passage. But the brewing and prestige of Scandinavian beer dates back to even earlier times. The sagas of the Vikings give a lively portrayal of the role beer played at sacrificial feasts, the old Norsemen having apparently regarded intoxication as a means of communing with the gods.

When the tenth-century Viking king Haakon the Good moved the mid-winter festival of *jól* to December 25 to coincide with the Christian Christmas celebration, he accompanied that decree with the mandate that every peasant brew a measure of beer for Christmas. The medieval Gulating Law continued and enforced that directive, calling for each peasant and his wife to hold a Christmas *gilde* (festive gathering) that featured beer. Failure to do so resulted in serious loss: a fine to the bishop for skipping one year and the confiscation of the property of any peasant who neglected the beer obligation three years in a row.

The wise peasant therefore set aside fields for growing high quality grain to make the malt. Many also kept a patch of leafy *humle* (hops) plants to flavor, color, and help preserve the beer. The brewing, involving numerous work-intensive steps, began soon after harvest. Choosing the heaviest, ripest barley, the brewer soaked it for three or four days, then kept it warm in the eldhus for sprouting.[31] When the sprouts had grown to about an inch, he untangled the grain, spread it out on the floor, and thoroughly dried it. This sprouted, dried grain, when ground and sifted, was known as *malt*.

Meanwhile the husmor assembled the extensive brewing equipment needed, giving each item a thorough washing with *einerlaug* (the ubiquitous boiling water infused with juniper) and making sure all the wooden containers were watertight. The night before the brewing began, she and her husband assembled all the equipment and ingredients, consisting—according to an old recipe for malt beer from Østfold—of one-fourth barrel of malt, one-fourth kilogram of hops, and at least eighteen liters of water and brewer's yeast.[32] They placed the malt in a wooden tub and covered it with lukewarm water. They also filled a large vat with water and juniper, then laid a fire, ready to light first thing the next morning.

Brewing began at dawn. Once the juniper water had almost reached the boiling point, they poured it over the malt, producing a thick soup that they stirred with a paddle, slowly and for a long time. Then they cooked up more juniper water to pour into the kegs.

Next they prepared the brewer's yeast in the *rostekar* (a three-legged mash

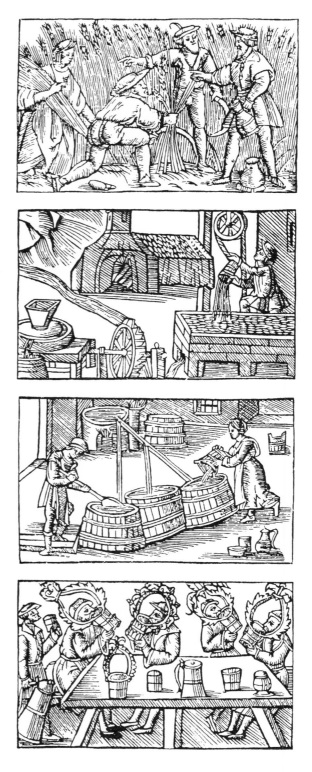

Making beer in Norway, 1500s. The sections show harvesting, drying the grain, brewing in wooden vats, and drinking from ornately carved wooden vessels.

tub). It had a bunghole in the bottom covered by straw and stones, which acted as a strainer. After transferring the malt and juniper water mixture to the large vat, they heated it almost to boiling, then poured it into the mash tub, topping it off with additional steaming hot juniper water. Brought to a boil and with the hops added, this mixture was known as the *vørter* (brewer's wort). It stood for half an hour before being tapped into the fermenting tub containing the yeast and a little sugar. After a couple of days of rapid fermentation, this mixture was finally tapped into barrels and put down into the cellar for storage.

Like slaughter and candle making, brewing had to be carefully timed. The finished beer needed to stand eight to ten days and had to be ready by December 21. Known during the Middle Ages as the day of St. Thomas, this date was popularly called "Thomas the brewer's day."[33] On it, all the farm's inhabitants and neighbors got their first taste of the Christmas beer. Since the farm's reputation rested on its ability to produce high-quality beer, this day loomed large in the yearly cycle.

With so much prestige at stake, Norway's preindustrial society counted brewing among the most important of the Christmas preparations, and a great deal of folk belief surrounded the process. Feeling vulnerable to the damage that hidden powers might rain down upon their art, brewers took many precautions. Working during the beneficial waxing moon and flood tide, they maintained a respectful attitude as they went about their task, treating it as a sacred act. They accompanied their devout demeanor with protective rituals performed largely in silence and, if possible, unseen by others. The brewer consecrated the brewing tub by waving hot steel or a burning branch around its interior. To keep evil from harming the beer, he made the sign of the cross over the metal brewing vessels and carved crosses in the wooden ones. He might also drive a knife into the beer barrel to protect its contents from invisible spirits.

As in so many of Norway's folk practices, sympathetic or imitative magic (the idea that actions produce outcomes of a similar nature, often expressed as "like influences like") abounds in brewing lore. Thus, much depended on the mood of the brewer, who should initially be silent, then boisterously scream and shout while adding the yeast, since this would make the beer stronger, just as smearing himself with ashes and dust would darken the beer.[34] Respectful of the mysterious fermentation process, the peasants took care during this phase not to tramp, slam doors, shout, or make any other loud noises that might disturb the beer and keep it from "working."

When Norwegian society changed its economic foundation from self-sustaining agriculture to industrial commercialism, professional breweries took over the beer-making process. The first breweries had appeared as early as the end of the 1700s, and their number grew steadily during the 1820s and 1830s. Industrial beer production resembles the process described above, adapted to suit modern techniques and larger volumes. Norwegian breweries have traditionally made their beer according to the "purity law," which allows only malt, water, yeast, and hops to be used in its production. Though some Norwegians still brew beer as a hobby, the household's reputation within the community no longer rests on the outcome, and brewing has ceased to take pride of place among the Norwegian family's holiday preparations.

HOLIDAY CLEANING

Once as much of a ritual as the brewing and butchering, an exhaustive basement-to-attic scrubbing and scouring of the house helped define the Norwegian Christmas. This custom, too, has given way to changing times, though a more thorough than usual housecleaning remains a requisite part of the pre-Christmas activity.

In Norway's preindustrial peasant society, cleaning followed the messy operations of slaughter and brewing. At a time when cleanliness presented an enormous challenge—confounded by sooty cooking fires, earthen floors, and the absence of running water—the results of the annual cleaning must have added enormously to the comfort of Christmas. But the process affected the family's well-being on an even deeper level, according to the pioneering Norwegian sociologist, Eilert Sundt (1817–75). In his 1869 book, *Om Rensligheds-Stellet i Norge* (On cleanliness in Norway), he argues that this "særledes Omhu for Rengjøring" (exceptional concern for cleaning) dated back to pre-Christian times. He related the wash water to the sign of the cross, fire, and steel—all endowed by folk belief with the ability to protect human beings from the *huldrefolk,* the normally hidden beings thought to infiltrate the human world, particularly at Christmas.

Clearly, the cleaning also conformed to the sense of renewal essential to the Norwegian Christmas: the dwelling shed its everyday appearance and emerged refurbished and refined. After scraping the soot from the walls and ceilings, the husmor often scoured the wooden surfaces with sand before washing and rinsing them. She brought in fresh hay for the beds, washed the linen, and hung the sheepskin coverings near the fire in the eldhus so the heat could kill the lice and fleas. Then she or her husband brought the handwoven wall hangings from the stabbur, chalked white decorations on the walls (a process called *kroting*), and spread spruce and juniper branches on the floor to freshen the air and absorb excess moisture. Finally they painted crosses of tar or blood (from the slaughter) on the doors of the stabbur and animal barns to protect the Christmas provisions and livestock from the *oskorei,* a terrifying species of hidden people thought to haunt the Christmas skies.

Not only the buildings but also their inhabitants took part in the Christmas renewal, as each of the farm dwellers (a group that, beyond the immediate family, included various long-term servants, hired hands, cotters, and wayfarers) all took a Christmas bath.[35] They fetched water, sometimes from considerable distances, and heated it (usually infused with the familiar juniper branches and berries) in massive cauldrons, a process too arduous to repeat for every bather. Those who had to use recycled water no doubt missed some of the warmth and juniper fragrance enjoyed by the first bathers.

Yet even they welcomed the refreshing bath and the donning of clean, soft clothes that concluded the ritual. The clothes they put on had been boiled in an immense cast iron cauldron. Here, too, juniper was added as a cleansing agent. Thorough washing and changing into clean clothes, far from being an everyday routine, could be counted upon only four times a year—in the early spring, at midsummer, after the fall harvest, and at Christmas.

Eventually soap came to augment and then replace the juniper in the bath and wash water. Made after the slaughter from tallow not deemed suitable for eating or candle making, the soap recipe also called for home-made lye. Hanna Winsnes's cookbook describes the arduous process:

> Boil 35 liters of good, white birch ashes in 12 pails of water, then let stand to clear until the next day. Boil down slowly but steadily until about 2 pails remain. This takes until evening, so you must resume the work the next day. For every 18 liters of ashes, use 1 kilogram of tallow and dissolve it completely in the lye. When the mixture is thick, pour some on a plate to test its firmness when cooled. When it is ready, pour the mixture into a large tub and stir until it has cooled and begun to thicken.[36]

Even after bathing became more frequent, the Christmas bath remained a special event, as the following memoir of a Nordfjord emigrant vividly recalls:

> This was by no means an ordinary Saturday bath. It was a genuine Norwegian Christmas cleansing with intense scrubbing and scouring that went beyond all rhyme or reason or measure. Grumbling got you nowhere. "You want to be clean for Christmas, don't you?" Then back into the tub went your curly head. But, my oh my, if you've never been a little boy getting a Christmas bath, you have missed one of the truly superb joys of Christmas. There you stand thoroughly prepared for Christmas. Minutes before you were just an ordinary kid dressed in everyday clothes that you'd worn to dirty, dingy rags; now you stood there cleansed for Christmas, a warm, vigorous feeling of contentment and celebration coursing through and wrapping all around you. Mother came with a new soft shirt, new stockings, Sunday-best clothes from top to toe. With grandparents, father and mother, sisters and brothers, all groomed and dressed for the holiday, the house clean and the floor fragrantly strewn with juniper, the singularity of the occasion surrounds you. What is old and commonplace has vanished. Outdoors the mystical *oskorei* and other Christmas goblins reign; inside we are safe and secure.[37]

THE LUSSI, OSKOREI, AND OTHER PREPARATION POLICE

The oskorei were only one group in the array of frightening, invisible beings that once terrified Norwegians at Christmastime. Strong convictions about these spirits regulated behavior in the preindustrial peasant society. Expecting severe reprisals if they failed to prepare for Christmas in just the right way or did not finish in time, the peasants made sure their preparations complied with community expectations.

Making life hazardous for laggards in Hardanger and Setesdal, the *lussi* was a fearsome witch who roared through the skies on December 13. For five hundred years that date had marked the winter solstice, when all work had to cease while—according to tradition—the sun turned in its course and henceforth brought longer days. The introduction of the Gregorian calendar in 1700 moved the solstice to its present date of December 21, but many traditions persisted that associated the lussi (and December 13) with the completion of Christmas preparations (especially threshing and slaughter). Numerous sayings reflected the belief that these pre-Christmas chores must be completed by December 13 lest the vengeful lussi wreak havoc. She also took out her wrath on disobedient children, who heard that she would swoop down the chimney and kidnap or punish them.

In other regions people told of the *julegeit* or *julebukk*, a half human, half goat who dwelt in the woods away from humanity during most of the year. Then as Christmas approached, it would gradually close in on area farms, expecting to sample the Christmas beer and food, quick to punish those who didn't have them ready.

Yet of all these preparation police, the most frightening were the oskorei, known in Setesdal, Telemark, and parts of western Norway. An unruly band of rambunctious spirits, they rode the Christmas skies on black, fire-eyed steeds. Too wicked for Heaven but not sufficiently evil for Hell, these spirits (also known as the *julerei* or *julesveiner*) were doomed to roam throughout eternity, but made a particular nuisance of themselves during the season of strong winter winds and storms, whose sounds and devastating effects they imitated.

Farmers tried to ward off visits from the oskorei, hastening to paint crosses on their stabbur doors before the sun went down, while uttering the words "kors i Jesu navn" (cross in Jesus' name).[38] They strove especially

Oral tradition includes many colorful descriptions of the oskorei (also known as the jolerei)
and the protective power of making crosses:

"The oskorei drank up the beer and refilled the barrels with something far worse. One Second Christmas Day the people of the Tolleiv Eptestøl farm were at the neighboring farm for a Christmas gathering. They had left a large bowl of beer standing on the wood stove at home. When they returned, the oskorei had been there and spilled beer all over the floor. My grandmother said that what was left in the bowl tasted like horse piss."

"The oskorei once came down Graanliaa at Konsmo and stopped on a hill there. Down on the farm below people heard it coming and started chalking crosses on the beer barrels and stable doors and everything else they were afraid it would take. When it left again, it left a man behind. His name was Helge and the place where the oskorei had stopped is called Helgodaa."

"One Christmas morning the farmer at Jostøl went to his neighbor Torjer and asked, 'How did it go with your horse last night? I can't use mine for driving because when I went out to him, he was dripping from every hair. I hadn't made a cross.'"

Oslo, Norsk Folkeminne Samling, NFS P. Lunde 36, 213; Bergstøl, Atterljom, *75, 77*

to protect the Christmas fare, particularly the *juleøl,* thought to be greatly savored by the oskorei. The custom remained strong until the 1860s and 1870s in parts of western and southern Norway, where crosses carved into aged wooden doors and vessels remain as evidence of this once widespread practice.

Fearing that the oskorei would damage their horses and sleighs, peasants sheltered these carefully, even as they placed steel implements in strategic locations for added protection: a sickle in the grain bin, a scythe in the hay, a steel blade by the well: all could ward off the marauding riders' fury. To ensure their own safety, peasants put axes, knives, leaf cutters, or scissors over the doors of their dwellings or drove these sharp implements into their walls, where they remained until the thirteenth or twentieth day of Christmas.

Numerous legends warned that the oskorei would kidnap those foolish enough to venture out on stormy nights. In lurid detail they told of individuals being snatched up, carried away and then turned loose in some far-off place, dazed and manhandled; other victims disappeared forever. Murder, foul play, or natural death soon visited any farm where the oskorei stayed long enough to dismount, such as in this account from Telemark recorded by the renowned Telemark minister, hymn writer, and collector of folklore, M. B. Landstad (1802–80):

> The people of the Dalen farm in Hvitseid were attending a Christmas gathering at Huvestad. Leaving no one at home, they had locked the doors, but left food on the table as is the custom at Christmas. Returning home a couple of days later, they could tell that the oskorei had been there. They had drunk up the Christmas beer and eaten greedily of the Christmas food, consuming all the lefse and pastries. But worst of all—they'd left a dead man hanging from the ceiling beam. That he was from Numedal could be seen from the silver buttons on his vest. The oskorei had abducted him there, and probably ridden so fast it had killed him.[39]

Belief in the oskorei has now vanished. Norwegians know of it today only through such sources as J. S. Welhaven's mid-nineteenth century poem "Åsgårdsreien" (The oskorei) or the equally famous painting by P. N. Arbo based on the poem.[40] Welhaven drew on Norway's folk beliefs in much the same way that his contemporary Edvard Grieg drew upon its folk music, as a way of defining and celebrating the uniqueness of Norwegian culture. Norway had recently drafted a constitution (1814) and—after centuries of being the weaker partner in a union with Denmark—was developing a sense of nationhood. During this period of what is now known as National Romanticism, folk traditions played a key role, and the Norwegian peasant came to be regarded as the embodiment of all that was genuinely Norwegian. Peter Christen Asbjørnsen and Jørgen Moe collected their folktales during this period, and these narratives, too, eventually became Norwegian classics.

Though belief in the oskorei has disappeared, remnants persist—not only in the thorough cleaning and other preparations that continue to accompany Christmas, but also in more tangible form. The still visible gouges that resulted from peasants driving metal implements into the wall for protection, as well as the crosses mentioned earlier, remain in some of Nor-

Peter Nicolai Arbo, "Åsgårdsreien" (The oskorei), 1872

way's oldest farm dwellings, bearing silent witness to the compelling terror
once struck by the oskorei.

SANTA LUCIA

Arriving in Norway on the thirteenth day of December, tourists might find
some Norwegians celebrating Santa Lucia, a custom that originated in Sweden. There on this day the oldest daughter in the family arises before dawn.
Dressed in a white, flowing gown and with a crown of glowing candles on
her head, she serves her parents breakfast in bed. The custom came to Norway in the 1950s, when it enjoyed great popularity in some places, then
largely disappeared.

The tradition is associated with a second-century Sicilian saint who died
a martyr's death. Many legends describe her piety and goodness. Committed
to remaining unmarried and a virgin, she donated her dowry to the poor
upon converting to Christianity. This action so enraged her brother that he

reported Lucia's conversion to the authorities, well aware of their merciless persecution of Christians. Intending to burn her at the stake, executioners covered her with oil, tree sap, and pitch. When her body miraculously withstood the flames, one of them finished the job by stabbing her in the throat. The Catholic Church conferred sainthood upon her, and she soon gained tremendous popularity, assisted perhaps by the resemblance of her name to *lux,* the Latin word for light.

Santa Lucia's name may also underlie the term *lussi* attached to the witchlike enforcer of proper Christmas preparation, since it was on her saint's day, December 13 (the former solstice), that the lussi's terrifying visits occurred. The fallen angel Lucifer seems also to have contributed to the lussi figure, which in turn has influenced the way people came to celebrate Santa Lucia: to protect livestock from the lussi's ravages, peasants used to give the animals an extra treat on St. Lucia's day, and eventually they came to provide an early breakfast for the farm's inhabitants as well.

The Lucia tradition of a young woman serving her parents predawn coffee may also have drawn upon the German *Christkindl* custom, in which a female figure similarly adorned in white gown and candle wreath comes to bestow gifts upon children. Though today's Norwegian families rarely perform the Swedish Santa Lucia ritual at home, family church services, schools, and *barnehager* (day-care centers) often do, selecting one of the older girls to be Santa Lucia. She wears the gown and candle-crown (often electric in this case) and leads a procession of girls and boys dressed in white robes—the girls with garlands, the boys in cone-shaped hats—as they all sing Christmas carols and seasonal songs.

A SHEAF OF OATS

One of the few traditional Christmas customs that today's Norwegians practice in its original form is that of erecting a *julenek,* or sheaf of grain for the birds. Equally widespread in both urban and rural areas, the tradition probably survives because it found a place in National Romantic artists' depictions of an idealized Norwegian Christmas and because it adapted easily to modern building styles.

Origins of the custom, however, remain obscure. One of the oldest known descriptions dates only as far back as 1753 and is attributed to Erik

Pontoppidan, a prominent clergyman and author of the *Forklaring* (the explanation of Luther's *Small Catechism,* which all Norwegians once had to memorize before they could be confirmed). He saw the julenek custom as the "Norwegian peasant's hospitality extending to the birds which he invites to be his guests by placing an unthreshed sheaf of grain on a pole above the barn door." The very next year, however, another minister railed against the identical custom that Pontoppidan had found so charming, decrying it in his Christmas sermon as "one of the most superstitious and therefore sinful practices."[41] This protest—possibly derived from an association of the julenek with the age-old folk belief in grain's power to ward off the supernatural—has led some scholars to think the custom had a pagan origin. Still others see a closer link between this gift of grain and the sense of Christian charity that motivated the commonly taken precaution to keep birds and other animals from being caught in animal traps and snares during the Christmas season. No matter what its origins, the julenek has become a symbol of Christmas generosity and commonly appears on Norwegian Christmas cards, wrapping paper, and gift tags.

CHRISTMAS MAIL

Packages arriving from far and near, letters and cards from relatives and friends heard from only at this time of year: the mail holds so many of the season's treasured pleasures. Writing Christmas letters and cards has become such a natural part of today's Christmas preparations that we easily forget what a young custom it is: not much over a century old.

An English businessman, Henry Cole (who later founded London's Victoria and Albert Museum), sent the first Christmas card in 1843. Unable to find time to write to all his friends and relatives that year, he commissioned an artist to make up a batch of printed cards. He used what he needed and sold the rest. The custom did not really catch on until the 1870s, when improved postal service and printing technology increased the practicality and popularity of cards. Soon mass-produced greetings made in Germany began pouring into both the United States and Great Britain.

For a long time most of the cards used in Norway, too, came from Germany, though the first Norwegian card did appear already in 1870. Yet it is the year 1883 that really marks the beginning of Norwegian Christmas card production. That year two cards appeared whose motifs became standard: Wilhelm Larsen's drawing of a *nisse* (gnome) throwing snowballs that stick to a fence and spell "Glædelig jul" (Merry Christmas), and Adolf Tidemand's famous 1843 painting *Norske juleskikk* (Norwegian Christmas customs), showing a stabbur, julenek, and wintry outdoor activity. Like most Norwegian cards until the 1970s, these greetings arrived as postcards.

The nisse, nostalgic Christmas scenes, and winter landscapes continued to decorate the cards of the 1880s and 1890s, while religious motifs occurred only rarely. Perhaps people regarded the new fashion of sending postcards too frivolous a partner for their earnestly practiced Christian faith.[42]

By contrast, the pig figured prominently on these early cards, a reference, no doubt, to the traditional Christmas slaughter. Its fundamental role in providing the yuletide abundance of meat-based foods gives sufficient grounds for its presence, but the pig's ubiquity on these cards suggests an even deeper meaning. The porcine image seems to capture the *festglede* (celebratory joy) that such a sumptuous meat—along with the other rich Christmas food—once conjured up in lean times. By extension, the pig eventually came to stand for good fortune, on a par with the four-leaf clover and horseshoe; it continues to appear on Norwegian Christmas cards as a symbol of abundance, celebration, and joy, despite the loss of the dominant role that the slaughter once played.

The baking that today in many ways has come to take the pivotal place of slaughter in yuletide preparations didn't make its appearance on Christmas cards until well after the turn of the twentieth century, when the requisite baking ovens, sugar, white flour, and other necessary ingredients had become widespread. Not until the 1920s, in fact, did cards picturing women and children wielding rolling pins and cookie forms abound, later joined by other motifs from the modern, child-centered Christmas, such as the Christmas tree and presents.

Of all the cards produced in Norway, though, by far the most popular have been those depicting the nisse. Making no pretense of documenting authentic folk belief, these cards have instead provided a venue for illustrators to express their sense of playfulness, absurdity, and originality. During the World War II Nazi occupation of Norway, however, these cards played a more serious role, becoming a forum for ridiculing the oppressive regime. The nisser cavorted in their red stocking caps amid outsized Norwegian flags and Constitution Day ribbons (all outlawed by the Nazi authorities) as the cards pointedly wished their recipients "God *norsk* jul" (Merry *Norwegian* Christmas—that is, Christmas as it had been before the occupation). The Nazi authorities banned the cards. First they rounded up those they could find at printers and at stationery stores, then they ordered all postmasters in Norway to confiscate any nisse cards that came through the mails. The fact that many of these cards still exist in private collections, public libraries, and museum archives all around Norway attests not only to the cards' appeal, but even more to a hunger for their vital message that Nazi intimidation could be overcome and that Norway would again be free.[43]

Some postwar nisse cards continued their traditional role of editorializing. A series by Arne Taraldsen, for example, commented sarcastically on wartime profiteering. But most often the nisse cards reverted to their role of providing a unique and welcome venue for the artistic release of childlike creativity. Following the example of Wilhelm Larsen, Nils Bergslien, and Trygve Davidson have also produced classic nisse motifs. Unlike American Christmas cards' heavy reliance on Santa, Norwegian cards rarely depict his Nordic counterpart, the tall, gaunt gift-bearing *julenisse*.

Today's Norwegian Christmas greeting typically arrives in a sealed envelope. Though nisse cards reached their peak during the 1960s, they remain popular, as do those showing wintry scenes, winter sports, and the sender's hometown or farm. Reflecting Norwegian social concerns, UNICEF cards, which raise money for the world's needy children, have become popular in recent years. But by far the most popular greetings now are the amateur snapshot photo cards and duplicated computer annual letters that with equal regularity—and the same self-deprecatory remarks about resorting to them—are sent by Americans. In highly computer-literate Norway, e-mail has joined these other ways of keeping in touch at Christmas, and on the Internet a Web site (www.interkort.no) invites people to send Christmas cards via e-mail free, offering a choice of several motifs.

More traditional is the *julehefte* (Christmas annual). Magazine-like in format, but with especially fine illustrations and paper, these booklets contain Christmas-related articles and stories, poetry, and artwork. The best ones feature literature and artwork from a particular area and reflect its local history and traditions. Peter Christen Asbjørnsen, Norway's renowned folktale collector, printed Norway's first julehefte in 1850 to publish some of the

God Norsk Jul!

This postcard—with others like it—was outlawed during World War II by Nazi officials.

folklore he had gathered. Many of Norway's most prominent writers contributed to *julehefter* in subsequent years, producing a treasure trove of Christmas-related short stories and verse. Norwegian Americans carried this tradition to the other side of the Atlantic, encouraging Norwegian immigrant writers to craft Christmas stories from their own unique perspective. In the process these annuals have become valued repositories of insights into Christmases past as celebrated by Norwegians on both sides of the Atlantic.

CHRISTMAS SHOPPING—GIFTS AND GOODIES

Statistics show that each Norwegian spends at least three thousand kroner (about five hundred dollars) extra during the Christmas season.[44] Of this spending, about 50 percent goes to gifts, while somewhat over 30 percent goes to food and drink. Products that sell particularly well during Christmas include watches, optics, clothing, textiles, and books. Norway's *Vinmonopol* (state monopoly on retail sales of wine and spirits) and chocolate factories reap their best earnings at Christmastime, too.[45] Taxation laws assist Norwegian Christmas shoppers by requiring them to pay only half their normally owed taxes for the month of December. What a boon to the extra spending that the modern Christmas requires!

To capitalize on this spending, the commercial sector has made valiant attempts to expand the pre-Christmas shopping period. During the first half of the twentieth century, Christmas shopping began on the Monday following the first Sunday in Advent. After World War II, shopping began progressively earlier until the 1970s, when the first Christmas displays started going up as soon as the end of October. Strong objection to this over-commercialization succeeded in pushing the date back to the last weeks of November.[46]

While gifts now occupy center stage, they have only recently become part of the Norwegian Christmas. Recalling the enormous anticipation of childhood Christmases spent in Østerdalen, Norway, former Luther College regent John Dieseth (born 1813) wrote: "The gifts we received had little to do with our great anticipation. A dollar would pay for all the purchased gifts I received from age five to age fourteen. These could be some wearing apparel, like mittens, socks and shoes that happened to be ready about that time and were called a gift, but these were things that we would have gotten anyhow."[47] Making such gifts rather than purchasing them constituted part of the Christmas preparations in the old peasant society, and simple, necessary gifts dominated until at least the beginning of the twentieth century.

The custom of giving presents at this time of year goes back, as we've already noted, to the ancient Roman New Year's celebration (the calends [first] of January), when the upper class bestowed gifts upon their servants to acknowledge work performed during the previous year. Exchanging New Year's gifts subsequently spread throughout Europe, especially to the royal courts and aristocratic circles. The sagas of the Norwegian kings tell of both Eirik Jarl and King Olav Haraldsson giving such gifts in the early eleventh century. New Year's gifts continued to be given throughout the Middle Ages, and the custom continued well into the eighteenth and nineteenth centuries.[48] By then the gifts served to convey good wishes for health and prosperity in the coming year and were exchanged among relative social equals. These New Year's tokens consisted of holiday cakes, apples, meats, nutmegs, eggs, or oranges stuck with cloves.

Christmas presents were added to the seasonal gift exchange during the Middle Ages. Stimulated by Catholicism's encouragement of charity and good works, Christmas gifts in the 1400s and 1500s consisted mostly of food. Christmas presents for children arose independently, influenced by customs associated with December 6, the Day of St. Nicholas.

Bishop Nicholas lived in Lydia (today's Turkey) during the period of Christian persecution. After his death, stories circulated portraying Nicholas as a protector of the weak and persecuted and of children. The church elevated him to sainthood, and by the year 1500 Europeans in several countries had consecrated more than three thousand St. Nicholas churches. But even as early as 1220, people had begun associating the well-established custom of giving New Year's gifts to children in monastery schools with St. Nicholas. Some time later this gift-giving moved to his saint's day, December 6, thus permanently entwining Nicholas with the giving of gifts.

By the 1400s the custom had spread from schools to families. The oldest reports come from Germany, where children left boots (and later shoes and stockings) in window sills and found them filled with gifts the next morning. From the 1500s come the first accounts of people dressing up like St. Nicholas and going door to door, now accompanied by a servant who carried a whip to thrash disobedient children.

Protestant Germans tried to replace this Catholic tradition by portraying the Christ child (Christkindl) as the giver of the gifts and moving gift-giving from the saint's day to Christmas Eve. Despite these reformation efforts, Klaus, Nikolaus, or Santa Claus remained an indelible part of the gift exchange. Though many of these practices came to Denmark and Sweden during the sixteenth and seventeenth centuries, giving gifts to children did not become common in Norway until the end of the nineteenth century. City residents had adopted it earlier, but the custom of exchanging store-bought presents took a long time to reach the countryside.

Eating special delicacies at Christmastime, however, has a long tradition all over Norway. The baked goods already discussed account for only some of the tasty treats that tempt palates during the Christmas season, when Norwegians buy: 250 tons of dates (*dadler*), 660 tons of figs (*fiken*), 739 tons of hazel nuts (*hasselnøtter*), 185 tons of Brazil nuts (*paranøtter*), and 409 tons of walnuts (*valnøtter*).[49] These foods may not stir the excitement they once did, as exotica seen at no other time of year than Christmas, but they remain part of the holiday season's definitive fun and flavor.

Norwegians continue to make Christmas candy, too, despite its daily presence at the grocery checkout stand. Nostalgia, the family fun of a shared activity, and the indulgence of childhood pleasures like licking the bowl all keep the custom alive. Oranges, too, still evoke yuletide memories; once appearing only at Christmas and Easter, their jet-age, year-round availability has not robbed them of their honored place on the Christmas Eve coffee table, which also features green and purple grapes, bananas, and pears.

Chocolate factories in Norway make 20 percent of their yearly sales at Christmas, when stores also sell 2,500 tons of almonds, much of which goes to making marzipan. Invented by the Persians (who called it *Mautapan*) around A.D. 600 to 700, this confection combines ground almonds with powdered sugar and egg whites. Marzipan came to Europe during the Middle Ages with the Christian crusaders who called it *Marci panis* (St. Mark's bread).

Much of Norway's Christmas marzipan appears in the form of *marsipangriser* (marzipan pigs). Available in a wide range of sizes, marsipangriser rank third in sales for Norway's Nidar Bergene Chocolate Company, which annually makes a profit of 75 million kroner (over 10 million dollars) on this confection alone.[50] A symbol of good fortune, the marsipangris is often presented to the person whose portion of Christmas Eve rice porridge contains a hidden almond.

LETTERS TO SANTA

Drøbak, a town on the Oslo Fjord about twenty miles south of the capital, has established itself as Norway's *juleby* (Christmas town). Since 1990, letters have arrived there from all over the world addressed to Santa. All are duly answered by *Nissens postkontor* (the Christmas elf's post office). Drøbak enjoys the additional distinction of being the only Norwegian town to have an official highway sign urging caution at *nisse* crossings. The official reply to the town's application for the sign reads:

> The Highway Department understands that there has been a significant increase of nisser in Drøbak and will therefore not oppose erecting a caution sign with the applied-for symbol: Running nisse with sack.[51]

Street sign, Drøbak, Norway, 1990s

The nisse depicted on the sign looks somewhat like the American Santa Claus, being considerably fleshier than the Norwegian nisse, who has an entirely different history and nature.

That history is full of twists and turns, the first complication being the name itself. *Nisse* stands for two distinct concepts that are frequently unwittingly intertwined, as they are in the Highway Department's letter quoted above. On the one hand there is the *julenisse*—the tall, gaunt giver of Christmas gifts, a direct descendent of Saint Nicholas and often dressed in a floor-length coat. Then there are the numerous barn *nisser*—diminutive fellows, sporting long white beards and dressed in knee pants, red stocking caps, and wooden shoes. Rather than giving gifts at Christmas, these nisser demanded them, expecting a bowl of porridge or other tribute for all the farmwork they had performed throughout the year.

The term *nisse* wasn't widely used until the 1820s, but the supernatural being most closely related to the barn nisse has ancient roots. Variably known in different parts of Norway as the *haugbonde* (farmer buried in the farm's *haug*, or ancestral grave mound), *gardvord* (farm protector), or *tuftekall* (the one who laid the farm's foundations), this being was known in Sweden and some parts of eastern Norway as the *tomte* (building site protector).

These names reflect the pre-Christian belief in the special power that rested with the ancestor who first cleared the farm. His descendants believed in his continued presence in the farm's buildings and landscape, as proprietor and defender. The farm dwellers made offerings to him at Christmas in hopes of receiving his help in attaining good crops, fertility, and peace.[52] When Norway became a Christian country around the year 1000, belief in the gardvord lived on, as did the pre-Christian custom of making offerings to him. Neither clerical objections nor ecclesiastical laws could discourage the belief that he should receive a tribute (usually beer or porridge) during the holidays, both in gratitude for his work and to spare the farm the misfortune thought certain to follow the custom's neglect.[53]

During the eighteenth-century Age of Enlightenment, belief in the gardvord began being replaced by stories about the nisse, usually personified as a little fellow who tends the livestock and guards the farm, but who also avenges ill treatment of the animals and any other practices inconsistent with traditional farm management.[54] This personification came to life in magazine and postcard illustrations during the mid-1800s, at the same time that Scandinavians were converting their Christmas into a more child-centered, family-oriented celebration. The nisse fit right in. Playful images of the nisse receiving his Christmas porridge proliferated. Meanwhile, the coincidence that the Scandinavian name Nisse is a form of the name Nicholas associated the nisse with the gift-giving St. Nicholas, long popular in Germany and Holland.[55]

While the nisse was attaining his new stature in Norway, the New York City literary club known as the Knickerbockers was inventing the American Santa Claus. The best-known member of this group, Washington Irving, published on December 6 (St. Nicholas Day), 1809, the immensely popular *Knickerbocker's History of New York*. The Knickerbockers belonged to the city's aristocracy; those in that social stratum felt their authority increasingly under siege as the city grew and modernized. Aiming to counterbalance the commercial bustle and "democratic misrule" of contemporary society, Irving satirically portrayed New York as a serene, slow-paced city ruled over by St. Nicholas himself.[56]

The next year another member of the group, John Pintard, who had founded the New York Historical Society on St. Nicholas Day, 1804, commissioned a broadside depicting St. Nicholas, "the good, holy man," in saintly, floor-length vestments with two children—a pleased little girl who has received a present and a tearful boy who has gotten a switch.[57] It was with this classical image of Nicholas that fellow Knickerbocker Clement C. Moore began when he created the new St. Nick in " 'Twas the Night before Christmas." Moore was a country gentleman and professor of theology. The seminary was located on his property in Chelsea (just north of present-day Greenwich Village), which just then was being converted from tranquil countryside into an urban landscape, subsumed by Manhattan's expanding grid system of streets and avenues. In Moore's hands, St. Nicholas lost his intimidating air of ecclesiastical authority, as already noted, and became a jolly old working-class elf ("a bundle of toys he had flung on his back, and he looked like a peddler just opening his pack").

In the years to come Santa Claus lost his miniature stature, becoming full-sized, even rotund; he also grew increasingly avuncular. Wrought by Thomas Nast, these changes appeared in *Harper's Weekly,* which first carried Moore's poem, illustrated by Nast, in 1863, then proceeded for thirty years to carry annual Nast Santa illustrations. In them Nast also created Santa's North Pole workshop. Innumerable reprints in magazines, newspapers, and books fixed the American public's concept of how Santa looked and behaved.

Before long, the idea that Santa Claus had a workshop where he received children's lengthy wish lists gained international acceptance and in 1946 youngsters from all over the world began associating Santa's North Pole workshop with Norway. That was the year Oslo began the now annual custom of presenting London's Trafalgar Square with a Christmas tree to thank Britain for its assistance during Norway's World War II Nazi occupation. Soon British children began sending their Christmas lists to Santa in "Oslo, the City of Snow," and the Oslo Tourist Office developed a brochure to send in return. This practice continued until the 1980s, when Finland cornered the Santa market in a blaze of international campaigning. More than five hundred thousand children began addressing their wish lists to Santa in Finnish Lapland rather than Norway.

With Norwegian honor at stake, something had to be done. In 1989, Drøbak municipal authorities declared their town Santa's birthplace. They established Santa's Own Post Office in 1990. About thirty of this small town's inhabitants work on Christmas year-round. The activity radiates from the main square and the *Tregården Julehus,* a large, painstakingly restored wooden house that sells a great variety of both domestic and imported Christmas goods. Though the post office goes by the name of *Nissens postkontor* (the nisse's post office), the image associated with it, like that on the town's nisse highway sign, shows strong influence of the American Santa Claus.

In whatever form you imagine him, letters to Santa may be addressed to:

> Julenissen
> P.O. Box 200
> 1441 Drøbak, Norway

The Internet also has a Julenisse Web site (www.julenissen.no), which proclaims that "the Julenisse answers e-mail. Do you have a question for the Julenisse? Write and send a wish list." It also offers a sneak peek at the Julenisse's workshop.

Thus three distinct figures claim the name *nisse* in modern Norway: the roly-poly American Santa, who is competing hard in the commercial sector with the two genuinely Norwegian nisser; the Julenisse, a gaunt, gift-giving man in the floor-length gray coat inspired by Saint Nicholas and still occasionally impersonated or depicted on Christmas cards; and the ubiquitous diminutive elf in knee pants and stocking cap who evolved from the once venerated but now largely forgotten gardvord. Growing together during the 1800s, the nisse and the Julenisse have become practically indistinguishable, while the international Santa Claus figure developed in America is increasingly taking their place.

JULEBORD: THE CHRISTMAS BUFFET

Yet another Norwegian Advent custom remains to be considered: the *julebord* (Christmas table). The annual highlight of the hospitality industry, this pre-Christmas buffet begins six weeks before Christmas, when

> hotels and restaurants compete with each other in making the best Christmas food they can muster. The julebord includes the most traditional Norwegian main dishes — *ribbe* [pork ribs], *pinnekjøtt* [steamed mutton ribs], *medisterpølser* [pork sausage], and *lutefisk,* along with cold cuts like *rull* [lamb roll] and *sylte* [head cheese]. All is washed down with generous servings of beer and *akevitt* [caraway-flavored spirits of potato].
>
> Serving one hundred different dishes is not unheard of, all at the same, one-time price, never to be repeated again — until next Christmas. Chefs set their pride in putting on the best table, and people flock from far and near to partake in this minor bacchanalia.[58]

It has become a tradition for couples, friends, business associates, and colleagues to meet over one of these pre-Christmas buffets. In addition, virtually every organization and place of employment arranges (at least one year in advance) a julebord for its associates, members, and employees.

One of the most high-profile recent developments in the Norwegian Christmas celebration, the julebord originated in the post–World War II period, stimulated by the nascent welfare state's innovative goal that individuals of all classes would share more equally in society's prosperity. Initially enjoyed only by the affluent, the julebord consequently spread to the majority of the population, and it has subsequently grown in concert with Norway's urbanization, expanding middle class, and growing service industry.

The julebord has also exerted a significant influence on the modern Norwegian Christmas celebration, moving part of it out of the home, giving it an earlier start, and diffusing its focus. Employers arranging the buffets for their workers, for example, frequently include an overview of the company's past year and recognition of key employees, along with the more seasonal speeches, group singing, and entertainment.

Though recent in practice, the julebord's roots reach back to the pre-industrial peasant society's custom of leaving the dinner table set all through the night on Christmas in deference to the family's returning dead, who could serve themselves at leisure while the family slept. The fare that stood on those peasant tables differs surprisingly little from the contents of today's julebord. In fact, the modern Christmas buffet frequently includes a dish that goes back even farther, a boar's head biting a real apple, a tradition said to derive from Viking banquets.

Then there's the *akevitt*. Not available in Scandinavia until the 1500s, spirits were originally used as medicine. By the 1600s people had discovered their recreational use and the "dosage" increased accordingly. Norwegians first made spirits from grain and built all kinds of contraptions for *hjemme-brenning* (home distilling). Every town and settlement produced moonshine (except during the hardship years from 1756 to 1816, when distilling spirits was forbidden to conserve the severely limited grain supply for planting). These years (especially the Napoleonic War years of 1807–14) taught Norwegians to value the potato as a replacement for grain.

Originally regarding the potato with great suspicion and superstition, the peasants shunned it, fearing it would cause leprosy. Civil servants realized the potato's possibilities more quickly. Seeing one bad grain crop follow another in the 1770s, they began increasing their potato acreage, so that by the 1780s every parish had at least one field devoted to the new crop. Ministers took up the potato's cause with special enthusiasm. Referred to as *potetprester* (potato pastors), they used their pulpits to overcome the peasants' mistrust and eventually convinced them of the potato's superior yield and sturdiness.

By 1845 the potato was a well-established crop all over Norway. In that year home brewing was forbidden. The production and consumption of spirits had gotten completely out of hand; public drunkenness had become an enormous problem. The monotony and hardships of life on the farms along with the gloomy weather contributed to widespread alcoholism and caused many a grain crop that should have been consumed as flatbread or porridge to end up in the still instead.

It is estimated that 11,000 distillation devices were in use in Norway in 1827. Thirty years later only 450 home stills remained. This was not entirely due to the prohibition of hjemmebrenning. The requirement that alcohol be distilled from potatoes instead of grain also played a role. Making spirits from potatoes required more advanced equipment and a greater volume of production.[59]

Originally the name *akevitt* had applied to all kinds of hard liquor, but it came to apply only to alcohol distilled from potatoes. The temperance movement that had prohibited hjemmebrenning in 1845 implemented in 1916 the prohibition of all fortified wine and whisky. By 1927, when these restrictions were rescinded, the Vinmonopol (state wine monopoly) had purchased all of Norway's distilleries, and all sales of wine and spirits had to go through it. The 1980s and 1990s have seen a liberalization of its policy restricting the number of sales outlets and liquor licenses, a development that will probably be reinforced under the influence of the European Union.[60]

Today's aquavit is made from neutral potato spirits and flavored with herbal essences, chiefly caraway along with varying amounts of anise, fennel, dill, and coriander. The filtered alcohol is blended to a strength of 60 percent, and this mixture is aged from three to five years in five-hundred-liter oak barrels that have already been used in sherry production. That's about as close to the exact recipe as we can get. Locked away in a fireproof vault to which only a tiny handful of people have access, the Vinmonopol's aquavit recipe may be guarded more closely than the nation's gold bouillon. What everyone does know is that it's the aging that gives the product its character, as the flavors mingle and blend.[61]

Taking that fact to its logical conclusion has brought fame to the Linie brand of aquavit. The *Linie* (or *linje,* line) in question is the equator, which this spirit crosses twice in the holds of Wilhelmsen Lines ships as they travel to and from Australia. Rolling around inside well-seasoned oak casks and subjected to sharp temperature changes, the aquavit grows ever smoother. When finally bottled in Norway, Linie Akevitt bears a label that tells the name of the ship on which it traveled and the dates of the voyage. How this custom got started no one really knows, but seamen in sailing ships probably noticed that their own aquavit improved with the journey.[62]

Well over half the aquavit sold in Norway is consumed at Christmas, and during the last few decades aquavit has assumed its place as Norway's Christmas liquor, significantly assisted by the simultaneous rise of the julebord. Though now a tradition in its own right, the julebord in many ways turns the old peasant Christmas upside down. While the Norwegian peasants decreased their already scanty diet during the weeks before Christmas in order to intensify their enjoyment of the rare delicacies served only at Christmas, many in today's Norway have already had their fill of these treats long before Christmas Eve arrives. Despite this change, Christmas Eve continues to contain unparalleled delights for both adults and children.

Christmas Eve
The Focus of the Feast

We bake cookies, although not everyone manages sju slags *[seven kinds] any more. We make marzipan, fill the freezer with meat, and make* kjøttruller *[luncheon meats] for use on open-faced sand-wiches. On Lillejulaften [December 23] everything is supposed to be ready: all the cleaning done, the Christmas curtains hung, and the house decorated.[1] Most still use a genuine* gran *[spruce] for their Christmas tree, though many older folks are going over to plastic for practical reasons. We ourselves usually get a* furu *[pine] if we can, or* edelgran *[silver fir]. It doesn't lose as many needles as the* gran, *but gran is the real Christmas tree.*

Karin Behr Skjævestad, Moss, 1997

Lillejulaften (Little Christmas Eve), the day most Norwegians put up their Christmas tree, is said to have been instituted by those who just couldn't wait for the twenty-fourth. Tradition even grants children (but, regrettably, not adults) permission to open one present that day. The Christmas tree is now a yuletide fixture in most Norwegian homes. Most still buy *gran,* or spruce, but for practical reasons, *furu,* or pine, and *edelgran,* silver fir, are quickly catching up. Norwegians often cut off the tree's lower branches and place them outside the front door as a festive and fragrant seasonal door-mat—and an echo (conscious or not) of past centuries' juniper-spread floors.

The prominent position of the tree in today's holiday would surprise a Norwegian peasant from the nineteenth century. Although the first decorated Christmas tree appeared in Norway in the early 1800s, more than fifty years passed before the custom really started to spread. Members of the upper class adopted it first, but received a great deal of criticism from more conservative circles, who viewed the tree as "sinful and blasphemous" and a form of "idolatry."[2] Others refused to adopt the custom simply because it *was* an upper-class custom, and the peasants did not want to copy *kondisjonerte* or city customs.[3]

Eventually schools and the media helped the Christmas tree prevail. Famous writers such as J. S. Welhaven, Henrik Wergeland, and Jørgen Moe mentioned the Christmas tree in 1836, 1840, and 1843, respectively, and Peter Christen Asbjørnsen's 1850 *julehefte* (Christmas annual) bore both the title *Juletreet* (the Christmas tree) and a cover showing people dancing around a festively trimmed fir.

Well before families had trees at home, schools began holding *juletrefester* (Christmas-tree parties) such as the one enjoyed in 1900 by five-year-old John Dieseth at Åmot in Østerdalen:

> The tree was in the center of a large room. It was loaded with goodies and many shining gold and silver balls. We started by forming rings around the tree, the smallest children in the inner ring and so on. As we were walking around the tree singing, I was eyeing all the things on the tree. . . . After so many rounds and minutes we would stop and each one would get one thing, the next time something else, and so on until the only thing left was some paper streamers and those shiny balls.[4]

As Dieseth describes, the early tree functioned as a "gift tree," holding edibles that the children harvested. Once acquainted with the Christmas tree, children urged their parents to adopt the custom at home.

But where did the Christmas tree come from? To Norway it came via Denmark from Germany. Though not widespread there until the 1830s, the Christmas tree custom was begun by sixteenth-century German Protestants as an alternative to the Catholic gift-giving associated with St. Nicholas. Parents told their children that it was Christkindl (the Christ child) who brought both the gifts and the tree. (The name Kris Kringle derives from Christkindl.) A market for Christmas trees existed as early as 1539 in Stras-

Lighting Christmas tree candles at the Salvation Army's orphanage, Oslo, 1910.

bourg (then a German city), where in 1605 a traveler made this entry in his journal: "At Christmas people in Strasbourg set up fir trees in their rooms with roses cut from multicolored paper, apples, cakes, tinsel, and sugar hanging from the branches."[5]

Then as now, however, protests arose that the folk custom was clouding the real meaning of the season. In 1642 the Strasbourg clergyman Johann Konrad Dannhauer complained: "Among the trifles to which people often devote more attention than the Word of God in celebrating Christmas is the fir tree, which is set up at home, hung with dolls and sweets and finally ransacked."[6]

Legends and myths helped make the Christmas tree acceptable. The best known tells how Martin Luther, on an evening walk in the forest, was struck by the beauty of bright stars shining through the evergreens. Wanting to share the vision with his children, he placed candles on a small evergreen and thereby invented the Christmas tree.[7] As the tree's popularity grew, the church eventually withdrew its objections. Attempting to remove any lingering pagan associations, the Church adopted the name *Christbaum* and also introduced Christian interpretations of the tree's decorations: the candles stood for Jesus, "the light of the world"; the star for the Star of Bethlehem (Matthew 2:9); and the glass balls for the world and God's love of it (Psalm 24:1).

At home, parents kept the family Christmas tree in a separate room, concealed from the children until the very Eve of Christmas. Then they would ceremoniously throw the doors open to reveal the seeming miracle of an already decorated tree. This custom eventually prevailed in Norway, as well.

The Christmas tree came to Norway in 1822. A family in Kristiania (Oslo) with connections in Denmark and Germany became acquainted with the custom there. Then it wasn't long before large landowners, ministers, and others of the kondisjonerte circles imitated the custom. In 1840 we hear of a tree at the University of Oslo, but the tree was not present in most Norwegian homes until about 1915.[8]

Though the Christmas tree itself arrived in Norway relatively late, Norwegian culture incorporated trees into its earliest myths and rituals. In Old Norse mythology, Ygdrasil (the world tree) provides the link that joins earth and sky. For centuries afterward the *tuntre* (farmyard tree, often growing on the grave mound of the farm's founder) constituted a sacred place on Norwegian farms, honored by the family (the founder's descendants), who ritually poured ale on its roots at Christmas and other special times of the year.[9] Ancient Roman winter solstice festival celebrants displayed the evergreen to symbolize the growing season whose return they sought; the Norwegian juniper branches on the floor may have conveyed the same hope, even as they freshened the air.

The Christmas tree, though not commonly found in all parts of Norway until after the turn of the twentieth century, had by World War II become Norway's most important yuletide decoration, replacing juniper boughs on the floor and weavings or *kroting* (lime drawings) on the walls. Today's Norwegian Christmas celebrations feature trees festooned with decorations (often store-bought) instead of with treats and gifts. The latter, increasingly more luxurious, now go under the tree.

In their growing affluence some families have begun decorating multiple Christmas trees, adorning an evergreen outside in the yard as well as the one in the living room. Some have even taken to decorating shrubbery other than evergreens, though this practice has so far not become widespread. The American practice of using strings of multicolored outdoor Christmas lights to decorate homes and yards rarely occurs in Norway, however, where white lights predominate and for the most part remain confined to one or two evergreen trees.[10]

Norwegian Flags, Heart-shaped Baskets, and Straw Decorations

Which decorations on a modern Christmas tree would identify it as Norwegian? We would have to look past an array of generic, store-bought, internationally produced (mostly East Asian) ornaments to find three items with roots in Norway. Norwegian flags found a place on the Christmas tree because of timing; the tree's introduction coincided with the development of Norway's identity as a nation during a period now known as National Romanticism. Having adopted its own constitution (on May 17, 1814) after more than four hundred years under Danish rule, Norway during the 1840s was celebrating those things that distinguished it from other countries. Edvard Grieg incorporated Norwegian folk melodies into his compositions, and painters like Johan Christian Dahl, Thomas Fearnley, and

August Cappelen glorified the quintessentially Norwegian glaciers and waterfalls, forests and mountains. Aided by these cultural developments, Bjørnstjerne Bjørnson and other influential politicians promoted national independence. Emblematic of that goal, *det rene flagg* (the pure[ly Norwegian] flag), Bjørnson urged, should replace the then official Norwegian flag, whose upper left panel displayed the Swedish colors (and which he derisively dubbed "sild-salaten" [a multicolored herring dish]). Norwegians obtained their pure flag in 1905, when they peacefully left the union with Sweden and gained full independence. By then the Christmas tree had become widespread, and Norwegians found it a suitable place to display their new flag.

As it turned out, however, 1905 would not be the last time Norwegians had to fight for their flag. When Hitler's soldiers marched into Norway on April 9, 1940, they replaced the Norwegian flag with the Nazi banner and made it illegal for Norwegians to fly their own flag for the next five years.[11] This prohibition only strengthened the Norwegians' resolve to display their country's colors once the war had ended, not least as a decoration on their Christmas trees.

The Christmas tree of old, festooned with gingerbread figures, apples, and oranges, also featured Christmas baskets (*julekurv*) shaped like cones and hearts to hold hard candies and raisins.[12] Some say that Hans Christian Andersen made the first Christmas heart. We do know that he was clever at making things with paper and scissors and that he made a *julehjerte* (heart-shaped Christmas basket) as a gift for Mathilde Ørsted in the 1860s; it is now exhibited by the Hans Christian Andersen Museum in Odense, Denmark. Though now entirely decorative, these woven heart-shaped baskets have not only remained popular, they have come to symbolize Christmas throughout Scandinavia. In Norwegian homes they provide a constructive activity to keep young hands busy during the final days and hours before Christmas.

Straw bent and sewn in various configurations is the third of the characteristically Scandinavian Christmas tree ornaments and has by far the longest roots. The association between straw and Christmas goes back to a time when the Christmas season held more fear and terror than glad tidings and joy. To protect themselves from the bands of ghosts and other such terrors as the *oskorei, lussi, julebukk,* and *julegeit* that they believed haunted the

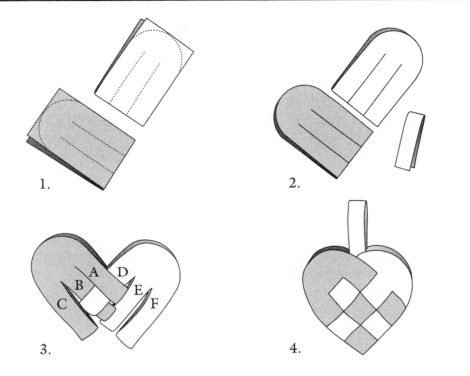

1. For each heart you need two pieces of paper of different colors. They must be three times as long as they are wide. The two pieces are placed on top of each other and folded. Then they are cut together to form two equal-sized, oblong pieces that are closed in one end. Draw lines to follow for cutting the three "ribs." Cut along these lines to form the ribs so they become a little longer than the width of the paper (see dotted line in drawing 1). Draw the rounded line using a compass or a cup, and cut out.

2. Now you have two identical parts. It is very important that they are exactly alike, otherwise you will have problems weaving them together. Cut out a handle, too.

3. Now start weaving. Pull the uppermost piece A (see drawing 3) around D, through E and around F. Push it in as far as possible. Then push piece B through D, around E and through F.

4. Weave piece C in the same way as piece A.

5. With luck, the heart can now be opened like a basket. Glue the handle on the interior of each side, and your basket is ready to hang on the tree.

Familiens julebok, *34, 36*

Folk wisdom from Østerdalen, collected before 1921:

No one must sleep in the barn at Christmas. Tjenestegutter [serving boys] and tjenestejenter [serving girls], who otherwise have their sleeping quarters there, sleep inside the dwelling house on Christmas Eve, as well as the three or four nights closest to it. All of the household members sleep together on the floor in the main room of the house on a bed of straw. This must be observed so the julerei won't get hold of anyone.

Nergaard, Gard og grend

dark nights of Christmas, all the farm's inhabitants gathered in the *våningshus* (main dwelling house) on Christmas Eve to sleep together on the floor, which had been covered with straw.[13]

Besides furnishing insulation and protection from the cold earthen floor, the straw could—according to widespread European folk belief—help ward off the evil spirits. This belief also accounts for the time-honored practice of fashioning straw mobiles or wall decorations, once a fixture in many homes. Straw's unchanging golden color seemed to provide a link between one growing season and the next. Seeing this connection, Norwegians closely examined the grains left behind when they swept out the straw the next morning, certain that these gleanings portended the coming year's crops.

Not all Norwegians interpreted the custom of sleeping on the straw-covered floor in the same way. Some gave up their beds less out of fear than to honor returning dead ancestors, while others felt the custom expressed the equality, on this one special night, of all the farm's inhabitants—from landowner to hired hand.[14] Rather than opposing a well-established yuletide practice, the church promoted sleeping on straw to commemorate the stable of Christ's birth. This interpretation helped preserve this venerable tradition after the fear of the supernatural had ceased to motivate it.[15]

Warmer homes, increased education, and stricter fire regulations eventually made the custom of sleeping on the straw-strewn floor obsolete, but "The Cat of Dovre," one of the folktales collected by Asbjørnsen and Moe, preserves the terrible fear of the supernatural that once lay behind it. The story also addresses the question of why the supernatural visits ceased:

Once upon a time a man up in Finnmark had caught a large white bear and was taking it to the king of Denmark. Now it just so happened that he came to the Dovre Mountain on Christmas Eve. He went to a house where a man named Halvor lived, and asked if he and the bear could stay there for the night.

"Lord have mercy!" the man exclaimed. "We can't let anyone stay here now, for every single Christmas Eve our house fills up with so many trolls we can't stay here ourselves, but must go without a roof over our heads."

Well, the Finnmark man wouldn't take no for an answer and they finally had to let him stay. As they usually did before they left, the family made things ready for the trolls, setting tables with *rømmegrøt* (sour cream porridge), lutefisk, sausage, and everything else that's good—just as for any fine feast.

Now it wasn't long before the trolls did come. Some big, some small,

---

Asbjørnsen and Moe collected oral tradition and used their transcripts as the basis for their stories. Accounts of the oskorei like the one that follows no doubt underlie their tale of Halvor's Christmas visitors:

The people on the Brastad farm in Konsmo were plagued in the old days by the oskorei. They lived near Borgeraasen but came down to Brastad and drank up the beer. The oskorei had made things so unpleasant at Brastad, the people living there finally had to move out of the house on Christmas Eve.

When the oskorei came, they went right down into the cellar and drank up the beer from the barrels there.

One year a stranger came to Brastad. He must not have been afraid of ghosts for he said he would stay there on Christmas Eve when everyone else ran away. He went up into the loft and took along his gun. There was a hole in the floor so he could see downstairs. After a while a large crowd arrived. They sat down around the table and started drinking. One of them said, "Now I'll drink a toast to Tron." Tron was their leader. But the man in the loft said, "Now *I'll* drink a toast to Tron," and with that he shot Tron who was sitting at the head of the table. Well, they all cleared out of there as fast as they could, dragging Tron along with them.

And that's the way they got rid of the oskorei at Brastad.

Bergstøl, Atterljom, *76*

some with long tails, some with no tail at all, and some with long, long, noses. They ate and drank, greedily tasting of everything.

Then one of the troll children caught sight of the white bear lying under the stove. He roasted a piece of sausage on a fork and poked it in the bear's face, burning its nose. "Want a sausage, Kitty?" the troll shrieked. Rising to its feet, the bear let out such a ferocious growl that all of the trolls, from the largest to the smallest, ran for their very lives.

A year later Halvor was in the forest gathering wood for the holiday on the afternoon of Christmas Eve, for he expected the trolls as usual. As he stood there chopping, a voice called, "Halvor, Halvor!"

"Yes?"

"Do you still have your big, white cat?"

"Sure do. She's at home, under the stove," Halvor replied, "and now she's had seven kittens, each one even bigger and meaner than herself."

"Then we won't be coming back to your house!" shouted the troll in the woods. And never again did the trolls eat Christmas porridge at Halvor's place in Dovre.[16]

Christmas Porridge

In the folktale, Halvor's family provides porridge for the marauding visitors. Eating Christmas porridge—now more often *risengrynsgrøt* (rice porridge) than the tale's rømmegrøt—persists in modern Norway, usually on the afternoon of Christmas Eve, as final preparations reach their completion.[17] Some Norwegians stir a blanched almond into the porridge as it cooks and reward the lucky person whose portion contains it with a marzipan pig. The custom echoes the Roman Saturnalia practice of placing a dried bean inside a cake and conferring the status of "king" upon the finder, who for the evening was permitted to order the other guests to make fools of themselves. A descendent of the practice lived on in Victorian England, too, where the finder of silver charms and new coins concealed in the Christmas pudding was promised a year's good fortune.[18]

Porridge has a long history as a festive food in Norway, but the custom of eating Christmas porridge may have grown out of the Catholic custom of Advent fasting. The medieval Christmas Eve, marked by eating lutefisk and porridge, signaled the transition from this period of abstinence to one of feasting on the abundant rich foods served on Christmas Day and the days to follow.

Regardless of its origins as a Christmas treat, porridge is the oldest warm dish known in Norway, and it constituted for centuries the main staple of the Norwegian peasant diet. *Vassgraut* (porridge of coarsely ground barley and water or skimmed milk) was eaten twice or even three times a day until about the 1850s, when the potato took over as Norway's dietary staple.[19]

To stir the porridge the husmor used a *tvare* (branched stirring stick) made from the trunk of a spruce tree, which her husband had selected, then shaped and smoothed into usefulness. Traditional Norwegian porridge had to be thick, some said "so thick you could dance on it," but at least thick enough to cling to the tvare or even make it stand up straight. They achieved this consistency by adding more flour after the already cooked porridge had been removed from the heat.[20] Everyone ate from the same large wooden bowl, each with a wooden or horn spoon taken from its place on the wall-mounted holder near the table, then wiped clean and returned to the wall after the meal.[21]

Special occasions called for a porridge of finely ground wheat flour cooked in cream—sweet (*fløtegrøt*) or sour (*rømmegrøt*), though these names are by no means consistently applied. This festive white porridge was served with a generous topping of the golden butter that had separated from the cream as it cooked.

In itself the generous amount of butter that appeared with the Christmas porridge distinguished the dish. A commodity the family could sell or use to pay taxes, butter was normally eaten sparingly and when possible done without. To stretch the supply the husmor replaced butter with *smult* (pig lard) after the slaughter and otherwise thinned it with potatoes. The sight of porridge swimming in butter thus signaled a special occasion.

Rømmegrøt varied widely from place to place, in both recipe and name. Some areas preferred a rather strong sour taste, others liked it sweeter; some places preferred the firmest possible consistency, while others wanted it thinner.[22] The amount of butter also varied. To cut the cost and richness of the dish, many served their rømmegrøt mixed with or layered on top of a blander porridge.

The final touches for presenting the rømmegrøt had local variations. Custom might call for sprinkling the sugar and cinnamon in prescribed patterns around the porridge surface. Similarly, the butter might be cut in stripes, placed in the center (called a *smørøye,* butter eye), or passed around in a separate bowl. Still other communities topped the porridge with raisins or egg wedges.

The difficulty of acquiring genuine *rømme* (nonprocessed sour cream) in America makes it virtually impossible to duplicate Norwegian rømmegrøt on this side of the Atlantic, says Astrid Karlsen Scott. Commercial sour cream is processed to prevent the butter separation that is key to the dish. She suggests circumventing this problem by making one's own rømme by adding lemon juice to sweet cream (two tablespoons lemon juice to two cups heavy cream) and letting it stand for fifteen minutes, then proceeding with the recipe as usual.[23] Norwegian peasants often used *smørgrøt* (butter porridge) instead of rømmegrøt for festive occasions; they often had more butter than rømme on hand because it was an easier commodity to store.[24]

Though rømmegrøt was the traditional Christmas porridge and remains so among most Norwegian Americans, many Norwegians have gone over to risengrynsgrøt (also called *risgrøt*) at Christmas. Rice had been known in Norway since the Middle Ages, but only the wealthy used this more expensive, imported grain. Nor did it much resemble the fine, white rice today's consumers have come to expect. Yet during the 1800s rice porridge became so popular on festive occasions among the urban affluent that it almost obliterated rømmegrøt. In rural areas, however, rømmegrøt retained its standing as Norway's most festive porridge. Though easily accessible today, risengrynsgrøt probably retains its position as a Christmas delicacy because of its former air of exotic luxury as well as its natural appeal to a wide variety of palates.

Porridge for the Nisse

Favored not only by visible Norwegians, a bowl of festive porridge also constituted the Christmas wages expected by the nisse for his faithful service throughout the year. Innumerable nineteenth-century drawings, folktales, and legends portray this elf's appetite for the treat. They also warned of dire consequences suffered by those who failed to provide it:

Somewhere—I believe it was in Hallingdal—a girl was supposed to take *fløtegrøt* to the nisse on Christmas Eve. She thought it a shame to give the nisse such fine food, and decided to eat the porridge herself, along with every bit of the butter. In its place she brought oat porridge and sour milk to the hay barn. Dumping it into a pig's trough, she muttered, "There's your fodder, you ugly thing!" Those words had no sooner left her mouth than the nisse appeared. He grabbed her and started to dance with her, singing:

> *Oh, you have eaten the porridge, you,*
> *and now you'll dance with the nisse, too.*

On and on he danced until the girl lay gasping on the floor. The next morning when the others came into the barn, they found her more dead than alive.[25]

Do Norwegian families still leave porridge for the nisse? Belief in the nisse has long since disappeared, but I wondered if any families still followed the custom, the same way an American family might leave milk and cookies for Santa. To find out, I placed a notice in one of Norway's largest papers, the Oslo daily *Verdens Gang* (The way of the world). Eirick Eid Olsson of Brummundal in eastern Norway replied: "As a resident of Hedmark, a major farming area in Norway, I know the tradition well. Whenever farms are passed true from one generation to the next for several centuries, the tradition of putting out porridge for the nisser is still living, but only on a few farms."[26]

Writing from Ådalsbruk in western Norway, Kjersti Pettersvold illustrated the practice with this example:

The tradition of *julegrøt* is still alive in our part of the country. Especially in families with small children. In our family we do not serve the *grøt,* but go to some friends' house, or rather their barn, to greet the nisse. Our friends are in their sixties with grown children. They used to bring the nisse *grøt* in the barn when their children were small and have kept up the tradition, inviting families in the neighborhood to participate. In the hayloft they find a real nisse. Nowadays one of their daughters returns home for this every year. The children are really excited because "he" looks like a real nisse.[27]

While most informants reported that the tradition of Christmas porridge for the nisse wasn't practiced in cities, it may have an urban counterpart, after all, at least in some families, judging by the answer sent by fifteen-year-old Cecilie Sanden:

I live in Porsgrunn, a city in the southern part of Norway with circa 31,000 inhabitants. . . . it's not usual to put out porridge for the julenisse in the middle of the city. That's more done on farms and such. But my little sister believes in the julenisse. And every Christmas Eve she puts out a bowl of risengrynsgrøt. She says that since Julenissen has been out an entire evening delivering gifts, he must be very hungry, and therefore she feeds him. . . . Of course, there's no julenisse to eat it, so my mom or my dad have to go out and take the porridge away. That is why on Christmas morning, when my sister goes out to the garage to see if the julenisse has been there, the bowl is empty.[28]

Going to Church on Christmas Eve

Of far more recent origin than Christmas porridge or the nisse is the Christmas Eve church service, instituted after World War II as a family-friendly alternative to the Christmas morning service. For most Norwegians, this afternoon service (usually between two and four o'clock) is the one time of year they do attend church. Norwegian American visitors, aware of Norway's normally scant attendance at Sunday services, would be surprised to find the church on December 24 packed with families in their best attire and resounding with children's voices reading the gospel or reciting lines from a Christmas pageant.

For the Norwegian church, Christmas is by far the busiest time of year, despite the theological position of the festival as second in importance to Easter. Because a high percentage of Norwegians prefer to spend their Easter holiday on skis at a mountain cabin (or, increasingly, in milder climes)—thus away from their parish churches—the services on Christmas Eve have become the most important of the year. Their portentous timing at the seam of the old and new year, as family gathers from far and near, adds to these services' prominence and popularity. Crisp evening air and newly fallen snow often lend the perfect backdrop to chiming church bells and voices raised in much-loved song.

In addition to Christmas Eve, the Norwegian State Church (which is Lutheran) now conducts services on Christmas Day (*første juledag*), and December 26 (*annen juledag*), as well as on the Sundays after Christmas and New Year's Day. The service most Norwegians attend on December 24 takes place in the late afternoon, but in recent years some churches have also revived the Christmas Eve midnight service. Its roots go back to the Catholic vigil tradition. Medieval Norwegians honored important saints' days by staying awake throughout the previous night; the Christmas vigil began with the Christmas Eve midnight mass.[29]

Modern clergy, noticing people's attraction to more "Catholic" (that is, spiritually expressive) forms of worship, have revived not only this service but many medieval liturgies as well. Further reflecting the Norwegians' new religious sensibilities is the growing popularity of lighting candles on graves at Christmas. The practice goes back to the years after World War I, when relatives of the fallen in southern Europe followed the Catholic custom of placing lighted candles on their graves during All Saints' Day. The custom spread to Protestant Europe and in the 1920s came to Norway, where the first Sunday in November substituted for All Saints' Day (which is not observed). After World War II, an increasing number of Norwegians adopted the custom and moved it to Christmas Eve.

Popular as the custom has become today, this way of honoring the dead has had vociferous detractors. The clergy initially rejected the custom be-

---

"Last Christmas I was in Norway. After the Christmas Eve service as we left the church the cemetery was beautifully lit up from all the candles that had been placed on the graves. Then it was our turn. Since my friend's husband was buried in another cemetery, by another church, we drove to that cemetery. Silently she and her daughters walked up to the grave and lit a candle. (The candles are especially made for this purpose and they burn for quite a while—maybe 8–12 hours.) All dressed in their bunads, they cleaned off the large rock that was Kjell's headstone so his name was clearly seen. The daughters spent a short time at the grave, but the mother spent about 5–8 minutes lost in her thoughts. In some ways I felt as though I was witnessing something that I shouldn't—a very private moment between two people. It was a very special sight. First of all, it was dark, but with a clear sky and millions of stars. The church was very old and it had one spotlight on the tower. Nearly all of the graves had a candle. It was only about 4:30 p.m., but it was dark as night. There were several families at the cemetery so we were far from being alone, but there was a reverent silence. It was special! During this experience the words 'Silent night, holy night, all is calm, all is bright' kept echoing in my head and heart."

Patti Goke, St. Cloud, Minnesota, e-mail to the author, December 19, 1999

cause of its Catholic origins, and cemetery authorities objected to the mess and bother. In 1958, for example, the Oslo supervisor of cemeteries purposely closed the churchyard gates too early for people to get in and light their candles. He reasoned that "while some people may think the twinkling candles in the cemetery create a beautiful display, for many the sight makes an eerily sinister impression in our winter darkness. Nor is it pleasant to see the cemetery the next morning when it has the feel of a living room after all the guests have gone home."[30] Objections proved useless, however, and by now the custom has firmly established itself. Grounded in the universal human desire to honor the dead, placing candles on the graves also conforms well with the ancient Norwegian practice of venerating the family's ancestors at Christmas time.

Christmas Dinner

Whether they have attended services and lit a candle on a loved one's grave or run some last-minute errands, most Norwegians return home by late afternoon or early evening on December 24. There, flickering candles brightly ward off the settling darkness, and mouth-watering aromas waft from the kitchen. When the clock strikes five, church bells all over the country *ringer julen inn* (ring Christmas in). Chiming steadily for several minutes, the bells signal that all work must cease. As their sound dies away, Christmas peace settles over farms and cities whose residents anticipate a prolonged period of peace and rest, fellowship and fun.

While other customs may vary by generation and belief, almost the entire Norwegian population unites in celebrating Christmas Eve with a traditional meal, following a prescribed menu.[31] What that menu might include for any one family, however, varies considerably by geographical location and tradition. For 60 percent it will be *ribbe* (roast rib of pork), while for 25 percent it is *pinnekjøtt* (steamed ribs of lamb); those in eastern Norway overwhelmingly prefer the pork ribs, while those in the west choose the lamb. In parts of southern Norway with close ties to the United States, turkey is more popular than anywhere else in Norway and now accounts for 15 percent of main dishes on Christmas Eve. In northern Norway and northern Trøndelag, lutefisk remains a popular part of Christmas dinner, while boiled cod is almost a must along Norway's south coast.[32]

Ribbe has the longest tradition of the various Christmas meats, dating back to the Viking Jól, when the pig figured prominently among the sacrificial offerings. Pork also figured prominently in the Old Norse view of paradise. There, said the myth, warriors would feast perpetually on boiled pork supplied by the boar Særimne. Consumed one day, this magical beast would reappear the next, as fat and meaty as before. Feasting on pork to celebrate midwinter, the Vikings found the high fat content necessary to sustain their hard lives of toil through the seasonal darkness.

As now prepared, ribbe became "traditional" only after bake ovens grew in popularity during the late 1800s and early 1900s. Prior to that, food was usually cooked in a *gryte* (cauldron) over an open fire. All-in-one dishes predominated, combining meat and other ingredients (today known as a *gryterett,* a hot dish or casserole). (Frying was a seldom used method; the requisite fat was a luxury item and was used in other ways.) A meal of this sort that was popular in great-grandmother's day called for one kilogram of *kalverygg* (calf back), two *rugkavringar* (rye rusks), and four to five tablespoons of good *rømme* (sour cream) to be cooked together until the meat was tender.[33]

When the *komfyr* (cookstove) became widespread, oven roasting replaced boiling as the preferred method for preparing meat. Today's method of preparing the Christmas ribbe (rubbing the meat liberally with salt and pepper before roasting and serving it in the rind) has changed little since then.

Norwegians make enough of the Christmas Eve ribbe to provide leftovers for the buffet meals served during the festive days to follow. Two additional delicacies, *medisterpølser* (pork sausages) and *medisterkaker* (pork patties), complement the ribbe and have equally long traditions. Many use the same meat *deig* (ground meat "dough") for both, making it with pork, pork fat, starch, and spices.

Medisterpølser may be made by placing the ground meat mixture into sausage casings. In times less concerned about cholesterol, Norwegians made their medisterpølse by mixing equal amounts of fat and meat. Chopping it twice until quite fine, they seasoned it with one or a combination of the spices then available: salt, pepper, *nelliker* (cloves), *allehånde* (allspice), *timian* (timothy), *ingefær* (ginger), or *muskat* (nutmeg). After mixing the meat with a broth cooked from the rind, they stuffed it into a casing of the

❖ ❖

Ribbe (Spareribs)

Use 4½ lbs. spareribs, 2 tsp. salt, 1 tsp. pepper, ½ quart water. Total roasting time at 355° F is two hours.

Do not remove the rind, but cut through it a pattern of 1-inch squares, and rub with salt and pepper. Let the meat steep refrigerated for 2 to 3 days, so the flavors blend. Pour 1 pint of water into a roasting pan and put in the roast with the rind down. Place in a pre-heated oven and cook for 20 to 30 minutes. Remove roast, rub it with salt and pepper and put it on a rack in the roasting pan with the rind up. The ribs are ready when the bones loosen easily from the meat. Norwegians serve the rind with the ribs; to make the rind crispy, leave the oven door open for 10–15 minutes before serving.

Medisterpølser (Pork Sausage)

Aase Strømstad gives this recipe for the pork mixture:

1½ pounds trimmed lean pork, ½ pound fat back, 1 tablespoon salt, 2½ tablespoon potato flour or cornstarch, 1 pint milk, 1 teaspoon pepper, ½ teaspoon ground cloves. Grind meat and fat back with 1 tablespoon salt, 2½ tablespoon potato flour or salt, once or twice. Stir in cornstarch, 1 pint milk, 1 teaspoon pepper, ½ teaspoon ground potato flour or cornstarch, add milk, cloves. and seasonings. Shape flat, medium large patties and brown them with the butter in a frying pan. Put the finished patties in the oven with the spare ribs and bake further about 20 minutes.

Pinnekjøtt (Lamb Ribs)

Rub lamb ribs well with salt. Put a layer of salt in a plastic tub, lay the entire rack of lamb on top and cover with salt. Place in the cold, 46–50° F, for three days.

Remove the meat and rinse it quickly in cold water. Dry it and hang in a cool, well-ventilated place for 6–8 weeks. (Lamb ribs are also available already salted and dried, and many Norwegians skip this preparation step, moving directly to the cooking.)

Cooking: Cut up the rack along the ribs. Soak for 1 to 2 days in plenty of cold water, until the meat has swelled thoroughly. Place the meat on a rack in a large pan, or as tradition dictates—on a lattice of birch or juniper twigs. Add water to the level of the meat. Steam covered over low heat until the meat loosens from the bone, approximately two hours.

Strømstad, Eat the Norway, *34–39 (pinnekjøtt), 41 (ribbe), 41–42 (medisterpølser)*

❖ ❖

thoroughly cleaned pig's intestine, which during the process lay in luke-warm water for ease of handling. The sausages were then either roasted with the ribbe or prepared separately by browning on both sides in butter, covering with boiling water, and cooking until easily pierced.[34]

While ribbe, with its roots in Old Norse mythology and sacrificial prac-tices, has long traditions all over the country, pinnekjøtt occupies a special position among the festive foods of western Norway. Its name comes from the small birch *pinner* (twigs) that form a platform to support the meat just above the water level in the cooking kettle. The recipe calls for a rack of lamb and four and a half pounds of salt, and the preparation entails layering the salt and meat and letting it cure for three days. Rooted in the Norwegian peasants' practice of preserving meat in dry salt or salt brine before aging it for the better part of a year, if not longer, modern recipes aim to duplicate the traditional saline flavor.

Today's hostess would not think of serving the Christmas dinner with-out at least one vegetable. In the preindustrial society, however, vegetables simply did not appear on the peasant's table.[35] Asbjørnsen, in his 1864 cook-book, *Fornuftig matstell* (Commonsense cooking), chided the peasants for their negative attitude toward "greens and roots": "It is much too common in our country that the people underestimate what they don't know and dis-parage what is good and beneficial, if it's not the style among their peers. Thus one hears greens and roots often referred to as 'grass' or 'cow- and pig-food' and those who eat them called 'clods.'"[36] Ironically, where veg-etables did appear was in towns and among the more affluent landowners, especially in eastern Norway. Noting this divergence of food preferences, Erik Pontoppidan had earlier noted in his *Norges historie* (History of Nor-way) (1752–54): "Of [vegetables] the common people here in Norway are no lovers, especially those in rural areas. Townspeople therefore import cabbage, onions, and other vegetables from Holland and England." People living in Norway's commercial centers prepared their meals according to the European pattern of a soup, a meat and vegetable course, and dessert. A popular dish at the time in the kondisjonerte (cultured) circles of eastern Norway was *majjæl,* made by adding potatoes, rutabagas, cabbage, and bar-ley to salted meat that had been boiled for a long time.[37]

This so-called conditioned class, influenced by study, friends, relatives or roots in Denmark (or Germany, England, or Holland), cultivated lifestyles that differed considerably from those of the peasants, and the "two cultures" (kondisjonerte and *almuen,* or commoners) continued to characterize Norway throughout the nineteenth century. While people in towns followed a fairly uniform diet, peasant cuisine varied considerably, each area developing local specialties according to the area's resources.

The continued preference for ribbe in eastern Norway (where raising pigs prevailed) and pinnekjøtt in western Norway (an area better suited to herding sheep) reflects this geographic variation. And as the main course varies, so do its complements. Thus ribbe always appears with *surkål* (sour cabbage), whose caraway seasoning is said to aid in digesting pork.[38]

As naturally as surkål goes with ribbe, *kålrot stappe* (mashed rutabagas) accompanies pinnekjøtt. The most commonly used recipe cuts the rutabaga with potato.[39] Only a few generations ago these dishes would have graced only the tables of the wealthy; now they are almost in every household. And today, even in the most affluent homes, peasant foods such as sausage links and meat patties retain a place of honor among the already abundant fare.

For dessert some families serve creamed rice with red fruit sauce; others prefer caramel pudding. Still, a dessert made with the distinctively Scandinavian *molter* (cloud berries) probably tops the wish list. Valued as a nutritional supplement since ancient times, these inimitable orange, crunchy berries taste of fall and provide a nostalgic reminder of hikes in colorful mountains or woodland marshes when the whole family may have joined in picking them.

Understanding the appeal of the molte berries is easy, but some of Norway's other "delicacies"—such as leathery dried fish soaked in lye or meats salted, dried, and aged beyond recognition—raise the question "Why"? Originally the answer was sheer necessity. Norway's food supply remained uncertain until well into the nineteenth century. The near famine that characterized much of the year would overnight suddenly turn to glut by dint of seasonal dairying and slaughter, hunting and fishing. Before electric refrigeration became common, methods such as salting, drying, fermenting, and even burying raw meat and fish in the ground provided the only means to preserve this bounty and make it last throughout the year. Milk was either soured or made into cheese and butter. Rarely were any of these foods consumed fresh, a practice long deemed unhealthy and, no doubt, one that permitted appetite rather than hunger to deplete limited supplies that had to stretch over time.

In recent years Norwegians have developed increasingly sophisticated palates through travel and immigration. Current Oslo tour guides list restaurants serving foods from twenty-seven different countries. Less than forty years ago, cabbage, carrots, and turnips were the only fresh vegetables available at Christmas, and oranges imported from Spain and Israel still seemed somewhat exotic. Today Norwegian supermarkets sell an array of vegetables and fruits from all over the world throughout the year. The many shops run by immigrants and other foreign nationals, moreover, sell the ingredients for the traditional dishes of their homelands.

At the same time, Norwegian chefs are increasingly garnering international acclaim, successfully competing for *Bocuse d'or* and other coveted culinary awards. These contemporary cosmopolitan eating habits notwithstanding, at Christmastime most Norwegians long for the foods that help define the season. It's just not Christmas without the dishes they have "always" had, prepared and served the traditional ways.[40]

How long will these rituals continue? The letter from Karin Behr Skjævestad quoted in the epigraph to this chapter goes on to present an alarming picture:

> Unfortunately the young generation is starting to break some of these traditions. I have heard that some people have started using pizza on Christmas Eve, and that what has always been a festive evening with the family has become an "evening out" for young people. Some restaurants now stay open that evening. That never happened before.[41]

The consternation aroused in one generation by the changing Christmas traditions of the next characterizes any discussion of Christmas. Yet, who would not want to maintain so charming a Christmas Eve as the one described by Thomas L. Juell of Ål in Hallingdal in a recent e-mail:

> The family gets together from far and near and we go to church to hear the Christmas *Evangelium* (Luke 2.1–21) and the sermon for children. The church is always filled with families that day. Then we go home for a nice Christmas dinner, we settle down for a cup of coffee or tea and

taste the various Christmas cookies that are made at this time of the year only. The norm is 7 varieties, but not everyone has the time for this anymore, although many wives still set a lot of store in doing so.

And if you have children, the high point is now to come. We walk around the Christmas tree holding hands, singing Christmas carols. Just to watch the children's eyes in the light of the candles is something special. Then lo and behold, if you have a good neighbor, he will now enter dressed as "julenissen" and give away a few presents. The rest of the packages will then be distributed one at a time so everyone can admire it. It is a lot of fun, and a custom not to be trifled with. Of course, bed time will come late on such a night.[42]

Christmas Music

As much as the adults enjoy watching the children, the youngsters themselves find the meal an endless preliminary to the real point of the evening—opening the presents. In some families yet another hurdle (from the children's point of view) lies ahead in the uniquely Scandinavian custom Juell mentions of joining hands and singing around the tree, the adults savoring the antics of the children and admiring the decorations on the tree, the children more concerned about what lies beneath it.

Special music has accompanied Christmas since the medieval mystery plays, and both religious and secular yuletide songs date back that far. The custom of caroling from door to door began during the 1300s, probably in Germany and Switzerland. Though some carols have roots in the Middle Ages, most of those sung in both Norway and America today took their present form during the 1800s, when many new carols were written and older ones revised and given new texts.[43]

Norway's most popular traditional carol, "Jeg er så glad hver julekveld" (I am so glad each Christmas Eve), written in 1860 and still well known among Norwegian Americans, may be found etched on the gravestone of its author, Marie Wexelsen (1832–1911), a loving tribute made possible by money donated by Norwegian schoolchildren.[44] More recent favorites include the songs by Alf Prøysen (1914–70) from the end of the 1940s, "Musevise" (the mouse-family Christmas, showing that everyone—even those who are poor as church mice—can find joy in Christmas), and the early 1950s, "Julekveldsvise" (Christmas Eve song, enumerating many of the

Christmas preparations described in chapter 2). The world over, no music sells as well as Christmas music, a rule proved once again by the phenomenal success of Sissel Kyrkjeboe's still enormously popular 1987 recording, *Glade jul,* which features "Silent Night" and other traditional favorites.

Presents and the Nisse

As the singing around the tree continues and the children eagerly eye the packages, their ears strain to hear the knock on the door that announces the arrival of the Julenisse with his bulging sack of gifts. While such julenisser may be hired for the evening from a firm, the usual pattern is for relatives or neighbors, both male and female, to oblige. This may be an elderly person enjoying a rare contact with the youngest generation or neighborhood parents taking turns playing Julenisse for each other's children to keep them from becoming suspicious.

But even if the youngsters do notice that the julenisse's voice sounds like Daddy's, *onkel* Johan's, or even *tante* Anne's, they'll eagerly answer with an earnest "Ja!" to the nisse's deep-voiced query, "Er det noen snille barn her?" (Are there any good children here?). Reassured by their answer, the nisse reaches into his sack for their presents. Almost half of Norwegian preschoolers receive gifts from the nisse personally, and on Christmas Eve more than one hundred thousand Norwegian nisser in both town and country perform this pleasurable masquerade.[45]

Dressed traditionally in either the Julenisse's floor-length coat or the barn nisse's knee pants and knitted wool socks, the gift bearer always sports a long white beard and red stocking cap. More and more often, though, in these internationalized times, an Americanized Santa shows up, as Thomas Juell describes:

> I bought my [Santa suit] in a store and am just like any other everyday American Santa you may encounter downtown collecting money for the Salvation Army. Since I am six foot six and not overly portly, I need a lot of padding, making me large enough to be more like a troll than a Santa. The idea is not to frighten the children, and even if I can Ho, Ho, Ho with the best of them, I don't think I fit the general idea of your everyday Santa. I do have a beard, however, and it is getting grey, so things may improve.[46]

Christmas in Christiania (Oslo), 1910

The increasing focus on children during the first half of the nineteenth century helped transform Christmas among the Norwegian upper class to the child-centered festivity we know today. By the end of that century, this Christmas—characterized by gift-giving and the Christmas tree—had also spread to the middle class. But not until well into the twentieth century did Norwegians in rural areas share this modern Christmas. Long resisting the Christmas tree as pagan, many rural Norwegians continued exchanging only necessary gifts of clothing, especially hand-knitted items. Since it was from this group in Norway that the immigrants to America predominantly came (during the early and middle nineteenth century), the customs most Norwegians brought along reflected the Christmas of the old peasant society. These immigrants adopted the Christmas tree and gift-giving only after they came to America.

"Surprise gifts" so common in Norway and America today did not become widespread among Norwegians on either side of the Atlantic until after World War I. Once introduced to the children, the modern Christmas caught on fast, and many Norwegian American memoirs tell with great fondness of the family's first *kjøpejul,* or "buying Christmas," when they exchanged store-bought gifts. As in America, grown-ups also receive Christmas gifts in Norway, where statistics say that each adult gives gifts to twelve people. In all, Norwegians exchange somewhere between 30 and 40 million packages, large and small, each Christmas.[47]

Christmas Eve in contemporary Norway lasts until about midnight for both adults and children. From the time the church bells *ringer julen inn,* through the festive dinner, singing around the tree, and opening gifts, until the concluding smaller meal or coffee, the time flies.

In the old peasant society, too, the evening lasted longer than usual and was distinguished by fellowship, flickering candlelight, a comforting cleanliness, and much finer, more abundant food than the family had eaten since the last Christmas. Savoring these treats, the peasants no doubt felt a peace settle over their farm. But to a far greater extent than can ever be imagined today, their peace was tempered by anxiety. Haunted by terrifying thoughts of the surrounding supernatural powers, chilled by whistling, icy winds, and saddened by memories of family members now absent, they somberly considered the uneasy question of whose place would stand empty on the next Christmas Eve. No wonder they sought solace by attending church on Christmas Day.

Freed from some of these fears, modern Norwegians no longer make church the entire focus of the day. For them, December 25 and *romjul*—the week that follows—continue the period of celebration and respite from work. Traditionally and to this very day, Norwegians spend this time visiting friends and relatives, savoring their company along with the season's culinary treats.

Christmas Day and Romjul
Taking Time for Family and Friends

Everyone got up early in the morning on Christmas Day to go to church. They rowed to Innvik, the parish's main church, which always had a service on First Christmas Day. The weather wasn't always the best, but that seldom kept them home. Once long ago such a terrible wind blew up on the homeward journey that they couldn't row over the fjord from Hildaneset; indeed they considered themselves lucky to get safely ashore at Frøholmstranda. From there they walked to Frøholm, where they stayed until Second Christmas Day, when they could finally row home.

Hans Øen, recalling nineteenth-century Christmases in Stryn

Serious challenges, both meteorological and topographical, faced them, but early in the morning on *første juledag* (First Christmas Day) the preindustrial Norwegians attended church services. The remainder of the day they usually spent at home. Even today, Norwegians tend to confine their Christmas Day activities to immediate family and closest friends. Skis or sleds unwrapped on Christmas Eve may get a workout, but Christmas Day remains the quietest of the season. Some still attend church on Christmas morning, but most Norwegians enjoy a prolonged Christmas breakfast with family and friends. Presented as a *koldtbord* (buffet, literally "cold table"), the food is served at room temperature, allowing guests to enjoy the meal at leisure with course-by-course returns to the table.

Christmas in the Norwegian countryside, as depicted in a broadside from 1881

No less than the church service, the buffet format of the Christmas Day family breakfast has roots firmly anchored in the past. Its form derives from the long-practiced custom of leaving food on the table to honor the returning dead, and the meal itself harks back to and combines two traditional early morning meals: a waking-up treat followed by a more complete breakfast. The traditional waking treat was described by the pioneering nineteenth-century Norwegian sociologist Eilert Sundt as it was enjoyed by residents of Hurum (Valdres) in 1858:[1]

> Between four or five o'clock in the morning people awoke, got partially dressed and gathered at the table for hymn singing, a sermon, and Bible reading. Following this simple service the *fjøsjente* [barn girl] went out to give the animals an extra meal of grain and fine hay before everyone went back to bed. The *husfar* and *husmor* [male and female heads of household] retired last, because first they had to make the rounds, serving treats to the others in bed, she serving *vortekake* [a cake made from brewers' malt] and warmed beer, he a glass or two of *brennevin* [hard liquor]. In some places the beer (but not the brennevin) was replaced by coffee [after its introduction in the mid-1800s]. After two or three more hours in bed, everyone got up for good. This custom was followed on First and Second Christmas Day and on New Year's Day.[2]

The remarkable Christian piety evident in this account accompanied the Norwegian immigrants to America, and reading the Christmas gospel also continues in contemporary homes in Norway, where this devout ritual still inaugurates the festive Christmas Eve meal. But, as Sundt's description shows, the Norwegians' home devotions from which these modern customs descend were once considerably more elaborate.

Usage varied widely all around Norway, but an early Christmas morning treat such as Sundt describes—consisting of Christmas sweets and coffee, known as "kaffe på senga" (coffee in bed), served to servants and children—provided the start of Christmas Day in many places. The full morning meal that followed usually consisted of the food that had been standing on the table throughout the night.

Peace and calm prevailed on Christmas Day in the old peasant culture, and Norwegians believed that if they went visiting, they would "skjemme ut" (spoil) Christmas. Anyone who did so risked being called a *julegris* (Christmas pig). Nor could the normally industrious Norwegian peasant lift a finger to perform work that was not absolutely critical. With this stricture in mind, families had carried in enough water and wood the day before to last at least until Second Christmas Day. Though milking and feeding the livestock could not be delayed, manure clearing and all other barn chores went undone.

The only permissible activity away from home on *første juledag* was the church service, universally attended until about one hundred years ago. While the idea of attending church seems tranquil enough in our day, in earlier times the journey seldom proceeded without event. Beer and other strong beverages, available in plentiful supply at Christmas, often came along to ward off both the cold weather outside and the damp chill inside the unheated churches. But even for teetotalers, the weather and natural conditions added enough complications of their own, as is evident in this chapter's epigraph, a vignette from Stryn in western Norway.

In other parts of the country as well, the journey to church often proceeded over water, which even in favorable weather could prove treacherous. From northern Norway comes this account of Landego Island dwellers on their way to Bodø on the mainland to hear the Christmas sermon:

> It was a long journey so they had to start out early in the morning. A light four-oared rig was launched from the boat house. Many shawl-clad women sat in the rear of the boat, while the men tended to the oars. A stone lay submerged on the south side of the island, and the boat was going at a pretty good clip when it hit that stone and capsized. One man managed to pull himself up onto the stone and there he stood until late the next day before some people from Ransvik rescued him. To this day the stone is known as Juldagen (Christmas Day).[3]

Those who traveled by land also had to proceed with caution, using a measured pace on the way to church to avoid leaving sweaty horses to freeze during the service. By contrast, the trip home proceeded quite quickly, the riders often competing to arrive first and punctuating their journey with loud shouts and laughter. In some places they said that the one who returned home first would also be the first to bring in that year's crops.

Romjul Pleasures

In contemporary Norway, family gatherings continue on *annen juledag,* Second Christmas Day, December 26. This day begins an extended period of hospitality, visiting, and celebrating that lasts through *romjul,* the term Norwegians apply to the days between Christmas and New Year's. School is out, and most adults, too, have abundant vacation time to spend with friends and relatives from near and far. "To me that is the most enjoyable part of the entire Christmas season: that we are together and have plenty of time for each other," says Erna Skarsbø of Undredal (Sogn).[4]

In the old peasant society, too, Second Christmas Day brought a new, more lighthearted mood, with customs and activities that signaled an end to the sacred solemnity of Christmas Eve and First Christmas Day. Food reflects this lighter mood; many eat fish pudding on *annen juledag* as a welcome and wholesome change from the rich and fatty foods that have come before and will soon follow.

As today, the Norwegian peasant farmers held an almost nonstop round

The custom of serving alcoholic beverages so as not "to carry Christmas out"—å bære julen ut—developed a bad reputation among the Norwegian Americans who worked for temperance. This editorial was published in a Norwegian-language women's magazine:

One of the customs designed for human ruin is the one that stipulates one must not "bære Julen ud." To avoid this, one is obliged to consume something in each home one visits. As a rule it is port wine and fattigmann that is served. If in a day one has half a dozen visits to make, this can reach quite a "fine" result. During Christmas when I see a man with rosy red cheeks, two eyes like the stars of Bethlehem, and his top hat perched precariously on the back of his head, I know that he has by no means "carried Christmas away," but like a good citizen has done his best to ensure that it remained safely ensconced inside each and every one of the places he has visited. . . . No matter how it originated, we have here a custom that we know claims numerous victims. The purpose of these lines is to encourage women to keep an eye on their husbands during the Christmas season and to keep them from making too many visits alone.

Kvindens Magazin (Cedar Rapids, Iowa), February 1906, p. 22

of parties and dances that lasted until either the thirteenth or twentieth day of Christmas. Anyone who dropped in during this period, invited or not, received warm hospitality and servings of beer, liquor, and food. Not to do so would cause the visitor's departure to "bære julen ut" (carry Christmas away; that is, destroy the Christmas spirit). Hospitality abides deep in the soul of the Norwegian people, a quality of their culture since time immemorial and still highly valued.[5]

Julebukking

Sudden pounding on the door, loud singing, or commotion may interrupt the Romjul visiting. The noise announces the arrival of the *julebukker* (pronounced *YOO-la-book-er*; literally, "Christmas goats"), neighborhood children disguised in store-bought or homemade masks and costumes. Before being invited in, they might sing a song or provide other entertainment. Once inside, the julebukkers receive candy, cookies, and other Christmas treats, which quickly disappear into the wicker baskets or plastic shopping bags they have brought along to collect their bounty. Those being visited, meanwhile, try to discover the masqueraders' identity, but will not usually find out if they guessed correctly before the still-masked children proceed to another home.

While julebukking in Norway is less common today than in the past and is usually practiced by young children, in the old peasant society it was the adults who "went julebukk." Halvor Floden of Trysil in eastern Norway highlights this difference in his 1890s memoir:

And just that night (December 26) was the right one for *julebukkene*. It was mostly adults who did this, but they disguised themselves the way children usually do. They took a white cloth and cut out holes for eyes and mouth, smeared on some soot and red paint, and that made a mask. Men put on women's clothes and some girls were so "fresh" as to put on men's pants and jackets. They didn't go from farm to farm, but visited only one neighbor. Altering their dialect and manner of speaking, they pretended to be travelers from afar and tried to stay in character for as long as possible. The children probably took them for the distant wayfarers they claimed to be, but the parents knew the score from the minute they came through the door, and they aimed to make the con-

Julebukkers, a drawing by B. Bergstrøm published in Norsk Folkeblad, *1869*

versation as amusing as possible in an exchange of quick-witted repartee. When the time came for the *bukkene* to go to the table, their masks came off and the children would yell in the greatest amazement, "No, was it *you,* Johanne!" The *bukkene* brought along their ordinary clothes and changed into them to become people again. Now everyone joined in ring-dancing that made the kitchen shake. The julebukk procession provided an excuse to go to other people's houses uninvited.[6]

So much for how the julebukkers behaved, but how did they get their name? Here their traditional disguise—a goat's head and skin (*bukk* means male goat)—comes into play, as seen in the following 1870 account from Valdres: "One of the group would wrap himself in a goatskin. It had a head with a tongue and horns and a string that could open the jaw."[7]

The question of why it was a *goat*'s head and skin these masqueraders employed has long puzzled researchers, who have in turn offered various explanations. Some have associated it with the goats in Old Norse mythology that pulled Thor's cart on its journey through the heavens; others have seen the image as harking back to ancient fertility rituals that involved the sacrificial slaughter of goats.[8] Impulses may have also come from medieval processions that featured a devil-like figure with horns and blackened, ragged clothes not unlike some julebukkers' costumes. Those who see the custom's function as supervising proper work habits relate the masquerading goats to the supernatural beings known as the *julebukk* and *julegeit.* These figures were thought to approach the farm as Christmas drew near, apparently to enforce timely and correct yuletide preparation.[9] Julebukkers performed a similar function, of course, as they went from home to home tasting each others' Christmas provisions.[10]

Though the origin of julebukking remains uncertain, the custom may first have functioned to ward off the hordes of evil spirits formerly believed to have slipped through the seam of the year to haunt the Christmas skies. Nowadays julebukking mainly provides entertainment. Disguise, surprise, and treats dominate, as seen in this description sent by Cecilie Sanden (aged fifteen) from the eastern Norwegian city of Porsgrunn:

In the days between Christmas Eve and New Year's Eve, Norwegian kids often dress up like little nisses or in various strange, old clothes. They visit their neighbors and sing Christmas carols. And then they get candy, fruit and cookies. I don't know why they did it in olden times, but every kid nowadays does it because of the reward they get for singing. Even "big kids" like myself and my friends have lots of fun, going around singing and collecting all sorts of goodies from people you don't even know! It's kind of like Halloween in America. . . . the only difference is that we sing and you don't.[11]

Carnival disguises have replaced grotesque animal masks, while traditional Christmas songs take the place of former, more raucous diversions. Hard liquor and beer have given way to hard candy as the julebukkers' bounty. How recently this relatively tame version of the custom appeared emerges from the description of julebukk etiquette published in the 1962 *Familiens julebok* (Family Christmas book):

Custom decrees that those going julebukk to "scare" their neighbors and other acquaintances on a dark evening during Romjul ought to dress as much as possible like the veritable old goat. Sheepskin, a long goat beard, and goat eyes are traditional; white socks work especially well, and the head should by all means have horns to arouse sufficient fright. When several go together, not all need to be disguised as goats. The visit must come as a surprise, and may include scraping on windows or sneaking into the house without knocking and making loud goat "bleats." Julebukkers used to sing traditional julebukk songs with general bleating as a refrain, but that custom has died out. The julebukkers expect to receive treats.[12]

Treats continue to motivate today's julebukkers, as once again confirmed by the following 1997 newspaper account from the west-coast city of Bergen. Here the custom—practiced strictly by children—has moved to New Year's Eve:

Witches, snakes, wizards, and rabbits. Male and female nisser and brave knights. The row houses of Bønes were crawling with julebukker during the last evening of the year—and with lots of Christmas goodies for everyone.

"We do this every year, and it's lots of fun," say Therese Oma (9), Marianne Demmo ($8\frac{1}{2}$), Adeline Skau (8), and Nathalie Reinhold Sand (9), who sat on their neighbors' steps singing a crystal-clear version of "På låven sitter nissen" (In the barn sits the nisse) about the nisse's liking for Christmas porridge.

*Sonja Innselsæt of Valdres Folkemuseum emphasizes the importance of the conversation
that took place between julebukkers and their hosts:*

Those being visited wanted to find out who the masqueraders were; they tried to get the
visitors to speak and thereby reveal a recognizable voice or characteristic word or expression that would help identify them. The conversation frequently had a standard range, from
the weather to where the julebukks had come from and where they were going next.

The julebukks took advantage of being masked as they hinted at knowing various things
about the household's inhabitants. Most often the talk was amusing and light-hearted, but
the masquerade could also afford people the opportunity to get something off their chests
they would otherwise never dare say.

"Julebukk," unpublished report, Valdres Folkemuseum

No one can resist their charm, of course, so everyone digs out their
very best treats to give them. . . . At one point we counted five separate
groups of julebukker singing in front of as many different doors. In a
couple of hours, they collected goodies that will see them well into the
new year.[13]

Though now largely a childhood diversion, julebukking among adults
has not entirely disappeared. In smaller rural communities, entire families
go together, as Kjersti Pettersvold (born in 1956) describes from Ådalsbruk
in western Norway:

Do we still go julebukk? Oh yes! The whole family gets dressed up with
masks and any kind of funny clothing we can find in the attic. This year
we went julebukk both the 4th and 5th days of Christmas. The idea is to
visit friends and have them guess who we are. I myself have a very recognizable voice, and can't speak too much. A dead giveaway! We usually invite some new friends to go with us every year, both to spread the
tradition and to confuse the people we visit. The custom is to treat kids
with fruit and candy and grown ups with "dram" shots. Shots might be
akevitt, liqueur, cognac or *kaffedoktor* (Irish coffee without the cream).
Going julebukk we get to visit 5–10 houses a night. Nice and really
social![14]

Julebukking has a particularly strong tradition in Valdres, says Sonja
Innselsæt of Valdres Folkemuseum.[15] Here as elsewhere it is now mostly

children who go julebukking, but the adult custom survives, though not without difficulty. Today's Norwegians, she says, are growing increasingly skeptical of being visited by adult julebukker. Times have changed. Small rural towns are not as stable and transparent as they once were; "no one can know for sure whose face the mask conceals, opening the possibility that undesirable, even dangerous individuals might enter one's home," says Innselsæt. Per Johan Skjærstad of Løten in eastern Norway confirms this new feeling of uncertainty: "Sure we still sometimes go julebukk, but it isn't often anyone goes inside now, out of fear that criminals may be hiding behind the julebukk masks. That's what it's come to in good old Norway."[16] In view of this new reality, says Innselsæt, "receiving julebukks has become something of an art." Fortunately it is an art that many—at least for now—still dare to practice, as this recent letter from Ester Leikanger attests:

> Where I live [Vikersund in Modum, eastern Norway] we continue the custom of going julebukk. Many do it, both children and adults. If you get a visit from the julebukks it is usual to invite them in, even though some of them, especially the adults, can seem very frightening.
>
> The children are served pastries and candy, while the adult julebukks tend to want something stronger like aquavit or whatever the house has to offer.
>
> Then the guessing starts about who is hiding behind the respective disguises. Some wear masks, while others have made themselves up to be unrecognizable. Most often it is friends, relatives, or acquaintances, but sometimes they can be totally unknown; then, of course, it's impossible to guess who has come to call.
>
> As a rule, julebukks visit several places in the course of an evening, so after refreshments and unmasking, it's on again with the costumes and off to the next house. The children get their baskets filled with pastries and candy, while the adult julebukks get more and more unsteady from the treats they receive. This sometimes sets a natural limit on how many visits the adult julebukks manage during an evening.[17]

Though many Norwegians think julebukking survives only in a few isolated areas, even this brief survey shows that the custom continues to exhibit the wide-ranging diversity of a living tradition.

Christmas Tree Parties

Even more than julebukking, these days the *juletrefest* (Christmas tree party) constitutes the Norwegians' major post-Christmas entertainment. Beginning during Romjul, these parties extend through January 13 or 20 and repeat the rituals of Christmas Eve.[18] Parents flock to the local *samfunnshus* (community center) with their children, who for the occasion have abandoned their usual jeans and sweaters for their best Christmas finery.

As they arrive, the families write down the name, sex, and age of each child accompanying them, information that comes in handy as the party progresses. They proceed into the auditorium, where an enormous, wellformed, and magnificently decorated tree captures their attention. A teacher or other community leader acting as master of ceremonies delivers

A Christmas tree party at the Oslo Freemasons lodge, about 1925

a talk or reading, then the children organize into a series of concentric rings—each going in opposite directions—as they slowly circle the immense Christmas tree, singing traditional songs of the season, both religious and secular. They also play *sangleiker* (song games) such as "Så går vi rundt om en enebærbusk" (Here we go around the juniper bush, which closely resembles the words and actions of the "Mulberry Bush" song), "Jeg gikk meg over sjø og land" (I wandered over sea and land, in which the children imitate a leader in limping, hopping, pointing, and so on). Some of the song games are traditional folk tunes; others were created especially for Christmas. In the early 1900s Margarethe Munthe wrote the *sangleik* now known best, "På låven sitter nissen" (about the nisse and his Christmas porridge). Traditional songs like "Pål sine høner" (Paul's chickens) and "Kjerringa med staven" (The old lady with a staff) became more widely known because of these Christmas tree parties. When Norwegian emigrants from the *kondisjonerte* class brought the juletrefest to America, they also ensured the memory of these songs.

The party's high point comes with the visit of the julenisse. His familiar query, "Er det noen snille barn her?" always receives a jubilant "Ja!" and he starts distributing gifts that—as if by magic—not only have a label with each child's name correctly spelled, but turn out to be appropriate to the recipient's age and gender, all thanks to the information each family supplied upon arrival. While the children hold their party, adult family members enjoy a chance to visit over coffee, hot chocolate, and Christmas cookies.

The Christmas tree party developed among the elite classes during the last half of the 1800s, as an outgrowth of the emerging children's culture. The parties came to Norway from Germany via Denmark. The characteristic Scandinavian custom of holding hands and dancing around the Christmas tree originated at these parties and made the song "Du grønne, glitrende tre, god dag" (You green, glittering tree, good day) Norway's most popular Christmas carol, sung to a tune by Edvard Grieg.

Both children's and adult festivities continue unabated through Romjul and reach another high point on New Year's Eve.

From New Year's Eve to Epiphany
New Beginnings as Christmas Ends

On New Year's Eve I watched wonderful fireworks in Hamar. All are set off by private individuals. I stood out in the middle of the field below our house and listened to the rumbling and watched the explosions from all over. You never knew where they would be coming from next. It was steady for half an hour until most people's hoards were used up. A spectacular show!

Jeanine Lorentzen, 1997

Most cultures welcome the New Year with noise, traditionally thought to scare off evil spirits. As recently as a century ago Norwegians fired guns into the air, but fireworks have now largely replaced shooting, certainly in urban settings. If the weather is not terribly cold or inclement, people of all ages come outside to see the fireworks. Children tend to be part of New Year's celebrations, especially in rural areas. Decades ago, the evening would have centered around *gnav* (an old-fashioned children's game using engraved wooden pieces, a game that the *kondisjonerte* also brought to America) and other parlor games, topped off by fireworks. Gnav has by now almost entirely disappeared, but the fireworks remain. Norwegians may legally purchase these devices only during the four days before New Year's Eve, and they must be at least eighteen years old to do so. Still, this country of 4.4

million people manages to shoot off about 100 million kroner (15 million dollars) worth of fireworks each New Year's Eve.[1]

Location helps determine how Norwegians spend the evening leading up to the fireworks. While those who live in rural areas will probably celebrate at home with a festive dinner in the company of neighbors and extended family, city dwellers will more likely go out for the evening with friends to a restaurant or house party. When the clock strikes twelve, the celebrants—often with glass in hand—wish each other "Godt nytt år" (Happy New Year), and they thank each other for the one just passed: "og takk for det gamle" (and thanks for the old one).

Jeanine Lorentzen, who gives her impression of New Year's Eve fireworks near Hamar in this chapter's epigraph, has recently moved to Norway. Together with her husband and three children, she lives on the Grefsheim Estate, whose livestock her husband manages. Owned and operated by Johan and Anne-Lise Mellbye, Grefsheim *gård* (farm) has a long history, rich in tradition, a heritage its owners lovingly cultivate. In her recent, beautifully illustrated book *Jul i Norge* (Christmas in Norway), Anne-Lise Mellbye says that on New Year's Eve at Grefsheim, "we always follow the venerable tradition of playing gnav with the old *trebrikkene* [carved wooden pieces]. There's also time for *juleleker* [Christmas games]. All those present, young and old, enjoy themselves tremendously."[2] The juleleker that people play are parlor games such as "My Ship's Loaded with . . . ," "Twenty Questions," "You're Getting Warmer," and "The Journey to America," popular with many Norwegian families during the relaxing Christmas vacation days spent visiting family and friends.[3] "At midnight," Mellbye continues, "we can look out at the fireworks being shot up from Hamar on the other side of Lake Mjøsa. Our wish is still for 'A good year and peace' [echoing the Vikings' 'Til árs ok fridar']. Before us lies a brand new year, filled with possibilities and challenges."[4]

Earlier that evening (at eight o'clock) many Norwegians will have also tuned in the king's televised *Nyttårstale* (New Year's address). Broadcast since 1965 (and previously on radio beginning in 1934), the royal speech has been a regular, annual tradition since 1954.[5] In addition to conveying the greetings of the royal family, it assesses the "state of the nation" and voices aspirations for the country's future course. The prime minister follows with a speech on New Year's Day, a day on which families have long enjoyed the orchestra concert broadcast from Vienna to homes all over Europe (and more recently to America via public television).

With New Year's Day, most modern Norwegians feel that the "real" Christmas comes to an end.[6] During the next few days, everyone returns to normal work routines. School resumes around January 5 or 6, but children still have some celebrating to look forward to. The *juletrefester* (Christmas tree parties), traditionally held during *romjul,* have increasingly moved to the first and second weeks after the New Year (while Romjul, which used to last from December 27 to January 6, now extends only through December 31). These parties still proceed much as they used to, but now take place on Sunday so the whole family may attend.[7]

Adults still have some celebrating of their own to do, too. Fancy dress balls, sponsored by the *bondelag* (farm organizations) or other local groups, dot the calendar during the first two weeks of the New Year. At one time these balls were reserved for wealthy landowners and other members of the kondisjonerte classes, and attendance signified a measure of prestige. In these more democratic times, the balls may have less social status, but they remain a tradition that many wish to perpetuate.[8] Throughout these first weeks of January, Norwegians continue to greet anyone they have not seen since the turn of the year with a hearty "Godt nytt år!"

As in today's Norway, the days after the turn of the year in preindustrial times saw a gradual return to the normal work routine. The peasants resumed the spinning and weaving, threshing and wood chopping, along with all the other work that had lain abandoned during Christmas. The customs practiced at the beginning of the year continued the social contact of the Christmas season, while they also predicted the nature of the year to come. Two New Year's traditions that once played an important role but have left no trace in today's celebrations are *å tigge nyårstråd* (begging New Year's thread) and identifying one's *rokkemand* (spinning-wheel man).[9]

Begging New Year's thread involved young, unmarried men who went from farm to farm asking the young, unmarried women for yarn they had spun for this purpose during the days before Christmas. These they made into small, multicolored skeins to present to the fellows they liked best, who wore them like trophies on their hats or jackets. This activity provided one of the few opportunities young unmarried people had to mingle with members of the opposite sex and possibly begin a relationship that might lead to marriage.[10] To show his interest in the woman, the fellow might offer a return gift, such as a carved wooden spoon or other handmade object.

The nature of these gifts was by no means arbitrary. Practical considerations played a dominant role in one's choice of mate. For a couple to succeed on the self-sufficient farm, the man had to be able to work wood well enough to make the necessary tools and utensils, while the woman produced all the textiles. To show his intention of asking a woman to marry him, a man often presented her with a hand-carved *mangletre* (utensil for smoothing textiles). Her acceptance of the gift indicated acceptance of his proposal. The folktale "Dukken i gresset" (The doll in the grass) portrays the other half of the equation, telling of a young man searching for a mate who had to spin, weave, and sew a shirt in record time. As patterns of socializing grew more relaxed during the nineteenth century, the custom of begging New Year's yarn lost its purpose, and by the turn of the twentieth century it had largely disappeared.

The rokkemand was the first man a woman saw after bringing out her spinning wheel (*rokk*) from its Christmas rest. The rokkemand was entitled to receive a gift from her wheel—hand-knitted mittens, say, or a pair of knee socks—and this custom, too, could eventually lead to marriage. But the rokkemand custom also served as a prognosticator, for certain things about the man could foretell the nature of the coming year: if he had a long beard, the sheep that spring would grow abundant wool, while their wool would be sparse if he were bald; a tall rokkemand signaled that the flax would be good and long, while a short man predicted the opposite.

Omens and Oracles

The predictions associated with the rokkemand are only a few of the myriad Christmas prognostications that claimed attention in the old peasant society. While part of a seemingly universal desire to know what the New Year will bring, the sheer number of omens the Norwegian peasants considered indicates the desperate uncertainty of their living conditions and their deepseated anxiety about the future.

Consulting omens at this time of year is another of the Christmas customs that goes back to the Calends of January, a New Year festival that concluded the pre-Christian Saturnalia and solstice celebrations in ancient

Rome. The Romans used both weather observations and dice throwing to divine the nature of the new year. In Norway, Christmas traditionally enjoyed far greater prominence than New Year's celebrations, and omens came to be associated with the earlier holiday instead.

The still commonly used phrase "Etter alle julemerker å dømme..." (Judging by all the Christmas portents) continues to reflect the once firmly held belief that these Christmas signs could predict the coming year. The saying relates to the old peasant belief that the weather during the twelve days between the first and thirteenth days of Christmas (others say it was from the thirteenth to the twenty-fifth day of December) foretold the weather during the coming twelve months: if the first day brought snow, January would be snowy, and if the second day were especially cold or warm, that's how February would be, and so on.

There were many other omens that Norwegians apprehensively studied in their uneasy quest to know the future. The remains of the straw that had been swept from the floor of the main house after serving as the household's Christmas Eve bed could foretell how the next season's crops would grow. Whole grains augured a good yield, while empty hulls predicted lean; whoever found the first grain would have good fortune throughout the year. How the candles burned on Christmas Eve received careful scrutiny, too; a clear and strong flame promised a prosperous year, but a smoking candle warned of unsettled conditions. The amount and nature of the smoke rising from the chimney made its own prediction: Norwegians hoped to see it thick and full of sparks, for that carried the best prospects. They also hoped to see many birds feeding at their *julenek,* for the size of the harvest varied with their number.

In coastal districts of the west and north, Norwegians filled a shallow bowl with sea water and around its edge wrote names of the most important fishing grounds. On Christmas Eve they covered the bowl and noticed the next morning where the greatest number of air bubbles had formed; the place-name closest to these would yield the most fish in the coming year.

Ø. Hodne, Jul i Norge, *93*

Young people, eager to know the identity of their future spouses, consulted various oracles. To see his future bride, a young man should walk backward around the table while silently saying the Lord's Prayer in reverse. Like so many other magical methods, this device contains ritual elements believed to strengthen its power. Items of religious significance and actions performed backward, silently, or in secret would multiply magical power. So could repeating magical acts three times in a row, as we can see in the once widely known custom of "dressing the Christmas chair."

Å kle julestolen, as the custom was known in Norwegian, was the method Norwegian women most commonly used to foresee their future husbands.[11] Existing in a variety of forms, the custom essentially went as follows: The young woman placed on a chair the clothing she planned to wear on Christmas Day. She walked three times counterclockwise around the chair, then sat down on it before a table set with three bowls, one filled with beer, another with milk, and the third with water. Sometime during the night a vision of the man she was to marry would come and drink from one of the bowls. The one he drank from told how her marriage would prosper: if the water, they would live in poverty; if the milk, in modest circumstances; and if the beer, in prosperity.

Because the identity and occupation of a woman's spouse largely determined the course of her own life and remaining single was not a desirable option in the old peasant society, thoughts of marriage preoccupied the young. The abundance of these Norwegian yuletide divining techniques provides a tangible measure of this preoccupation in a time and place far removed from our own.

While the young considered their marriage prospects, their elders looked for omens of death, attempting to discover who among them would be taken in the year to come. During the Christmas brewing they noticed how

---

A young woman could discover her future husband's occupation by standing at a crossroads on Christmas Eve. If she heard wood chopping, he would be a lumberer; if sawing and hammering, a carpenter; if jingling bells, a merchant; and if rustling papers, a businessman.

Myking, "Juleminder," 70

soon the yeast started working: any delay predicted death—either for the brewer himself or a member of his family. Crossed straws under the table boded death for the one who sat there. A candle that suddenly went out signaled an equally sudden demise. Anyone who dared venture outside during the Christmas Eve dinner could look through a window back into the house and see those who were *feige* (soon to die) sitting with a shroud over their heads, without heads, or in shadows. If a cock crowed on Christmas night, one should feel its feet; if they were cold, the farm would soon have a corpse.

Norwegians took notice of portents not only as they brewed the yule ale and on Christmas Eve, but during each of the vital preparations leading up to Christmas. Tradition had taught them to pay these portents serious heed. Many stories gave persuasive accounts of the instances when the omens had predicted the future accurately. Through frequent repetition (and by ignoring all the times the predictions failed), folk tradition created a durable impression of the omens' reliability. During the eighteenth-century Age of Enlightenment, printed almanacs with more advanced (though often equally fallible) predictions began to proliferate. These have not yet entirely disappeared. In fact, the belief in prognostications of all kinds seems once again to be on the rise on both sides of the Atlantic, reflecting our own growing need for reassurance in a quickly changing world.

The use of oracles or runes was part of the pre-Christian Scandinavian religion, as well. Christianity specifically tried to forbid them (in the medieval Gulating's Law, for example), but the Christian position on predictions remained somewhat equivocal, given the prominence of prophecy in biblical accounts, not least the role of the Wise Men in foretelling Christ's birth.

Astrology was closely intertwined with astronomy during the Middle Ages, when both flourished, and European astrologers devised sophisticated systems of prognostication. Little evidence of this type of forecasting exists in Norway, where the omens tended to confine themselves to simple sympathetic magic (the doctrine underlying the methods I've described in this chapter, that "like actions produce similar outcomes"). Norwegian omens mostly concern three general areas of interest: the fertility of fields and health of livestock, marriage and prosperity, and illness and death. They retain their pertinence by accurately reflecting their users' deepest concerns, thereby providing a rare interior view of past generations.

In the twentieth century, predictions came to be associated with the turn of the year, and professional prognosticators—and more recently futurists—have taken over the role of interpreting the omens. Their profuse forecasts flood the media during the final days of the old year and first days of the new.

Epiphany: Thirteenth Christmas Day

January 6 marks the end of the Christmas period in most Christian countries. Many Norwegians use the day to take down their trees. As they carefully put away the star, glittering garlands, handcrafted paper baskets, strings of flags, straw figures, and glass ornaments for another year, some Norwegians have recently revived the custom of burning a *trekongerslys* (three kings candle), a three-armed candle representing the three Wise Men). In Catholic countries, this date—known as Epiphany—ranks in importance alongside Christmas Day (as it once also did in Norway). Epiphany is the oldest celebration of Christ's birth; its name comes from the Greek *epiphania,* meaning "coming into view" or "revelation."

When the bishop of Rome (during the first half of the fourth century) instituted December 25 as the day to celebrate Jesus' birth, a conflict arose between the Eastern Church and its Western counterpart. The Eastern Church wanted to retain Epiphany as the date for celebrating Jesus' birth, but it ultimately accepted December 25 as the church feast day. The Eastern Church nevertheless continued to celebrate Epiphany, now as the day of Christ's revelation as the son of God through his baptism in the River Jordan. Epiphany remains one of the most significant festivals in the Eastern Orthodox Church.

The Holy Three Kings

In the Catholic Church, Epiphany developed into a celebration of the so-called *hellige tre konger* (holy three kings), a festival that over the centuries grew to be almost equal in stature to Christmas. It included gifts for children, inspired by the gold, frankincense, and myrrh brought by the Wise Men to the Christ child.

The Reformation subdued the celebration of Epiphany. In Norway a church ordinance officially did away with its celebration in 1770, but the day remained a folk festival as late as the nineteenth century. Norwegians celebrated with feasting and drinking that almost equaled that of Christmas Eve, although with less solemnity. The celebration persisted in the folk culture because it coincided with Old Christmas, a name many people associated with January 6. In Hardanger, for example, the name *gamle joli* (old Christmas) applied to this date as recently as the 1870s.

Why did Norway have both an old and a new Christmas? When the country converted from the Julian calendar to the Gregorian in 1700, twelve days disappeared from the year (specifically the days between February 19 and March 1) and Christmas Day came twelve days earlier. Not everyone accepted the change, however. The peasants, always more conservative than the authorities, continued to observe the twelfth day of Christmas as Old Christmas Day, with drinking parties and other festivities. Since this celebration fell close to Thirteenth Christmas Day, also a holiday, the revelry often extended into that day, as well.

The reason Denmark and Norway, along with many other Lutheran countries, did away with the celebration of Epiphany was the lack of scriptural authority for the centuries-old story about the Three Kings. The only biblical citation occurs in Matthew 2:1–12, which tells of wise men coming from the East to worship the Christ child after having seen the star marking his birth. They bring him costly gifts of gold, frankincense (a mixture of tree resins), and myrrh (a fragrant camphorlike balsam), and they foil King Herod's attempt to find the Christ child by keeping their visit a secret from him.

Over time the story acquired several additions: by the middle of the second century church fathers set the number of wise men at three and declared that they must have been kings. In the fifth century the three received the names Gaspar, Melchior, and Balthasar, as well as biographies describing their lives and journey to the stable in Bethlehem. In 900 the church began celebrating January 6 in earnest, though it never canonized the Three Kings as saints. Later historians have pointed out that they weren't kings at all,

The custom of the *stjernegutter,* or Star Boys, procession was common all along the coast of Norway, though not in inland communities, and it had roots in medieval liturgical dramas presented on Thirteenth Christmas Day that featured processions of the Three Kings into church to visit the Christ child. Pupils of the cathedral schools (known as *latinskoler*) later conducted these processions to raise funds to replace the church support that had disappeared with the Reformation. People invited the Star Boys into their homes, where they would perform special songs and sing Christmas carols. In the 1800s many objected to this old-fashioned and "Catholic" form of organized begging, and officials began forbidding the practice; by the 1900s it had largely disappeared.

but Babylonian magi (astrologers), a prestigious occupation at the time of Christ's birth.

Though the story of the Magi officially receded in Norway after the 1770 ordinance, the celebration of the Holy Three Kings remained a strong folk tradition. Perhaps the most lasting manifestation was the *stjernegutter* (star boys), schoolboys who dressed as the Three Kings and processed through the streets following a leader who carried a paper star illuminated from within. By now, though, these processions, too, have almost entirely disappeared.[12] Of the three Scandinavian countries, only Sweden continues to celebrate Holy Three Kings Day.

Epiphany Folk Traditions

Notwithstanding the church's efforts to downplay the significance of Epiphany, folk traditions about Thirteenth Christmas Day abounded in the old peasant society. The number and variety of work taboos attached to that day show the special position the date continued to occupy in the popular imagination as late as the twentieth century. In Gudbrandsdal, for example, men were to undertake no form of physical labor on either Thirteenth or Twentieth Christmas Day; they should do no work in the wilderness nor cut down trees in the forest. Women should similarly refrain from carding and spinning, shearing sheep, and churning butter. Farm workers thus essentially had the day off, except for vital animal-tending chores. From a modern point of view, taking such a vacation would require no enforce-

ment. Who doesn't want a break? Self-sufficiency farming presented different challenges. The intense labor required just to survive made it tempting
to continue working. The body needed rest, however, even more than now,
since it was the peasants' most important tool; overwork could do serious
harm to the individual and ultimately to the farm and community. The
peasant society therefore designated certain times of rest and devised sanc-
tions against those who failed to keep them. Cautionary tales helped enforce
these strictures, describing accidents or signs experienced by those who ignored them: "A woman who sat carding wool on Thirteenth Christmas
Day found a warning written in blood on her carding paddles; another
woman was shearing sheep, and blood appeared in the wool though she
had not pierced the animal's skin; yet another churned but could get no
butter." Tradition also tells of a man who went with his servant boy to
gather moss for fodder, then had no end of ill fortune while trying to return
home with the three sledloads they'd gathered: "The first spilled out when
they tried to drive through a snowdrift and broke both runners. The runners on the second sled broke further along as they descended a steep
mountainside. They got the third sled as far as the edge of the home fields,
where one of its runners flew off, so the men came home with no moss and
three unharnessed horses."[13]

Good work habits mattered in the old peasant society; customs that supported them supported survival. Tasks had to be done at certain times and
in certain ways or sometimes had to be avoided entirely. Taboos regulated
most undertakings and settings. When rules were broken and something
bad *did* happen, people remembered it and talked about it. In this way the
event became part of oral tradition. Frequent recounting of the event reinforced the importance of doing work properly. These folk legends went
into decline as self-sufficiency farming gave way to industrialization. During
this time, too, fewer people extended their celebration as late as the twentieth or even the thirteenth day of Christmas.

St. Knut: Thirteenth or Twentieth Christmas Day?

According to some accounts, Christmas ended on Thirteenth Christmas
Day, but others specify Twentieth Christmas Day. Couldn't the Norwegians agree how long Christmas should last? Apparently not. What every-

one did agree on was that its conclusion was linked to St. Knut (Knut Lavard of Denmark, martyred January 7, 1131, canonized in 1169, and the patron saint of many medieval Scandinavian merchant guilds).

All over Norway people once knew the saying "Sant Knut jagar jula ut" (St. Knut chases Christmas out).[14] In the old peasant society a boy dressed to represent the saint led a procession of disguised young people who enacted the chasing out of Christmas. Though the St. Knut masquerade has no direct connection to *julebukking,* it was probably influenced by it.[15] Rather than a goat's head, the St. Knut masqueraders carried brooms to sweep Christmas from all the nooks and crannies of each and every house as they proceeded from farm to farm.

Less clear, however, is how they knew on which day to perform this masquerade. St. Knut's name and the idea of chasing Christmas out have been associated with both Thirteenth *and* Twentieth Christmas Day, depending upon when local custom deemed the holiday to end. The twentieth day probably had the oldest roots, and in some places St. Knut went by the name *Tjueendedagsknut* (twentieth-day Knut). Still, several factors favored the thirteenth day, January 6; it lay closer to Knut's saint's day (January 7) and also coincided with the old (Julian calendar) Christmas Day.[16] The growth of industrialization toward the end of the nineteenth century also encouraged an earlier conclusion of the Christmas holiday, the more quickly to resume ordinary work operations.

Collecting tradition mostly among the *almue* (peasant and working classes), Norwegian folklorists have uncovered relatively little oral tradi-

---

Observers have noted both the thirteenth and the twentieth day of Christmas as the occasion for the St. Knut masquerade. Pastor Blom of Valle in Setesdal (1828–1912) wrote, "On the eve of the thirteenth day costumed boys arrive calling themselves *Sankt Knut* and saying they have come to sweep Christmas out." Describing the same custom, Johannes Skar (1837–1914) wrote: "The twentieth day of Christmas Sankt Knut chases Christmas out. With his bishop staff he chased Christmas out of every nook. If there was beer left after that, it would go bad. Sankt Knut should look as tattered as possible—a visible result of his wholehearted celebration of Christmas."

Quoted in Bø, Vår norske jul, *155*

tion about Twentieth Christmas Day, suggesting that the observance of it by these classes may have largely died out before such information began being systematically collected in the nineteenth century. The material pertaining to the end of Christmas that they have managed to collect emphasizes two phases: driving Christmas out and consuming the remaining yuletide food and drink. The importance of the twentieth day comes out most clearly in the medieval Christian laws from Gulating and Frostating, which stipulate that *julefred* (Christmas peace) should last through Twentieth Christmas Day.

Nowadays most people accept January 6 as the last day of Christmas and recognize its origin in the church calendar, while designating January 13 as Twentieth Christmas Day tends to raise modern eyebrows in disbelief. Though growing obscure, the once widespread custom of celebrating Twentieth Christmas Day originated in the Catholic practice of observing the eighth day (known as the octave) after a significant celebration. Since January 12 was the old Christmas Day, its octave was the twentieth day, which also became known as *Octavia epiphania Domini*. Modern skepticism notwithstanding, all of Norway must once have venerated Twentieth Christmas Day.

Families that treasure tradition still do. Anne-Lise Mellbye recalls how eagerly she looked forward to Twentieth Christmas Day in her childhood: "On that day Mother arranged a *juletrefest* for the children. We were served the remainder of the Christmas goodies. Holding hands, we walked around the Christmas tree and sang carols as we emptied the tree's baskets of their treats. (They had been specially filled for the party.) That was our farewell to Christmas and the Christmas tree."[17]

Now Mellbye keeps the tradition alive at Grefsheim, where she says:

Christmas never concludes before Twentieth Christmas Day. Then our neighbors gather and *bærer julen ut* [carry Christmas out]. Along with the last of the Christmas food and what's left of the Christmas cookies, I tempt my guests with a large platter of Norwegian cheeses garnished with fruit and vegetables. We burn a *helligtrekongerslys* [three-armed Epiphany candle] and say farewell to Christmas, but who knows? Maybe Christmas does last [as a familiar Scandinavian song claims] all the way to Easter.[18]

Mellbye mentions that their neighbors at Nes also keep up the Twenti-eth Day tradition, assembling at each others' homes and finishing off the Christmas leftovers. That the Twentieth Christmas Day juletrefest still con-tinues in some homes is attested by Ragnar Wislof (born 1973), from Kol-botn, Norway, a student at Luther College in 1993: "Twenty days after Christmas the trees come down on a day called Christmas Tree Fest Day. Your entire family sings songs around the tree and Santa brings candy to the children."[19]

Though observing Twentieth Christmas Day may be growing increas-ingly rare, the custom of burning the three-armed Epiphany candles actu-ally appears to be reviving.[20] Not so the game of *gnav* that Mellbye mentions playing on New Year's Eve, though it may have been known to ancestors of present-day Norwegian Americans, for along with Epiphany candles, it accompanied the immigrants to America. We hear of their use in the memoirs of Pastor Vilhelm Koren's daughter, Caroline Mathilde Koren Næseth, who wrote from the Washington Prairie, Iowa, parsonage in 1869: "The evening of Twelfth Night we also had a celebration. One of the most important parts of candlemaking was the three-branched light which was to be burned that evening. We ate nuts and small cakes, played gnav and enjoyed ourselves. And then Christmas was ended."[21]

In memory of the Three Kings whom these special candles celebrate, peasants in medieval Norway had carved three crowns to indicate Epiphany on their *primstaver* (calendar sticks). Looking not unlike a yardstick, these perpetual calendars predate both the Julian and Gregorian calendars. Divid-ing the year into two halves, winter (beginning October 14) and summer (beginning April 14), the calendar had notches along one edge for each day of the week. On each flat side special carvings indicated saints' days and other holidays that required abstinence from work and attending mass. Norway's conversion to Christianity, around the year 1000, had added thirty-seven such days and eventually fines for neglecting to observe them, making the primstav necessary to keep track of these obligations.

Even before the Reformation put an end to the veneration of saints, the peasants had begun giving alternative meanings to the primstav's symbols, making them more relevant to their daily work lives. Thus St. Katharine's Day—November 25—became known as *Kari med rokken* (Kari with the spinning wheel), the knife-bearing wheel by which she was martyred having become a cue to begin spinning the fall's wool so they could finish it before putting the wheel away for Christmas. The ax that signified St. Olav's day, July 29, received a similar reinterpretation; it was no longer the weapon of his martyrdom, but a reminder that at least in some places the farmers should harvest the grain.[22]

Since agricultural conditions varied considerably in differing areas of the country, peasants carved local variants of the primstav that accorded with local conditions. When the Reformation ended official church recognition of the precise dates of many primstav *merkedager* (days of demarcation), peasants came to observe these occasions on dates more appropriate to their own climatic conditions. The resulting variance in times of celebration helps account for the differing ending dates for Christmas in various parts of Norway. No doubt the degree to which industrialization had touched an area also had an effect, as it increasingly demanded an earlier return to the normal work routine. Cities and more mechanized rural areas would thus favor January 6 as the end of Christmas, though this circumstance may not have precluded celebrating Twentieth Christmas Day as a feast day in a work year that had already begun.[23]

Surprisingly, Twentieth Christmas Day appears in some of the Norwegian immigrant accounts of Christmas, showing that at least some parts of Norway continued to observe this date until well into the nineteenth century. It was customs such as this, deeply embedded in the lives of home and farm, that the Norwegian emigrants took along with them. How these centuries-old Norwegian traditions weathered their encounter with the newly invented American Christmas tells much about the competing pressures of assimilation and preservation faced by any immigrant group. Norwegian Americans, especially nostalgic at Christmastime, tended to express their deepest feelings about adjusting to their new culture while celebrating or writing about Christmas.

PART TWO
The Norwegian American Christmas

The Norwegians' greatest desire is to celebrate Christmas in the land of their adoption as it was celebrated in distant Norway.

G. M. Bruce, "Christmas on the Prairies," 1912

Pioneers
Christmas on the Prairie, 1850–1900

An immediate need arose in the hearts of the Norwegian immi-
grants to preserve the Christian faith and doctrine acquired in
their childhood and inherited from their forefathers. . . . [But] since
everything about us was shabby during those pioneer days, so too
was our Christmas celebration, and it was to only a limited extent
that we here in this country were able to observe the ceremonies and
customs of Christmas back home in Norway. . . . As small settle-
ments and colonies were created, [however], they shaped their cele-
bration to resemble the Norwegian observance as much as possible,
and they aimed to prepare festive foods and drink in precisely the
Norwegian way.

C. R. Remme, "Jul blandt nybyggerne," 1912

During the first half of the 1800s Norwegians began hearing about vast
tracts of fertile soil and cheap land available in the United States. Over-
population had left too many with too few opportunities in the homeland,
and "America fever" spread like a contagion. The first group of emigrants
embarked in 1825, and after 1836 a steady stream left Norway for America.[1]

Since Christmas meant so much to the Norwegian immigrants, they
often took great pains to write about how they and those around them observed it. These documents retain value not only as chronicles of earlier
customs, but also as a measure of the immigrants' degree of Americaniza-

tion. Providing a glimpse of the pioneer context in which the early immigrants observed Christmas, I. F. Grose (born around 1860 in Goodhue
County, Minnesota) writes in the 1919 issue of *Jul i Vesterheimen:*

> To the south and east of our house lay miles of rolling prairie, covered
> with occasional patches of hazel brush and containing gentle depres-
> sions. . . . An occasional house dotting the prairie looked at a distance
> like a big box. The willow and cottonwood and maple groves of today
> were then nowhere to be seen.
>
> Our house was a conventional white washed log dwelling with a log
> shanty attached. Its cellar held potatoes, cheese, barrels of salt pork and
> kegs of butter. The first floor, making up one room only, performed po-
> tentially the functions of parlor, living room, dining room, bedroom and
> kitchen. . . . The upstairs attic served as a sleeping room and as a place
> for stowing away emigrant chests, boxes, wearing apparel, "wadmol"
> [homespun] blankets, and other things not needed for immediate use.

Though situated in an unfamiliar, desolate landscape, the one-room, all-
purpose farmhouse had much in common with the *stue* the Norwegian immigrants had left behind, but now the attic took over some of the storage
function of the separate *stabbur.* The pioneer home also resembled the farms
from which they had emigrated in providing for its own needs: "They made
cheese, churned butter, baked bread, boiled soap, carded wool, spun yarn,
wove cloth, and sewed clothes. Canned fruit and vegetables were not then
on the market. Home prepared food and home made furniture and garments were largely in vogue."[2]

The similarities were deliberate; many had left Norway not so much to
find something new as to cultivate a lifestyle no longer possible for them in
Norway. By traveling in groups or entire households and usually settling in
small rural communities in the United States, emigrants hoped to enjoy both
greater material wealth and the reestablishment of old values in the New
World.[3] They therefore made a conscious effort to continue their way of
life—and not least their Christmas customs—in the New Land. How well
their effort succeeded varied according to the differing needs they felt, sometimes to preserve their traditions and other times to fit into the new culture. Even immigrants from the most economically strained backgrounds
strove mightily to recapture the solemnity of Christmas practiced according to the customs of home. Their material circumstances, however, did not

always match their aspirations, as C. R. Remme's words in this chapter's epigraph confirm. With time, though, as he also notes, conditions grew more conducive to practicing the customs they had brought from home.

Preparing for a Prairie Christmas

Just how well the pioneers managed to imitate the Norwegian Christmas emerges from the writing of three men, A. A. Veblen, Knute Løkensgaard, and Knut Teigen. Their memoirs (dated 1916, 1919, and 1899, respectively) weave a tapestry that depicts Christmas preparation and celebration during the 1850s to 1870s.

A. A. Veblen—the brother of the influential economist and social theorist Thorstein Veblen and a prominent physicist in his own right—emigrated as a child with his family. Arriving from Valdres, Norway, in 1854, the Veblens lived in a simple shanty in the north woods of Manitowoc County, Wisconsin, where they supported themselves by producing white cedar shingles. Veblen emphasizes the almost indescribable anticipation of Christmas, which he says the Norwegian immigrants regarded as "the greatest celebration for both adults and children," and which therefore served as "the constant topic of thought and conversation for weeks in advance."[4]

The same high-voltage yuletide anticipation emanates from the memoirs of the children's book author Knute Løkensgaard, who grew up in the pioneer settlement of Lake Prairie, Minnesota, in the 1870s: "Oh, how we small children *longed* for Christmas, whose approach was signaled by the slaughter of a pig. From then on, everyone grew increasingly busy with preparations."[5]

THE SLAUGHTER

The Christmas slaughter emerges most graphically (if not always entirely factually) in the memoirs of Knut Teigen. Born in Koshkonong, Dane County, Wisconsin, one of the first Norwegian settlements in America, he, too, describes Christmas during the 1870s.[6]

"Heart-rending squeals" pierced the air from the cornered pig, whose heart was pierced by the *husbond* (man of the house) deftly burying "his freshly sharpened long knife, clear up to its shaft."[7] As he cut along the breastbone, the housewife knelt holding a tin platter, stirring the rich blood to keep it from clotting as it cooled and preserving it for later use in making blood sausage, "a satisfying food," Teigen asserts, as he details a process his parents had learned in Norway: "Now they scalded the carcass, split it open, and removed the innards before hanging it up to stiffen. Regarding the lymph glands as poison, they removed and discarded them, but not before scraping them for every morsel of tallow and flesh." The spleen and liver they also removed; "these were good food and salted down with the rest of the meat in a barrel." The kidneys, heart, and lungs they chopped fine and cooked in broth, producing a dish known as *lungemos* and deemed a great delicacy. The thoroughly washed and cleaned intestines, meanwhile, made casings for *spekepølse* (cured sausage).[8] Not only the process but also the attitude toward it had roots in the Old Country. As there, work habits counted for a lot on the prairie, and a great deal of personal prestige rested upon doing the job right:

> To split the hide correctly and get it smoothly off the animal without damaging tears, to cut along the breastbone *paa folkavis* [in a humane manner], to split the carcass without serious injury, to find the joints— all demanded practice and agility.

Folklore enforced these norms:

> The butcher who could not hit the joint on the first cut was said to have lied that day! And the one who could not manage by the third try to break out the ribs without using an ax was called a miserable *vesalkrok* [wretch].[9]

BEER BREWING

Folklore played a role in another Old Country practice continued by the pioneers—brewing. Like his Norwegian forebears, Løkensgaard terms it "unthinkable" to celebrate Christmas without homemade ale.[10] Again Teigen provides colorful details:

> After the slaughter and a little closer to Christmas came beer brewing. Several had their own *bastu* [bathing house, used for washing clothes and drying grain, as well, and also known as the *eldhus*], where they and

Beer was an important part of the early Norwegian American Christmas celebration. In this January 1857 letter, Caja Munch, a pastor's wife, bemoans the absence of Christmas ale: "I should have brewed some beer for Christmas, all preparations were made; but a keg is very difficult to get hold of here. We had finally been promised one from a man, but when this same man wanted a christening a couple of months after Munch had conducted his marriage and was accosted for this, he got angry, and we lost the keg. I had been afraid this would happen, and I asked Munch to consider that we were to borrow this keg, but he would not even listen to me, although he dearly wanted that beer. Thus we had trouble for our pains instead of Christmas brew."

Munch, The Strange American Way, *64*

their neighbors could dry their Christmas malt when the malt grain had sprouted sufficiently. Meanwhile they picked hops, scoured copper kettles and brewing vessels with ashes and sand, and washed them with *einebærlaag* [boiling water infused with juniper berries, as in Norway]. Stone supports were erected in the yard to cook on. Then early one morning the man of the house would begin brewing his Christmas beer.

Teigen says the best brewers in Koshkonong used at least as much malt as water, and equally generous amounts of hops. Before cooking the wort, the brewer drove his sheath knife into the wooden barrel above the tap "to keep *troldskab* [supernatural mischief created by the *huldrefolk,* or hidden people] away, so the brew could proceed without the interference of *djævelskab* [bedevilment]." The brewer's use of his knife this way belies commonly made assertions that the immigrants left their folk beliefs behind in Norway. The evidence shows instead a high degree of continuity with Old Country ways, including this behavior derived from belief in the hidden people.

Down in the cellar, meanwhile, the scrubbed beer barrels stood ready. Later that evening they would receive the brew as it was strained through their four-sided bungholes.[11] Then came the yeast, and for the next few days "the brewer kept close company with the fermenting barrels, attentively placing his ear against them as a doctor would a patient needing constant care." "Thick and strong," says Teigen, "but also healthy and invigorating was the beer brewed by the pioneers out here for the greatest holiday of the church year." Teigen's blithe mixture of beer brewing and church celebration might raise eyebrows today, but the association has long roots in Norway, reaching back to the earliest Norwegian Christian laws, the Gulatingslov, which exacted stiff fines from any landowner who failed to brew a sufficient quantity of ale to suitably observe the yuletide celebration.

BAKING

Finding a use for even the by-products of brewing, the always resourceful housewife (on the American prairie as in Norway) made *vortekager* by adding rye flour to the fermented wort. Veblen recalls his mother etching invisible markings in the pastries' raw dough, then placing them by the coals after she had allowed a roaring fire to burn down on the hearth (still lacking the cast iron cooking stove that would soon revolutionize food preparation on both sides of the Atlantic). The pastries stayed on the hearth throughout the night.

❖ ❖

Rømmebrød is popular in the valley of Hemsedal, the ancestral home of Ade Docken, professor emeritus of chemistry at Luther College. His great-grandmother brought the following recipe from Hemsedal when she emigrated to America in 1861. Her daughter, Randi Gjerde (born 1859), married Ade's grandfather, Torolf Dokken, in 1880.

Rømmebrød

$\frac{1}{2}$ cup sugar
1 cup whipping cream (originally sour cream, *rømme*)
1 cup butter
2 cups flour (or enough to make a soft dough)

Chill dough in refrigerator several hours. Remove small amounts at a time. Roll out thin, bake on top of stove with very low fire. (Ade notes that he and his wife Orene use a Teflon-lined frying pan.) Sprinkle with sugar, either before baking or after baking while still warm. Break off pieces to serve.

Letter to the author, January 10, 1999

❖ ❖

The next morning the family awoke to the appetizingly browned vorte-kager, ready to be put away until Christmas Eve, with the once impercepti-ble markings—family members' initials, crosses, and other symbols origi-nally relied upon to ward off the hidden people but which eventually became merely decorative—now transformed to embossed prominence.

Løkensgaard makes no mention of vortekager, but says that his mother baked "*rumebrød* [*rømmebrød*, or sour cream bread], *lefse,* and *flatbrød.*" Like the latter two, rømmebrød (whose ingredients included sour cream, butter, and a sweetener) was made on a *takke* (griddle) and varied widely from place to place. Rømmebrød continues to enjoy well-deserved popularity in Hallingdal, Løkensgaard's ancestral home, and is usually presented stacked high on a stemmed, wooden cake platter decorated with traditional Nor-wegian rosemaling.

Immigrants from preindustrial, rural Norway rarely mention the now common, oven-baked Norwegian cookies like *sandbakkels* and *Berliner-kranser,* since the ingredients and technology needed to prepare these pas-tries remained unavailable to the peasant society until at least the turn of the twentieth century.

MAKING CANDLES

As in rural Norway, immigrant candle making constituted "an enormous undertaking," which, says Veblen, "occupied virtually the entire family long into the evening": "In addition to the two or three candles that were to stand in the middle of the table for the whole family, individual Christ-mas candles would be dipped or molded for each of the older children. When they were all lit on Christmas Eve, the house fairly glowed." Different from the daily method of lighting the house (which, according to Grose, often consisted of "rags dipped in fat and placed in tins"), candles sig-naled—like so much else—that Christmas was no ordinary time.[12]

NEW CLOTHES

The pleasure derived from wearing clean and newly made Christmas clothes, a luxury as welcome on the prairie as it had been in the Old Country, also set Christmas apart as a special time. Long before the holidays, Veblen says, his mother would be busy cutting and sewing new garments for every member of the family: "They had to have new shoes, too, and new socks and mittens—all spun and woven at home by Mother herself, who also cut and sewed and knitted everything except the shoes." Ideally each member of her household would wear only brand-new garments on Christmas Eve, a preventive measure taken in light of the well-worn phrase that "whoever does not have a new article of clothing will have to sit on the chopping block."[13]

CLEANING, CHOPPING FIREWOOD, AND SPECIAL TREATS

Modern Norwegian Americans would probably not consider housecleaning a Christmas ritual, but their prairie predecessors—like their Norwegian ancestors before them—certainly did. As part of this ritual, Løkensgaard says, his sister used their father's subscription to *Skandinaven* (a widely circulated Norwegian-language newspaper, published in Chicago from 1866 to 1941). Putting the issues aside throughout the year, at Christmastime she covered the walls with them and thereby gave a new twist to the Old Country custom of decorating the freshly scrubbed cabin walls with weavings or chalk drawings: "[*Skandinaven*] was the only wall covering I knew as a child, when the house consisted of a 12 x 14 foot space. . . . Once [its pages were] on the walls and the floors scoured, it meant just one thing: now we must kindly keep out until further notice." Not that they lacked for things to do outside. As in the Old Country Christmas, wood had to be chopped and carried into the shed during Christmas Eve day, says Løkensgaard: "The work proceeded from early morning till late afternoon with great intensity, for the firewood had to last through Thirteenth Christmas Day." Veblen echoes: "All the adults had long been at work before the children awoke that day. The men out chopping so the wood chips fairly flew, while inside Mother and the newcomer girls, who usually stayed with our family, swept and scoured; it was no easy matter to find a place we weren't in the way." On this gendered division of labor between inside and outside chores, Teigen comments: "The women, poor things, had so much to tend to inside that all the outdoor work—chopping wood and seeing to the cattle—rested on the menfolk."

Later that afternoon, with every nook and cranny scrubbed and the floor steaming dry by the crackling fire, the men cut each other's hair and shaved.

They would change clothes once they'd finished the evening chores in the outbuildings, to which the thorough cleaning also extended.

There, too, the traditional Norwegian practice persisted of providing a special Christmas Eve feeding for all the farm's animals, "from the horses down to the lowly cat in the barn." "Sometimes a wheat *nek* [unthreshed sheaf] was set on a pole outside for the birds of the air," says Teigen. Løkens-gaard adds, "They cleaned inside the animal barn and out in the farmyard because the animals had to receive special treatment at Christmas so they, too, could know that this night was out of the ordinary."[14] Løkensgaard's explanation of the reason for the animals' Christmas treats was the one given in Norway as well.

THE CHRISTMAS BATH

The Christmas bath was another tradition brought from Norway. "More than at any other time, on Christmas Eve cleanliness was next to godli-ness," quips Teigen, referring to the bathing ritual, which in his home be-gan as soon as they had strained the evening milking. Veblen and his siblings bathed one after another, "with the cleanest water going to the most obe-dient, usually one of the littlest." Still, the bath held its attractions in a tub that was homemade, "both wide and deep, so you could sink down in water all the way up to your chin and splash around with merry abandon."

Celebrating A Prairie Christmas

Once the men had also finished their chores, bathed, and changed into clean clothes, the celebration could begin. "The husbond served beer to the house-hold," says Teigen, "while his wife set the table and the children danced around, getting only a little taste of the *juleøl* [Christmas ale] when their father came around with his tankard wishing everyone *glædelig jul* [Merry Christmas]."

As in Norway, the Christmas Eve atmosphere grew more serious as the meal began. After the mother invited everyone to the table, saying "Vær så god, da," they began their devotions, as Teigen describes: "Next to the father's plate eyeglasses lay atop the *psalmebok* [hymnal]. Ceremoniously putting them on, the father respectfully opened the book and with melan-

Frida R. Nilsen remembered Christmases in the home of Pastor Ole Nilsen of Scandinavia, Wisconsin, in the 1890s.

Christmas was celebrated on a splendid scale. When November's cold froze the ponds and lakes, and our thoughts were centered on skating and coasting, Mama would ask, "Are there any dolls, wagons, or other toys that need repair? If so, bring them to me tonight or before you go to school tomorrow." It was hard to part with beloved but battered treasures though we knew that in a few weeks they would return to us beautifully renewed.

Finally Christmas *did* come! The house was shining from top to bottom, everyone's hair had been washed, everyone had taken a bath, the pantries and store rooms were stacked with special food, and a sheaf of wheat was tied to a post for the birds. The men gave extra rations to the horses, cows, and chickens. The whole family could now sit down in their best clothes at the long festive table for the family dinner on Christmas Eve. The white linen gleamed in the flickering light of the candles in their brass candlesticks from Papa's home in Norway. They traditionally had the place of honor, rather than the candelabra, on Christ's and Papa's birthdays.

In the sonorous language of his homeland Papa read the old, old story of the birth of our Savior. We all participated in concluding part of the prayer that followed. Then the hired girl brought in the traditional dishes—rice pudding topped with a big pat of butter and sprinkled with sugar and cinnamon, roasted ribs with many-colored vegetables. As we waited our turns we savored the aroma of the festive food mingled with the fragrance of the lighted candles. We smoothed the slippery linen napkins over our best clothes and then almost forgot the beauty of it all in our first taste of the delicious food. We tried to remember our manners at this meal of all meals, to take small bites, to eat slowly and chew well.

choly solemnity everyone sang a couple of Christmas verses followed by the recitation of the Lord's Prayer or a table grace. Christmas had once again come and been consecrated." Suddenly back in his own childhood Teigen enthusiastically recalls: "How marvelous that *julegrøt* [Christmas porridge] and Christmas fish on lefse could taste! And what enormous portions we children managed to find room for!" Likely he gave little thought to the history of the fish and porridge meal, its roots stretching back to pre-Reformation Advent fasting, when the Christmas Eve meal marked the transition to the abundant feasting that would characterize the remaining holidays.

Of course, no one put elbows on the table, shoved or stretched for this or that. As we looked around the table we saw eyes shining almost as brightly as the tips of the candles.

Dessert came later. The men put on heavy wraps and disappeared. We knew they were going to bring the tree in from its sheltered corner on the long porch. Mama disappeared into the bedroom adjoining the living room. The hired girl and children were busy in the dining room and kitchen doing dishes, cleaning up after the dinner, and filling containers again with wood and water. Never had we done our work so fast and so well. The minute we were through we ran to the two doors which opened into the living room. There we peeked through the keyholes hoping to glimpse some of the glory within. The suspense was unbearable!

At last the big door opened! We stood wide-eyed, mouths agape! In the middle of the floor stood the tree, its shining star reaching almost to the ceiling. Dozens of colored candles winked at us from the fresh green branches. Down below on the floor were our old dolls and other toys, beautiful almost beyond recognition, toys resplendent in new paint and restored parts! We could hardly wait to hug them to our hearts once more.

But Papa and Mama were already forming a circle around the tree and who would want to be left out of that? We sang one carol after the other, holding hands as we marched around the tree. Just as we were becoming dizzy with delight, Papa swung the circle sharply in the opposite direction.

Dessert was served near the tree. There were Christmas cookies, nuts, and even a whole orange for each one, saved until morning by the more self-disciplined of us. We could take one gift to bed with us, with the rest piled in close proximity. Our evening prayers that night were mostly filled with thanks.

Nilsen, Growing Up in the Old Parsonage

After the meal came a lengthier religious service and hymn sing, introduced and concluded by readings about the shepherds and the Child in Bethlehem. Then came beer, aquavit, or wine for the adults and *sukkerpinner* (sugar sticks), nuts, and fruit for the young people. Teigen continues: "Around ten o'clock the children, satiated and exhausted, hung their stockings on the chair backs and dreamed of dolls and pocket knives, which they would indeed find in place the next morning, even though Sankte Klaus was at that time [1870s] not a well-known figure among the Norwegians." While Santa Claus and the Christmas tree had not yet arrived in Koshkonong, gift-giving in a way unknown to Norwegian peasants already characterized the American Christmas.

It had, in fact, arrived even earlier, for Veblen, describing Christmas in the 1850s, also mentions store-bought Christmas gifts. After eating the Christmas Eve meal in the kitchen, he says, they went into the "*'levings-rummet'* [living room], as we called the room with the large fireplace.[15] . . . Then came gifts for all of us. These could be handkerchiefs, mouth organs, a drum, books, dolls for the girls. And then there were tasty treats like raisins, nuts, stick candy, and some large, flat, round candy disks, striped in red, yellow, and blue, and up to three inches in diameter." About the absent Christmas tree, Veblen comments: "Our parents were not taught the custom of putting up a Christmas tree with things hanging on it, for they emigrated before the middle of the [nineteenth] century, and they took along the Christmas customs that existed in their homes then and followed those as closely as the new conditions allowed."

While Veblen emphasizes how closely his parents and other early immigrants replicated the Old Country slaughter, brewing, candle making, ritual cleaning, and bathing, he fails to note how the gift-giving they practiced in America differed from the home country's peasant culture. There gifts consisted of handcrafted clothing items the recipient would have received anyway, rather than the more frivolous, store-bought gifts of the type Veblen describes.

The custom of hanging up Christmas stockings was no doubt stimulated in America by Clement Moore's 1822 poem, "'Twas the Night before Christmas," but it originated in Old Country German and Dutch practices. Otherwise the child-centered Christmases that Veblen and Teigen describe resemble the celebrations that had been developing during the nineteenth century among Norway's *kondisjonerte* classes, but which did not appear until after the turn of the twentieth century in most Norwegian peasant communities and in some places remained unknown as late as the 1940s.

The immigrants probably adopted the Christmas gift-giving custom as soon as they could, both because of its prominence among more established Americans and because Christmas gifts represented a departure from their homeland poverty, a concrete demonstration of the immigrants' new status as landowning Norwegian Americans on the way to joining the middle class.

PASTORAL MEMOIRS

How did Norwegian immigrants become acquainted with the middle-class Christmas? Even those untouched by American magazines and newspapers and living in isolated, solidly Norwegian communities could gain glimpses of middle-class yuletide rituals by visiting the parsonage. As members of the kondisjonerte class, the clergy had enjoyed more comfortable circumstances in Norway than the majority of the immigrants and had during the early 1800s adopted the modern child-centered Christmas, featuring gift-giving, the Christmas tree, and Christmas tree parties. Because of the central role played by the church in the Norwegian American community, these more urbane celebrations and customs inevitably came to influence the way their parishioners celebrated the holiday, as well.[16]

At first few clergy had immigrated, being reluctant to risk the security of their relatively prestigious positions and assured incomes in Norway to minister to their countrymen in a strange land. Those who took the chance were often motivated by a strong sense of mission, as was Pastor Ulrik Vilhelm Koren, who at twenty-seven accepted a call in northeastern Iowa near Decorah.

The first Norwegians in this region of Iowa had come in 1849. Their

This cabin, shared by the Koren and Egge families in 1853, now stands at the Vesterheim Norwegian-American Museum.

number grew so rapidly that by 1852 the first missionary pastor west of the Mississippi, Nils O. Brandt, could organize no fewer than three congregations. It was a call letter signed by 105 members of these congregations that brought Vilhelm Koren and his wife Elisabeth to America. With no parsonage ready for them, on December 24, 1853, they moved into a tiny log cabin that they would share with earlier immigrants, Erik and Helene Egge and the two Egge children (three and four years old). Here they would live for two and a half months in a fifteen-by-sixteen-foot space "divided by curtains of calico into two rooms, one of which affords the space for two beds." Later that evening the twenty-one-year-old Elisabeth, married only a few weeks before their September departure to America, confided to her diary the couple's impressions of their first Christmas in America: "This was a strange Christmas Eve, indeed, so different from any I have ever known before. Here we sat, Vilhelm and I, separated for the first time from relatives and friends, in a little log cabin far inland in America."[17] Though she constantly makes the best of her drastically changed circumstances, she did admit some sixty-one years later, in 1914, that on that Christmas Eve in 1853 she had gone up to the attic and found in their trunk the last little piece of chocolate and eaten it. "To me that was almost like a last reminder of civilization."[18]

Newly ordained, Vilhelm spent much time on the road looking after his far-flung parish and holding religious services "in the settlers' small houses, where many a time the rose-painted emigrant chests had to serve both as altar and pulpit."[19] Not having to do "any housekeeping," Elisabeth tended to "correspondence and her diaries," which she kept to show her husband upon his return. On New Year's Eve, 1853, she continued:

> My pen has been resting a little, while I sat thinking of Father and all the dear ones in our distant native land; and I am sure we have been constantly in their thoughts this evening. On such occasions they are doubly missed. May God bless this year for them too! Last year I began the new year clad in a bobbinet [lacy dress], dancing away with roses in my hair. This year I am sitting here with Vilhelm in this bare room, where tomorrow he is to conduct divine services for all these people who so long have lacked a pastor. Still, this is best.

How quickly her life had changed from the background of relative privilege she had known!

CHRISTMAS AT THE PARSONAGE

Almost a decade later another Norwegian pastor arrived in the area to help relieve Koren of some of the constant travel required to serve the more distant congregations in his charge. Ove Jacob Hjort brought his family from Norway in 1861. He was ordained at Wisconsin's Norwegian Koshkonong settlement in 1862, and later that same year began his ministry in Paint Creek Parish in Allamakee County in northeastern Iowa (another of the three parishes organized by Brandt in 1852). The Christmases spent in that parsonage come to life in the memoir of his daughter, Lulla (Hjort) Preus.

Describing the period around 1870, Lulla notes the parsonage's close contact with the students at the nearby, recently founded Luther College (whose future president, C. K. Preus, she would later marry).

The parsonage needed a goodly supply of meat at Christmastime for there were always many guests—especially college boys from Decorah, who brought along healthy appetites. Several sleighs were usually sent

Christmas Eve at the Preus parsonage, 1861, from Linka Preus's sketchbook

each Christmas vacation from Paint Creek to Decorah to fetch Christmas guests from the college. A number of families had sons at the school, and they would invite a group of their friends home to celebrate.[20]

According to Lulla's sister, Dikka, the thirty miles took almost the entire day to cover because of poor roads. A frigid journey, besides, even with all the parsonage's clothing and blankets to keep them warm and straw stuffed into the bottom of the sled together with some heated stones. Still they had to stop several times during the trip and run around to keep their circulation going.[21] Four Luther students were usually invited each holiday. Among them, Lulla mentions such prominent future educators and clergy as L. S. Reque, Pastor O. A. Normann, Professor R. B. Anderson, Professor W. Pettersen, Pastor P. T. Hilmen, Professor O. G. Felland, Pastor Olaf Mandt, Pastor Johannes Ylvisaker, and writer and educator Peer O. Strømme.[22]

Years later memories of these Christmas vacations remained vivid for Lulla, especially their keen anticipation of seeing the splendidly adorned tree on Christmas Eve. Though this particular recollection must have brought mixed sensations, having once gotten them all into trouble: "The Christmas guests had arrived and my parents were busy getting the Christmas tree ready. Meanwile we children were supposed to get dressed and be at the ready for the ceremonial moment when the door to the parlor would be opened to reveal the radiantly shining tree."[23] The European practice of concealing the tree until the last minute prevailed in America as well, but this time the waiting proved too long, and both her brother and Johannes Ylvisaker fell asleep on one of the beds. Felland (later a highly respected clergyman and St. Olaf College professor) was, Lulla reveals, "in those days quite a tease." He began pinching the sleeping boys, causing a great commotion. "Father had to come upstairs to investigate," Lulla wrote—an outcome that no doubt marred the spectacle the children had been anticipating.

The Christmas tree, once revealed, was "always the largest the parlor could hold" and stretched from floor to ceiling, adorned with a multitude of candles, says Lulla. Her mother considered the candles "the tree's most important ornament because they represented Christ, the True Light."[24] The tree also held an abundance of colored baskets and other paper decorations, gilded walnuts, and so on, prepared by Lulla's mother "in all secrecy during the evenings before Christmas once we children were in bed." Sister Dikka, four years younger, remembers this differently, saying that the children themselves decorated the tree.[25] This change in custom was no doubt hastened by the tragic death of their mother in an 1873 kitchen fire, though in other families, too, the decorating eventually transferred from the parents to the older children.

In the Hjort household, the period between Christmas and New Year's Eve went by the Norwegian name *romjulen*. As in Norway, this period marked a time of great merriment, including a *juletrefest* (Christmas tree party) held on the fourth day of Christmas at the parsonage by Lulla and Dikka's parents for "as many young people as the house could hold." Arriving in the afternoon, more than fifty guests would stay through the evening, mostly in the basement, where her father otherwise held confirmation class; the Christmas tree had been moved there for the occasion. Reminiscent of the Norwegian *juletrefester* which by then had begun among the kondisjonerte in Norway, the Paint Creek parties included games to play as they danced around the tree: "Here we played 'sip nip' and with great glee harvested the Christmas tree once we had sung our Christmas songs," Lulla recalls. "Then the guests were invited up to the dining room for supper: What a table was laid! I can still see the large platters with the decorative open-faced sandwiches we had prepared that morning with the college boys' help and a great deal of laughter and fun." The Norwegian delicacies she names differ considerably from those the peasant classes of her time would have known in Norway. While the latter feasted on *lefsekling* (lefse spread with butter or sour cream) and *rømmegrøt*, Lulla's family served *fattigmann* (thin, deep-fried cookies) and *julekage* (Christmas bread), *siripskager* (syrup cookies, somewhat like ginger snaps) and *snipper* (diamond-shaped syrup cookies topped by a blanched almond). Contrasting these delicacies with the American ones that eventually replaced them, Lulla uses English names in her Norwegian text: "Dishes such as 'salads,' 'pickles,' 'jellies,' and 'layer cakes,' which now seem so essential, we did not know, and not 'sherbet' or 'ice cream,' either." Referring to the proffered fare as "simple treats," she assures her reader that their simplicity "in no way dampened either our enjoyment or appetite, both of which were always beyond reproach."

After the meal they returned to the basement, where, adds Dikka, her parents taught them *barneleker* (children's singing games) and her mother sang and played the piano (which they had brought from Norway). "The children thought they'd never heard anything lovelier, and they were probably right," she says. "Then Father held service, we all sang a hymn, and parted very well satisfied," Lulla concludes. The Luther students would stay at the parsonage for fourteen days and then were brought by sleigh back to Decorah, "enriched with happy memories."

The memoirs of Lulla Hjort Preus and Dikka Hjort Koren portray Norwegian American parents, born and raised in the kondisjonerte class of Norway, consciously perpetuating upper-class, Old World customs among Norwegian-speaking people in their adopted land.[26] It was in such families that the first Norwegian American Christmas trees appeared.[27] Considerable time would yet pass before Norwegians of the less affluent classes on either side of the Atlantic adopted what we now see as an indispensable part of the Christmas celebration.

INTO THE MIDDLE CLASS: THE CHRISTMAS TREE

The immigrants' entry into the middle class changed their holiday customs, says Veblen, "so that eventually Christmas became quite different." As the painstaking preparations made by the peasant culture began to disappear, the child-centered Christmas—manifested by the Christmas tree—took over.

A community's first tree usually arrived via the school or church. Løkensgaard recalls the tremendous impression made by his own first encounter in the late 1870s:

> The community had gotten a new schoolteacher, who announced that—among other innovations—there would be a Christmas tree. Many wondered what a Christmas tree might be. When Christmas Eve finally arrived, the entire settlement and all their children gathered in the church—oh, how we packed it in! The tree was beautiful and its candles made it glow with a spectacular radiance.[28]

Surprising as it may seem that some communities as late as 1870 had yet to see a Christmas tree, others had to wait even longer.

Sometimes, even if they had heard of the custom, the lack of indigenous evergreens prevented its adoption.[29] Such was the case of Viking Settlement,

Professor O. G. Felland with the family Christmas tree,
Northfield, Minnesota, December 29, 1910

North Dakota, whose first Christmas tree did not arrive until the 1890s and
then suffered a sad fate:

> It was Christmas of 1894 or thereabouts that we had a teacher from the
> East who began talking about a Christmas tree celebration in the school
> house. Of course we all wanted a tree. We had read about Christmas

trees all these years and had seen many pictures. Now we were really going to have one at the school house.

The school directors were all against it: there was too much danger from fire. Only a year or so before a tree trimmed with cotton batting for snow had caught fire and burned up a church at Oberon.

Prodigious powers of persuasion eventually enabled the schoolmaster to succeed, say family historians Hilda Wisness and Levard Quarre. Imagine, then, the teacher's chagrin when on the afternoon of the party, long before the settlement's citizens would arrive eager to glimpse their first Christmas tree, the pot-bellied stove—generously stoked with coal against the chill of the day—felled every last needle from the tree and left its wax candles dripping on the floor.[30]

CHRISTMAS DAY

While the Christmas tree had initially been unfamiliar to many nineteenth-century immigrants, the practice of attending church on Christmas Day had accompanied them from the Old Country. As in Norway, the weather did not always cooperate: "In sub-zero temperatures, with the wind lashing against their faces and driven snow blinding their vision, they crossed the countryside by open sleigh to perform their sacred duty."[31] "Sacred duty" it was to many, not least because of their veneration of the pastor, who in their view "frequently stood face to face with the Lord [and] . . . spent a large portion of his time in the presence of the throne of Jehovah."[32]

Much of that awe passed with the pioneer generation, according to Grose. Still, most felt an urgency, says Løkensgaard, to attend Christmas Day services in order to give the minister the payment they owed him: "Even if they otherwise never went to church, people went on Christmas Day so they could contribute to the offering." Teigen agrees: "As long as the roads were passable, few stayed home from church, if for no other reason than the offering—the venerable minister should at any rate have his due on time." The Christmas offering provided a necessary supplement to the minister's salary and was calculated into the sum offered by the letter of call that constituted his legal contract with the congregation. As its members filed around the altar and deposited their money, the pastor knelt in an attitude of reverence.

Though Veblen agrees that "everyone went to church on Christmas day," he adds this important proviso: "if there were services there." As in post-Reformation Norway, the Norwegian American pioneer minister typically served more than one congregation and rotated his preaching during the period between December 25 and 27. Teigen mentions that West Koshkonong Church had services on First Christmas Day, East Koshkonong Church on Second Christmas Day, and Third Christmas Day services took place at either Liberty or McFarland.

If the local church had no service on Christmas Day, Veblen says, "People held their own service at home, as they did on Sundays, though perhaps with more hymns and more readings from the Bible. They would always include a sermon from the *postill*." The postill, a collection of sermons intended for home use, is one of the most frequently found items in Norwegian American book collections.[33] The practice of holding devotions in the home had also accompanied the immigrants from Norway.

Since not all Americans observed Christmas Day as a holy day or even a holiday in Veblen's time, he emphasizes that "Christmas Day was fully as *hellig* [sacred] as Sunday in our little neighborhood, and the commandment that it be kept holy was strictly observed. While on Sunday there would be cheerful visits among the neighbors, people never had guests on Christmas Day." Breaking the quiet solemnity of Christmas Day, the ride home from church could be great fun. Accompanied by shouts, screams, and laughter, it proceeded at top speed, perhaps influenced by the tradition in some parts of Norway predicting that the one who arrived home first from Christmas Day services would also be the first to bring in the coming year's harvest. Veblen says: "After the services the horses could never get back home fast enough, for now the serious part was over and the actual Christmas joy could begin, though the real socializing didn't start until Second or Third Christmas Day." As in Norway, Christmas Day initially confined the social circle to the immediate family.

ROMJUL SOCIALIZING

Though they never had guests on Christmas Day, says Veblen, "on the Second Christmas Day, the partying erupted with visits, good food, and drink." Teigen echoes the contrast of Christmas's solemnity with the raucous days to follow and describes how, once begun, the Norwegian American Christmas socializing exceeded any sort of celebration familiar to Americans.[34] For the Norwegians, says Veblen, "Christmas was above all a season of parties, and the revelry continued for at least a couple of weeks until Thirteenth Christmas Day." As in Norway, all work was left undone during this period, all tools and implements put away, and only absolutely critical chores got done. Veblen continues: "The third day was like the second, but the fourth was 'children's day' and then we could 'rå oss selv' [rule ourselves] according to old custom. Usually it meant we could visit as many of our friends as possible and share opinions about our Christmas gifts."[35]

Meanwhile the *gjestfrihet* (hospitality) for which Norwegians have been known since Viking times reigned: "The houses were small, but they always had enough room for the guests," says Løkensgaard. Raising a toast had long cultural roots, derived from the Viking belief that alcohol facilitated communication with the gods, and put into practice by their midwinter-feast toast to Thor, Odin, and Frey for "peace and a good year." Nor was heavy drinking entirely unknown at these pioneer house parties, as Løkensgaard's account shows: "Things got pretty lively, as liquor was present in every home, and the bottle made busy rounds. Drinking in moderation had never been the Norwegians' way—it was at any rate not the custom among the Lake Prairie Hallings in those days." The liveliness of these Romjul get-togethers also figures in the memoirs of Thurine Oleson (born in 1866 to immigrant parents from Telemark who settled in Winchester, Wisconsin):

> During the Christmas holidays, my folks always had a real party. Everyone would drink the malt beer and homemade wine that Mother had made, and eat all the good food she had been preparing for weeks. Then they would talk about Norway, and after a while it would get pretty lively, at least among the men. If the downstairs of our little house got too crowded, the men would take off upstairs where they could smoke and drink and play cards in peace. They played mostly Euchre and Pedro, but I never heard that there was any gambling amongst our people.[36]

Euchre and Pedro remained popular card games among the Norwegian Americans for generations to come. Teigen mentions other games and entertainments of the Koshkonong parties, principally five-card, *sveis* (another card game), and *svingom* (dancing):

After several table seatings of guests had eaten, the fiddles struck up, and the party held forth fueled by alcohol punch. The oldest of the assembly played some hands of five-card and *sveis* in the corner of the parlor or upstairs, while all through the night and until the next morning the young people danced on, whirling around the floor with their chosen partner, exercising the usual coquetry and flirtation.

STORYTELLING AND FOLK BELIEFS

Along with these other amusements, storytelling, especially about the Old Country, played a vital role at Romjul parties. Veblen—echoing Oleson's comment that her parents' guests "would talk about Norway"—observes, "During Christmas we heard much about the old folks at home." These stories concerned not only the folks back home, but equally often the hidden people and powers, which the Norwegians took no less seriously: "Folktales and legends about the huldrefolk and trolls, *julesveiner, rokkemænd,* many kinds of superstition—what one had to do and what was dangerous to do . . ." Such tales, says Veblen, enlivened many a Norwegian American Romjul gathering.

These observations further contradict any notion of the emigrating Norwegians having abandoned their folklore when they left Norway. On the contrary, these stories constituted a treasured part of their cultural cargo. As if to document the case, Thor Helgeson of Iola, Wisconsin, assembled and published (in 1923) a sampling of folk stories told by his Wisconsin neighbors during the period from 1850 to 1880.[37]

In addition to preserving a wide array of the now mostly forgotten immigrant narratives, Helgeson's collection is valuable for recording the context in which the stories were told and in portraying the varying degrees of belief this lore enjoyed among the pioneers.

The men talked first about the wind and weather, and then about the wheat crop, wheat prices, stock for butchering and timber dealings. When these topics, which are so interesting to farmers, were exhausted, they gradually began to talk about other events—about trolls, elves, fairies and ghosts. Many of the older pioneers still believed in the power of the underground folk (*de underjordiske*) and all that was said about

Andreas Ueland, who emigrated in 1870 at the age of eighteen, recalls the ghost-story-telling sessions from his childhood: "How they could tell stories in the days before the minds had been filled with trashy books and newspapers! The ghost stories would not only make me afraid to go out alone in the dark, but even to keep my legs out of sight under the table. The ghost stories became more frequent as Christmas approached." Ueland credits these narratives as the start of his "real education," which, he says, began "during the long winter evenings listening to the talk going on between the members of the family and the servants sitting around the light of a tallow candle or of an open three-cornered iron lamp burning bad-smelling cod liver oil. The women sat there carding, spinning, and knitting, and the men whittling out some household implement, or doing nothing except their share of the conversation."

Ueland, Recollections of an Immigrant, *3–5*

them as sure as God's truth. But others believed they were nothing but nonsense.[38]

The stories most likely to have accompanied pioneer Romjul socializing are of two types—those set at Christmastime and ghost stories, whose telling once constituted a favorite yuletide entertainment. Such a ghost story Helgeson collected from an immigrant shoemaker in Scandinavia, Wisconsin. When the shoemaker was a youth "reading for the minister" (preparing for confirmation in the Lutheran church, the rite of passage to adulthood), he was apprenticed to a shoemaker with a drinking habit. Given to letting his work slide, then making it up with all-night work sessions, the master shoemaker sat sewing one Lillejulaften (December 23) with his apprentice, long into the night, trying to finish a batch of shoes and boots promised for Christmas. When the shoemaker remarked that they'd have to keep working through Christmas Eve and Christmas Day as well, the apprentice refused, and that is how he came to be walking home at dawn on Christmas Eve: "Going down the hill by the church, I noticed a woman several paces ahead of me. I was close enough to see she wore low boots, a long skirt, and a cape over her head. But halfway down the hill she suddenly disappeared. When I went to see what had become of her, I found a hole in the middle of the road."[39] Certain that she had sunk into this hole, "for I could see her foot prints in the snow," he decided to investigate. "I followed her prints back to the church gate, where I could see that she had walked several times around the church." He spotted some more prints that went through the woods to the cemetery; "following those I came to a newly dug grave that had a large opening in one end. The prints stopped there. She had clearly emerged from this grave," the legend confidently concludes, serving like many such legends chiefly to confirm the reality of the hidden world.

A tale of a different sort and one familiar to most Norwegians even today concerns the Christmas Eve ride of Johannes Blessom on an airborne sleigh driven by a *jutul* (giant troll).[40] Helgeson's collection includes a closely related account of a Slidre (Valdres) man taking a Christmas Eve ride through the air on the sleigh of a nisse. Helgeson attributed his story to a Valdres emigrant living in Helvetia, Wisconsin.[41] "About to sit down to Christmas dinner, the family heard a knock on the door. The man of the house went to see who it was, but failed to return." Outside the door, the Slidre man saw a "little, tiny" fellow who introduced himself as their neighbor, saying he had saved the man's *eldhus* (grain-drying house) from burning down many a time when the man had put too much wood in the stove. "The nisse asked if the man would fancy a Christmas Eve ride, and no sooner had he asked than a magnificent horse appeared, sporting harness and reins so fine their like had been seen in Valdres neither before nor since." The man climbed into the nisse's sleigh, which "took off like the north wind in autumn, so the snowflakes fairly flew about their ears." Coming to a farm some eighteen miles distant, the nisse brought the horse to a halt. The owner of the farm brought out an enormous wooden beer tankard, "ornately painted and intricately carved." Both the nisse and the man drank deeply before climbing back into the sleigh, which now "sailed so speedily the man from Slidre sometimes thought they were on land and sometimes in the treetops. Then the nisse suddenly disappeared and once again the man stood outside his own cabin door." This story, too, functions mostly as testimony that the normally unseen nisse does in fact exist and may as soon be encountered by any human being as by the man from Slidre.

Another popular story type common all around Norway tells of a human woman serving as midwife to a jutul. Helgeson attributed his version to a Waupaca County, Wisconsin, resident from Gudbrandsdal, who sets the story in the archaeologically significant parish of Hole in Buskerud County.[42]

Such sites of long habitation, documented by rich grave-mound finds, often play a role in stories about trolls, giants, and the hidden people. This story is no exception. One Christmas Eve, Ola Hole heard loud pounding on his cabin door. Opening it, he found the Hole jutul, looming large before him, wanting to see Ola's wife, Kari. The jutul invited Kari to go with him inside the mountain (the traditional realm of the supernatural), but refused to say why. Nevertheless she complied and, "when she got inside Hole Mountain, found the jutul's wife lying in childbed, struggling with the worst pains of labor. Presently Kari delivered the mother of a baby jutul—son and heir to all of Hole Mountain. Then, studying the jutul's wife more closely, Kari recognized her own daughter, now married to the Hole jutul and living happily and well inside Hole Mountain." Again affirming the existence of the hidden world, this story belongs to a large class of legends about human beings marrying the huldrefolk. The motif of a human woman acting as midwife to the huldrefolk also abounds, reinforcing the concept crucial to the preindustrial peasant society of "reciprocity" (balanced giving and receiving of help among members of a community) and newly pertinent to the immigrants, who put it into practice as they assisted and depended upon their neighbors—whether seen or unseen.

All three of Helgeson's stories share the once standard view of Christmas as the seam of the year when the barriers between the visible and hidden worlds break down, facilitating contact between human beings and the normally invisible denizens of other realms. Though modern readers might muse about the role alcohol played in some of these accounts, previous generations of Norwegians once took the hidden world very seriously. Belief in the *underjordiske* (undergrounders, as the huldrefolk were also known) strongly influenced their behavior. Sleeping on the straw-covered floor on Christmas Eve, placing decorative (once protective) markings on baked goods, bringing porridge to the nisse, and consulting omens were among the Christmas customs that grew out of the peasants' fear of these beings and their desire not to offend them.

OMENS AND ELVES

While most of the stories in Helgeson's collection have settings in Norway rather than America, some immigrant narratives spanned the Atlantic.

Jerome Field heard the following account from his mother, who had learned it during her North Dakota childhood from her Norwegian immigrant mother, Ingeborg.[43]

Ingeborg had left Oslo (then known as Christiania) during the latter half of the 1880s, intending to return home after a short visit in America. Instead she fell in love. Marriage followed, and she settled down in a North Dakota farming community to raise her family. Other Norwegians had been "coming in droves" to this part of the country with the common aim of "hewing out a pattern of Christian living." Like most of the women in the community, Ingeborg "dedicated her life to the home, the children and the church," but she also delighted in telling the mystical tale her grandson here recounts about how she and her husband had met: "Near Christiania during the 1880s, people believed that if a girl went to any cross-road at midnight on Christmas Eve and remained perfectly quiet, she would get a glimpse of her future husband." Encouraged by a girlfriend to engage in this "adventurous lark," Ingeborg dressed warmly, and the two young women left the house unnoticed. Approaching the crossroads at midnight, they saw two shadowy figures:

> They were conversing with one another and one of them laughed. The laugh rang out so clearly on the night air that the girls became frightened and ran back home.
>
> Two years later Ingeborg, now nineteen, had arrived in America. She was invited to a Christmas Eve ball at the local opera house in the North Dakota town where she was staying. Relatives and friends took her there to introduce her to the townspeople. They arrived a little late. Many people had gathered and the dancing had already begun. Above the noise of the crowd she heard the same ringing laugh she had heard two years ago at the cross-road. Turning around, her eyes met those of the violinist in the orchestra. The violinist threaded his way through the crowd toward her and, after introducing himself as Peter, he asked her to dance with him. They both felt that they had met before, but they realized this was impossible as she had just arrived from Norway.
>
> They dated each other after that time. Eventually Ingeborg learned that Peter had been ill with typhoid fever two years previously. He had lapsed into a coma on Christmas Eve and had been given up as lost. At twelve o'clock midnight, however, he had taken a miraculous and startling turn for the better.

Ingeborg's story builds on the widely accepted folk practice of divining one's future spouse's identity. Many Norwegians on both sides of the Atlantic seemingly found no conflict between such folk customs and their profound Christian piety.[44]

With time, though, these customs, along with belief in the hidden beings, faded. Industrialization and more widespread education took its toll on superstition, both in Norway and among the immigrants in America. Helgeson's stories record and address this transition. He portrays two storytellers, Per, a true believer, and Ola, the doubter, to whom Per tells the story of a certain family from Valdres who had always been on good terms with their invisible neighbors and consequently enjoyed great prosperity. They emigrated to a Norwegian community near Manitowoc, Wisconsin, where one day the housewife received a visit from a strange woman who asked to borrow a spinning wheel. The stranger turned out to be one of her invisible neighbors from Valdres, who explained why they left Norway: "We had to leave because when they began to build a new road, there was so much commotion and blasting that the mountain shook. We could not live there any longer." Industrialization had driven the *huldre* (hidden) woman from her familiar life in Norway; before long she suffered the same fate in America, and after that, "no one [again] saw anything of the hill people in the Norwegian settlement near Manitowoc."

Per believes this story, telling the doubtful Ole in his mixture of Norwegian and English that "det meka ingen differens [it makes no difference] whether you believe it or not because I know it to be a fact." Despite Per's protests, "progress and education had scared both the trolls and elves so far into the ground that they never dared show themselves again."[45] Though many of the early immigrants retained their folk beliefs, changing times, and the change of place, did not support their continuance. Yet, as the immigrant narratives reviewed here demonstrate, storytelling vividly infused with these beliefs long continued to enliven Romjul celebrations and to evoke meaningful memories of home.

GOING JULEBUKKING

No matter how much enjoyment the old stories aroused, though, "of the many Romjul amusements," Veblen asserts, "going julebukking was the most fun." Despite its notable absence in historical accounts, Christmas masquerading not only survived in Norwegian immigrant communities, it thrived. In the Koshkonong settlement of the 1870s, says Teigen, "some came walking, some riding, in groups of fifteen to twenty apparitions of both sexes, visiting house after house in the entire neighborhood, [in guises ranging from] rotund brewers or women in far advanced pregnancy [to] terrible bandits with mustaches of calfskin and beards of blackened wool." Only a few sported their horns and calf tails as they "sashayed" down the road, but "all had their masks on when they came knocking on the door—until well after midnight—their hideous appearance scaring women and children half to death." A musician might come along, and they'd waltz at each place while refreshments were served, then either proceed to another house or take off their masks and stay.

Its rollicking social delights aside, when seen through the eyes of a child, the custom could terrify and confuse. Veblen recalls his first encounter with these masked marauders:

> It must have been the evening of Second Christmas Day that we suddenly heard noise out on the porch and people pounding on the door, growling and bleating. My younger brother had no sooner opened the door, than he beat a hasty retreat. In the lead came a figure that looked like a bogeyman, except that in addition to his hideous head, he had two enormous horns. Now the house filled with all kinds of limping, twisted, hunchbacked, or outrageously fat human figures dressed in the most fantastic costumes and masks. Some crowed, grunted, and brayed like speechless animals; others spoke with hoarse, gruff, or snuffling voices.
>
> Pandemonium reigned for a while, granting neither inhabitants nor furniture a moment's peace. Beer was offered, but not everyone wanted to taste it. The *bukk* [the group's leader in goat disguise] tried to take a sip, but spilled it on the floor. At last the procession went on its way, probably to make further visits.

The bukk sometimes carried an actual goat's head, saved from the fall slaughter, but more often it was carved out of wood:

> The bukk himself was the strangest of the lot. I spotted a pair of boots under his wraps and realized then that the julebukks were nothing more than disguised people. In the lamplight I soon recognized some red

cloth I'd seen mother give Ingrid, and surmised that the bukk must be Gudbrand. . . . He had constructed a very clever goat head, around whose neck he had nailed a fur skin; he was carrying the head on a pole that he held under the fur. He moved the lower jaw by pulling a string so the bukk could open and close its mouth at will.[46]

Veblen's account echoes in surprising detail the julebukking custom practiced in Norway during the same time period. Apparently the immigrants didn't lose their sense of fun on the transatlantic passage.

THIRTEENTH CHRISTMAS DAY

Along with the Christmas customs themselves, the immigrants brought to America the Old Norse (Viking) concept that the celebration should last at least until Thirteenth Christmas Day and then *drikkes ut* (be escorted away with drink). Some beer should still remain in the bottom of the barrels, but the experienced knew to handle it with care, says Teigen. Those foolish enough to be seduced by the yule ale's sweet taste found that the fourteenth day dawned as a day of trial. More often than not the womenfolk had to add the men's chores of watering and feeding the livestock to their own labors until their husbands had recovered from "chasing Christmas out."

Their raucous behavior notwithstanding, Teigen argues, the Koshkonong pioneers were "good Lutherans in their own way": "They took pleasure with those who were happy and enjoyed what was joyful, all the while loving their women—along with wine and song. Though they might lose their inhibitions on especially festive occasions, it was seldom more than was good for them or than they could handle." Teigen's remarks reflect a tension between the kind of behavior characteristic of the old peasant society and that which suited the middle-class lifestyle to which the immigrants aspired. While the clergy and established middle-class Yankees objected to the Norwegian immigrants' Christmas drinking habits, Teigen and his fellow immigrants viewed their drinking as appropriate to the holiday, which had since the time of the Vikings been observed with considerable quantities of beer.

Besides adjusting to new attitudes about intoxication, the immigrants' (like the Norwegians') transition to the middle class brought a change in the established gender roles of the old peasant society. Teigen's assertion that watering and feeding the livestock constituted men's work contrasts with the division of labor in Norway's old peasant society, where the farm animals (consisting of a few dairy cows known individually by name) had received their care exclusively from women. With the transition from subsistence to cash-based farming (including large-scale cattle raising in America), tending the livestock became men's work; as machinery took over (in both countries), outdoor operations fell more exclusively into the male domain while women's work increasingly moved indoors.[47] Creating a comfortable home and carefully rearing their children had become core values among Norway's kondisjonerte during the 1800s and by the 1920s also became commonly held goals among the Norwegian working and peasant classes. In America immigrant women of peasant origin typically encountered these middle-class values earlier than if they had stayed in Norway. Helped by such guides as the widely circulated *Buckeye Cookery and Practical Housekeeping* (published in thirty-two editions between the years 1876 and 1905), they turned their attention to keeping house, caring for the children, and becoming informed consumers of goods and services.[48] Though the women still "pitched in" when necessary, as Teigen suggests, industrialization had transformed their ordinary sphere of operation.

American industrialism changed Christmas, too. New arrivals from some parts of Norway came expecting the holiday to last until the twentieth day, says Veblen, but "practical considerations made it impossible for the pioneers to extend the holiday that long. The women seem to have observed the old rules most faithfully. To weave before the thirteenth day was unthinkable, nor was the spinning wheel to turn, though knitting was permissible." Though women could sometimes keep the old ways, men, whose work was more deeply intertwined in production networks, had no choice but to resume normal operations much more quickly than they had ever done in Norway. Veblen continues:

> Even if we tried to extend it to the two weeks we had grown up with . . . the demands of building a home and acquiring the necessities of life got in the way. People had entered a new reality where the old customs didn't always fit in. The circumstances required a greater intensity of work and permitted less leisure than had the Norwegian conditions, which the Christmas customs had originally developed to accommodate.[49]

Adjusting to the Western Home

Do Veblen's words mean that homesteading on the prairie demanded even more than the self-subsistence farming in preindustrial Norway? Probably not in terms of actual backbreaking labor, but added to the stress of the move, adapting to new surroundings, and absence from family—not to mention establishing a new home and livelihood—it must have seemed more intense. But the marked lack of leisure in America more directly derived from the new country's push for development: opening the frontier, growing cities, expanding businesses—all created a relentless push to grow, earn, and work longer and harder. America was no place for the Norwegian Christmas customs, which served to enforce a much needed rest in the context of a hand-to-mouth peasant culture. These customs worked at cross-purposes to the American imperative to develop, produce, and expand.

DISAPPOINTMENT WITH THE AMERICAN CHRISTMAS

The differing circumstances between the Old Country and the New Land had caused the American Christmas to develop along different lines than the Norwegian *jul*. In the eyes of many Norwegian immigrants, the American holiday suffered by comparison. Nor did they keep this observation to themselves. Spanning the period from 1856 through the turn of the century, the following reactions share a common sadness and deep disapproval of the way Americans failed to keep Christmas.

Caja Munch, who accompanied her minister husband to Wiota, Wisconsin, wrote letters home complaining of the Americans' disregard for Christmas (and her own valiant efforts to continue observing the holiday as she had in Norway). She writes in 1856: "Before the holidays we were just as busy as everybody at home (here they pay no attention to Christmas, and many even work right through the whole holiday season). Naturally even in this respect, the Norwegians are just copycats." The next year she documents the difficulty: "[Mrs. Holmen's] husband was unable to come until a few days later as he could not leave the store, which was kept open both Christmas Day and Boxing Day; there you see how the Americans observe the great Christmas holidays."[50]

"Is there any difference between weekdays and holidays here?" wondered

Twenty-year-old Gro Nilsdatter Skrattegård, even before she emigrated from Ål in Hallingdal in 1862, had already singled out Christmas as the time she would especially dread being
parted from her loved ones: "Never to be with you again on Christmas Eve, that festive,
exalted and holy night, when we were all so happy. I can't think of it without weeping."
When she encountered the Americans' indifference to the holidays, her homesickness only
grew worse, as she observed that, on Christmas Day, "work was being done on many of the
farms as on an ordinary work day, with people chopping wood and doing other work."
She found it "strange and blasphemous to treat Christmas Day like a work day."

Svendsen, Frontier Mother, *32*

a Norwegian visiting Audubon, Minnesota, in an 1883 letter. Her first Christmas Eve in America had gone pleasantly enough: "We had a Christmas tree
in the Norwegian Lutheran Church here on Christmas Eve. It was very enjoyable, and the organ sounded glorious in the cold, quiet evening air. Pastor Myhre preached, and we sang both Norwegian and English carols.
Both children and adults received presents." It was the troubling Christmas
Day that provoked her question: "Myhre preached again the next day. Since
Americans keep only Sunday, that day was rather strange. The shops were
open all day, as were the saloons—these unfortunate, miserable saloons,
the cancer of America. We Norwegians went to church while dancing and
music could be heard in those buildings."[51] The reader may note a changed
attitude toward drinking expressed by this visitor compared with earlier
emigrants such as Teigen. This difference reflects changing attitudes in
Norway. Drinking had changed from being an occasional occurrence with
ritual overtones to being an everyday occurrence, with the result that the
collateral social problems had gotten out of hand. This situation prompted
the founding of a teetotalers movement in 1859, which gradually gathered
steam and by the turn of the century had become quite influential. Further-
more, brewing on the farm ended around 1880, as professional brewers began taking over the industry.

H. H. Borgen, who arrived in Minnesota in 1887 and gained employment on a work crew building a grain elevator in St. Anthony Park (between
Minneapolis and St. Paul), also found his first Christmas troubling. He
identified the cause of the lack of Christmas celebration that he encountered

as the relentless pursuit of monetary gain, and his indignation seemed just as fresh more than fifty years later, in the early 1940s, when he wrote:

> Christmas came, but there was none of the festivity of Christmas. As on other days, I got up before five o'clock on Christmas morning, downed a little food, and then ran from northeast Minneapolis to reach St. Anthony Park by 7 A.M. . . . What longing I felt then, thinking of my home and community and the comforting pleasures we enjoyed there, compared with the harsh surroundings here, and I thought: what an ungodly land this was. Only Sundays were regarded as holy days, and even two-thirds of them were work days—the only thing anybody thought about was money. Money was the god here and to a great extent still is.

Echoing the same distress over the American emphasis on commerce, the Telemark emigrant N. N. Rønning (a future editor and author of note) spent his first American Christmas, in 1887, in a dejected frame of mind. Used to a holiday spent amid an extended family and a neighborhood social network, he learns to his disappointment that his more Americanized sister would be away with "a stranger," leaving him to spend the holiday alone. Before leaving, she acquainted him with the American commercial Christmas:

> My sister had heard that people gave each other Christmas gifts in this country. She handed me a quarter and told me to buy myself a suitable gift. On the way home I went into a bookstore and bought the first book I saw. I don't think I understood the meaning of the title, but it expressed the sentiment of a newcomer on his way to a cold, cheerless room to spend his first Christmas away from the lights and laughter and love of the old home; the title was: "Is life worth living?"[52]

Less dejected than Rønning but all the more indignant, the voice of O. A. Miller joins the chorus of alienation and accusation. Emigrating from northern Norway in the 1890s, he found that Christmas in America seemed "no more than an ordinary Sunday during the rest of the year," though Christmas Eve did offer some of its familiar delights: "At Mother's there was a little holiday spirit as she had prepared special Christmas food and we had morning and evening devotions as well as the table prayer, as had been our custom in Norway." It was Christmas Day and those that followed that left him disgusted and discouraged: "We went to church on the morning of Christmas Day, but just imagine what we saw on the way to church—we met farmers driving along with huge loads of timber and firewood. Seeing them you'd never know Christmas had come or that a Savior had been born for them and to us all." Offended by the lack of respect for the holiday's religious significance, Miller is also frustrated by its brevity: "It certainly turned out to be no long holiday, my first Christmas in America. Though I had been free to go home and celebrate Christmas Eve, on Christmas Day I had to walk forty miles back and go to work on December 26. I heard no ringing of church bells such as there was in Norway during the holidays."[53] Nor did his longing for the Norwegian Christmas ever cease: "By now I have experienced fifty-one Christmases in America and only seventeen in Norway, but this much I can say: those seventeen in Norway far outweigh the fifty-one here in America."

Miller's enduring disappointment with the American Christmas certainly seems to bear out the dire warning sounded by Thoralv Klaveness that Norwegians would never attain "human happiness" in America. Traveling among the Norwegian Americans around the turn of the century, Klaveness published his observations, *Blandt udvandrede Nordmænd* (Among emigrated Norwegians), in 1904.[54] Strongly opposed to emigration, Klaveness saw the American Christmas holiday as symptomatic of a larger problem that afflicted American values and general way of life.

The isolation of those living on the frontier, he said, presented one of the chief hindrances to their happiness. Bereft of the extended family and highly structured social network of neighbors that had characterized life in rural Norway, the settlers could not expect to find happiness. To back up this contention, Klaveness quotes a South Dakota housewife who complains: "We have not had one glad day since we came here. How could we have out here on the prairie? It is so far to neighbors that we get no contact, but have to live alone. It's different back in Norway." This isolation precludes celebrating Christmas in the traditional way:

Christmas is coming. At home in the Old Country friends and neighbors can get together and enjoy themselves during the holidays; they have enough time for this and feel they can afford it. But we? Here we sit out on the prairie. We have enough food and money for ourselves and our families. But *hygge* [social and aesthetic comfort, enjoyment of life, pleasure]? We don't know what it means to live.

Hygge being so highly valued in Norwegian culture, especially at Christmas, its absence seems to sour all other aspects of the woman's existence. But it is not just the loneliness that is problematic, says Klaveness. The American emphasis on making money also stands in the way. Again he cites the South Dakota housewife:

We have been lucky over here. We started out empty-handed, but now make a comfortable living. But what haven't we paid for all this? . . . And how hard haven't we worked to earn what we have? Would people in Norway work this hard once they had sufficient means to manage? Here people have to work like dogs all their lives, and when they get old they're left with broken-down bodies, far from home; that's the reward.

Though now well off, her family's prosperity has come at the expense of their health and happiness, and she advises prospective Norwegian emigrants not to come: "Tell them this. Tell them to stay home!"[55]

What are we to make of such a tortured account? The housewife's American-born son explains it away as residual depression resulting from a recent illness. Yet backed as it is by other accounts of disappointment, indignation, and frustration over the American Christmas, the South Dakota housewife's account leaves little doubt about the immigrants' distress over their inability to celebrate Christmas in the traditional way.

Isolation on the prairie, the disturbing presence of others who observed the holiday in unfamiliar, seemingly blasphemous ways, and employers' demands that work continue—all prevented the Norwegian immigrants from celebrating the Christmas they knew and yearned for. The depth of their resulting disappointment reveals how important Christmas was in Norwegian culture; the season intensified their feelings of homesickness and nostalgia. For the Norwegian Americans, Christmas, a celebration firmly centered around family and neighbors, could only sharpen their awareness of other frustrations in adjusting to the New Land.

GROWING COMMERCIALIZATION

The Norwegians had their own reasons for being discontented with the American Christmas, but even well-established Yankee families had begun to react to the growing commercialization of American life, not least at Christmastime. Worried observers had noted how the trend for Americans to express themselves through money also manifested itself in American Christmas gift-giving. As early as 1850 Harriet Beecher Stowe created a modern-sounding character who bemoaned the stressful nature of Christmas shopping:

> Oh dear! Christmas is coming in a fortnight and I have to think up presents for everybody! Dear me, it's so tedious. Everybody has got everything that can be thought of. . . . There are worlds of money wasted, at this time of year, in getting things that nobody wants, and nobody cares for after they are got.[56]

The commercial Christmas that Stowe's character sounds so wearied by had been in existence for almost thirty years: people on the East Coast had begun exchanging store-bought Christmas gifts as early as the 1820s and advertising had started to proliferate at about the same time. Though the same degree of commercialization came much later to the Midwest, there, too, businesses increasingly depended on Christmas for their profits. By the late nineteenth century, Midwestern store owners had joined their Eastern counterparts in developing strategies to make the Christmas season more enjoyable for their customers—and more lucrative for themselves.

How this development of the gift-giving Christmas manifested itself within a comfortably well-off family in the small town of Decorah, Iowa, emerges in a set of letters written during the 1880s by Mrs. Axel Smith (Gertrude Christopher, known as Jane) to Anna Bugge, her Norwegian sister-in-law. Jane had married Axel, the Luther College physician, in 1878.[57] Her early letters describe a mixture of handmade and store-bought presents, with store-bought ones already seeming more special. At this point, though, relatively little is being made of Christmas, and the gifts remain quite small. In a letter of December 14, 1880, she writes: "Well, the holidays are soon here. We are not making much preparation. I am making a dark red long scarf for Axel. I would like Carsten [their son] to have a silver cup. . . .

the little fellow should have a nice present the first Christmas." Her 1880 letter made no mention of a Christmas tree, but by 1887, the family had one. The tree was a sufficiently new phenomenon to deserve special mention, and the number of presents had increased. In a letter of January 18, 1887, she writes: "In speaking of Christmas I should perhaps have mentioned that it did not pass without being noticed a little by us. Last year, you remember that we had our people here, had also a Christmas tree; this year we were all in my sister's home, and there had a tree, to the great joy of old and young. Our boys received many presents that evening and not a few the next day." With the children getting older, their anticipation of the holiday becomes the focus. While one of her sons wants a tree, the other prefers the more traditional means to receive his gifts, the Christmas stocking. Jane assumes that the Christmas stocking custom is American and wonders if her Norwegian sister-in-law is acquainted with it:

> Dec. 7, 1887
> My dear sister Anna:
> . . . Tonight we had a nice [bedtime] story of a Christmas tree. How the boys plan for Christmas; they talk of it every morning before daylight. We tell them that they may choose their own way of celebrating, so Carsten is going to hang up his stockings (you know what that means, don't you?). But Laurence wants a tree.

By 1889 Christmas for this comfortably well-off family is sounding very modern, with a tree "loaded" with gifts, including some rather expensive luxury items:

> Feb. 24, 1889
> My dear sister Anna:
> . . . We were all invited to brother Martin's to supper Christmas evening, and had a nice tree well loaded with gifts for all, the children in the four families being particularly well remembered. We gave Laurence a good iron train locomotive with four cars. Carsten gave Laurence a pretty red drum; besides this he got books, handkerchiefs, and toys. Carsten got a dark brown plush cap from us and a game of Lotto from Laurence, from others a pretty inkstand, box of stationery, book, handkerchief. The boys and I gave Axel a sort of boot polishing concern, box and table combined.

We got on the tree a pretty little caster with two bottles for salt and pepper, one striped rose-colored and crystal, the other milk white and crystal. We also got a few pieces of decorated china. Axel gave me a beautiful little table, top Italian marble about twelve inches square, two small places below, frame cherry. To all these presents is added a most beautiful lamp shade from our dear sister in Norway.

The child-centered Christmas had clearly become a welcome fixture in this upper-middle-class family, showing little trace of the handmade items of necessary clothing exchanged in the preindustrial Norwegian peasant society. Still, conditions continued to vary by location and means, sometimes seeming not so far from that peasant Christmas after all. Such were the Christmases spent by my uncle Einar (Fred) Fretheim (born 1916) growing up in relatively difficult circumstances in Albert Lea, Minnesota: "I don't recall presents wrapped up under the tree—nothing fancy and not many. Those were hard times. I remember my gift one Christmas was a pair of homemade mittens and another was a warm, wool coat made by my mother from used clothing of my brothers."[58]

How long it took for the Christmas tree and the child-centered, gift-giving Christmas to become the norm is also suggested by a December 22, 1908, advertisement in the Albert Lea *Evening Tribune,* offering advice on negotiating the still somewhat mysterious ways of the commercial Christmas: "To be real happy and cheerful at Christmas, you must buy presents for the little folks; they expect it, so don't disappoint them. To help you select what would be appropriate for your children, we have secured extra clerks, and they will be more than glad to wait on you and give suggestions.

Mary Paulson King recalls the simple Christmas gifts from her childhood in Fillmore County, Minnesota, in the 1870s: "We never got much for Christmas those days, but mother always managed to give us a little something. Father would get a piece of leather and make us shoes and they were nice ones, too. He made shoes for us quite often, and it didn't take him very long either. Mother would have a pair of mittens or stockings for us and we had a good supper on Christmas Eve, and we could stay up a little longer and play games too. Even grandfather would play games on Christmas Eve."

King, "Memories of a Prairie Girlhood"

Our entire force of clerks are waiting to serve you." A time when people needed to be told that children expect presents at Christmas now seems very far away and did not last very long.

The gap between the child-centered Christmas adopted during the nineteenth century by the kondisjonerte and the Christmas celebrated by immigrants of peasant stock had begun to narrow. As more and more immigrants began exchanging Christmas gifts, later adopting the Christmas tree and finally Santa Claus, they also realized that their customary celebration would not last. Few immigrants could celebrate Christmas for thirteen days (as Teigen managed to do in the homogeneously Norwegian Koshkonong settlement); immigrants in closer contact with the dominant American culture experienced the much abbreviated and commercialized American Christmas as a threat to their own customs and an affront to their religious faith.

Though many Norwegian immigrants and their offspring welcomed the commercial Christmas, it was already alarming critics who sounded dire warnings about its impact. The loss of many Old Country traditions caused many immigrants to view the changes with confusion and even pain and regret. Warnings notwithstanding, the changes were not all bad; they brought new and now beloved family traditions that have stood the test of time.

The New American Christmas
Twentieth-Century Changes

In the early years of settlement, Christmas was celebrated in poverty, but anyone now visiting our Western expatriates during the Christmas season will find the table laden with both Norwegian and American Christmas treats and the home in festal array. Children circle the tree singing songs taught by their mother: Jeg er så glad, Glade jul, Deilig er den himmel blå.

G. M. Bruce, "Christmas on the Prairie," 1912

In their growing affluence, early twentieth-century Norwegian Americans struggled with two warring aspirations: they wanted to become Americans as quickly as possible, but they also wanted to maintain their Norwegian heritage.[1] The Christmases they celebrated not only reflected this essential conflict; they also elicited some of its most acute reactions.

Having by now significantly improved their economic footing, Norwegian Americans increasingly entered the American middle class. Though a growing number of observers at the time warned of a corresponding loss of moral grounding, the immigrants' attitudes continued to be influenced by Old Country Christian piety and folkways.[2] The combined influences of their ancestral background and contemporary setting had a profound effect on the immigrants, making it impossible for them to remain purely Norwegian or to become fully American. All immigrant groups undergo this struggle and respond by creating a unique culture specific to their time and circumstances. Like other immigrants, Norwegian Americans adapted their traditional background to their new environment. They thereby created a Norwegian American culture, valid in its own right.

The Mingling of Traditions

The first three decades of the twentieth century saw an increasingly rich mixture of the immigrants' traditional Christmas customs with those adopted in America. Christmas trees and gift-giving grew in popularity, as was also happening in Norway by this time. The turn-of-the-century Norwegian American Christmas celebrated by the family of Borghild Estness in Chippewa County, Wisconsin, does not differ so very much from the one her family by then would have known in their native Hardanger, except for its emphasis on shopping:

> Christmas was a happy event with a religious observance in the home as well as in the church. Preparations for Christmas included shearing sheep, carding wool, spinning, knitting and sewing, besides shopping for additional gifts. Then there was the cleaning and baking. For the children, no shopping trip all year could compete with the excitement of selecting five and ten cent gift items for the entire family at Simons Brothers Bazaar.[3]

While Estness's account shows the commercial aspect of the American holiday playing a more pronounced role than it would have in Norway, the family's tradition of keeping the tree concealed until after the Christmas Eve meal closely parallels the Norwegian practice that developed among the city-dwelling *kondisjonerte* during the nineteenth century, with the difference that the role of decorating the tree passed from the parents to the older children:

> The decoration of the tree was a semi-secret operation performed by the older girls. Not until after the festive supper on Christmas Eve would the disclosure of the tree be allowed, when the finished masterpiece with its burning candles shone in full splendor. With the chores done early, the family then assembled, sang their hymns and children's songs and gave their recitations.

A Christmas tree with all the trimmings in Northfield, Minnesota, 1900

A program in the home, such as Estness describes, gradually became part of the Norwegian American Christmas, the recitations often coming from the children' parts in school and church programs.

> After the reading of the Christmas story, the climax of the celebration finally arrived—the opening of the gifts. Equally as exciting as receiving the gifts was watching the reactions of recipients of one's gifts—the brother who received a pencil box and the mother who was given a salt box to hang on the wall beside the kitchen range.

The gifts had become the "climax of the celebration," yet amid their enchantment with the American commercial Christmas, the family also preserves the Norwegian practices of handcrafting woolen textiles, cleaning, baking—and julebukking: "From one farm house to another they would go, giving each household a chance to guess their identity, and hoping for a bit of lunch."

Continuing Traditions in the First Generation

Another child of Norwegian immigrants, Ethel Odegard, grew up in Merrill, Wisconsin. Her mother (born in 1849 in Hillestad, Buskerud County, Norway), who had emigrated in 1883, kept a map of Norway on the dining room wall, a telling detail of strong Norwegian ties, further confirmed in Odegard's description of the family's intricate Christmas preparations.

Unlike the accounts of nineteenth-century Norwegian immigrants (whose poverty had prevented such treats), Odegard's description includes the cookies now customarily associated with the Norwegian Christmas. "First came the baking"—of Christmas bread, "with its distinctive flavor of cardamom, raisins and citron," of *fattigmand bakkelse,* "a thin cookie fried in deep fat, coming out a golden-brown color with curlicue tips," and of *gorokake,* "baked on a special iron which transferred a leaf pattern to the cookie."[4] Next came the preparation of beef and pork delicacies, "which required skill and knowledge of the types of meat best suited." These included *sylte,* "hog's head cooked with spices soaked in cold water brine, packed and sewed in a cloth," and *rul,* "beef or veal flank, cut into strips, cooked, seasoned and formed into a loaf, bound with cloth, then cooled and placed under a heavy weight."

The food preparation climaxed, says Odegard, with the lutefisk: "Sixty years ago [circa 1910] it was a common sight to see frozen cod fish hanging in long strips outside the meat market in the below freezing weather. One or more of these was purchased and brought home to be chopped up or sawed into convenient pieces, and then, as a first step, placed in a brine or lye solution." Because knowledge of the procedure for making the lye solution had generally disappeared by the time Odegard wrote her 1974 account, she describes in detail how her mother collected clean hardwood ash from the dining-room heating stove for this purpose. Her own role in the lutefisk preparation consisted of changing the water in which the lutefisk soaked. In a time before sinks with running water and drains, this procedure involved frequent trips up and down stairs from the kitchen to the basement, where the fish was soaking, with buckets of water. Emphasizing the arduousness of the preparation, Odegard reminds her readers that "the water had to be carried from the pump outside the kitchen porch in the first place," and she speculates that it was this advance preparation that sharpened their appetites for the "heavenly taste which could only be satisfied when the fish, cooked to just the right consistency, was brought steaming to the dining room table."

While some celebrants of the early-twentieth-century Norwegian American Christmas recall its painstaking preparations, others dwell on the Christmas meals themselves and their accompanying rituals. Norman Reitan was born on the Øien farm near Melhus, Trøndelag, in 1894, to parents who soon immigrated to Shawano County, Wisconsin. Apart from the notable absence in America of an extended vacation from work, Reitan's parents practiced "in almost every other way the traditions that for centuries had been followed on the farm in Norway": "Lutefisk and Norwegian meatballs made up the principal course of both [Christmas and New Year's Eve] meals. Cranberries took the place of *tyttebær;* flatbrød and lefse replaced leavened bread. There were several kinds of pastries—*fattigmand-bakkels* and *krumkake.*"[5] As much as he enjoyed the taste of these delicacies, Reitan found even more meaning in their accompanying rituals:

After the meal a hymn was sung three times, always the same song, *Et barn er født i Bethlehem* [A child is born in Bethlehem].[6] Then Father read in Norwegian the passage from the Bible containing the Christmas

Thurine Oleson (born 1866 in Winchester, Wisconsin, to immigrant parents from Telemark)
writes about the ritual aspects of meals in her childhood home:

There was quite a ceremony attached to eating even a simple meal among the Norwegians, and it stemmed from the idea that food was a gift of God. Before the meal was begun, this prayer was usually said by Father:

> In Jesus' name we go to the board
> To feast and drink upon His Word;
> God to be honored, and us to be given,
> So have we food in the name of Heaven.

It was the mother's duty to press food upon her guest again and again, saying, "*Vær så god*" (be so good). When a guest had had enough, he would usually lay his hand lightly on the stomach and say, "*Nei tak, jeg er mett,*" which meant, "No, thanks, I have enough." When the meal was finished, the guest stood and went to the back of his chair, put his hands upon it, bowed to the hostess and said, "*Tak for maten*" (Thanks for the food). To omit any part of these ceremonies was to admit that you didn't come from nice people.

Oleson, Wisconsin My Home, *105 (Oleson's translation of prayer)*

story. Following this, at a signal from Dad, we would rise to our feet and Dad would shake Mother's hand and say, *Tak for maten* [Thank you for the food]. Then each of the rest of us would shake Mother's and Dad's hands and each other's hands and say *Tak for maten.*

Concluding meals with the phrase "takk for maten" remains a daily ritual in most Norwegian homes (though the accompanying handshakes occur only on special occasions). The degree of language retention Reitan's family displayed declined sharply in succeeding generations. The Reitans had apparently known the Christmas tree while still in Norway and therefore practiced the custom of caroling around it: "After the Christmas Eve dinner the tree would be decorated and each one would bring his presents and place them under the tree. . . . When all had been opened, we would pull the tree into the middle of the room and all join hands around it and sing Norwegian Christmas carols."

The Reitan family's early-twentieth-century Christmas Day breakfast ritual closely resembles the one Eilert Sundt observed in late 1850s Valdres,

Mealtime at the home of Norwegian American photographer
Martin Morrison, Ames, Iowa, 1880

except that by now coffee often replaced beer and *brennevin* (hard liquor) as the beverage of choice (as it would by then also have done in Norway):[7]

> Early Christmas morning, long before any of the family was astir, Mother would arise and cook coffee and serve it with *fattigmand-bakkels* and *krumkake* to each of us in bed. After the chores were done, came the Christmas morning breakfast, which had always been the same so that it had become a tradition. The main dishes were pigs feet pickled in brine and blood sausage fried in fat with milk added. Breakfast over, the entire family crowded into the long bobsled and covered the five miles to church to the music of tinkling sleigh bells.

Like the custom of dancing around the tree, fattigmann and krumkake had probably become familiar to the Reitans in Norway, given their later date of immigration and more comfortable means while there. For many peasant families in Norway the high cost of white flour and sugar kept these pastries from being available until around 1920. Indeed it was the pastries' initial expense that made them special and therefore immediately associated with Christmas.

Breaking with Tradition

Customs were thus changing in Norway as well. While many immigrant families themselves took great pains to preserve the traditions they had brought from Norway, succeeding, American-born generations often could not or chose not to follow their ancestors' ways. Some immigrants also made this choice. C. R. Remme of Luverne, Minnesota, writing in 1914, proudly distances the Norwegian Americans from the Old Country's arduous Christmas preparations: "As we recall, the folks in Norway used to engage in the tremendous toil of lengthy yuletide preparations many weeks in advance with brewing, baking and everything else imaginable, which we here in this country don't find necessary to imitate."[8] There's no need to prepare all the meat dishes, he says, for reality lives up to the stereotype that "over in America they live so well it is like Christmas every day"; the abundance of beef and pork that in Norway only existed at Christmas, in America constituted the daily diet.[9] Not totally oblivious to their heritage, however, Remme says that at Christmas they would prepare a small keg of home-brewed beer and a little flatbread, lutefisk, and lefse in an effort "to emulate the Norwegians in Valdres by living a little better at Christmas than otherwise." Lutefisk had thus become "soul food"; its association with the past and (for the immigrants) with Norway making it seem "better than ordinary" fare, despite its original, medieval function as a fasting food.

While bowing to his ancestor's foodways, Remme finds their folk beliefs too antiquated for the New Land. Not wishing to offend, however, he hastens to soothe the sting of his scorn:

> If any of the old folks at home who still believe in these [invisible beings] happen to read this piece, I don't wish to insult them by insisting that

they are utterly mistaken in asserting that they have seen and experienced such things. They know what they have seen and have the right to believe as they like. I don't want to deny or affirm anything of the sort; their experiences must stand on their own merit. But here in America these invisible beings have not had a chance to settle, so I firmly believe that they do not exist here among us.

To prove that the Norwegian Americans did not occupy themselves with "any such superstitious things," Remme insists: "We never think of carrying on with such old-fashioned customs as making the sign of the cross over every act and every object throughout the Christmas season, whether livestock or inanimate objects. Nor have we ever placed tar crosses or steel on all the doors of the farm."[10] The change Remme documents is in many ways one more of time than of place; the move to America may have accelerated the immigrants' distance from the folk practices he describes, but by the time of Remme's 1914 remarks, they had largely passed from the scene in Norway as well (as Remme's references to "old folks" and "old-fashioned customs" suggest).

As already documented, however, Remme exaggerates the extent to which the immigrants had abandoned their folk beliefs and stories. Folk narratives continued to play a prominent role at Christmas gatherings, and in this chapter I will document the persistence of lore about the *nisse*. It is true, however, that the once dominant role these folk beliefs played in regulating daily behavior greatly diminished in the New Land.[11]

The Price of Breaking with Tradition

Watching old beliefs and customs begin to fade, a chorus of Norwegian American voices rose up to predict the dire consequences of such a loss. In 1923 Pastor D. G. Ristad of Manitowoc, Wisconsin, warned:

No one would melt down the family silver; only vandals and robbers do. Nor ought a people destroy their customs, especially those relating to Christmas. Preserving their customs is what gives a people dignity and refinement. Vouchsafed in these traditions are a people's finest sentiments. What they feel most deeply and are most sincerely devoted to, finds expression in their customs and traditional practices.[12]

Ristad's fears notwithstanding, the Norwegian Americans had actually done an extraordinary job of retaining their Christmas customs. Their accounts show remarkable continuity with the past, even retaining traditional customs already abandoned in some locations in Norway. In addition to the pressure of Americanization, the immigrants (along with Norwegians in Norway) were confronting modernization. New materials, methods, and attitudes were changing both cultures. Another influence on the immigrants was a more strictly enforced insistence (in the wake of World War I nativism) that immigrants conform to American ways. Compounding these external pressures were those from within their own families, as American-born children urged their parents to drop their strange Old Country traditions and adopt the new ways that so attractively beckoned—especially at Christmastime.

A Midwestern Christmas

As immigrant families added more and more American elements to their observances, the purely Norwegian Christmas inevitably became a thing of the past. The resulting blend of American and Norwegian customs emerges in a remarkable document prepared by Orel R. Winjum, the son of first-generation Norwegian parents who settled in the northern Minnesota community of Deer Township in Roseau County. Winjum's manuscript, lovingly drafted for his descendants, preserves the memory of their family's multifaceted Christmas during the period from 1903 to 1925.[13] Showing an increasing presence of American foods, factory-made materials, and Santa Claus, his account details the simultaneous preservation of traditional Norwegian ways—beer brewing, ritual Christmas bathing, special treats for the livestock, and Christmas masquerading. Nor does he overlook the Christmas tree programs at both church and school that so profoundly came to influence the way American families kept Christmas.

Given the church's central role in the settlement, Winjum begins by documenting the congregation's founding and growth, from primitive beginnings to the eventual, long-awaited construction of a church building:

> One of the first things the Norwegian settlers did was to organize a Norwegian Lutheran congregation, ca. 1900. In the absence of a church building, services were held in the homes of the congregation mem-

bers. . . . The circuit pastor lived 25 miles away and he drove or rode this distance to conduct the service. In 1905 the district school was built, and services were conducted there until 1911 when the Poplar Grove Church was built. . . . Regular church services in Norwegian continued until 1924.[14]

Beer Brewing and Other Advent Preparations

Winjum's account reveals the immigrant ideal of emulating the Norwegian Christmas, even as it acknowledges departures from that goal necessitated by the pressure to adapt ethnic principles to American realities: "According to oral tradition Christmas in Norway started with the First Sunday in Advent and ended the Sunday after Christmas Day. While we did not follow this cultural pattern, it was in the background of our Christmas celebration." It is interesting to note how the foreshortened American Christmas season has influenced Winjum's concept of the traditional Norwegian Christmas, which actually extended far beyond the Sunday after Christmas Day to Thirteenth or even Twentieth Christmas Day. In their brewing, however, Winjum's family remained more consistent with the Nordic Christmas, though here, too, their practice had to adapt to American circumstance. Having no *eldhus,* the separate outbuilding dedicated to brewing, washing, and baking that had been a fixture of the Old Country farmsteads and even of some pioneer prairie settlements, the Winjums used available space in attic and cellar:

> Shortly after Thanksgiving, two low square flats were taken into the granary and filled with barley. These were taken into the house and sprinkled liberally with water, and then taken upstairs and placed near the chimney, where it was warm. The flats were kept moist until the barley sprouted, and grew green to about an inch. The flats were then taken downstairs, and the contents dumped into the copper boiler, and about six gallons of warm water added; plus dried hops and black molasses.

In place of Norwegian juniper, they flavored the beer with American molasses, while store-bought, factory-made utensils—crockery (the stone jar) and glassware—have replaced the handcrafted wooden containers and ladles Winjum's parents would have known in Norway:

The mixture was placed on the back of the stove to simmer all day. It was then taken off, and allowed to cool to a tepid state, and a solution of dried yeast added. The mixture was then taken upstairs and put into an eight gallon stone jar placed near the chimney. The mixture was allowed to work until Christmas, when it was strained through flour sacking, into a smaller stone jar.

As in Norway, the resulting brew was shared with each and every holiday visitor. Years later Winjum still relishes its taste and regrets the loss of the recipe: "Mother never wrote down the recipe, so the art of making Christmas beer passed with her passing. I wish it hadn't as it was a fabulous drink."

Fortunately the baking recipes enjoyed a better fate, but the treats Winjum mentions are notably American rather than the Norwegian krumkake, fattigmann, and goro we might expect:

The baking was done the day before Christmas Eve day, as on the following day the wood stove cooking range was fully utilized for other purposes. Baking was not elaborate: white and brown bread and biscuits; always white sugar cookies and molasses cookies, Santa Claus cookies with currants as eyes and buttons, raisin-filled cookies, sometimes ginger cookies, mince and apple pies. Mother's sugar and molasses cookies became traditional in the family.

While the baking shows an unmistakably American influence, the family's continued practice of the fall slaughter harks back to their Norwegian roots. Several carcasses of pork and beef resulted from the slaughter, says Winjum, and his mother "usually made a large head cheese [sylte] and a stone jar of pickled pigs feet, which they set aside for Christmas."[15] Once prepared by necessity—a way of preserving every scrap of scarce meat—these dishes, too, had become soul food, eagerly anticipated as Christmas treats despite the abundance of meat in the American daily diet.

The School Christmas Tree Program

In the immigrants' adjustment to American ways, the public school—and not least the school Christmas program—played a central role. Besides promoting the use of English, it enhanced social skills and community involvement. The school program was the first of a series of events that after 1912,

"The school Christmas program always started out with fourteen of the youngest children each holding an alphabet letter spelling out Merry Christmas and reciting a line denoting the letter, such as 'C is for Christmas, a season of Joy,' 'H is for Happy holidays, merry and bright.' Thereafter came individual recitations, by grade. Around the middle grades someone nearly always gave the perennial favorite, 'Twas the Night before Christmas . . .' Interspersed was the singing of Christmas songs, usually by an ensemble of all the pupils. Most of these songs were religious in character, and the same ones were later sung in Norwegian at the church Christmas program, always including 'Silent Night' and 'Jingle Bells.' Near the end of the program, the Christmas tree candles were lit, accompanied and followed by songs. The program ended by a pupil saying a piece thanking the audience for attending."

Winjum, "Christmas on the Farm"

Winjum says, assumed a fixed order and content in his community: the district school "Christmas Tree Program," the Christmas Eve celebration at home, Christmas Day visiting and Christmas dinner with neighbors, Christmas masquerading (julebukking), and the Christmas program at the church. While Christmas Day—both in Norway and on the nineteenth-century prairie—had once been limited strictly to family, Winjum mentions having the company of neighbors at Christmas Day dinner. Perhaps the lack of the extended family characteristic of the peasant society encouraged Norwegian Americans to more readily include neighbors in the family circle. In 1913 Knut Takla comments on this difference, too, as well as on the overall lack of American observance of Christmas:

> The great festivals of the year—Christmas, Easter, Pentecost—are made much less of in the States than in Norway. . . . Christmas Day goes like any other Sunday during the year. If there's a sermon, people go to church, if not, nothing special is made of the day. The dinner tends to be a little better than usual, and Norwegians customarily have lutefisk in addition to the standard roast. They might invite friends home. Beer or hard liquor is seldom on the table, even among the non-teetotalers.[16]

Other traditions they modified, too, such as the timeworn necessity that each person of the household have new clothes for Christmas. In Winjum's family the new Christmas clothes received their debut, not on Christmas Eve, but at the school Christmas program: "The school Christmas program was one time we knew we didn't have to walk to school in winter. Looking our best in our Christmas outfits, we rode in the bobsled box, cushioned with clean straw and robes to keep us cozy and warm." During the program itself, the "dialog" constituted the chief entertainment and occupied the pupils—not to mention their teachers and parents—for weeks in advance:

> Preparation for the "dialog" started just after Thanksgiving. The School Marm selected the play, the principal characters and other participants. The older girls vied for the best parts and the boys were "drafted." Participants selected, the School Marm sent home instructions to their mothers as to costumes required [understanding that the mothers would make them].
>
> On the day of the program the stage was in front of the classroom, with the stage curtain stretched across the room half way between the School Marm's desk and the front row of "recitation" seats (to which we marched during the regular school day when called upon). From this line, where the muslin curtain was hung, to the end wall blackboard, was our performing area.
>
> The Christmas tree (which had to have a prominent place and therefore took up much of the "stage" area) was not lighted until after the "dialog" because flimsy costumes might brush against the tree and catch fire.

Involving the entire community—mothers sewing costumes, both parents helping children practice their lines, and entire families making up the audience—the school program performed a significant role of its own in socializing the immigrant families in early-twentieth-century communities.

After the dialog came the gift exchange. Having previously drawn names and purchased an inexpensive present for the name drawn, the pupils now received these gifts from under the tree along with a red mesh bag of candy, nuts, and an apple. Judging from the period's memoirs, these red netting bags enjoyed enormous popularity, seeming never to have missed an appearance at any school or church Christmas program throughout the Midwest.

Preparations on Christmas Eve

Though the red mesh bags originated in America, the preparations made by the Winjum family on the day of Christmas Eve strongly reflected their Norwegian roots. This certainly applies to their ritual bath, whose symbolic significance of renewal and consecration ("recycled" water notwithstanding) Winjum clearly realizes:

> It was a rule (apparently of long standing) that on Christmas Eve day everyone was renovated; all members of the family had to take a tub bath, and have their hair washed. The bath tub was the familiar round galvanized portable laundry tub; nineteen inches wide at the bottom, twenty three at the top and eleven or twelve inches high.

Taking a bath in it was a challenge, says Winjum, and he describes the process in some detail:

> Early in the morning the twenty gallon copper laundry boiler went on the cook stove range, was filled, and replenished throughout the day by repeated trips (about twenty) in the winter cold and snow to pump and carry water. Likewise, repeated trips had to be made to the woodpile to keep a good fire in the range.
>
> Shortly after noon the bathing production line started. The tub was brought in and placed on the cellar trap door in front of the kitchen range. The girls were bathed or took baths in order of age, and as the water heating capacity was limited, two baths were taken for each wash water. The wash water had to then be carried out, and dumped in the snow among the yard trees. As each one bathed they were dispatched upstairs to dress or be dressed. Privacy was maintained for the older girls, and this meant us menfolk (dad, my older brother and I) couldn't enter until an "all clear" was given.

A Special Treat for the Livestock

As the human beings enjoyed their special yuletide treatment, so did the animals. Embracing the Norwegian philosophy that they be included in the Christmas celebration, the Winjums erected a *julenek* for the birds: "During threshing time a sheaf of wheat was saved and placed in a granary bin. On Christmas Eve this sheaf was placed on a long stick which was nailed to a fence post in the barnyard [after barn chores were finished, around five o'clock] so the birds would have a Christmas morning feast." They also gave all their livestock a special Christmas treat:

> For the hogs we had around (usually between one and three at Christmas time) there was a special feeding Christmas Eve of barley boiled in

a cast iron kettle, or ground barley mixed with hot water, so the hogs would have a warm meal on Christmas Eve. For the chickens the feeding floor in front of the roosts was cleaned, new straw laid, and sprinkled liberally with wheat.... Even the farm dog and cat got special feedings.

But the horses fared best of all:

The farm horses (which we first got in 1912) were like persons who had everything; they had timothy or good uplands hay, two feedings of oats a day, and were curried and brushed and had fresh bedding almost every day as it was. However, on Christmas Eve we gave them an extra half measure of oats, and extra heavy straw bedding for their stalls.

The privileged daily care given to the horses reflects their vital role in the preindustrial agrarian society. Before the advent of machinery, the horse bore the brunt of the farm's labor, and many a Norwegian nisse legend served to reinforce the notion that if the horse did not receive proper care, the nisse would take revenge. In America, too, horses enjoyed special status. Immigrant families unable to afford horses initially settled for oxen. The family's purchase of their first horse represented a significant step toward prosperity. Increasing reliance on machinery to perform the work eventually transferred favor to the cattle, which American farmers raised for profit. Winjum's account reflects their consequent high status: "All the cattle were given good quality hay, ground feed or wheat bran on Christmas Eve. Dad was the one who perpetuated this special feeding of the animals, but we ceased this practice except for the cattle in 1918. The practice for cattle continued until about 1921 or 1922."

The nisser had a special fondness for horses. This tale comes from Østerdalen:

Teodor Torp had a horse the nisse really liked. One day when Teodor came back from the market at Vinger, he had been driving the horse rather hard, and it was dripping with sweat. This infuriated the nisse. Teodor had no sooner released the horse from the shafts and put it into the stable, than he was boxed so hard on the ear that he staggered into the stable wall. "Never before nor since have I received such a hard blow."

Nergaard, Hulder og trollskap

The Nisse

The animals' special Christmas feeding derived, says Winjum, from belief in the nisse:

> If the animals were not given something extra for Christmas Eve, the nisse would do such mischief as letting the cattle loose in the barn, opening the barndoor, drying up milk cows, or having an animal break a leg. On the other hand, if the farmer was good hearted and just forgot or didn't have the extra rations, the "nisse" would see to it that the animals were specially fed. During the earlier years there were many stories told at Christmas about these elves and their doings during visits of neighbors.

Evidence of the surviving nisse lore once again contradicts Remme's assertion that the Norwegian Americans had abandoned their folklore. It also raises a question: Why—of all the supernatural beings Norwegians once believed in—was it particularly the nisse that persisted in the New Land?

Understanding this lore requires taking seriously the preindustrial Norwegians' view of life lived in a constant tension between good and evil powers, conceived of as *huldrefolk*, hidden beings. Sharing the universe with human beings, these supernatural creatures could either promote or impede human endeavor, depending on how the humans behaved. The amount of deference people showed to traditional ways largely determined how the hidden people would treat them (that is, the extent to which their endeavors would succeed). Though only one of a host of supernatural beings, the nisse occupied a vital position, for he acted as overseer of the farm, the family's entire basis for existence and survival. Since the farm usually remained in the family for generations, its first cultivator was considered the family's progenitor. On many farms this individual was traditionally thought to be present in the farm's burial mound. To show reverence for his spirit, the family made holiday offerings of beer, porridge, or other valued foods, placing the tributes at the roots of the *tuntre*, the venerated tree growing in the burial mound. In folk stories, this spirit came to be personified as the *gardvord*, the farm guardian. With time, beliefs about the gardvord came to be associated with the nisse. In many places the figure of the nisse thus subsumed the gardvord lore that embodied the family's traditions and lineage.

In these places the nisse thus came to stand for the very essence of the farm. Portrayed in legends as having the farm's best interests at heart, the nisse was thought to bring prosperity to the farm and to avenge anyone who worked at cross-purposes to the farm's well-being. The association of this lore with the farm's origin and prosperity no doubt accounts for the long survival of the nisse and why he joined the emigrants as they set out for America.

For come to America he did, as numerous Norwegian American accounts reveal. Ethel Odegard's immigrant mother, for example, spoke so frequently of the nisse that in the 1960s Odegard decided to send her relatives a Christmas letter attempting to "recapture the mood and the spirit" of her mother's stories:

> They were funny little folks, the Juleniss[er]. Always up to pranks of one kind or another. You never really saw them—but you thought you did! They would be underfoot, that is, you might accidentally stumble over one, especially when your hands were full trying to get the baking done. In that case you gave him a good cuff on the ear. Or if you happened to lie awake at midnight on Christmas Eve, when all was quiet, and deep snow covered the ground, you just knew they were down in the *fjøs*, that is in the barn, where the cattle were talking among themselves, and where everything was warm and cozy.

Rounding off with the classic description of the nisser in knee pants and red stocking caps and the oft-heard advice that they be given *risengrynsgrøt* at

---

*For Enid Ringdahl of Fergus Falls, Minnesota, and her family,
nisser remain a big part of Christmas:*

We never had Santa Claus as part of our Christmas, but the nisses were everywhere. In the mornings when we would come downstairs we all had a story to tell about the "carrying on" we had heard during the night—if one of us was still sleepy in the morning we blamed the nisse for keeping us awake. The nisse were always doing something—we had them hanging from light fixtures, decorating their own small tree, serving cookies and drinking coffee, rocking a baby nisse, reading to their youngsters, etc. . . . One year I made red yarn nisses like my grandfather had done—that was all we had on the tree.

Letter to the author, March 24, 1997

Christmas, Odegard urges her family to preserve this lore: "I hope you, too, will hand down to your children and grandchildren the many ancient customs and beliefs which add to the sparkle and color of the Christmas season."

Not articulated in Odegard's account, but fundamental to it, is the evolution of the nisse from the gardvord, venerated farm progenitor and protector, to the barn nisse, diligent promoter of good husbandry and vengeful foe when crossed, to the playful "funny little folks" that developed once actual belief in them had disappeared. As so often in modern descriptions of the nisse, Odegard intertwines the barn nisse and the julenisse, a Santalike figure, a confusion that also abounds in present-day Norway.

Odegard's reference to the animals' being able to speak at midnight derives from a different Norwegian folk belief. Henry Field (born 1913), a descendent of Norwegian immigrants and a dentist in Decorah, Iowa, explains: "They believed that on Christmas Eve the cattle could talk, because Christ was born in a manger and the cattle had seen it. At midnight they were given the gift of understanding and speaking human language." Though Field said this was both "believed and not believed," his uncle apparently numbered among the believers, for at the age of five or six this uncle "stayed in the barn almost all night, and was disappointed because he didn't hear a word."[17]

Corrine Schoien of Elgin, Iowa (born 1927), amplifies both accounts, reporting that her grandfather, Ole Torkelson, a mid-nineteenth-century emigrant from Hallingdal, always advised his descendants to leave extra food for the animals on Christmas Eve, "because at midnight all the animals would talk, and tell the nisse how they had been treated for the year. He also said you couldn't stay in the barn to hear them, because if you did, you wouldn't be around for the next Christmas."[18] Torkelson's comments combine three distinct ideas from the old Norwegian peasant society: the necessity of appeasing the nisse, the animals' ability to speak on Christmas Eve, and the yuletide preoccupation with death. We recall that Winjum, too, mentioned the notion of the animals' tattling to the nisse if they didn't get their Christmas treat, an idea that seems to have enjoyed greater currency in America than in Norway, where the initial motivation for giving the animals these special feedings was the length of the nights around the winter solstice, an idea that subsequently generalized to the philosophy that like human beings, they too should enjoy the blessings of Christmas. The nisse, meanwhile, received a bowl of porridge to thank him for having brought prosperity to the farm in the current year and to retain his goodwill so that he would continue his good work in the next. This view of the nisse seems to have continued on the farm near Ridgeland, Wisconsin, run by the parents of Guy Jacobson (born there in 1918), who grew up hearing that "if we set out rømmegrøt in the barn on Christmas Eve, good luck would come to our family and good health to the animals."[19]

Equally anchored in Old Country ways were the practices handed down to Leif Lie, whose father and mother immigrated in 1912 and 1914, respectively, eventually settling in Hoople, North Dakota: "We always had cows, pigs and horses, and always left food for the nisse who fed and cared for our livestock. We put up a grainbundle for the birds. Mother always had names for the animals as they do in Norway. Dad and Mother told stories of Norway and our relatives, trolls, huldrefolk and the fables."[20] This ranking of trolls and *hulder* along with one's relatives (all joking aside) appears in other accounts, as well, and underlines once again the firm grasp that these supernatural beings, though now foreign, had on the Norwegian immigrants' worldview. While they gave the nisse his Christmas treat as much in fear of reprisal as in gratitude, recent accounts place more emphasis on his beneficial nature; as actual belief in these beings faded, so did their threat.

The friendlier nisser became a living, lasting tradition in Decorah, thanks to Laura Hoeg (born 1907), who created a whole series of nisser inspired by the one said to have stowed away in her grandfather's shirt pocket the day he emigrated from Norway. Colorfully painted on flat wood and propped up in windows by a small crosspiece, Hoeg's nisser peek out from most homes in Decorah—and by now from windows in many other parts of the world, as well. The note Hoeg wrote to accompany her nisser insists that they be treated with respect: "The Nisser are extraordinary creatures that can bring good luck to whoever owns one, but only under the proper conditions. The most important rule for a Nisse owner to follow is to treat his Nisse with kindness. If a Nisse is not treated properly, he becomes mischievous, and a Nisse's trickery knows no limits."[21] Hoeg's guidelines conform to the original Norwegian tradition, requiring deference to the nisse or gardvord. Besides honoring the family's founder and the farm's established customs, this age-old lore emphatically demands that humans recognize and show respect for powers beyond their control, whether in following principles of good husbandry or working in harmony with the environment.

CHRISTMAS EVE DINNER

Like their acknowledgment of the nisse, the Winjum family's Christmas dinner had its basis in Norwegian models, deriving as in the Old Country from a seasonal abundance of food: "At Christmas time we had ample food resources for the finest of Christmas feasts." Traditional Norwegian delicacies remained at its core, but the Winjum Christmas repast also included distinctly American dishes.

The meal began with *søtsuppe* (sweet soup), "which had been simmering on the back of the stove all afternoon. It was served every Christmas and consisted of sago, raisins, currants, prunes, lemon peel, spices and sugar. It was traditional and became so for all members of the family." Though Winjum, like most Norwegian Americans, considers søtsuppe "traditional," earlier immigrants from Norway's preindustrial peasant society have not mentioned it. During the nineteenth century such fruit compotes remained the province of the kondisjonerte and became familiar in the rest of Norway (and Norwegian-America) only after the turn of the twentieth century.

Winjum's family made their fruit soup with sago, a thickening agent (consisting of the rinsed, dried, and ground starch of the sago palm) that enjoyed great popularity in early American puddings. Present-day recipes usually call for quick-cooking tapioca. After the søtsuppe, the Winjum family Christmas meal continued with

> a choice of beef or pork roast, or a huge pan of baked pork spare ribs and a pan of baked beans; mashed potatoes, gravy, peas, string beans, beets, biscuits, jam and jelly, relishes, a variety of pickles; pickled herring, pickled pigs feet, head cheese, and mince and apple pies. This feast was served about eight o'clock, under the mellow light of a sparkling clean kerosene lamp in the middle of the table.

Along with the scrupulous Christmas Eve cleanliness from the Old Country came the classic pork rib, which joined Yankee baked beans, mashed potatoes, and gravy, while the traditional Norwegian peasant delicacies of pickled pigs' feet, herring, and head cheese shared the table with modern

❖ ❖

There are probably as many variations on søtsuppe as there are cooks who make it.
This recipe was used by Arlene Brumberg Stokes of Eau Claire, Wisconsin
(born in 1928 in Meridean, Wisconsin). Arlene's daughter, Diane House
of Eau Claire, provided the recipe.

Søtsuppe

4 cups water

2 cups grape juice

1½ cups raisins

½ cup golden raisins

½ cup currants (Arlene substituted apricots)

1 cup prunes

1 tablespoon lemon juice (or ½ lemon, sliced)

½ to ⅔ cups sugar

¼ teaspoon salt

2 cinnamon sticks

5 tablespoons quick-cooking tapioca

Bring all ingredients except the tapioca to a boil; reduce heat and simmer 20 minutes or until fruit is tender. Gradually stir in the tapioca and simmer about 15 minutes more. (Some cooks do not add the grape juice until this point; they then let the soup simmer another 15 minutes.) Serve warm or cold. Arlene served the søtsuppe sprinkled with cinnamon and sugar; some top it with whipped cream.

❖ ❖

dishes like pickled fruits and vegetables, jam, relishes, and biscuits. And what could be more American than apple pie?

The Christmas Tree

What *could* be more American, by some accounts, was the Christmas tree, which—O. E. Brandt declared—"only in America received such universal acclaim."[22] Bearing out this claim, the breathless descriptions that Winjum and other memoir writers devote to this originally German custom leave no doubt about the enormous impression the Christmas tree made on Norwegian Americans. Not realizing how recently the tree had gained widespread acceptance in Norway, Winjum wonders why his family and others delayed having a "home tree" for so long:

> After the meal the living room door was opened and we scrambled in to celebrate the Christmas tree. While we lived in an area where evergreen forests were close by, and a Christmas tree could be had for the cutting, we did not have a home Christmas tree until 1916 (but had one each year thereafter). Nor do I remember any of the neighbors having a home Christmas tree before about that time. Just why this was so, I do not know, since having a home decorated tree was part of the Norwegian custom.

Whether a Norwegian custom or not, the Christmas tree had by this time certainly become a Norwegian American icon. Brandt wrote in his 1918 article: "For most of *Jul i Vesterheimen*'s readers, a Christmas without a Christmas tree would seem like a diamond ring without a diamond. The entire Christmas holiday stands for us like a glowing setting for the Christmas tree." Contrary to Winjum's assumption that his parents had known the custom in Norway, the pre-twentieth-century peasant culture had, as already noted, shunned the tree, some because they saw it as blasphemous idolatry, others because they refused to adopt the fancy customs of the kondisjonerte.

Given the tree's enormous popularity in America and their middle-class aspirations, most Norwegian Americans adopted the custom as soon as possible, so Winjum's conjecture that a lack of space accounted for his family's lack of a tree is probably correct:

> Our homestead farm house consisted of a main room about 16 by 20 feet, with a lean-to kitchen of about 16 by 10 feet. The main room was the family bedroom, living room, and dining room when we had company. In 1909, our last Christmas at the homestead place, this provided the living accommodations for our parents, six active youngsters and a baby. In 1910 we moved to the farm house of an adjoining rented farm, where the house was two storied with larger rooms. Here the downstairs room was a combination of kitchen, dining and living room, and

the same size room upstairs was our sleeping quarters. Space was short to start with, but by 1914 these two rooms had to accommodate an enlarged family of twelve.[23]

The situation changed in 1916 when a two-storied, two-room addition doubled the size of their home: "The bottom room of this wing was solely a general purpose living room and for the first time we had the space not only for a respectable seven to eight foot evergreen tree, but room to dress it, conduct the associated mysteries in privacy and an ample area for the evening celebration." Winjum wisely realizes the need for space extended beyond just a corner in which to place the tree, for, according to that time's custom, it had to be decorated in private, to be revealed only on Christmas Eve, when the family might circle around it to sing Christmas carols, according to Scandinavian custom.

This last practice receives no mention by Winjum, however (another clue that his parents probably had not known the tree in Norway), nor did his family's tree bear any distinctly Norwegian decorations. Instead they improvised from available materials:

> A day or so before Christmas Eve the tree was brought into the living room (after Dad, my older brother and later I had cut the tree off square and fashioned and spiked on a cross piece wood stand). The tree decorations came out of mother's mystery trunk: a strand of heavy gold tinsel and a like strand of silver tinsel that would circle the tree from top to bottom; gold and silver tinsel, icicles, red cotton icicles; the star for the very top of the tree. . . . The trim was supplemented from time to time by home-strung strands of pop corn, small squares of red and green construction paper separated by short wheat straw cylinders.

Imagining the tree erected in its stand and decorated, Winjum recalls the awe a candlelit tree inspired—and the vigilance it demanded:[24]

> After the tree was trimmed and the candles in place, they had to be inspected so the candle flame would not be too near the tree needles, trim or the tissue paper bells.
> We all stood around as the tree was lit; the candle lighting up the star at the very top being lit first and then the rest, with all of us watching that none of the candles was missed. Suddenly the tree became a beauti-

ful sight, seemingly alive with a spirit of its own. Mother and the girls sang Christmas carols and then each of us were given a red netting bag of mixed hard candies, peanuts and mixed nuts from under the tree. Each of us received a single gift (from Santa Claus) from under the tree.

Looking very American with its horizontal strands of popcorn, gold, and silver tinsel encircling the tree (rather than descending in vertical garlands, as in Norway), the tree towered over the sparse gifts from Santa Claus, says Winjum. Santa Claus? How had *he* become a part of this Norwegian American family's Christmas?

SANTA CLAUS

Santa's presence seems all the more remarkable in that Winjum's parents—both first-generation Norwegian Americans who spoke Norwegian in the home almost exclusively until 1912—neither called the bearer of Christmas gifts a julenisse nor portrayed him in the nisse's gray clothing and red stocking cap, but had instead adopted the fully American Santa: "One of my elder sisters remembered that when she was five or six years old, Dad played Santa Claus and brought gifts on Christmas Eve. Mother had made him a typical American red and white trimmed Santa suit, peaked cap and white whiskers. Our gift from Mother and Dad always came from Santa Claus."[25] This evidence clinches the argument that Winjum's parents had not known the child-centered Christmas in Norway with its gift-bringing nisse; they had more likely celebrated the traditional peasant Christmas, with a barn nisse who expected respect and a tribute for his hard work, rather than a julenisse who brought gifts. Yet they had quickly adopted the American Santa, perhaps referring to magazine features like "Home-made Santa and a Christmas Tree" in the December 1907 *Ladies' Home Journal* for useful tips. Describing how to make a Santa mask from flesh-colored, wax-coated cloth, cutting holes for eyes and mouth and attaching white whiskers, the article further advised that Santa could wrap a simple toga of red muslin around his body and wear regular trousers underneath, covering his shoes with high black boots of felt or waxed cloth.[26]

In so quickly adopting Santa, Winjum's parents showed an enthusiasm for the commercial Christmas shared by many other Norwegian Americans whose memoirs spill over with glee in describing their first store-bought gifts. Alida Johnson writes: "I remember a Christmas long ago when my sister and I were given big dolls by our Grandpa and Grandma Thompson. One had a pink dress and the other one had a blue dress. We were so surprised, thrilled and happy. We played and played with them for a long time, undressing and dressing them and 'playing house.'"[27] In urban areas Santa became big business around the turn of the twentieth century.[28] Climbing into the lap of a flesh-and-blood department store Santa Claus quickly assumed ritual significance for urban children, as merchants suddenly seemed able to transform fantasy into reality. The 1901 *Dry Goods Reporter* described the then novel scene at Chicago's Siegel-Cooper department store: "One of our attractions is a live Santa Claus right in the middle of our toy stock. He has all the regalia credited to the real Santa of story and sits in a booth . . . from which he distributes presents to the little folks. This booth is built so that a procession can pass through up the front steps, past Santa Claus, and out the back steps.[29]

In smaller towns and rural areas, by contrast, Santa waited much longer to become a commercial force. Alida Johnson says: "I don't remember anything about a Santa Claus coming to town during those days of the early thirties. The only exposure to Santa Claus was in school through stories, pictures and songs."[30] In some families, though, like the Winjums, Santa was

The author with Santa at a department store, 1948

quickly becoming an important presence. Chrystene Nordness Weedman writes: "On Christmas Eve we told Christmas stories and sang carols. Then about 9:00 p.m. a knock came to the door and here was Santa Claus with the gifts. The gifts were useful items—stockings, a tablet, pencils and maybe a sled. The gifts still tended to be practical rather than 'fun.'"[31] Other families mixed the Santa and nisse traditions together, as Ruth Halbert recalls:

> In the evening before I went to bed, I put out some cookies and milk for the nisser. Before we went to bed, we hung our socks up. Since we did not have a fireplace, we hung our stockings on the rung of a chair next to the stove. The next morning I usually got an orange and pair of homemade mittens; Mother a handkerchief and an apple; Dad a pair of socks and a can of snuff. One year Santa pulled a good one: he put the snuff and socks in my stocking![32]

True to their differing traditions, the nisse *receives* the cookies and milk in the rituals Halbert describes, while Santa *gives* the gifts. Snuff notwithstanding, the "surprise" and luxury gifts so common today and already present in affluent circles had not yet become a feature of the average Norwegian American rural Christmas.

THE CHRISTMAS EVE PROGRAM AT HOME

With commercialism rumbling in the distance, Christmas for rural Norwegian Americans still remained a family affair, and it often included a short program put on by the children. Recalling a Minnesota Christmas around 1919, Lois ("BJ") Bjelland says:

> In our home my father read the Christmas gospel and then we children put on a program. At first this was in Norwegian. [An oft-performed verse began] *"Jeg er en liten pike/gutt bare tre år gammel"* [I am a little girl/boy only three years old]. When we were a little older, and my older sister and brother went to school, we spoke more English.[33]

The custom of a home Christmas program—often containing Norwegian-language selections—continued for quite a few years in many places. Irma Chamberlain (born 1932) tells of Christmas Eve in small-town North Dakota: "The big meal came first—and afterwards, before we could open presents—we had a program where the children entertained with their 'pieces' and songs. Then we all sang carols—including Norwegian ones. It was faithfully observed every year."[34] Having Christmas programs put on by the children seems to take the place of the Scandinavian custom of encircling the tree while singing carols, a custom then still confined to Norway's kondisjonerte circles and apparently unfamiliar to these immigrant families.

THE CHURCH PROGRAM

The home program frequently rehearsed or reprised the children's "pieces" for the public programs at church and school. These public programs united the community and always featured a sizable Christmas tree. The vivid and lasting impression made by these trees comes through clearly in Winjum's detailed description:

> I remember the big church tree best, trimmed with a star, two ropes of thin ruffled paper, one green, the other red, draped starting at the top, criss-crossing each other in ever bigger diamonds, and strands of tightly woven gold tinsel, draped in a circular fashion from the top to bottom, gold and red cotton icicles . . . , candle holders filled with red, white, pink, blue and green candles, as many as the tree could hold. Also varied colored glass balls—small and large—gold, silver, red, blue, green, plain and frosted. Red tissue paper bells, which opened from a flat state to make a bell of intricate connected diamond shaped openings. But what I remember best—blue cherub angels (made of glazed post card stock) blowing on a trumpet.

With the tree as a backdrop, the program began after the pastor had conducted the liturgy and given the Christmas message. Norwegian remained the program's sole language of presentation until just before World War I, says Winjum. The elimination of Norwegian as the language of these programs reflects the pervasive suspicion of everything foreign that washed over America as World War I began. To some, the slow pace of "Americanization" within the ethnic communities posed a threat to national security. Sustained by this nervous sense of danger, a campaign arose that was designed to transform U.S. citizens into pure Americans; it included active

Christmas Tree 1918

In 1918 a patriotic Christmas tree decorated Trinity Lutheran Church,
founded by Norwegian immigrants in Dawson, Minnesota.

measures against non-English-speaking groups in the population.[35] Probably the most extreme example of legislation toward this end was Iowa governor William L. Harding's May 1918 ordinance that prohibited the use of any language but English as the medium of instruction, in conversations in public places, over the telephone, in public addresses, and at church services. The governors of at least fifteen other states introduced similar, if less radical, legislation, restricting the use of languages other than English to private religious meetings in the home. These restrictions account for Winjum's report of a gradual shift from Norwegian to English in the church Christmas program before the war. By 1924, he says, the regular Norwegian-language church services had also ceased. This loss of language constituted for many a significant part of the "anguish of becoming American."[36]

Anguish of a different sort derived from the pieces the children had to memorize and recite at the church program.[37] Despite detailed instructions received at home about how to bow and curtsy and to speak in a loud, clear voice, "what 'came out' in front of the congregation," says Winjum, "was largely a matter of fate," depending on shyness and other distractions. "A child would know his 'piece' perfect at practice," Alida Johnson adds, but "at the program the words did not seem to come. The teacher would help with

A children's performance of "Julekveld i Quieaasen" (Christmas Eve at Quieaasen) at the Chicago Norske Klub's Christmas party, December 27, 1921

the lines or skip to the next child." Decades later Winjum could still feel "shamefaced" recalling how a "ghostlike pale faced woman" sitting in one of the front rows made him forget his lines. "Being prompted, I made it through," he says, but the embarrassment lingered on.

If their "piece" loomed as the children's most dreaded part of the program, its highlight came afterward, "when each of us received a bag filled with candies and nuts and also a nice big red apple," says Alida Johnson.[38] Santa came to distribute treats during the early years, but "it wasn't within church doctrine to have Santa Claus around during the religious Christmas celebration, so he was later eliminated," says Winjum. A significant controversy had raged throughout the country during his childhood. Should parents continue to teach their children about Santa? Some worried parents reported that their children confused Santa with Christ, praying to the former for Christmas gifts and even for help in difficult situations.[39] In response, Protestant clergy launched a crusade during the first two decades of the 1900s to minimize Santa Claus's presence in churches. The *Sunday School Times* carried on its own crusade, calling for attention to be more squarely focused on the nativity: "Christmas is not Santamas," the paper insisted, chiding Victorian Protestants for making Santa the center of their Sunday School entertainment.[40]

HOME CHRISTMAS TREE PARTIES

Having survived these controversies, though perhaps without Santa, the church Christmas program remains familiar today. Not so the home "Christmas tree" party, which in some places was once an equally popular custom. Though not practiced now, this custom—a direct descendent of the medieval and Renaissance *julestuer*—embodies so many Norwegian American values that it deserves attention here. Recalling the zest these home parties added to the holidays, Mabel Braton (born circa 1900) of Lawndale, Minnesota, says:

> As a very young girl "The Christmas Tree" meant going to a neighborhood gathering one evening between Christmas and New Years. Each family took its turn in entertaining. A nice tree would be bought and the decorations would be saved from year to year and passed on to the next family who would have the celebration next year. The decoration

*A Christmas tree in the home of Peter Rosendahl, the creator of the popular
"Han Ole og han Per" cartoon in the* Decorah Posten, *about 1914*

included green and red crepe paper for streamers, to decorate ceilings in
the rooms, bells to be hung in the center of the rooms and doorways,
fancy glass balls for the tree, clip-on candle holders and colored wax
candles.

   Each family brought a gift for their own family and perhaps for all the
women. There would be so many presents that there would hardly be
room to move about. The candles would be lit and Mrs. Strand would

read the Christmas story from the Norwegian Bible, then a delicious lunch would be served.

Without indoor plumbing there was always a problem when so many little folks would run to their mothers and whisper in her ear, then an older sister or brother would be summoned to dig through the huge heaps of coats on the bed to find wraps and take the little one "out."

It never seemed too cold to go to the "Christmas Tree" [party]. The horses would be harnessed and hitched to the sled, robes would be warmed and covered over everyone but the driver and away they would go.[41]

A veritable archive of Norwegian American character traits—the vital role of hospitality, equality, evenhandedness in sharing hosting obligations, resourcefulness, the ability to make one's own entertainment, a concern for aesthetics, and the attention accorded Christian piety—this custom embodies qualities still valued in Norwegian society. The northern Minnesota "Christmas tree" party could hardly have expressed its roots more explicitly.

JULEBUKKING

As much as Norwegian Americans enjoyed these other post-Christmas entertainments, they most gleefully looked forward to going julebukking.[42] Since the early Norwegian immigrants rarely wrote about this colorful Christmas masquerade, Winjum and others had to depend on oral tradition. As a result of this and the uncertainty about what the Norwegian term *julebukk* (Christmas goat) actually meant, memoirs exhibit a wide variety of spellings, including "yulebook," "Yule Bok," "juleboek," "julbock," "yulebokk," and "julebakk." Winjum calls it "jul-brukk."[43] Descriptions of the custom, however, remain surprisingly consistent:

Young men disguised by dressing foolishly, coats and overcoats turned inside out (often exchanged so clothes couldn't be identified with the wearer), odd garments and masks, stocking cap or kerchief over the face. They would approach the house singing Christmas songs or howling like wolves and then when invited in, would make funny noises, imitate animals (especially a goat), dance a jig, ask and answer foolish questions in disguised voices and when it was guessed who they were, they would unmask and be served coffee and Christmas goodies. By their antics and dress they would frighten the young ones in the household, who usually hid behind Mother and Dad. After the unmasking they would try and coax the children to be friends.

The terrorizing of children aside, "all in all," says Winjum, "it was good entertainment and harmless fun."

Yet the custom was so much more. Beyond being just plain fun, julebukking provided a way of cementing relations among individuals who lived and worked closely together, as Tina Olson in Prairie View Township near Barnesville, Minnesota, notes: "When pioneers from the Scandinavian countries settled in the area between Pelican Rapids and Barnesville, they became a close knit community. They helped each other in many ways and also enjoyed social gatherings together. Christmas fooling (*Yule Bok*) was a common way of enjoying evenings from Christmas Day on for 10 days or more."[44]

Though once a common way of socializing, the widespread julebukking Olson recalls began to decline rapidly after the 1930s. Many observers blame tractors and cars for the decline: "[Julebukking] was discontinued when roads were cleared for motor vehicles," says Chrystene Weedman. Without the horses, sleighs, and jingling bells, julebukking just didn't seem the same, agrees an interviewee in a 1930 Clinton, Wisconsin, newspaper article: "'It

---

"Every Christmas my parents had lots of fun with julebukking and I remember it well. Dad was a professional accordionist, and Mother an expert cook and baker. So . . . this meant the julebukking ended at our home. My parents' Norwegian friends would go from house to house dressed as outlandish as possible; laughing, joking, singing, and just plain having fun. When the group had reached a large number, they all went to [our place] for the party. When I was about 10 years old, I was dressed as they were—old ragged and spotted clothes, too big or too small, beat-up hats and our hair was all messed up. Mother placed a smudge of soot on her cheek and some on my nose. There was home brew, dandelion wine, blood sausage, pickled herring, sylte, bløtkake, lefse and all kinds of cookies (seven different kinds, a tradition!)—homemade everything."

Ruth Halbert [born 1917], letter to the author recalling her childhood
in east-central Minnesota, May 15, 1997

was most fun' say the older ones, 'when we could go in a bob-sleigh. Nowadays the youngsters go in automobiles, stop for only a minute or two at each
place, and finish with a party at some home where it has been planned.' "[45]
Julebukking never did entirely die out (and in some places even seems to
be making a comeback), but it never again achieved the almost universal
participation it once had in some areas.

The Generation Gap: How Will Norwegians Be American?

Times were changing. By the 1920s Norwegian visitors as well as new
immigrants and their children perceived a cultural divide between themselves and the earlier immigrants and their children, whom they found old-
fashioned. As early as 1904 Thoralv Klaveness had perceived a *kløft* (chasm)
between the Norwegian immigrants and their American-born children.
While a South Dakota housewife he interviewed complained of the terrible
isolation and hard work, her children, he says, "listened to her comments
uncomprehendingly," blaming her bitter words on residual exhaustion from
a recent illness. Klaveness explains their conflicting perceptions: "To the
children, America is a land of opportunity, the best country on earth, even
though it has cost their parents' life and health. The young dream the dreams
of the prairie and feel the joy of life in the land of their birth."[46] The generation gap grew wider during the second decade of the twentieth century.
While the American-born generation turned their backs on old ways,
the parent generation increasingly decried their children's materialism.
Remarkably often they expressed these evolving views as they related to
Christmas.

Christmas intensified Norwegian American sentiments about both their
ancestral home and their adopted one. Their growing concern over American materialism and sorrow over what had been left behind blossomed in
nostalgic accounts of earlier yuletide celebrations. Writing in the 1914 *Jul i
Vesterheimen,* for example, B. F. Bergesen admonishes parents to hand down
to their children a traditional Norwegian Christmas: "Not least here in
America we need the old-fashioned, cozy Christmas Eve, because the high
degree of materialism here robs life of its sweetness and the soul of its
faith. . . . Those homes in which children can amuse themselves in the old-
fashioned way . . . remain the happiest." "A vital part of the attraction these

homes hold for little ones and young people," Bergesen concludes, "is the correct celebration of Christmas in the traditional Norwegian manner."[47]

Knute Løkensgaard agrees, recalling in a 1919 issue of *Hallingen* the charms of Christmas past:

> It seems to me that Christmas in those days meant a great deal more both to children and adults than it does at present. Though they may not have had Christmas tree parties and carloads of Christmas gifts for the children, there was nevertheless something about Christmas then that cast a festive mood over the entire community—a festive mood that permeated the homes and settled on a child's mind like a life-giving dew.[48]

The development these writers trace seems dire, but is tempered when compared with remarks that Marcus O. Bøckman would make some twenty years later in the 1936 issue of *Jul i Vesterheimen.* For there he urges the preservation of precisely the modern, tree-centered, commercial Christmas that Bergesen and Løkensgaard bemoan: "Shall we protect the beautiful tree with its flickering candles or shall we let it wither and the light go out, as is happening with so much else in our time? We would suffer a profound loss if this happened."

While these writers disagree about the precise form Christmas should take, they do agree on its vital importance; Bøckman continues: "Christmas contributes strength, as do few other things, toward establishing the home as the solid foundation of our people. This foundation needs all the fortification it can get, for more than anything else in our day, it is under attack from all sides."[49] What is most striking about all these passages is the sense of being under siege that their writers share. In part this may be due to the universal human wish that time could stand still, especially as it affects beloved traditions. Who does not regard his or her childhood Christmas as the one worth perpetuating? What "tradition" means to any one of us, it seems, is the way *we* did it before. Certainly today many, both in Norway and America, see Christmas growing too commercialized. Yet, as Stephen Nissenbaum points out in *The Battle for Christmas,* few realize how many generations prior to their own have had the very same feeling. The perception goes back at least to the time of Harriet Beecher Stowe (born 1811), who in the short story "Christmas; or, The Good Fairy" has her narrator muse: "When I was a child of ten the very idea of a present was so new [that a child would be delighted] with the gift of even a single piece of candy." The narrator clearly believes that children of the next generation should feel the same way, but how can they if they grow up in different circumstances—in a different world? Though the conversion to the commercial Christmas actually took place in Stowe's time, each succeeding generation, says Nissenbaum, has perceived the corruption of Christmas as taking place since their own childhood.[50]

Even beyond this universally perceived threat, however, the Norwegian American writers I've quoted had additional reasons to feel themselves to be under siege, oppressed as they were by the powerful Americanization movement surrounding World War I. The unrelenting coercion to conform could not help but affect them, and it met with a variety of Norwegian American responses. Two opposing views stand out: One group saw danger in the melting pot, feeling that a variety of distinctive cultures would serve the nation better, with each culture contributing something unique to the American society. The other urged that Norwegians assimilate into the American mainstream, adopting American values and conforming to American ideals to cultivate a sense of belonging.

Representing the former view, Klaveness emphasized as early as 1904 the importance of maintaining a Norwegian identity, especially among the coming generation:

> It is essential to win and keep the youth. Their understanding of the land of their ancestors is essential because when emigration stops in fifteen to twenty years, Norway's name, language, and memories will soon be forgotten. When emigration ceases and the pioneers are gone, their descendants will quickly be swallowed up by the American nation until there are few or no memories left about the time when Norwegians played their great role in building the American society.[51]

Taking the opposite view, Carl Roan (writing in 1921) warned that embracing Norwegianness too enthusiastically could cause no less harm:

> Clearly many things draw us to Norway. I feel drawn there myself, since from childhood I have inhaled so much Norwegian that in my youth and until quite recently I didn't know exactly where I belonged—here or in Norway. Many years have thereby been lost during which I could

have gained a knowledge of my country's history, constitution, and goals to a far greater extent than has been the case, if only I had realized that this is where I belong.[52]

Providing a context for the kind of confusion Roan describes, Andreas Ueland wrote in 1918 objecting to the "romanticization" of Norway:

> The Norwegian clergy, schools and newspapers in America have nursed this national tendency and the Norwegians here have come to see Norway and what appertains to her in a romantic light. Their imagination and ideals have come to cluster about what is Norwegian to the exclusion more or less of what is American. This has retarded the development of a stronger sentiment of American nationality.[53]

Articulately balancing these views, I. F. Grose, writing in the 1919 *Jul i Vesterheimen,* rejects the notion that Norwegian Americans can embrace only one of their cultures. Rather, he says, they must look to *both* the "rock from which they have been hewn" and the "land by which they have been adopted": "They owe much of their comfort, competence, education, position and prestige to enterprising ancestors who through intuitive foresight, patient sacrifice and unremitting toil acquired lasting benefits both for themselves and their posterity." But while remembering their past, they must also look to their future, for "this country offers our young people great advantages. Their opportunity for development and service recognizes no bounds except those set by the capabilities of their own faculties."

Arguing that the Scandinavians had perhaps done too good a job of becoming Americanized while neglecting their heritage, Mary Wilhelmine Williams, professor of history at Goucher College in Maryland, published her views in *Jul i Vesterheimen* two years later. Her article, titled "Scandinavian Qualities and American Ideals," scolded the Scandinavians for not teaching their children to take pride in their origins. Williams suggested that the Scandinavians' admirable adaptability had almost perversely worked against their adjustment to the New Land. For while they had smoothly assimilated into the American culture, their easy integration had kept them from living up to their "superior social inheritance":

> In their zeal to become Americanized, Scandinavians cut themselves too completely loose from their past and fail to give their children an

appreciation of the history and culture of the ancestral lands. Nor has this knowledge been adequately supplied by the schools. As a result the children born in this country, instead of being proud of their ancestral descent, as they might well be, are often ashamed of it and of their parents with their broken speech and "queer foreign ways." Lacking the respect of their children, the parents have little means of controlling them, which lends credence to the charge that the second generation lacks "moral fibre."

Voicing complaints about the younger generation familiar to parents since the age of Socrates, Williams did, however, see encouraging opportunities for improving upon past performance. Aids had appeared to help parents teach their children about their heritage; books about Scandinavian history had been published in English, as had translations of Scandinavian literature. These, along with the American Scandinavian Foundation and Society for the Advancement of Scandinavian Study, wrote Williams, would "make it easier for the parents to train up the youth in the way that they should go, and inspire those of Scandinavian descent with greater sense of responsibility and self-respect, and do much toward lifting standards and creating ideals." In no way shirking the responsibility of her own generation, Williams concluded that making these ideals a reality rested "especially on the second generation whose pioneer parents—often at the price of heavy toil and sacrifice—gave us better opportunities than they themselves enjoyed."

The issue of assimilation continued to haunt the immigrants, especially at Christmastime, and the Christmas annual *Jul i Vesterheimen* continued to address it in fiction no less than in opinion pieces. D. G. Ristad's 1923 sketch "Slik holder vi jul" (How we celebrate Christmas) portrays a Norwegian immigrant grandfather sharing with his grandchildren tales of Christmas in the Old Country. Rejecting notions of the Norwegians' overassimilation, his sketch demonstrates how American Christmas customs parallel Old Country ways and concludes that America has so fully adopted these traditional ways and interwoven them into its own cultural fabric that they no longer realize the customs' actual origins: "The old Christmas customs are still being maintained in America's Norwegian communities. In the oldest Norwegian communities they have taken firm root—so much so that people no longer think of them as being 'Norwegian.' They have become

'American.'" Those who sound alarms about Norwegian culture being subsumed by American culture thus underestimate that culture's endurance.
Instead of losing themselves in nostalgia for a lost past, Ristad suggests,
they might better appreciate the unique freedom America allows its people
to intertwine strands from both old and new cultures into their own traditions. "Thank goodness," says his story's grandfather, "for this good America where we can have the good old customs with us—and," he utters under his breath, "on top of that so much we couldn't afford in the old
country."

Jul i Vesterheimen
Mirroring the Norwegian American Experience

I have spent the day browsing through the illustrated Christmas publications of past years, which Mother has already brought out. It is her way of preparing instead of the butchering, brewing and baking of my boyhood.

Andreas Ueland, *The Recollections of an Immigrant*, 1929

The nineteenth-century tradition of the Christmas annual took root among the Norwegian Americans after 1910.[1] Their bright covers, adorned with folk art or religious motifs, added much visual cheer to the home, while their contents—colorfully illustrated stories, poetry, travelogues, and music—enlivened its yuletide celebration. To this day, families like Enid Ringdahl's in Fergus Falls, Minnesota, retain the old issues, handing them down like heirlooms to generations no longer able to decipher them: "We have several *Jul i Vesterheimen* magazines that I 'put out' but sadly, none of us reads Norwegian."[2]

Jul i Vesterheimen (Christmas in the western home) began in 1911 as the pet project of Andreas Sundheim (1861–1945), head of Augsburg Publishing House. Its contents blended English- and Norwegian-language fiction, poetry, and articles until 1931, when it became entirely Norwegian, thereby providing one of America's only venues for Norwegian-language fiction,

Intricately embossed and illustrated, books emerged on the scene and flourished as New Year's and Christmas gifts. In the antebellum period no holiday gift was more typical than books, and these annuals, with their fine bindings, literary offerings and pictorial embellishments, were among the most prominent seasonal mementos and most successful holiday commodities.

Schmidt, Consumer Rites, *116–17*

besides *Decorah Posten*'s *Ved Arnen. Jul i Vesterheimen* continued appearing solely in Norwegian until publication ceased in 1957. Eighteen years after the annual's start, the new editor, J. A. Holvik, wrote of its mission: "It is significant that an annual bearing the name *Jul i Vesterheimen* come as a guest to the Christmas table; it embodies the emigration experience, homeland, inherited customs, and traditions—the bridge between home and abroad. Surely Christmas is the most essential span on that bridge."[3] Once again we see how central Christmas was to the Norwegian American experience.

Jul i Vesterheimen could appear exclusively in Norwegian after 1931 because in that year Augsburg also began issuing the English-language annual *Christmas*. This publication sparked immediate response and continues to circulate widely both within and far beyond the Norwegian American community. What these Christmas annuals meant to earlier generations of Norwegian Americans can be clearly seen in the words written in 1921 by Judge Andreas Ueland in the epigraph to this chapter.[4] Associating these annuals with the preindustrial peasants' painstaking Christmas preparations, he captures the profound anticipation invested in the Norwegian Christmas, then and now. These annuals, his words suggest, deserve an honored place in the Christmas celebration.

Harboring similarly optimistic views of his annual's potential, Sundheim commissioned some of the most insightful Norwegian American writers of his day—including Waldemar Ager, O. E. Rølvaag, Simon Johnson, Dorothea Dahl, and George Strandvold—to write for it.[5] The authors' charge to develop stories relating to Christmas joined with their own concerns as sensitive observers of contemporary society to produce fiction that meaningfully reflects the prevailing mood and pressing issues of their time.

Cover of Jul i Vesterheimen, *1925*

Representative narratives from the pages of *Jul i Vesterheimen* give readers insight into the Norwegian American experience, from poverty and hardship, through growing prosperity and materialism (with its accompanying concern for lost idealism), to an ultimately enhanced understanding and appreciation of the immigrant ordeal and legacy. Each decade of the annual seems to be characterized by a particular theme.

Pioneer Sacrifice and Aspiration

The pioneers' sacrifices for their children's and grandchildren's future happiness recurs as a theme in the annuals issued before 1920. O. P. Vangsnes's "Jeg glemmer aldri den første jul" (I'll never forget the first Christmas) from 1914, for example, tells of a father who during the winter of 1870 undertakes the formidable journey from the family's isolated South Dakota dugout to Sioux Falls. This year, he vows, his children will have storebought Christmas gifts, now that his status has risen from lowly cotter in Norway to American landowner. A snowstorm blows up and strands him in town. When he finally gets back home, he finds his dugout entirely buried under the snow. Seeing no signs of life, he imagines the worst. But the story ends happily when he learns that a neighboring family has saved his wife and children by taking them to their own farm on higher ground. Like O. Henry's "Gift of the Magi," the story contains the inspiring theme of the sacrifices we willingly make for those we love. Vangsnes's story also shows the neighbor-to-neighbor help that was essential to survival on the prairie and that became a major aspect of the Norwegian American experience. (Both stories also raise the more sobering question of whether the impulse to exchange Christmas gifts does not sometimes obscure other necessities and priorities. Was buying Christmas presents worth risking the life and limb of this family's provider?)

Simon Johnson's story "Blaa øine" (Blue eyes) also appears in the 1914 issue and contains similar motifs of early hardship and hopes for a better future. The Northland settlement is preparing for a *juletrefest,* a Christmas party, and the community's wealthiest man, Ole Breiseth, is making his way from farm to farm collecting money for the children's gifts. Though the father of the main character, Sigurd Graalien, is worse off than most of his neighbors, he donates generously to the fund.

On the day of the party, the community eagerly fills the church. Inspired by the sight of the magnificently decorated tree, the schoolmaster speaks grandly about Norway, the land of Christmas that "we have brought with us to America! . . . Mother thinks of Norway while keeping house, and Father remembers Norway as he walks behind plow and reaper. When we speak of Norway, our children's eyes widen, though few of them have been beyond the prairie! Norway is with us at this moment as we gaze upon the Christmas tree, for it, too, derives its essence from the North." The speech over, the children receive gifts from under the tree—all except Sigurd. When Sigurd's father hears that his son has received no present, he assumes the "big shot" stole his money, but Sigurd sees the oversight as part of a larger pattern of poverty destined to plague him throughout life.

Haunted by this thought, Sigurd withdraws from the others and spends his time reading Horatio Alger rags-to-riches stories. He begins imagining a time when the rich Breiseth and his daughter, Klara, would notice his accomplishments. A few days later he receives the missing Christmas gift. It had been there all along, rolled under the foot of the tree, and no one had seen it. To Sigurd, an aspiring writer, the pen he receives holds great promise. Gazing toward the Breiseth's prominent home, pen firmly in hand, Sigurd muses that though "it was a long way there, . . . the intervening stretch now seemed to him like a snowy plateau . . . glittering in the sun, the sky above as blue as Klara's eyes and the snow already beginning to melt."

Primarily a story of immigrant aspiration, Johnson's narrative also hints at the generation gap that was opening between the immigrants and their offspring. In describing the community's sharply divided sex roles, the story shows the immigrant generation already settling into the American middle-class norms of men dominating the outside sphere of production, and women, the indoors. At the same time it tacitly questions the schoolmaster's easy assumption that the children will retain their parents' strong ties to the Old Country; Sigurd's aspirations are already moving in quite a different direction.

The Generation Gap

The gap between the immigrants and their children grows more overt in Dorothea Dahl's 1919 story, "Det gamle bokskap" (The old bookcase).[6]

The protagonist, Herman Diesen, is building a legal practice in Seattle while consciously distancing himself from his roots. Christmas approaches, and his girlfriend Edith loses herself in a whirl of preparations and parties. But Diesen finds little meaning in the season, having abandoned his childhood faith as a hindrance to professional success.

A telegram announces his father's death, and Diesen travels back to his Midwestern hometown to settle the estate. Intending to discard the father's treasured collection of old books from Norway, Diesen puzzles over how such an abyss could arise between two generations: How could these anti- quated, alien volumes have held such deep meaning for his father?

Slowly he begins to perceive the answer. Realizing he has given little thought to Edith since his arrival, he also notes a growing attraction to Margaret, an idealistic young nurse who had befriended his father. Finding several of his father's books inscribed either to himself or to Margaret, Diesen wonders what his father could have meant and eventually reaches two pivotal decisions: He will settle down in this town, taking over the legal practice recently vacated by a friend of his father's, and he will marry Mar- garet and join her in cultivating the values bequeathed to them both through his father's old bookcase.

The Generation Gap Widens

Though Dahl's 1919 story ultimately reaffirms the bond between genera- tions, the stories of the 1920s increasingly despair of this possibility. They chide Norwegian Americans for having cut themselves off from their past, and accuse them of failing to give their children an appreciation of their an- cestral land.

Again it is one of Dorothea Dahl's stories, "The Beckoning Distance" in the 1926 issue of *Jul i Vesterheimen,* that most clearly articulates this theme. Set in a time "scarcely half a century since the conquest of the great North- west had first been undertaken by Norsemen," Dahl's narrative tells of a gen- eration that "rarely takes the time to look beneath the surface of anything." Evelyn Kilde belongs to this generation. Her grandparents had come from the Old Country with all their worldly goods packed in a massive, home- made chest, while Evelyn herself "went to college with a wardrobe trunk that cost more than her grandfather's first reaping machine," and its con- tents more than the house that had replaced their homestead shack.

Illustration from Dorothea Dahl's "The Beckoning Distance," Jul i Vesterheimen, *1926*

Relegated to the sidelines, her grandfather sits rocking on the porch pondering how things have changed. He hardly recognizes his increasingly prosperous son anymore, and "his daughter-in-law so successfully met the demands of the new order of things that the old one seemed no longer to count"; the grandchildren have no time for him at all.

Evelyn's mother lacks pride in her heritage, wanting to forget as completely as possible that she herself once arrived in this country by steerage. From college her daughter writes proudly that Cynthia, her roommate—whose mother is a Daughter of the American Revolution—has given her the great "compliment" of saying she'd "never thought of her as being a foreigner." Deeply satisfied that her daughter associates on equal terms with such a fine girl, Mrs. Kilde now faces a terrible dilemma. Evelyn wants to invite Cynthia home for Christmas and asks if her mother can't somehow get rid of the grandfather during the visit to spare their guest his "queer and old-fashioned ways." He would insist on having his foreign newspapers all over, Evelyn whines, and could not be depended upon to stick to "his weird version of English," but might "burst forth into uncensored Norwegian at any moment."

No less than her daughter, Mrs. Kilde wants to impress the potential visitor, but how can she send her father-in-law away at Christmas, the season in which he finds such childlike joy? The story ends back on the porch in the grandfather's musings about life in a distant past when there had been something to work for, something to look forward to, and something worth the sacrifice.

The theme of the younger generation failing to appreciate the immigrants' sacrifices and values also underlies Waldemar Ager's story "Bare mor" (Only mother) in *Jul i Vesterheimen*'s 1928 issue. As the title character trudges home, shunning the streetcar as "the young folks' conveyance," she reminisces about her childhood cabin on the prairie. After long anticipation the family had eventually built a large, fine house, which, however, never compared in coziness to that primitive cabin. Now her younger brother has inherited the farm, built a home with all the latest conveniences, and "unforgivably" converted the original cabin into a pig shelter. To console herself, the mother concentrates on planning a party for her children around an especially meaningful Old World tradition. During the weeks of preparation that follow, she is hardly able to contain her joyful anticipation. On the day of the celebration, however, she finds herself alone and bereft. Having neglected to mark the date on their calendars, her children have made other plans.

Though its sympathies lie with the mother, the story also asks the pivotal question of the immigration experience: How can a generation born into dissimilar circumstances ever understand their parents' world, especially when that world lies on the other side of the ocean?

American Nativism

The world across the sea—and its sons and daughters' commitment to it compared with their allegiance to America—is a topic that informed and inflamed the political rhetoric of the period surrounding World War I. *Jul i Vesterheimen* contains no accounts about Norwegian immigrants related to this issue, but Ernst W. Olson's 1924 "Loyalty under Fire: A Story of Yesterday" about a Danish settlement reflects the wrenching turmoil that characterized this turbulent era, as "Americans of certain stock sought to brand good Americans with the stigma of disloyalty."

The story's crackling indignation responds to the hurt and confusion engendered by the contemporary rhetoric, such as Theodore Roosevelt in 1915 scolding: "Many elements of our nation are not yet properly fused. The absolutely certain way of bringing this nation to ruin . . . would be to permit it to become a tangle of squabbling nationalities . . . each at heart feeling more sympathy for Europeans of that nationality than with citizens of the American Republic. [Those] who do not become American and nothing else are hyphenated and there ought to be no room for them in this country."[7] Reflecting this rhetoric, the Yankees in Olson's narrative view their Danish American neighbors as a threat. He sets the story in Burr Oak, Iowa, where he says: "Secret scavengers collected the garbage of neighborhood gossip for what they could make of it. When no evidence of sedition could be found, there were always expert shysters willing to manufacture it, [deeming it necessary] to make charges of disloyalty as a means of arousing patriotism and to dishonor the citizens in order to honor the flag." The plot follows the differing fates of Jens Carling and Tom Quigley. As the Danish American Carling goes off to war eager to defend his country, Quigley, the Yankee rich man's son, manages to get a deferment and, staying behind, tries to win away Carling's girlfriend, Doris Madsen. His efforts intensify when Carling is reported missing in action, and the story pointedly faults his failure to grasp the "old ethical law still written in the conscience of the Northern races . . . , the old-fashioned faithfulness unto death," that keeps Doris true to Carling.

Meanwhile the town's old Danish Lutheran pastor Rasmussen delivers a sermon on Christ's words "Blessed are the peacemakers," which prompts certain elements of the community to brand him an "un-American renegade" who takes orders directly from the Kaiser. Vandals cover Rasmussen's church with graffiti: "Hun-American," "Damn the peacemakers," and "Reverend Rascalson preaches by order of the Kaiser." The community's Danish Americans find the last charge unfathomable. Their ancestors, after all, had fled their native province of Schleswig when the Germans took it over. But common sense holds little sway in the prevailing atmosphere.

The story accurately reflects the pro-German sympathies some suspected the Scandinavians of harboring because their home countries had remained neutral. The fact that the Scandinavian cultures observed Lutheranism as their state religion only added to the suspicion, for, as the 1917 issue of the *Lutheraneren* magazine observed: "Everyone knows that the Lutheran Church originated in Germany, [which] does not enhance its popularity here in America at the present time."[8]

The language issue fueled the fire even further, as Yankee community members now deemed as un-American the Danish language, which worshipers at Rasmussen's church had for decades "used without prejudice to their citizenship. . . . Every child in the settlement had attended [the American] district school, but these farmers and their wives, while engaged in developing their share of American soil to three-hundred-fold its original value, had found no time to go to school themselves."[9]

The order comes that the minister must conduct services in English. Fearing his broken English would mock the solemn service, Rasmussen posts a sign on the church: "Closed by Order of the Governor." The congregation's families subsequently worship in Danish individually at home, as the law so "generously" allows.

When the community launches a fund drive in support of the American war effort, they discover with great surprise that the Danish American population far outgives its Yankee counterpart. Then it is the Danish American community's turn to be surprised: At the Christmas Eve vespers service, Jens Carling, hospitalized all this time in France, comes marching down the church's center aisle with Doris on one arm and the soldier who had saved his life on the other. Both soldiers wear the prestigious French War Cross, and now each receives one of the stars that were that evening to be placed on the church's flag in their memory.

Stacking the deck against the Yankees in the same way that some Scandinavians felt contemporary political rhetoric had been stacked against them, the story emphasizes the insanity of the wholesale suspicions leveled against immigrant groups. Though the Scandinavians suffered far less of this discrimination than did other ethnic groups, the story reveals that they did not entirely escape the sting of the period's zealous nativism.

Into the Melting Pot of Financial Ruin

Like members of the Burr Oak Danish American community, Scandinavians had originally settled with pockets of people from their own home area, but by the 1930s their pattern of settlement had grown more wide-spread, and many had moved to larger cities. *Jul i Vesterheimen*'s fiction re-flects these changes. For example, its narratives in the 1930s draw less at-tention to the Norwegian heritage of the characters, who frequently bear generic American names rather than distinctly Norwegian ones.

Though all the post-1931 stories appear in Norwegian, their plot situa-tions seem more universally American, with urban settings outnumbering placements in homogeneous Norwegian farm communities. The frontier, when it appears, has moved farther west and north. Strong female characters lead several of the narratives, reflecting recent progress in women's rights. Written in the wake of the 1929 stock market crash, many stories feature the theme of economic reversal. The financial hardship the characters face, however, usually leads to their spiritual growth, and the narratives often bear witness to a revival of community that was absent during the 1920s.

Anna Dahl Fuhr's 1935 story "Severini and Company," an example of some of these characteristics, takes place in a northern Minnesota logging camp. The narrator has gone to work there because it's "better than being unemployed in Duluth." The inscription on his six-year-old calendar—"Holt and Severini, Imports, Exports, Wholesale and Retail"—recalls his past, spent in mahogany-furnished offices. He and Holt had achieved tre-mendous financial success, shooting for the moon and never shying away from even the most aggressive deals. Then came the crash of 1929. Faced with financial ruin, Holt tried to drown himself in Lake Superior. When the cold water changed his mind, he managed to rescue himself but succumbed to pneumonia. Now all that remains of Severini's former life are his fine name (deliberately changed from the unmistakably Scandinavian Severin-sen) and the outdated calendar.

True to his roots, Severini holds Christmas Eve in high regard, seeing it as a special time of extra treats. Prospects seem dismal, though, with almost all his neighbors on relief. Triangle, the local combined store–post office–telegraph, would have the usual slim pickings—peas and cabbage, salt pork and bread, fresh once a week. Still, he figures he can at least buy some rice and raisins to make the traditional *risengrynsgrøt,* rice porridge.

Severini skis the two miles to the store. Counting out his pennies to pay for the ingredients, he learns that a letter has come for him. It contains par-tial repayment of a long-forgotten loan. Feeling flush, Severini decides to ski the six miles farther into town to do some serious shopping.

Later, his money spent on purchases, Severini's backpack hangs too heavily to get all the way back home. Unloading it a little at a time at each of his neighbors' homes, he leaves the pork rib at the Finn's cabin; the lutefisk, Christmas tree lights, cheese, and chocolate with the Swedish couple who live with their eight children in a tar paper shack; and the head cheese and anchovies with the Norwegian neighbor. In each case, Severini leaves the very items the recipients have missed most. Home at last, only the rice and raisins of his original purchase remain, but Severini finds the resulting rice porridge uncommonly satisfying. Beyond emphasizing the rewards of charity, the story expresses the importance of solidarity and sharing of limited goods consistent with the philosophy of the workers' movement just then gaining momentum.

The theme of redemption through impoverishment also appears in Hans Rønnevik's 1932 story, "Det gaar saa underlig til" (Things turn out so strangely). We meet Carl Olson, who lives alone in a miserable ten-by-twelve-foot shack on the Dakota prairie. The English phrases "Down and out" and "dead broke" in the Norwegian text underscore his plight. On his fortieth birthday, made all the more poignant by falling on Lillejulaften (December 23), he dejectedly concludes that life has passed him by.

Things had not always looked so bleak. Twenty years earlier he had arrived on the prairie, young and full of hope. The hut seemed a palace then, and he ridiculed his neighbors' lack of daring. In particular he mocked a newcomer named Berte. Obstinately declaring that women did not belong on the Dakota prairie, he ignored her requests for help and refused her offers of friendship.

Impatient with his own progress, he took out a loan to buy a better tractor, a bold move from which he never regained his financial footing. With no fine car to show off back in Minnesota and no new house, he now has only a debt that continues to grow. Despite his constant criticism of Berte's "old-fashioned and inferior" farming methods, she had long continued to show him kindness, even as she realized that she would never penetrate his stubborn pride. Both had suffered crop failure that spring, but while it had reduced Carl to a subsistence diet of barley porridge, Berte had saved her money during more prosperous times and managed to maintain a more comfortable lifestyle. Having seen no light in Carl Olson's cabin, she stops by on that Lillejulaften to see if he is all right. The ice between them finally

Illustration from "Maleriet" (The painting) by Georg Strandvold in Jul i Vesterheimen, *1938*

melts; he admits his errors, and she her caring for him. After all these years, they decide to wed.

The story's theme of finding spiritual renewal through material loss hinges on the historically accurate pattern of Norwegian immigrants moving on to the Dakotas for better land and greater prosperity after having initially settled in Wisconsin, Minnesota, or Iowa. Like those immigrants, Carl Olson had dreamed of returning with flashy new possessions to "show off" and brag about. Though these goals did not materialize, Olson receives the more valuable reward of having his priorities rearranged so that he can finally accept Berte's love.

The apparently irresistible theme of salvation through economic reversal appears yet again in "Maleriet" (The painting) by Georg Strandvold in the 1938 *Jul i Vesterheimen*. Henrik Karstens, a thirty-year-old immigrant from Stavanger, is a talented painter, but having never found a truly engaging subject, his work remains without distinction. The prospect of Christmas only adds to his dejection. Unable to make a living from his art, he had been forced to take an office job. Then the stock market crash forced the firm to close, and Karstens joined the ranks of the unemployed.

Walking from his stop on the elevated railway one evening, Karstens sees two needy children transfixed by a department store window display. Hand in hand they stand, in ragged clothes, as their eyes gaze longingly at the artful arrangement of dolls, electric trains, stuffed Santas, tin soldiers, building blocks, horses, skates, and skis—a world of toys that can never be theirs. The children's poverty resonates with Karstens's own dire straits. Staying with wealthy friends during the Christmas season, he feels every bit the powerless witness of all he cannot own. Karstens spends the next few days pouring his soul into a painting based on the scene. The deep empathy that radiates from the finished piece moves its viewers. The painting soon sells to an influential buyer—the first acclaimed work of a subsequently renowned artist. Like several other stories that appeared in the 1930s issues of *Jul i Vesterheimen,* Strandvold's narrative posits the need for thorough engagement in life as a prerequisite to achieving its rewards. At the same time (and also in common with much of the annual's other fiction) the story leaves no doubt that of life's rewards, spiritual growth consistently outweighs financial gain.

The Immigrant Experience Reappraised

The stories of the 1940s, as one would expect, abound with references to World War II, but at least as commonly these issues of the annual reflect a growing appreciation of the Norwegian immigrants' accomplishments and a greater sympathy for their ordeal. "Minner fra en norsk bygd i Minnesota" (Memories from a Norwegian community in Minnesota) by Knute Knutson (1941) strikes the keynote. Recounting impressions of Camp Lake Township in Swift County, Minnesota, during the 1860s, the author emphasizes the significance not only of the Norwegian, but equally of the Norwegian American heritage:

> Also we who grew up in Norwegian settlements here in America have
> childhood memories that in their own way are Norwegian, though not

Two observers of the immigrant scene, who were immigrants themselves, thought that the Norwegian Americans' initial feelings of inferiority were caused by the condescension with which they were treated by both Americans and Norwegians, and they argued that that feeling was subsiding. Addressing the experiences of the immigrants themselves, Andreas Ueland noted in 1929, "Americans knew very little about the Scandinavian countries at the time of emigration in the 1870s, and it was inevitable that when the immigrants arrived, poor and bewildered, during the height of the hot summer season in their heavy woolen homespun of strange make and not too clean after many weeks of being on the way, the Americans should consider them not only less fit, but in every respect inferior."

By 1935 Birger Osland saw a change in the attitudes of Norwegians in the home country: "The feeling of condescension, long nurtured in the souls of many 'old country' Norwegians of the educated and wealthy classes toward their emigrated countrymen, now is very much on the wane. The better understanding has come from American official recognition of the merits of the Norwegian pioneers and by the acknowledged standing of their descendants in the American community of today."

Ueland, Recollections of an Immigrant, *48; Osland,* A Long Pull from Stavanger, *228*

exactly in the same way as our fathers' were, still *Norwegian,* and Norwegian in a way that no longer has any counterpart in our present Norwegian American communities, and which—perhaps precisely because it belongs to a now vanished period of transition—shines with its own radiance.

The new sense of pride notwithstanding, the 1940s issues of *Jul i Vesterheimen* exude an air more of looking back than of future promise. An article by N. N. Rønning in the 1943 issue both exemplifies and explains this mood. "Når et folk mister sitt morsmål" (When a people lose their native language) refers to the present as a "post festum" period. The party is over for a Norwegian American literature written in Norwegian, he says, regarding this as a tragic loss and one that will damage the immigrants to their very souls. Nothing can replace the Norwegian language, he says, colored as it is by the country's rugged landscape, its rhythms, and a vocabulary that embodies the people's struggle for survival; the language is as natural as it is irreplaceable.

English simply does not resonate in the same way with the Norwegian soul, Rønning argues. Learning it, moreover, presents a significant challenge for which Norwegians are unprepared. For while both English and Norwegian arose from the same linguistic source, English subsequently added many Latin-based words whose meanings do not immediately suggest themselves to those unfamiliar with Latin. Rønning gives as an example the Norwegian word *medfølelse* (literally meaning "feeling with"), which explains itself, while the equivalent English word *sympathy* remains opaque to anyone who does not understand its Latin (and Greek) root words. The resulting linguistic uncertainty, says Rønning, has produced a rootless generation of Norwegian Americans, raised by parents who have been deprived of the leadership they could have shown in their native language.

Making matters worse is the confused state of Norwegian itself, says Rønning, specifically the large number of dialects the immigrants brought to this country, as well as the dominance of Dano-Norwegian over these dialects in both Norway and America. Growing up speaking a dialect but finding only Dano-Norwegian (the only official written language in Norway until the end of the 1890s) used at church and school, Norwegians lost confidence in their linguistic moorings.

In the face of this complicated language situation and lacking a common spoken language, Rønning seemingly leaves his argument to note with pride the Norwegian Americans' considerable accomplishment of having nevertheless produced a larger number of books than any other group of Americans besides the British. But all is not well in this realm, either, for now this fruitful period has ended. Rønning blames the premature demise of this once flourishing Norwegian American literary activity on the Norwegian American press, which has not kept up with the Norwegian language as it developed in Norway. Clinging to its cherished Dano-Norwegian as the literary expression of its heritage, it ignored the series of nationalistic orthographic changes in the homeland (in 1907, 1917, and 1938) that aimed to make the written language better reflect Norwegian speech habits (removing silent consonants—for example, *kunde* became *kunne*—and changing certain vowels—*vejr*, for example, became *vær*—and replacing the Danish infinitive marker *at* with the Norwegian *aa* or, later, *å*). The stiff, old-fashioned, convoluted style better suited to Bibles and *postiller* (sermon books), Rønning charges, persisted in the Norwegian American press and eventually strangled the once "fertile flowering" of Norwegian-language literature written in America. As a result, writers such as himself, "who once were a part of" that flourish, had come to feel "utterly abandoned."

Against this background of disappointed promise, the fiction contained in the 1940s issues of *Jul i Vesterheimen* also looks more backward than forward, yet it also portrays Norwegian immigrants who, having endured impoverished backgrounds and economic reversals, are at long last financially well established. Though some of the 1940s fiction expresses regret that their greater economic ease has distanced many Norwegian Americans from their forefathers' sound values, the stories more often celebrate the legacy the pioneers bequeathed through their hard work and sacrifice.

Einar Lund's "Solstrålen i nybygget" (The sunbeam of the settlement) in the 1945 issue belongs to this appreciative category. It sets out to explain the mystery of how an enormous, lone Norwegian spruce came to be growing next to an old wooden cross, as the only conifer in an old oak grove near Decorah's Washington Prairie Church. When asked about this unusual sight, old-timers tell the story of Ingebjørg.

Ingebjørg had accompanied her husband Per Nyjordet over the sea from Norway, enacting the familiar tale of the landowner's daughter and the cotter's son, who because of class differences met with opposition to their marriage in Norway. Though they lived quite primitively in their prairie home, their happiness overcame any physical privation. Yet at Christmastime they could not help feeling homesick. Wanting to at least give his bride a Christmas tree, Per searched the area, but finding neither pine nor spruce, settled at last for a tiny red cedar. On Christmas Eve they slowly circled this sapling, straining to sing the words of "Jeg er så glad" despite their tears.

Ingebjørg became the darling of the settlement. To return the community's goodwill, she conducted summer parochial school for the children, teaching them Norwegian language and religion.[9] When she became pregnant that fall, her pupils' mothers helped her in any way they could in gratitude for her teaching.

Meanwhile Per worried about how a newborn could thrive in their crude cabin where no ceiling boards separated their living space from holes in the roof that went clear to the sky. He saw how Ingebjørg admired the ceiling their neighbor Hans Nordset had recently installed, but saw no way

Illustration from Einar Lund's "Solstrålen i nybygget," Jul i Vesterheimen, *1945*

of replicating this accomplishment. It was the same Hans Nordset who only a few months later opened his door to find a grieving Per; Ingebjørg had died giving birth to the child. To honor her, Hans willingly tore down his much admired ceiling and used its boards to make her coffin.

People consoled themselves that despite Ingebjørg's early death, she had lived more fully than if she had stayed in Norway and married the man her father intended. Instead she had followed her heart, and her life would continue through their daughter, who had survived the birth.

Roads and a schoolhouse were later built in the settlement, and little Ingebjørg followed in her mother's footsteps and became the local schoolteacher. She married the recently arrived young minister from Norway. Hailing from the same Old Country community her parents had left, he told Ingebjørg much about her own family background. He also disclosed his own identity as the son of the man her grandfather had wanted Ingebjørg to marry.

The descendants of Per and Ingebjørg spread far beyond the local settlement to many other parts of America, where legends perpetuated Ingebjørg's memory. Unable to give his wife a real Christmas tree during her lifetime, Per had planted a genuine Norwegian spruce on her grave, and it is this tree whose enormous dimensions came to attract so much attention. The old folks said that every Christmas Eve the tree's radiance illuminated the forest, just as Ingebjørg's teaching once enlightened the settlement.

The values of the immigrants receive further affirmation in the 1948 narrative "Glade jul" by Mona Aanrud. Underscoring the power of tradition to bring personal renewal, the story tells of John and Ellen Opdal's visit to their older son's family living in California. Descendants of Norwegian immigrant parents, the senior Opdals reside in Wisconsin. They have come to California so that their younger son, William, who runs the family farm, can receive treatment for an injury he incurred during his World War II service in the Pacific.

Originally intending to stay no more than a month, they learn that William's therapy will take four times that long, and face the daunting prospect of spending Christmas far away from all they know. The outlook remains dreary until their young granddaughter, Susan, introduces them to Lois, the local librarian. Lois was also raised in Wisconsin by Norwegian parents and lives in California only temporarily. Her mother has recently died and she herself is about the age the Opdals' own daughter would be had she not died in childhood. The Opdals' granddaughter has heard nothing of her Norwegian heritage from her parents, and she finds her grandfather's descriptions of Old Country traditions enchanting. She decides to give her grandparents a genuine Norwegian Christmas. Lois enthusiastically joins in the plan, helping to make the lefse and raising the family's spirits in many other ways.

On Christmas Eve Susan surprises her grandparents by singing "Glade jul," the Norwegian version of "Silent night." This she has painstakingly learned from Lois, whose company William, too, seems very much to enjoy. Topping off the joyous evening, John Jr. announces that he has accepted a position in his company's Oshkosh, Wisconsin, branch. Now they can all look forward to spending next Christmas in Wisconsin—together.

Like the 1941 "Memories from a Norwegian Community in Minnesota," Aanrud's narrative argues the value of a Norwegian American heartland in the Midwest that has retained immigrant sensibilities. Reaffirming these values, the story also reprises the theme of spiritual rewards eclipsing those brought by financial gain, a theme that had also characterized *Jul i Vesterheimen*'s fiction during the 1920s and that reflected the ongoing debate within the Norwegian American community that pitted immigrant idealism against American materialism.

The struggle between idealism and materialism emerges even more powerfully in the 1949 story "Vegen tilbake" (The way back) by Otis S. Peterson. Here we meet Olaf Dahle, who finds happiness far more elusive than the wealth he had assumed could buy it. The son of a Norwegian immigrant father and himself now a grandfather, Dahle awaits the arrival of his grown children and their families. For the first time in years they will be coming home to the Minnesota farm for Christmas. Fred, the youngest, studies theology at Luther Seminary; Paul, now a doctor, lives in Des Moines, Iowa, with his two children; Carl, an engineer, has married and settled in Chicago; and Mary has a well-paying job in New York.

Happy at the prospect of seeing his children again, Dahle is also worried. The others all share their mother's Christian faith, from which he feels excluded, having years ago consciously rejected the religion of his immigrant father. Growing up poor, Dahle had suffered the other children's taunts for being a "Norskie" and for his father's overt Christian piety. Dahle came to associate his father's Christianity with the poverty and derision he so desperately wanted to leave behind. At this he has succeeded, having securely established himself and his family both economically and socially.

The children arrive, and Dahle can't help feeling proud. But when his wife takes down the Bible to read the gospel after the festive Christmas dinner, his usual sense of alienation takes over, heightened by shame over his inability to lead his family in the religious realm. For it is no longer for want of trying that Dahle feels excluded. Painfully aware of the way his attitude has isolated him from those he loves, he has during the last eight years made a conscious effort to regain his childhood faith, only to find it still eludes his grasp.

Leaving the dinner table to think his dark thoughts alone, he finally gains the perspective he needs. Suddenly realizing that he must put God's will before his own, he ultimately succeeds in establishing a healthy relationship to the Deity and thereby also to his family.

Standardization of the American Lifestyle

Like the story of the Dahle family, much of *Jul i Vesterheimen*'s fiction since the 1930s emphasized the value of a good education, but during the 1950s the stories often portrayed characters who had attended one of the Norwegian American Lutheran colleges. Unlike the fiction of earlier years, however, some of the selections from the 1950s suggested that growing away from old customs was a necessary, even positive development, as individuals from varied cultural backgrounds increasingly blended and the American lifestyle became more homogenized.

"Den sterkeste vant" (The strongest won) by Eyvind Johnson Evans in the 1953 issue contains the characteristically American theme of a working-class boy marrying the rich man's daughter. The distance from Norway—where a cotter's son could seldom marry a landowner's daughter—could not be clearer. Far from objecting to the match, the father in this story has long admired the young man's diligent work in the northern Wisconsin forest that the father owns, and he welcomes him warmly into the family. The couple announce their engagement, but plan to postpone the wedding until the young man fulfills a previously made commitment: he will attend St. Olaf College, supported by his own father, who is by no means a wealthy man, but who regards education as the key to his son's future success.

Young love joining initially disparate elements also features in "Naar hjertet begynner å banke" (When the heart starts beating) by Haakon Martinsen from the 1955 issue. Here, a young woman brings home for Christmas her boyfriend, who has flaunted his disdain for religion. Sitting down to Christmas dinner, the woman's father—his own eyes now too old to read fine print—asks the boyfriend read the gospel story. Instantly apprehensive, the young woman is surprised and relieved that her boyfriend not only pleasantly agrees to the task but reads the text with remarkable sensitivity.

Asking him later if he was just playacting, she learns about her boyfriend's abusive upbringing, so different from her own, and the way he has used sarcasm to mask his frustrated longing for a family just like hers. Though the story revolves around the retention of an old custom, the custom operates more to illustrate an individual character's psychology than to suggest the value of retaining traditional practices.

For contrary to extolling the virtue of retaining traditions, the fiction in the 1950s issues of *Jul i Vesterheimen* tends to demonstrate the inevitability of losing them, as well as the joy new ones can bring. In the 1954 issue, "Jul hjemme hos mor" (Christmas at Mom's) by Hilda Nelson tells of the narrator's widowed mother, who had emigrated to America to improve her children's prospects. On her first Christmas—homesick for the familiar customs of home—she invited several other newcomers to her apartment for a traditional celebration. As they circled the tree singing the old, familiar yuletide songs, the shaking caused by so many feet stopped the clocks in the watchmaker's shop downstairs. In response to his banging on the ceiling, the Norwegian dancing abruptly ended.

On that first Christmas her mother had been too poor to buy any Christmas gifts, says the narrator, remembering how eagerly she herself had looked forward to the time when they would be able to afford such a luxury. That time finally arrived several years later when a package arrived from her oldest brother, who by then had a job in the city: "Though I recall with joy every Christmas from my childhood home, that American Christmas when we gave each other presents for the first time holds a special place among those memories that I will never forget." In its wholehearted embrace of the American commercial Christmas, this story belies the dire warnings spoken by other Norwegian American voices of the "spiritually deficient," "costly and store-bought" Christmas that would "destroy the family structure."[10] At the same time the story could hardly state more clearly the stifling effect tradition can have on progress: the mother's Old Country dancing around the Christmas tree literally stops the hands of time.

Similarly refusing to lament the loss of a distinctly Norwegian American culture, another story, the last to be considered here, frankly embraces the melting pot. "Det ble jul lell" (Christmas came after all) by Erik Hetle, from *Jul i Vesterheimen*'s 1951 issue, portrays the first meeting between a mother and her daughter-in-law. The young woman has no Norwegian roots, something that so upsets the mother that she actually dreads the visit, especially since the son himself will not be present. When the two women meet, though, the mother realizes their shared love for the same young man creates a powerful bond between them. The mother suggests that they read the Christmas gospel together, an experience that proves deeply moving to the mother. Seeing once again how much they share despite their lack of a common heritage, she ultimately concludes: "They could say what they would about the melting pot. It wasn't really as dangerous as they thought." Transcending the opposing views of the melting pot that stirred Norwegian American rhetoric during the previous decades, Hetle's story shows that tradition, heritage, or customs must not be allowed to stand in the way of love, the noblest of human emotions. At the same time it reflects the reality that Norwegian Americans had joined the mainstream of American life both economically and socially. Viewing themselves as simply "American," many Norwegian Americans, like the story's mother, had learned to place less emphasis on the distinguishing features of their ethnic background than previous generations had done.

While not necessarily great literature, *Jul i Vesterheimen*'s fiction remains valuable for accurately reflecting significant aspects of the Norwegian Americans' changing moods and perceptions during the first half of the twentieth century. Through the unifying theme of Christmas, its writers addressed the major issues of assimilation versus preservation and idealism versus materialism, along with the widening generation gap between the immigrants and their offspring. Core immigrant values emerge in these stories as they assert the necessity of a Christian foundation, the value of a solid education, and the mutual benefit of neighbor helping neighbor.

Julebukking
Christmas Masquerading Norwegian Style

"Julebukks! Julebukks!" my brothers yelled as they ran pell mell down the stairs into the living room. "They're coming! They're by the mailbox now."... Mama quickly disappeared into the pantry to take from the shelf some of the Christmas cookies,... freshly baked and frosted chocolate cake... and the jar she'd hidden filled with hard Christmas candy. We were beside ourselves with excitement.... They jabbered and laughed as they came in, shaking the snow off their wraps, and tried to disguise their voices so we would be unable to guess who they were. They had tried to make this difficult with homemade disguises—stocking caps over their faces, or a dish towel with holes cut out for the eyes and nose. Coats had been turned inside out.... Papa and Mama joked with them and, of course, very soon saw it was Carl and Halvor and some of their children.... The masks were coming off as Mama handed out treats and everyone laughed about how they had tricked us. The men pulled Papa aside, and they quickly dashed down to the basement for a few minutes.... We heard hearty laughs as they came up the steps, and they were jollier than ever as they picked up the children and with many goodbyes, went on their way to another home.

Eva Mykleby Pearson, born 1921

A julebukk head displayed at the Vesterheim Norwegian-American Museum in Decorah, Iowa, in the late 1970s

So you've never gone julebukking? Neither had I before coming to Decorah, Iowa. In the late 1970s the Vesterheim Norwegian-American Museum in Decorah displayed a strange artifact.[1] Carved of wood and resembling a goat's head, it stood propped on a four-foot-long pole. Cows' horns sprouted from the top of its head and a horse-tail beard dangled from its chin. It came equipped with staples around the neck for attaching an animal hide that the user would wrap around his body. Museum curator Darrell Henning wanted to know more about how this artifact had been used and suggested I do some research on the *julebukk*. *Julebukk* literally means "Christmas goat," but most Norwegian Americans soon forgot the meaning of the term and misspellings abound.[2]

Initially I couldn't find any articles in Norwegian American newspapers or magazines that so much as mentioned julebukking, nor did the custom appear in any historical writing about the immigrants. Since few immigrants had written about the custom, most scholars assumed it hadn't survived. When preliminary results of our julebukking research (conducted by interviewing Norwegian Americans who had practiced the custom) were eventually presented to the 1993 meeting of the Norwegian-American Historical Association in Voss, Norway, most of the audience expressed surprise that the custom had continued on the other side of the Atlantic.

The reason julebukking survived in America but remained obscure may have to do with the twin Norwegian American aspirations of fitting in with the culture of their New Land and of preserving certain Old Country practices, especially at Christmastime. While the immigrants willingly publicized achievements that seemed most in keeping with middle-class status in the New Land—founding churches, hospitals, and colleges; pursuing successful careers in law, politics, and medicine; and producing serious works of literature—they tended to keep their more homespun customs to themselves, leaving precious few traces of them in the written record.[3]

Even as we at Vesterheim began our interviews in the 1980s, informants

---

The Norwegian American reticence to discuss julebukking made it difficult to find printed sources about the custom. At first I found only three accounts, all originating in private memoirs and the more valuable for covering three distinctly different periods and areas. One of them, Eva Pearson's lively account from Eldred, Minn., opens this chapter. The others are similarly evocative:

Clara Jacobson described her experience in the 1870s in Dane County, Wis.: "One evening during the Christmas holidays . . . some unbidden guests came, the so-called julebukker. . . . They were some young boys dressed in ridiculous fashion with squirrel tails for beards, etc. They did not speak but kept mum. They were treated to cake and drink. Such mummers were usually well received. I, a child of five, badly frightened, climbed into Mr. Nuave's lap and clung to his neck."

Around the turn of the century at Hatton, N.D., Aagot Raaen, writing in the voice of her sister, showed the custom: "Aagot dressed Tosten and me. She put a long white dress of her own on him . . . and made a mask out of part of a flour sack. . . . After she put the mask on Tosten, she put Mor's old black hood on his head. Tosten was a witch. She fixed me up so they would think I was a boy dressed like a girl. I had Far's old coat, cap and mittens. Mor's old skirt and Aagot's old shoes, so large they looked like boys' shoes."

Jacobson, "Childhood Memories"; Raaen, Grass of the Earth, *112*

seemed reluctant to mention their participation in the custom. Perhaps they felt embarrassed to tell about a custom that had brought them such pleasure but that flew in the face of the reserved image Norwegian Americans had prided themselves upon projecting. Gradually, as we ourselves grew more confident that Norwegian American julebukking had in fact once been quite widely practiced, our informants grew more numerous and their descriptions more eager. At last we gained a rather complete notion of the custom's variety and scope, finding a general pattern of large-scale julebukking in many Midwestern Norwegian settlements until around the 1940s, and scattered revivals during and after the 1970s.

Quite a variety of practices emerged from our interviews: Entire families might participate together, or julebukkers might go in uniform age and single-sex groups. Though a few mentioned a goat's or sheep's head, such as the Vesterheim Museum artifact that had originally sparked our quest, most described costumes not unlike the cast-off clothing and masks used on Halloween.[4] Refreshments served during the visits varied as well, from heavily favoring alcohol or avoiding it entirely. Singing or instrumental music might accompany the julebukking, but just as often did not. Everyone in a particular neighborhood might be visited, or only selected, close friends. In general the custom probably varied according to established patterns of socializing within individual communities.

Amid all the diversity, however, some elements of the practice remained consistent, notably the use of disguise and the consciousness of the custom's Norwegian origin: "We were aware that it was Norwegian while growing up [in the late 1930s and early 1940s]. We had German neighbors and I grew up knowing that Germans just didn't do this, but Norwegians do. So when we did it, we didn't stop at their homes."[5]

Multicultural Masquerading

Christmas masquerading or "mumming" has thrived in a number of European countries besides Scandinavia, including the British Isles, Germany, Austria, and Switzerland.[6] As practiced in tsarist Russia the custom figures in Tolstoy's *War and Peace,* but it was subsequently suppressed by the Communist regime. The fall of Communism brought a revival of Christmas mumming in many Eastern Bloc countries, perhaps most notably in Bulgaria, where the so-called *kukeri* tradition had managed to survive despite Communist oppression and has now become a yuletide tourist attraction drawing a steady stream of chartered tours.

Immigrant groups brought Christmas masquerading to many parts of North America: In small fishing villages in Newfoundland, the descendants of English and Irish immigrants continue to this day to go *mummering* or *janneying;* a radio station in St. John's even plays a song about the custom throughout the Christmas season.[7] Christmas masquerading once occupied a central place in the Christmas revels of New York City, but that was far from the only place: in Rock Springs, Georgia, and Randolph County, Alabama, English and Scots-Irish immigrants used to go "a-sernatin'"; in southern Pennsylvania and the Shenandoah Valley of Virginia, German immigrants masqueraded as *belsnickles;* and in Philadelphia, immigrants of English descent went mumming.[8]

All these practices resemble the Norwegian American julebukking enjoyed in the Upper Midwest. Common to the locales in which North American Christmas mumming endured is the characteristic of being predominantly settled by a single immigrant group in an isolated area. These features continue to characterize the custom as practiced today.

A Julebukker's Initiation

Some Norwegian Americans in Spring Grove, Minnesota, have ardently retained the julebukking custom, and during Christmas 1985 they kindly invited three outsiders to join them: Vesterheim's Darrell Henning, Bill Moore of the University of Minnesota Art Museum, and me. We acquired a revealing initiation into the art of Christmas Fooling, as they also call the custom. We learned that veteran julebukkers abandon their usual coats and boots since these can quickly give them away, they wear gloves or mittens because hands can betray identity as easily as faces, and they adopt a limp or slouch or otherwise disguise their walk and stance to avoid being identified by characteristic body movements.

These instructions we received early that evening at the home of the town's veterinarian, where we were joined by a local farmer and his two teenaged daughters. Costumed to give no clue of our identities, eight of us set out, switching off our car lights as we entered the driveway of the first

Julebukker, Vesterheim, 1988

farm to heighten the surprise of our arrival and to prevent the car's identity from giving away ours. Before going inside, we ran around knocking on windows, making menacing faces and wild noises. Then we tramped into the house, snowy boots and all, without waiting to be invited.

We could tell by the occupants' expressions that they were surprised to see us, but also pleased to be included in that year's round of visitations. Quickly dropping other pursuits, they readily joined in the game of trying to figure out who we were. Needing no coaching, family members of all ages knew the tricks. They tried to get us to say something, hoping to recognize our voices, all the while scrutinizing every inch of our persons—poking and prodding and sometimes making rather provocative gestures and comments—all in an effort to identify us.

Before long, names were being correctly guessed and masks were coming off. No sooner had the identifications been made than plates of treats and glasses of wine appeared and made the rounds, while conversation turned to tales of other memorable julebukk adventures. Suddenly all but two of the family members scurried off to other parts of the house. They reappeared in amazingly short order disguised in costumes ranging from nightgowns, underwear, and old clothing to more painstakingly designed witch or criminal outfits. Most often the costume represented the wearer's opposite sex. Face masks ran the gamut from grocery bags or panty hose to heavy makeup or store-bought disguises. Seasoned julebukkers, this family "just happened" to have three wigs on hand as well!

Joined by our recent victims, we headed off to several other households. The decisions about whom to visit were made on the spur of the moment, and our arrival at each household came as a surprise. The inhabitants nonetheless entered willingly into the game, knowing exactly what to do and following remarkably similar patterns of guessing, serving refreshments, and conversing. Some of the participants would throw in a Norwegian expression here and there, and a few could even carry on fluent conversations; others knew none. But all seemed aware of the Norwegian roots of the julebukking custom, and remarks affirming Norwegian heritage abounded.

By 9:30 our group had grown to fifteen, with our ages ranging from fourteen to seventy-five. One twenty-six-year-old woman declared that she had been julebukking since before she was born—her pregnant mother, disguised as Santa Claus, had even been complimented on the authenticity of "his" paunch! By now we had sampled glasses of champagne and red and white wine (no wonder the face masks were getting so warm!), and we'd eaten an amazing array of meats, cheeses, candies, nuts, pretzels, and popcorn, all produced with remarkable speed and served with well-practiced ease.

Making our last visit at 10:30, we found only the housewife still up, her husband having retired after an exhausting workday. Much to my amazement, that did not keep her from rousing him out of bed to join in the "fun" of helping discover our identities; even more astonishing, he didn't seem to mind, but joined right in the festivities as eagerly as any of our earlier victims.

That not all Spring Grove residents welcome the practice equally enthusiastically, however, is suggested by the commonly used alternative term: "julebugging."[9] Nor have all Spring Grove residents even heard of the practice. The story is told of a startled homeowner who pushed a disguised visitor off his doorstep and sicced his dogs on the rest of the group. Only later did he learn from his wife about the custom of julebukking and that the visitor he'd pushed had been a woman! A more recent story told in Spring Grove tells of julebukkers dressed up in their most fanciful gear stopping to aid a motorist who had slid off the icy road. (Julebukkers don't let things like inclement weather stand in the way of having fun.) In their eagerness to help, they forgot how they looked, remembering only when the terrified man waved them off, more alarmed than he'd been about going into the ditch.[10]

Julebukking tends, then, to remain confined to close-knit groups within communities.[11] Its continued practice suggests that it must fill some social need besides merely providing entertainment. Fun can be had in any number of ways, a folklorist would say, but the ways we choose reveal our needs, desires, and values. What does julebukking reveal?

The Hows and Whys of Julebukking

In the preindustrial peasant society julebukking—essentially a tour of inspection through the community—provided an opportunity for neighbors

---

Marion Oman (born 1917), Waseca, Minnesota, writes:

I was born and raised in a Norwegian settlement in Moland Community near Kenyon, Minnesota. My mother, Maria Aase Benson, was a fun-loving soul. On crisp, clear winter nights she would organize a group of folks to go julebukking, either the week after Christmas or the week after New Year's. She preferred going to a house where a party was being held. All julebukkers would ride in a horse-drawn sleigh. Everyone would dress in goofy clothing, face covered with a stocking with holes for eyes, nose, and mouth. Some heads were covered with scarves. We would quietly walk to the door of the house and rap loudly. In we would walk, never saying a word, making our way around in the house. We would answer questions in falsetto voices and perhaps sing a song. If and when we were recognized, off came the face mask! Then we were treated to cookies and wine. Afterward, we'd go off to the next farm where there was a light in the house. Though we arrived by horse-drawn sleigh in the earlier years, later we traveled by car.

Letter to the author, April 7, 1997

to check on each other's timeliness and proficiency in making Christmas provisions. To a certain extent this function remains, as the custom allows neighbors to drop in unannounced, see each other's homes, and sample each other's food and drink. While the tour is now just for fun, in the traditional, interdependent peasant community it gave assurance that each family complied with social norms and could, therefore, be relied upon in times of trouble.

The custom's most prominent feature, reversal—the cross-dressing and outrageous behavior—nowadays provides fun and entertainment. But in the enforced confinement and conformity of earlier times, it provided a much needed release, permitting participants a rare opportunity to act just as they pleased, protected by the cloak of anonymity.[12]

The pattern of reversal emerges most clearly in the julebukkers' apparently unconscious choices of costume: they'll go outdoors in clothing normally reserved for the indoors or private (nightgowns, underwear, aprons, dish towels) and wear their clothing inside out or back to front, shoes on the wrong feet, and so on. Normally painstakingly well-kept in public, Norwegian American julebukkers appeared in worn and tattered clothes with faces dirtied by charcoal or heavy makeup.

Participants reversed their identities as well, either by becoming the opposite sex or emulating criminals, village idiots, or other types far removed from their normal selves. Tall people stooped and short people attained height from grocery boxes on their shoulders or wooden blocks underneath their feet. "I remember wearing my father's WWI Army uniform one year, and my husband walked on small wedges inside his boots, thus confounding people with his height," reports Elaine Nelson (born 1930) of Holmen, Wisconsin.[13]

Julebukkers reversed their behavior, too; the adjectives "crazy," "ridiculous," "foolish," and "silly"—terms not typically associated with Norwegian American demeanor—abound in their descriptions of the custom: "One Julebukking I remember well. Mother, a roly poly short person, dressed in a well-padded suit of grey underwear. When we stopped at the home of the Moland buttermaker, he whooped, grabbed Mother, put her over his knee and spanked her! When he found out who she was, he was mortified! But that was the fun of going julebukking, and Mother had a good story to tell after that."[14]

Abandoning their usual good manners, they barge into homes without knocking, remain silent when spoken to, and leave messy footprints on formerly well-scrubbed floors. Dropping their normal reserve, they dance around, play taunting tricks, and frighten children. "If they'd see something they wanted," says one informant, "they'd just eat it right off your table."[15] Those being visited acted in uncharacteristic ways as well, taking extraordinary liberties as they touched, stared, and asked pointed questions in their attempts to unmask the visitors.

The fact that the ritual involves two different phases is significant. While the first emphasizes the already mentioned reversal of appearance and behavior, the second phase—after the masks have come off—abandons the deception. People assume their customary roles and identities, politely serving and accepting refreshments and engaging in pleasant conversation. The feeling of solidarity grows as the participants merge roles and the original visitees join the visitors on their further rounds.[16]

One man's description from his 1990 julebukking session (initiated by Lee Grippen of Caledonia, Minnesota, and including friends from Norskedalen near Coon Valley, Wisconsin) illustrates the custom's reversal and two-part structure:

> The third place we came to, the people weren't home—well, we didn't think they were—so we went in. The doors were open, lights were on and everything. We went in, but we couldn't find anyone. So Lee Grippen said, "Let's turn everything upside down so they know we've been

Several people recall being terrified by the julebukks as children. Elaine Olson, Coon Valley, Wisconsin, says: "I can remember being a child in Timber Coulee and I was really scared when my folks would get julebukkers. They would come tramping on the porch and making all this noise, and I didn't think it was too funny, really. They didn't look very friendly and they made a lot of noise and I remember we would go hide, then my sister would peek around the corner.... We were really leery of the whole thing."

Richard Staff (born 1946), Pigeon Falls, Wisconsin, had an older sister who built on this fear and convinced him that the julebukkers stayed around all year: "I believed an entire family of Julebukk lived in our attic and was deathly afraid of going upstairs alone."

Olson interviewed by the author, February 16, 1991; Staff interviewed by Steve Ringlien, April 29, 1989

here" [reversal]. So we started putting chairs up on the tables upside down and hadn't done very much of it before here the people had gone out the back way [and] came in and caught us. So they had a lot of fun—kind of surprising *us* again [exchange of roles]. Of course after we were through with that, then they joined us too and went to the next place [the roles merge].[17]

Granting an opportunity to break out of normal roles and identities, the custom afforded the immigrant residents of close-knit communities a welcome release. By becoming unknown strangers, the julebukkers briefly escaped the sharply defined expectations of the small, rural community in which they were well known and part of a cooperative economic unit: "We all depended on each other. Like at harvest, we all had to get together to harvest. In the fall of the year, when we did the threshing . . . every farmer furnished one team. . . . You needed the neighbors, you were all one . . . just like one big family even if you weren't related."[18] As necessary and desirable as this mutual dependence was, it could prove confining and build up hostility. Julebukking allowed people a chance to vent some pent-up aggression,

---

Julebukkers' memories hint at some of the socializing functions of the custom.

Ensuring timely Christmas preparations: Marlis Høines (born 1910), Cresco, Iowa, recalled, "At Christmas if we didn't have the house and ourselves clean, then the julebukk would come and harm us."

Controlling children's behavior: Hannah Lee (born ca. 1923), Austin, Minn., said: "At Christmas time parents used the story of the 'julbock' to keep the children in line. They told them that the julbock would come and get them if they were not good."

Shunning the unsociable: Individuals who do not appear to accept the good-natured behavior of the Christmas Fools may be set aside as marginal in status. Others who have achieved an unfortunate degree of ill will might be omitted from the Christmas visits or receive unmerciful treatment by the Fools: "Julebukk was quite common in our neighborhood. The pious folk, however, were ignored. In our area [Goodhue County, Minn.] this included Methodists and then there were households who simply were no fun or anti-social."

Høines and Lee interviewed by Steve Lee and Steve Mattson, Luther College folklore students, 1988;
Lloyd Hustvedt, letter to the author, December 20, 1990

without jeopardizing the carefully maintained relationships essential in the small, isolated community. At the same time, however, the custom affirms the values and accepted rules of the community since the participants ultimately revert to their ordinary roles and demonstrate their proficiency at them. Cementing their solidarity, visitors and visitees join in a shared visit to the next home.

Besides reasserting community unity, the custom also helped initiate newcomers, and still does, as the experience of our Spring Grove hostess illustrates: Home alone while her husband was making a veterinary call during their first Christmas in the community, she suddenly heard several pair of feet stomping resoundingly through their house and headed her way. Then she saw them—a group of monsters, each more frightening than the last, standing in silence, expecting her to identify them and serve refreshments. Her ready willingness to accept and participate in the custom quickened the process of acquaintance in the new community in which she and her husband now enjoy a prominent place.

Julebukking continues to promote good feeling and fellowship among longtime members of the communities where it is practiced, with the custom's annual repetition producing a backlog of shared experiences and memories to be retold year after year. As a visual experience, the custom emphasizes solidarity, at first displaying unfamiliar and even frightening disguises, then giving way to recognizable faces and gestures, familiar personalities, and expected behavior, all accompanied by the coziness of shared food and conversation.

Opposition to Julebukking

Despite the attractive, even laudable social functions of julebukking, its participants' turbulent behavior has frequently led authorities to disapprove of and even ban the practice. We have seen how the modern Christmas actually grew out of middle-class aversion to Christmas mumming in early-nineteenth-century New York; julebukking came under similar fire in the Norwegian American Midwest. An article criticizing the custom appeared in the January 11, 1894, *Spring Grove Herald*.[19] Headlined "Stop it!" and written by a certain Frank Bartholomew, the article appealed to julebukkers on behalf of the area's Yankee settlers who were unfamiliar with

Julebukkers at
Madison, Minnesota, 1908

julebukking. It urged the mummers to consider the potentially dangerous consequences of their actions:

> During the holiday season it is a common custom among our young sports to put on false face and all the outlandish toggery to be had and make the rounds of the village—and sometimes a part of the country— during the evening hours, calling at residences and other places of habitation, regardless of the wishes or condition of the inmates. This they call "Jule buk" or perhaps more appropriate, "Christmas Fools."
>
> On last Friday evening, some of these characters called at the residence of station agent D. R. Moore and they may be very thankful if they escape the penalty of their folly. As Mr. and Mrs. Moore were expecting friends that evening, Mrs. Moore answered the knock at the door and was so horrified and frightened at the unexpected sight of hideous faces that she was only able to give one scream and was instantly overcome with nervous prostration. She was so badly frightened that a physician had to be called. As a rule, these parties are composed of good boys—and we are sorry to say sometimes girls—who start out for

an evening of innocent fun and amusement, little thinking of the possible injury their thoughtlessness may inflict upon others, to say nothing of the risk they are taking themselves.

Bartholomew goes on to describe the "sad experience" of two such parties from the neighboring state of Iowa (only a few miles away) who visited local households. In one instance, three julebukkers entered a home unannounced to find a mother holding her eight-year-old daughter, who was "sick with fever." The child "was so badly frightened," says Bartholomew, "that she went into spasms, and before a doctor could be secured, she was a corpse." The young men were convicted of manslaughter and sentenced to the penitentiary.

In another instance, two julebukkers visited the home of one of their uncles who had recently been warned that burglars were abroad. When the young men in masks appeared, Bartholomew writes, "he grabbed his gun and shot them both." The article concludes, admonishing: "Don't do it any more. It is not only silly and dangerous, but a direct violation of the law."[20]

Why the vehemence of Bartholomew's objections? Possibly he, like the Puritans, reacted so strongly because the revelers' antics seemed to threaten prevailing community values. Certainly Bartholomew's condescending tone shows that he feels a difference in social order between the original English settlers in the area and the Norwegian newcomers. His article seems to be an effort to educate the immigrants by appealing to established social norms, to which the author urges the Norwegian Americans to comply.

Comments like Bartholomew's must have further convinced the immigrants that julebukking did not suit the middle-class status to which they aspired. A January 14, 1885, letter written by the Norwegian immigrant Gunnar Høst of Caledonia, in the Dakota Territory (now North Dakota), indicates a similar perception of this disjunction: "I have had a most pleasant Christmas with dancing and other fun, yes, I have even been out Christmas Fooling. What do you think of the worthy schoolmaster as a Christmas Fool?"[21]

Nor was it only the original Yankee settlers who objected to julebukking. The custom had staunch opponents among the Norwegian Americans themselves, especially within the ranks of the clergy. This clerical antagonism, no doubt, contributed to the scant attention the custom received in the historical documentation of the time. Ministers understandably objected to the revelers' excessive drinking and accompanying social abuse. Accounts of drunken julebukkers being found in snowbanks abound in julebukking lore, such as this anecdote told by the father of an anonymous Norwegian American informant (born 1910) about julebukking in Norway:

> There was a glass factory in town and they had three open-hearth furnaces. Around midnight the workers had a break for lunch and they went outside where they found a julebukker who was buried in the snow and seemed sound asleep. They were scared he would freeze to death. So to help him, they picked him up and brought him inside the factory and set him in front of the big open blast furnace. Eventually the man woke up. Seeing this, the glass workers came over and asked him if he was comfortable or if he should be closer to the fire. He said, "No thanks, kind Devil. It's fine just the way it is." Evidently the man thought he had died and gone to hell.

Still, the custom didn't always include such raucous behavior and—as noted—often provided enjoyable and even valuable socialization. This, says Luther College professor of religion R. S. Hanson, was something Mrs. Z. J. Ordahl understood. Her husband, the learned pastor of the Rush River (Wisconsin) Lutheran Church during the 1930s, condemned julebukking as a "pagan custom that had no place in a true celebration of Christmas." He therefore strictly forbade his children from participating in it. Mrs. Ordahl, however, sympathetic to her growing sons' desire to do as their friends did, would arrange for the good pastor to go to bed early, then cheer the julebukking youngsters on their merry way, whispering that what her husband didn't know wouldn't hurt him.

The Demise and Revival of Julebukking

Though the disapproving voices may account for the scarcity of references to the custom in press accounts and formal histories of the day, they did not stop julebukking. What, then, did bring the widespread practice of the custom to an end? For in most Norwegian American communities it died out during the late 1930s and early 1940s. Informants cite various causes. Some blame the increasing mobility that diluted ethnic distinctions as

neighborhoods became less homogeneous and lifestyles more standardized. Marlys (Thorstad) Charles (born 1936) says her parents practiced
julebukking all the while they lived in Sacred Heart, Minnesota, but when
they moved to Morris, which was not a Norwegian community, they didn't
dare to do it. They often talked about "going julebukk," she says, but figured they'd "hear about it" if they actually did.[22] Tracing the varying fate of
julebukking over a longer period, Elaine Nelson writes:

> My parents grew up with [julebukking] and spoke of the fun they'd
> had. . . . In the 1930s our family lived in communities with few Norwe-
> gians, thus no Julebukking. . . . Coming to Holmen, my husband's life-
> long home, gave me the chance to actually experience Julebukking. . . .
> With 1000 people at that time, this entertainment was safe and it was
> fun, not only for the visitors but also for the visitees. With a present
> population nearing 4000 and multicultured, we have few Julebukks.[23]

Other informants mention a growing suspicion of strangers that resulted from robberies and other crimes said to accompany julebukking.
Whether in practice or rumor, this suspicion grew even stronger in the wake
of World War II. Clifford Dopson of Coon Valley, Wisconsin, says: "Times
changed—people were being robbed, not in our area, but I heard about
it. . . . They were julebukks and then they'd rob the place and stuff like
that. . . . It takes just a few people to spoil things." Inez Rude of Blair, Wis-

---

*Arnold Elvestrom (born 1907), Blue Earth, Minnesota, elaborates on
the delights of the horse-drawn sleigh:*

The sleighs were usually painted dark green with some color trim and the sled runners were
usually orange or red. They were a beautiful sight and were also used to go to church and
town in. The sled horses would sometimes be decked out in holiday finery with jingle bells
and plumes or tassels on their heads. They would put hay bales in the back of the sled and
you could get 10–15 people in there. . . .

Naturally the young men would have their girlfriends along, because they too liked the
fun. If you had your girl sitting with you on a bale of hay and singing with the rest of the
guys, you were enjoying yourself.

Quoted by Charles in "Art of Julebukking"

---

consin, adds: "After the World War started, julebukking wasn't allowed, people didn't let other people in. They were suspicious, too, because more and more people were moving into the area."[24]

Several informants also blame the effects of technology, as cars and tractors replaced the more romantic horse and sleigh: "It stopped when we quit horses and went to tractors, about 1937–38. It was the horses that made it, hearing the bells on them. That was the fun of it—going jingling with the bells in the moonlight. Julebukking seemed to go out with the horses."[25]

Still others point to the end of prohibition, which eliminated the need to use julebukking as a legal way of obtaining alcohol. According to Lloyd Hustvedt, executive secretary of the Norwegian-American Historical Association, who knew the custom growing up in Goodhue County, Minnesota: "[Julebukking] flourished during prohibition because the brewing of Christmas 'øl' was legal. Those who did this received 'julebukker' from far and wide, to the point of exploitation. I suspect that the repeal of the Volsted Act put a first dent into the practice."[26] Hustvedt also suggests that as Halloween developed, it, too, may have helped diminish julebukking. Arnold Elvestrom similarly mentions the competition of other pastimes: "People stopped julebukking when television and radios and other forms of entertainment became more widespread."[27]

In their descriptions of julebukking, informants often inject a note of social criticism, contrasting today's lifestyles with those of a society more hospitable to julebukking. They note the increased dangers of the present compared with the innocence of times past, and compare today's wastefulness with the resourcefulness and self-sufficiency of former times.[28] Not least they differentiate the isolation and alienation of the present from the neighborliness, cooperation, and mutual dependence of earlier days. As Orville Bakken laments: "Everyone is so independent now. It was like one big family even if you weren't related in those days. . . . Television has ruined it. Now you can sit home and entertain yourself. Then you went with each other and had fun."[29]

With nostalgic longing for the kind of society where julebukking once thrived, more and more communities and individuals are reviving the custom's infectious fun. Some Sons of Norway lodges have found julebukking a popular activity, and Decorah's Vesterheim Museum has begun incorpo-

Julebukking at Vesterheim, 1988

rating the masquerade into its annual Christmas festival, always held the first weekend of December.[30]

A few groups are even reinventing the practice to fit local needs. This is a significant development to folklorists, since the reinvention or evolution of a custom identifies it as one that is growing to fit an existing need. Proof of this development came in a March 16, 1994, letter from Sheryl Hammel, telling of julebukking in Denver, Iowa. Snapshots accompanying the letter showed a dozen adults wearing festive sweatshirts reading "julebukk" ordered to celebrate this group's tenth anniversary. Hammel writes:

> Our julebukking started in 1983 with two couples who began the night with a little information about julebukking. Ours has always been associated with some element of surprise, a goal of socialization and fun mixed with singing Christmas carols. We had surprises the first couple of years, going to people's homes unannounced, singing and inviting them to come along. Over the years, however, it has become somewhat more structured. We usually gather at someone's home, practice and warm-up on some music and then set out spreading Christmas cheer.

Over the years, we've gone to the nursing home yearly, to shut-ins, wheelchair-bound community members. One year, a three-year-old girl from Denver [Iowa] was undergoing chemo[therapy] and we went to her home. One elderly man, who was bedbound for the last three years, was visited by us for two years. We stood outside and sang and one of us rang the doorbell. His wife invited us in, stating that he could hear better if we came in, so 16 of us streamed through their home to his bedroom. As we stood around his bed, he sang along, mouthing the words. In Dec. '92 when we went to his home, his condition had deteriorated. She again invited us in and we stood around his bed. He was unable to sing along, but he was alert and had tears streaming down his cheeks. We had a tough time getting through the songs, but it was so gratifying for us.

We have three or four homes we go to regularly. Two of them are parents of some of the participants. They greet us with treats, drinks, hot cider and sing along. We've gone in good weather, icy, foggy or snow conditions. We usually go out a week or two before Christmas. Some of the people we usually see even ask us ahead of time when we're coming so they will be home and ready.

People have been very gracious and excited to have us come and await our return. We have invited a variety of people to come with us. We usually return to the hosts' home, have a warm meal and gift exchange.

We realize it is not the true or genuine way to follow the julebukk custom, but it has worked wonderfully for us.

Not true? Not genuine? On the contrary. Although Hammel's group wears neither costumes nor masks and their activity differs little from ordinary Christmas caroling, their self-identification as "julebukkers" seems to convey a deeper layer of meaning to everyone involved. "True" and "genuine" in its own right, their practice is a wonderful example of a traditional custom adapting to a new context and function. Is there any better way for a custom to survive?

The function of julebukking has changed over time. In an era of mutually dependent farm communities, Christmas masquerading gave people opportunities for social control and release, while also fostering a renewed commitment to neighbors, family, and friends. Today julebukking provides mostly entertainment, but continues to offer group initiation and fellowship. Readers who have not yet gone Christmas Fooling ought to give it a try!

Lutefisk, Lefse, Rømmegrøt
The Culinary Emblems of Ethnicity

Norwegian dishes have been a source of much enjoyment in thousands of homes throughout America since the first descendants of Norway came to this country. Particularly at Christmas...have these good things been so regularly and generally used that they have become a part of the happy and proper observance of the event.

George Mohn, *Cook Book of Popular Norse Recipes*, 1924

Ethnic foods provide a strong bond for immigrants in a strange land, especially when enjoyed together with those who share their roots. Practical considerations usually make these delicacies unavailable on a daily basis, however, and while the early Norwegian American pioneers tried to prepare the dishes familiar to them, purely Norwegian meals had all but vanished by the end of the nineteenth century. Thus, Elisabeth Koren writes in her diary on February 3, 1854: "We cannot say that we live so exceptionally well here. The dishes vary from boiled pork to fried pork, rare to well done, with coffee in addition (milk when we can get it), good bread and butter. . . . But our appetites seldom fail." Still, she cannot help adding on June 15: "Oh that I had some new potatoes and a little mackerel from home!" Three days earlier, Koren had decried "this land of pork."[1] The prominence of pork also figures in the memoirs of Mary King (born 1869) about her prairie childhood in Minnesota and South Dakota: "We always had plenty

A pioneering effort in keeping Norwegian food traditions alive in America, especially at Christmastime, was made by two sisters who published the women's magazine *Kvinden og Hjemmet* (The Woman and the Home) in Cedar Rapids, Iowa, from 1888 to 1947. This monthly magazine achieved the largest Midwest circulation of any Scandinavian periodical. Ida Hermanna (born 1853) and Wilhelmine Amalie (born 1857), who emigrated from Ringerike with their parents in 1870, advised their readers as to which stores sold lutefisk and other Scandinavian Christmas foods. Hermanna and Amalie maintained close contact with Scandinavia and arranged for implements and ingredients to be shipped over to America, enabling their readers to order goro, krumkake, and waffle irons, pastry tracing wheels, rolling pins for flatbread and lefse, cheese planes, and other specialty items rare in the United States.

to eat, but it was plain, substantial food and nothing fancy; salt pork, bread and butter, potatoes and milk were the main articles of our diet."[2]

The difficulty of obtaining familiar Norwegian foods on the prairie also emerges in an 1895 newspaper notice placed by K. K. Hande, advertising for an apprentice from Slidre, Valdres, for his Spring Valley, Minnesota, blacksmith shop: "Free lodging with all the food you can eat—of American food. Don't expect *rakefisk* [fermented fish] or *gammelost* [sour milk cheese]. *Spekekjøtt* [cured meat] and *rømmegrøt* can be gotten occasionally, but they are delicacies and not as good here as in Slidre."[3]

Given the scarcity of the familiar foods from home, Norwegian Americans turned to special occasions for ethnic meals and began concentrating their efforts on the Christmas season. This seasonal focus, along with the Scandinavian tradition of abundance at Christmastime, produced the rich yuletide feast that their descendants continue to enjoy. A few delicacies became both ethnic markers and definers of the season. How and why did these foods achieve that distinction?

Lutefisk

The roots of lye-soaked cod go back at least to the Middle Ages, when it came into prominence as an Advent fasting food. Though its significance subsequently diminished in Norway (and has only recently revived), for

Norwegian Americans the dish has always held special meaning. Many contemporaries no doubt share memories similar to those of Crystal Lokken (born 1929): "We had lutefisk and lefse at Christmas time. It was available in barrels at the local grocery store. Grandma would make a white sauce to accompany it, and boiled potatoes. I remember Grandpa rolling the lutefisk and boiled potatoes into his lefse and eating it with great satisfaction, accompanied by a loud munching sound!"[4]

Mrs. Andrew A. Olson soaking lutefisk at home in St. Paul, 1936

Meat department managers of Midwestern grocery stores say that once the lutefisk season starts in November, they can sell any quantity they can obtain, usually between five and six hundred pounds. Not only will Norwegian Americans drive great distances and spend much money for the delicacy, they'll risk their lives on icy roads going to lutefisk dinners in faraway communities. Then they'll turn around and purchase intricately cross-stitched, gothic-lettered samplers proclaiming "Lutefisk, the gift of cod that passeth all understanding," along with myriad T-shirts, cartoons, jokes, songs, and bumper stickers ridiculing the dish and anyone who would willingly consume it. Clearly lutefisk is more than just something to eat.

The early Norwegian immigrants went without lutefisk until almost the end of the nineteenth century, when dried cod began being shipped from Massachusetts.[5] Individual families would then take it upon themselves to make the final preparations at home, each autumn buying sheets of stockfish—as the dried fish is known—and soaking it in lye as part of their Christmas preparation. In the mid-1920s, prepared lutefisk, all ready for cooking, appeared in stores,[6] and during the 1930s Minnesota lutefisk processing companies experienced phenomenal growth. In a typical year, Olsen Fish Company, only one among at least eight others, soaked one hundred thousand pounds of dried cod. Through the 1950s many families continued to process their own lutefisk, passing down the directions orally, using recipes never written down, and always looking forward to the meal with great anticipation.

But "with the anticipation came also a pleasant tension," says Gary Legwold in his book on lutefisk; "one mistake in your soaking process and you ruined the meal."[7] This uncertainty, along with America's beginning romance with convenience foods and the disappearance of the generation who knew the process, led to a sharp decline during the 1950s in the number of families able or willing to prepare lutefisk themselves, whether presoaked or not.

The declining popularity of lutefisk (and other traditional foods) had actually begun years earlier, as this December 27, 1925, letter from Andreas Ueland suggests: "We had the customary Norwegian dishes the evening of the 23rd—the lutefisk, rulle pølse [sausage], goat cheese, gammelost [old cheese], lefse, flatbrød, rice mush, all excellently prepared by Inga, each dish sniffed at more or less by all except me."[8]

Nor has this scorn abated. Writing in 1997, Avis Holmgreen Ruhnke of Fond du Lac, Wisconsin, says, "None of my girls or their families, or my husband will eat the lutefisk with me as they never acquired the taste for it."[9] Joyce McCracken of Macomb, Illinois, echoes, "Both my daughter and I have lutefisk in our freezers, but we gave in to my grandsons' pleas of 'No, please, no lutefisk this year.'"[10]

Lutefisk suppers served by churches and Sons of Norway lodges address this generational gap, maintaining tradition as well as providing a "lutefisk fix" without subjecting the entire family to it. (In much the same way, restaurants in Norway have taken over the preparation and serving of the newly popular lutefisk.) Recognizing the less-than-enthusiastic reception that lutefisk often receives, churches and lodges wisely offer *kjøttkaker* (meatballs—more closely resembling smaller, rounder Swedish ones than the Norwegian variety) as an alternative dish to extend the fellowship of their meals to a broader base.

But the Norwegian American church basement dinners, prepared and served by volunteers, provide much more than a culinary experience, having in themselves become a significant folk tradition. One worker put it this way: "Preparing for this dinner and working here now bring back the tradition of hard work and loyalty to the community. . . . People don't necessarily eat lutefisk for the taste. They eat it as a rite of passage each year, a tradition to pass on to their children. It's a reminder of the courage it took to come to America."[11] To ensure that this message gets passed along, some make the dinner an intergenerational affair by recruiting younger family members to help with serving, a feature everyone appears to enjoy.

Chrystene Weedman of DeForest, Wisconsin, writes, "Our congregation still has an annual lutefisk dinner for the public. This past November we served 1650 people."[12] With numbers like that, church dinners have taken up the slack in lutefisk orders, and Minnesota currently produces more lutefisk than all the Scandinavian countries combined, says Legwold, basing his information on an interview with Mike Field of Mike's Fish and Seafood in Glenwood, Minnesota. Field processes some 50,000 pounds of stockfish each season, from which he makes 350,000 to 400,000 pounds of lutefisk.[13] The stockfish comes from Norway's Lofoten Islands, where it is dried in the air and sun on wooden frames (*heller* or *stokker,* therefore the name *stokkfisk*), in a climate perfectly suited—too cold for insect damage, but not cold enough to freeze the fish—to produce a shoe-leather-hard product. Wrapped in burlap and shipped in hundred-pound bales, the leathery stockfish looks more like a load of shingles than something to eat. After arriving on the East Coast, the fish comes by train to Minneapolis; then in August and November Field trucks it up to Glenwood, where he unloads the bales and soaks the fish for three to four days in water-filled livestock tanks. During the company's busiest time, from August through February, Field stacks the fish tanks three deep and hires eight people to tend them.

After the first water soaking, the workers drain the tanks and refill them with a solution of lye water. They stir the fish twice daily, keeping them in the lye solution for eight to ten days, depending on their size. Field says he goes through two and a half tons of lye each season. With luck, the alternating lye soaks and water rinses produce beautiful, flaky white fish.

Much can go wrong, however, and it is the chancy nature of the dish's outcome that gives rise to much of the humor that surrounds lutefisk. Lutefisk humor also derives, says Lise-Lunge Larsen, from the immigrants' initial unease about fitting into American society. Jokes about this most distinctive Norwegian food developed as a coping mechanism, she argues, helping the immigrants deal with hostile criticism, while strengthening their own sense of group identity; laughing at it themselves relieved embarrassment and eased relations with the dominant Yankee population.[14] (This origin, of course, helps account for the lack of a counterpart to the self-deprecatory lutefisk humor in Norway.)

The role of humor in strengthening relations within the immigrant group itself recently became an item of personal interest to folklorist Roger L. Welsch. While being initiated into his fiancée's family's lutefisk-eating ritual, Welsch puzzled over the predinner joking about the dish. Gradually the realization dawned on him that "for this family's single most important meal of the year, they were about to eat something they not only didn't like, but actually found disgusting."[15] Jokes flew thick and fast, he says, as they awaited the feast, with the stories growing "increasingly offensive." One told about the old days when the dried, boardlike sheets of cod would be stacked in front of the country store, where the town's dogs would "add their own special contribution" to lutefisk's distinctive taste. Another recounted the conversation between two old Norwegian settlers that took place outside the store: One commented that the other's dog must have a

Fish drying on heller *or* stokker, *Lofoten Islands, 1994*

Soaking lutefisk in preparation for the seasonal rush, Lyons Food Products, Golden Valley, Minnesota, 1971

bad case of worms since he was constantly licking the base of his tail. No, replied the other, the dog had been eating lutefisk and was merely trying to get rid of the awful taste.

Learning later that the family recited the very same stories and gags every year at the Christmas meal, Welsch realized that the humor belonged to the ritual every bit as much as the food itself did. He also observed that, as in Norway, the method of eating lutefisk displays considerable variation in the United States, even within a single family. People eat it with a fork, plain or mixed with potatoes, on bread, or mixed with potatoes and butter on a large sheet of lefse rolled up like a burrito and eaten with the hands.

Yearly repetition of the Christmas dinner ritual provides continuity; whatever other changes the family has experienced in the year past—death, birth, marriage, divorce, prosperity, economic reverses—the lutefisk remains constant. Nor, says Welsch, could the Christmas meal ever be mistaken for any other meal of the year. It can therefore never be eaten casually.

Although the humor that accompanies lutefisk seems to suggest a unique talent for self-torture on the part of Norwegian Americans, they are by no means alone. Most ethnic Americans eat foods that they don't necessarily find appealing, as an affirmation of their heritage. Never on the daily dinner table, these foods appear only on ritual days when ethnicity is being deliberately observed.

Strongly associating lutefisk with their heritage, many Norwegian Americans discover with surprise how rarely Norwegians (at least until recently) eat lutefisk. Indeed, many in Norway dismiss the dish as lowly peasant fare. Norwegian Americans, by contrast, see lutefisk as "a touchstone," says Bill Andersen (president since 1977 of North Minneapolis's Olsen Fish Company): "It's a reminder of the best of times and the worst of times. It's a food that touches us all, it reminds us, and takes us home. . . . When you eat lutefisk, there's a click in the head—all those fond memories of Christmas—the talking around the table, the friends coming over and so on."[16]

Welsch agrees, saying that lutefisk's ability to evoke times past gives the dish a religious aura almost equaling that of the Norwegian prayer that begins "I Jesu navn . . . ," which often accompanies the Christmas meal. Once recited as part of a larger language repertory and later the only Norwegian-language item remembered, then eventually haltingly read or said by rote in a language no longer understood, the prayer further confirms the ethnic

For many Norwegian Americans, this table prayer is still part of the Christmas Eve tradition:

> *I Jesu navn går vi til bords*
> *å spise, drikke på ditt ord.*
> *Deg, Gud, til ære, og oss til gavn.*
> *Så får vi mat, i Jesu navn.*
>
> In Jesus' name we go to the table
> to eat and drink at thy word.
> Thou, God, to honor and ourselves to gain.
> Now we shall eat, in Jesus' name.

association of the meal and venerates the early immigrants' deep Christian faith.

Lutefisk evokes that faith and symbolizes Norwegian tenacity in the face of hardship as the family recalls its humble past. But the lutefisk ritual does even more, says Welsch. It also recognizes the family's migration and celebrates the distance it has traveled from those impoverished circumstances. As such, lutefisk has become a powerful expression of what it means to be a successful Norwegian living in the New World.[17] (These associations—in addition to clever marketing—may also account for lutefisk's recent surge in popularity in an increasingly multicultural, internationalized, and affluent Norway.)

The connection between lutefisk and former times of hardship is the basis for some of the irrepressible lutefisk humor, such as this common takeoff on "'Twas the Night before Christmas":

> Tvas da night before Christmas and each little Norsk
> Vas dreaming of lutefisk, lefse and torsk.
> Our stockings had holes and dey hung by da door;
> Dere vasn't no fireplace because ve vas poor.[18]

Humor of this sort is now so much a part of the lutefisk experience that readers may not realize how recently it appeared or recognize its direct connection to marketing the product. Though the decline in sales of lutefisk following the 1950s had been effectively reversed by church and lodge suppers, fewer than one hundred tons annually were being exported to the Midwestern states by the 1980s. Then, as Americans grew increasingly in-

Lutefisk TV dinner, available at a local grocery in Decorah, Iowa, 1999

terested in their ethnicity, the media both responded to and fed the trend. Books, poems, and jokes linked the funky fish with Nordic identity, while humorous bumper stickers and T-shirts (demanding "Legalize Lutefisk" and warning "This vehicle brakes for Lutefisk suppers") promoted it as a fun food.[19] Between the growing ethnic interest and the clever marketing, the volume of stockfish exported from Norway to America was once again on the rise. Appealing advertising and increased contact between Norway and Norwegian America achieved similar results in Norway, which, as we've noted, is now experiencing a lutefisk boom of its own.

Still, there's no escaping the central fact about lutefisk—it *smells,* as Joyce McCracken (born 1927 in Norman County, Minnesota) once experienced so memorably:

About two years after our [1950] marriage we were living in Lincoln, Nebraska. We could not afford a car so travel for any distance was by city bus. Christmas time was again approaching and Christmas was synonymous with lutefisk, even though I was not particularly fond of it. I managed to locate a shop where I could buy some. Having made my purchase and boarded the city bus for the homeward trip, I could not help but notice the puzzled looks of the other passengers. The rather bulky package of fish was loosely wrapped in butcher's paper and definitely not the neat, fresh frozen and odor-free package which we can find in the stores today.[20]

Expanding on the theme of lutefisk *lukt* (odor), Avis Holmgreen Ruhnke remarks: "There are many 'Lutefisk and Lefse' suppers throughout Wisconsin at this time of year. They say if you don't know where they are, just follow your nose; you can smell lutefisk for miles. It isn't a pleasant smell. Something like boiled ammonia. Only a Norwegian could love it!"[21] Lutefisk's olfactory assault naturally also figures prominently in lutefisk humor, such as Don Freeburg's "Lutefisk Lament":

> From out in the kitchen an odor came stealing
> That fairly set my senses to reeling.
> The smell of lutefisk creeped down the hall
> And wilted a plant, in a pot, on the wall.
>
> The scent skipped off the ceiling and bounced off the door
> And the bird in the Cuckoo Clock fell on the floor.[22]

Ridicule and upturned noses notwithstanding, lutefisk is here to stay. Consider the experience of Jo Ann Kana of Fargo, North Dakota. Describing her struggle to continue Nordic Christmas Eve traditions in the face of her family's annual "griping about lutefisk" and her having to "watch everyone pass it under the table," she eventually decided to drop the dish from the holiday menu: "I thought everyone would be happy. When the food was passed I heard, 'Where's the lutefisk?' I informed them I was tired of hearing them carry on about it. [The] answer to that was a chorus of voices saying, 'But, Mom, that's a tradition.' Needless to say, the griping is back, along with the lutefisk."[23]

Lefse and Flatbrød

While lutefisk requires some getting used to, most people take an immediate liking to lefse, Norway's unleavened soft bread. Somewhat thinner than a commercially produced tortilla, lefse rounds are also much larger and softer than the Mexican bread. It has a mottled brown and white surface because of uneven cooking of the flour, potatoes, or other ingredients.[24] While a great variety of lefse types exist in Norway, potato lefse dominates almost exclusively in the United States.

Like lutefisk, lefse now serves as a badge of Norwegian ethnicity, but the crispened *flatbrød* actually got here first. Crystal Lokken recalls its arduous preparation atop a polished wood-burning stove:

> We didn't have potato lefse. Grandma would make flatbread on the kitchen range. She would tie a kitchen towel around her head and go to work. It would take her all day and she made a boiler full. Then it was stored in the cellar. She would bring some upstairs, sprinkle it with water to moisten it, and warm it in the oven a bit. Then it was flexible, and you could butter it and roll it up to eat it. Mostly we enjoyed it with sugar or brown sugar. But not Grandpa. He liked it with lutefisk and potatoes. I didn't make potato lefse until after I was married.[25]

A wood-burning stove and contained storage in the cellar had replaced the Old Country hearth griddle and open storage in the *stabbur,* but the resulting bread, like a cross between crisp flatbread and soft lefse, was made, as Marion Oman (born 1927) points out, with the same specialized utensils used in Norway and still favored by Norwegian American lefse makers today: "Each Christmas Mother baked *flat brod.* . . . To roll out the dough, she used a special grooved rolling pin which was kept just for the occasion. The top surface of the big wood- and coal-burning kitchen range was cleaned and polished to a high gloss, for that was where the flat brod was baked." The recipe called for 1 heaping cup flour, 1 teaspoon salt, and 1 tablespoon shortening, to which enough boiling water was added to make a stiff dough while stirring constantly. When cooled, egg-sized balls of dough were rolled out very thin into round sheets about 15 inches across, on a piece of canvas sprinkled with cornmeal.[26] Oman continues:

> When the flat brod was placed on the stove to bake, it was carefully watched until light brown. Using a long pointed stick made from the sanded-down handle of a broom, Mother turned the flat brod in half, then in fourths and placed it on a clean towel on the warming shelf above the stove. The flat brod could be frozen and kept for weeks. When it was used, Mother sprinkled the brod lightly with warm water to make it pliable. She then cut it into fourths with a scissors and put it between the folds of a clean dish towel on the warming shelf. Was it ever delicious with potatoes and lutefisk on it![27]

Oman's mother also made lefse, and Oman distinguishes the two breads as follows: "[Lefse] was made with slightly warm mashed potatoes, flour, milk and just a little salt. It was made like flat brod but the rounds weren't as big. Potato lefse was pliable. It was eaten with butter and brown sugar. It was served at coffee parties and also for dessert. Now people use potato lefse with lutefisk but the flat brod is really much better with lutefisk while potato lefse is more of a 'sweet.'" In America the mingling of traditions from different parts of Norway together with the passage of time has resulted in a generalized practice probably unlike any single tradition originally brought from the Old Country.

Lefse was not available in stores during the 1940s and 1950s, when the custom of making it at home, handed down by oral tradition since pioneer days, began dying out. Suddenly Norwegian Americans were desperate to get it for the holidays, and, to respond to the demand, every town had at least one woman who became the local lefse maker. Like the itinerant bakers in Norway's preindustrial peasant society who traveled twice annually from farm to farm, the American lefse lady would cover three to five miles or maybe two different towns as she prepared the soft bread for the Thanksgiving and Christmas season.

Still, need exceeded demand, and lefse factories began to take up the slack. Noting an escalating interest in all kinds of ethnic foods, grocer Merlin Hoiness founded Norseland Lefse in Rushford, Minnesota, in 1981. By 1985 he was delivering lefse to more than 167 stores.

Before long, Al Spande bought the business from Hoiness; he enjoys watching people see the lefse being made. Gary Legwold's book on lefse shows why:

> Behind the glass wall, conveyer belts were moving rows of rounds. Nine rolling machines, made by Jim Humble right there in Rushford, were automatically rolling, then turning the rounds and rolling and turning again and again—about thirty-six passes per round—until the rounds were seventeen inches in diameter; they shrank down to fourteen inches by the time they were grilled.
>
> A woman with flour-covered eyelashes lifted the rolled-out lefse onto one of the half dozen gas ranges that were blazing away in blue. One baker was turning and checking and flipping the rounds, and then feeding the finished ones onto an eighty-five foot cooling conveyer. In the back a woman was sealing the cooled rounds in a plastic bag filled with nitrogen gas, which retarded spoiling but didn't affect taste. . . .
>
> Back farther in another room was a potato peeler that basically looked like a big bowl with the insides covered with metallic sandpaper. This

rough surface rubbed off the skins of a hundred pounds of spuds—in three minutes flat. Next to it was a steam cooker that cooked three hundred pounds of potatoes in forty minutes.[28]

The factory sells 250,000 to 300,000 rounds a year, says Spande, and ships to all states of the Union. He attributes the growing demand to the increasing number of women in the workforce and an aging, increasingly mobile society. More women working leaves fewer with the time to make lefse; others who used to make it are no longer able to or have moved away from communities where lefse is in demand.

When Legwold asked why lefse is important, a woman in Story City, Iowa, told him that lefse makes her remember former times in Norway, "when things weren't always so good": "Lefse is unique to our roots and more and more people are interested in their heritage. Lefse is a tradition, a thread running through the family."[29] Avis Ruhnke agrees: "Each year before Christmas my four daughters and I start thinking about our yearly traditional get-together to prepare our lefse for the Christmas season. . . . My daughters and I each have our own lefse grill, rolling pins and lefse stick. Two of us roll the lefse out and the others can bake it. . . . We usually make one hundred in a day."[30] Family ties thus strengthen the tradition, which in turn strengthens the family ties. Retirement can also have a positive—and prodigious—effect, as Chrystene Weedman writes: "I am now 86 years old and when I retired I started making lefse for sale. One year I made 137 dozen, but am slowing up as I only made 85 dozen this year."[31]

As with lutefisk, Norwegian Americans discover with surprise the dismissive attitude shown toward lefse by many Norwegians, who for their part find the Norwegian Americans' fascination puzzling. Once again the food's peasant origins cause the conflict. While most Norwegians prefer to focus on their country's phenomenal twentieth-century progress instead of its poverty-stricken past, Norwegian Americans celebrate their roots in those bleak past times and fondly credit lutefisk and lefse with having seen their ancestors through.[32] They consequently revere these foods as venerable symbols of a brave and honorable heritage.

This reverence, though sincere, allows plenty of room for laughter. Lefse humor, employing the same self-deprecatory style, echoes the mockery of lutefisk humor, deriding anyone who would willingly consume such a silly substance:

*The Englishman H. K. Daniels, writing in 1911, also remained unimpressed by lefse,
its status as a "national food" notwithstanding:*

This lefse is likewise a national food and about the most primitive of its kind as you will
ever meet with in the proverbial day's march. It is really nothing more than a dough of
flour and water, rolled out more or less thinly—and served. The surface is then coated with
margarine, or sugar, or treacle, and the dough (rolled up, like a small petition) is held in
the hand and eaten as a jam roll is occasionally devoured by our London waifs. It is a common enough food in the uplands, and I have found it very useful in the pocket when there
was any prospect of getting lost among the fjelds; for its staying, or rather intimidatory
powers are almost up to the standard of gjed ost [goat cheese]. But it must not be kept un-
duly, or it will take unto itself the appearance of old parchment, and the consistency of
shellac.

Daniels, Home Life in Norway, *278–79*

Lefse's good for many things, we can give you proof.
For tiling on the kitchen floor and patching up the roof.
Some people even use it as the soles upon their feet
And some folks even think that it is good to eat.

Chorus:
Just a little lefse will go a long way,
Gives you indigestion most all of the day.
Put it on your menu, you'll be sure to say,
Just a little lefse will go a long way.[33]

Since lefse actually tastes good, though, most of the humor about it falls
flat (so to speak). Unlike lutefisk, lefse is something people would rather eat
than laugh about.

Christmas Cookies

Fattigmann, sandbakkels, krumkaker, Berlinerkranser, goro, and *rosetter*—the
cookies produced by today's Norwegian Americans bear a remarkable similarity not only to those served by the more prosperous Norwegian immigrants a few generations ago but also to the Christmas cookies served in
Norway today.[34] Still, this is the Norwegian Christmas tradition that has
shown the most change over time. Up until the mid- to late 1800s, cele-

❖ ❖

Goro

1 egg
6 Tbsp. sugar
6 Tbsp. heavy cream
1 Tbsp. cognac
grated peel of ½ lemon
½ tsp. cardamom
1 heaping cup butter
4 Tbsp. potato flour or cornstarch
approx. 2 cups flour

Beat egg and sugar light and fluffy. Beat cream stiff. Add to egg mixture with cognac and spices. Stir in a little flour, melted butter, and remaining flour. The dough should be quite thin. Cover well and refrigerate over night.

Cut a paper pattern the exact size of the iron. Roll out dough and cut it the same size as the pattern.

Put cakes on the iron and bake on both sides on top of stove. In an electric iron both sides are baked at once. The cakes should be a delicate pale yellow. Trim edges while cakes are warm.

Krumkaker

12 Tbsp. sugar
¾ cup butter
4 eggs
1 tsp. cardamom
approx. 1¾ cups flour
3–4 Tbsp. cold water

Cream sugar and butter light and airy. Add eggs, one at a time, alternatively with flour and cardamom, mixed. Add water.

Pour a spoonful of batter on iron, press it shut and bake cookies on each side (or both sides at once on electric iron).

Curl them around the wooden cone or in a cup while they are warm.

Strømstad, Eat the Norway, *91*

❖ ❖

brants would not have known most of these cookies, enjoying instead *pepperkager* (ginger snaps), *kavringer* (rusks), *vortekager* (pastries made with brewing wort), *honningskager* (honey cakes), *sirupskager* (syrup cookies), *kringler* (anise-flavored twists), and *vafler* (waffles).[35] In some parts of Norway, the cookies that Norwegians on both sides of the Atlantic now associate with Christmas remained unavailable until the 1920s, their ingredients and method of preparation costing too much to be widespread. As a result, earlier immigrants from peasant backgrounds did not come equipped with this baking tradition, but learned it in America.

Fattigmann, sandbakkels, krumkaker, Berlinerkranser, goro, and rosetter all share the same basic ingredients—flour, butter, eggs, sugar, cardamom, and almonds—yet each pastry has its own unique form, something that adds to the challenge of making them.[36] Goro, one of Norway's oldest cookies, were mentioned by the prominent Dano-Norwegian poet and playwright Ludvig Holberg (1684–1754), who called them *Gode Raad*. That name, or its variant *godråd,* also appears in old cookbooks; the ingredients were so extravagant that you had to have *gode råd* (good means; that is, be well off) to bake them. The recipe my own immigrant great-grandmother, Gertrude Fjelbroten Guldbrandson (1845–1920), used for this attractive, rectangular cookie impressed with a decorative leaf motif came from the *Minneapolis Tidende's norsk-amerikanske kogebog* (1907):

> A teacup of clarified butter is stirred to cream with a teacup of fine sugar. Three eggs are beaten, first alone, then with a teacup of sweet cream, and these are added to the butter, followed by three teacups of wheat flour. Lemon peel and cardamom are then added according to taste. Of this, one places a spoonful in the iron and sees the first time if it should be more or less full.

This recipe's less than precise measurements and experimental instructions, typical of its time, attest to the skill of pioneer cooks and the knowledge they had acquired through oral tradition. Measuring cups and spoons were unknown, says Barbara Levorsen: "Every cook learned by trial and error how to handle the oven and what size spoons and cups were best suited to her needs."[37] Though now purely decorative, the goro's intricately flowering design once functioned to keep the hidden supernatural beings from undoing all the labor that went into making this cookie.

❖ ❖

Rosetter

9 Tbsp. flour
2 Tbsp. sugar
3 small eggs
12 Tbsp. milk

Beat all ingredients to a smooth batter. Let it stand and swell a few minutes. Dip the rosette iron into the hot fat. Shake off extra fat and dip the iron into the batter. Dip the iron into the fat again and fry cakes golden brown.

Drain on absorbent paper.

Berlinerkranser

yolks of 2 hard-boiled eggs
2 raw egg yolks
8 Tbsp. sugar
approx. 2 cups flour
1 heaping cup of butter
2 egg whites
coarse sugar

Oven temperature 355° F. Baking time approx. 10 minutes.

Mash hard-boiled egg yolk with a fork, add raw yolks and beat with sugar until light and fluffy. Alternately add flour and softened butter. Handle dough as little as possible. Roll dough into pencil thick ropes. Cut into 5½ inch lengths. Shape into rings. Dip rings first in lightly beaten egg white, then in coarse sugar. Bake golden brown in middle of oven.

Strømstad, Eat the Norway, *89, 93*

❖ ❖

Unlike goro, krumkaker are thin rounds; initially flat, they are curled while still warm around a wooden cone (*krum* means "curved"); *strull* are made the same way but rolled into a thin, cigarette-shaped roll, though this distinction between krumkaker (as cone-shaped) and strull (as cigarette-shaped) by no means remains consistent throughout the country.

The special iron needed to make rosettes (*rosetter* or *rosetbakkelse*) is wheel-shaped, with a long, thin handle for dipping into the batter and then into the deep fat that fries the batter into crisp, lacy flowers. *Minneapolis Tidende's kogebog* gives the ingredients (2 eggs, 1 teaspoon sugar, ¼ teaspoon salt, 1 cup milk, and 1 cup flour) and the method (beat the eggs a little with the sugar and salt, add the milk and flour) and the yield (40 rosetter), but makes no mention of the dipping process, this cookie apparently being so familiar as to make such instructions superfluous.

Needing no special iron, Berlinerkranser (Berlin wreaths) result from a challenging recipe blending hard-boiled and raw egg yolks. Attesting to the cookie's popularity, George Mohn's 1924 cookbook contains five different recipes for Berlinerkranser. It remains one of the most popular Norwegian Christmas cookies on both sides of the Atlantic.

Sandbakkels, another of the popular baked cookies, owe their sandy texture to finely chopped almonds added to the dough, which is baked in fluted tins. The spartan *Minneapolis Tidende's kogebog,* however, leaves out the almonds, advising simply that "some drops of almond extract gives good taste"; it also allows substituting lard for half of the butter.

If it economized elsewhere, Great-grandmother's cookbook gave the full range of rich ingredients for *fattigmandbakkelse:* six egg yolks, two whole eggs, and one-half pound white sugar to be beaten well, then stirred with two tablespoons cream, one spoon of clarified butter, and "as much of one pound of flour as one can get into it." With nothing spared on their ingredients, no wonder these cookies became such a prairie favorite!

Despite the rich ingredients, *fattigmandbakkels* achieved early and widespread popularity among the Norwegian immigrants in America. Elisabeth Koren mentions them several times in her diary, noting that Helen Egge served them when the Koren couple arrived to share their cabin near Decorah on Christmas Eve in 1853. Two days later, on Second Christmas Day, their neighbor's wife, Ingrid Haugen, brought out wild grape wine and fattigmandbakkels, leading one person after another to the table and urging

❖ ❖

Sandbakkels (Sandkaker)

¾ cup butter
10½ Tbsp. sugar
1 egg
½ cup almonds
approx. 3 cups flour
¼ tsp. baking powder

Oven temperature 365° F. Baking time approx. 20 minutes.

Cream sugar and butter light and fluffy. Add egg, ground almonds, and dry ingredients. Press pieces of dough along bottom and sides of well-greased tart molds.

Put molds on baking sheet in lower half of oven. Bake golden brown. Cool on a rack. Turn upside-down and tap with back of knife to loosen cakes from molds.

Fattigmann

4 egg yolks
1 whole egg
4 Tbsp. sugar
3 Tbsp. heavy cream
1 Tbsp. cognac
½ tsp. grated lemon peel
½ tsp. cardamom
approx. 1¼ cups flour

Beat egg yolks, egg and sugar light and fluffy. Beat cream stiff and add it to egg mixture with cognac. Add spices and flour. The dough should be somewhat moist. Cover well and refrigerate over night.

Roll dough thin and cut in diamonds. Cut a lengthwise incision in the middle of each diamond and pull one pointed end of the cookie through the cut to give the cookies their characteristic shape.

Bake golden brown in deep fat or oil for 2 to 3 minutes. Cool on absorbent paper.

Strømstad, Eat the Norway, *90, 92*

❖ ❖

them to eat and drink. "Why, come now, you must not be bashful; drink all of it, this will not harm you." Such urging of the guests to eat was also the custom in many parts of Norway, and the proper guest waited to be urged three times before "giving in."[38]

People apparently gave in to fattigmann early and often, though, since no fewer than eleven different fattigmann variants appear in Mohn's 1924 cookbook, the highest number for any item. These recipes differ not only in ingredients but also in the treatment of the dough before frying. This ranged from cutting it into triangles, squares, or diamonds (preferably using a tracing wheel to give the cookies notched edges) to slicing "a slit near one point through which [to] draw that point back along the same plane." Uff da!

Like fattigmann, all these Norwegian Christmas cookies have unique and precise forms that can be achieved only with a great deal of practice and patience. Their difficulty gives rise to the frequently heard Norwegian American lament echoed by Mary Ann Braaten Snyder (born 1930 to a Norwegian immigrant mother in McVille, North Dakota): "I do a great deal of Christmas baking—krumkake, pepperkaker, fattigmann, sandbakkels and rosettes—but never get them as nice as my mother did."[39]

The very same words were spoken by Vesterheim Museum's Darlene Fossum Martin when she described her great-grandmother's cooking: "No one could beat her cooking. I can just see her going into the back pantry and bringing out her large jar of hartshorn cookies." Those cookies are a tradition Martin intends to pass down: "Hartshorn has been a very traditional Christmas cookie in my life and I intend to carry it on with my family. Hopefully they will acquire a taste for them as I have." Yet she warns that the ammonia-like aroma and taste of hartshorn cookies can take some getting used to. Fondly referring to them as "the lutefisk of Christmas cookies," Martin says: "People either hate them or can't get enough. It seems to depend on being raised on them." The cookie's namesake ingredient, hartshorn salt (ammonium carbonate), predates baking powder by several centuries; it saw much use as a leavening agent around the turn of the century. Once actually made by distilling deer antlers,[40] hartshorn salt is the secret ingredient that gives Scandinavian cookies their characteristic crispness. Now chemically produced as *aqua ammoniac* (more commonly known as

❖ ❖

Hartshorn Cookies

*Darlene Martin's great-grandmother, Amanda Fossum of
Spring Grove, Minnesota, used this recipe.*

2 cups sugar
1 cup home-rendered lard
3 eggs (slightly beaten)
3 Tbsp. hartshorn dissolved in 1 cup warmed half and half
7 cups flour
1 tsp. salt
1 tsp. lemon extract

Cream sugar and lard, add rest of ingredients, and mix well. Roll on a floured surface about ½ inch thick. Cut with cookie cutter. Bake at 450 degrees for about 5 minutes.

Darlene sprinkles the cookies with sugar after baking.

❖ ❖

"baking ammonia"), hartshorn salt is sold in pharmacies, there not being sufficient call for grocers to stock it in this country. (In Norway, where groceries regularly stock hartshorn salt, you must similarly go to the *apotek*, the drugstore, to buy cream of tartar.) Still, many American cooks continue to use hartshorn salt, finding the lighter and crisper pastries it produces worth the nostril-crinkling ammonia odor emitted during baking.

Like hartshorn cookies, fruitcake may be a treat or a threat, depending on the beholder. More often than its heavy American counterpart, however, Norwegian *julekake* meets welcoming palates; there are five recipes for it in the 1924 *Cook Book of Popular Norse Recipes.*

The high quality of the ingredients used in the Norwegian pastries and the degree of control required to successfully execute them are key to their nature and the message they convey. Never overly sweet or garishly colored, they are served undecorated, with the possible exception of a little white sugar sprinkled on top, elements that also reflect the Norwegians' characteristic self-control and reserve.[41]

❖ ❖

Julekage

1 cup butter
¾ lb. raisins
4½ cups milk
2 yeast cakes
1 cup sugar
¼ lb. citron
1 tsp. cardamom
flour

Melt butter and sugar in milk. While lukewarm, add flour and the dissolved yeast cakes. Knead well and let rise until light. Add raisins and citron and knead again. Shape in loaves and let rise and bake in moderate oven one hour.

Mohn, Cook Book of Popular Norse Recipes

❖ ❖

Coffee

What goes better with these pastries than good, strong Norwegian coffee? In the American Midwest, coffee arrived a decade or two earlier than even among the *kondisjonerte* in Norway; brands such as Mocha and Java began appearing in Minnesota grocery stores as early as the 1850s.[42] Contradicting the stereotype of coffee as "Norwegian plasma," Elisabeth Koren, herself a tea fancier, actually found the American reliance on coffee rather plaguesome, complaining on June 12, 1854: "They use only coffee—coffee for breakfast, coffee instead of soup for dinner and, when things are really topsy-turvy, coffee for supper too." Though homemakers could get commercially ground coffee by the 1860s, most continued to purchase whole beans well into the twentieth century. Household guides advocated purchasing raw beans and home roasting them "to a dark, rich brown," free from burned grains that would ruin the flavor.

Egg coffee—still popular in many Minnesota households and Lutheran church basements—was made by mixing the yolk of an egg with sufficient cold water to moisten the ground coffee, then adding it to hot water, boiling rapidly for five minutes, and simmering for fifteen. Instead of egg, some housewives used a codfish skin that was washed, dried, and cut into one-inch pieces.[43] The reader's suspicion that this custom *must* have originated in Norway is confirmed by H. K. Daniels's thorough description of Norwegian coffee use in his *Home Life in Norway* (1911):

> A Norwegian peasant of the better class buys a high grade of coffee in the bean, unroasted. It is then roasted by installments and at night in the stove or any fireplace, in a long handled iron container. . . . The coffee is then ground, not too finely, and immediately before use. The coffee kettle is half filled with fresh cold water, in order that it may not afterwards boil over, and sufficient coffee for the requirements is put in. When the water comes to the boil, it is kept boiling for four minutes. The kettle is then placed on one side of the hot range and the grounds allowed to settle. This is hastened and perfected by the addition of a tiny piece of dry, salted fish skin, and in a few minutes the coffee is ready for pouring—hot, clear, and brown as a berry, and as delicious as only Norwegian coffee may be.[44]

Relishing the image of his readers' discomfort on learning this news, Daniels comments: "You didn't know about that tiny piece of dry, salted fish skin, did you, oh my tourist, when you drank and be-praised your Norwegian coffee?" Present readers may take comfort in knowing that the practice of using fish skin has by now passed from the scene, as has the use of *knupp,* the method nineteenth-century peasants resorted to for stretching their coffee with roasted bits of potato dough. This custom, too, accompanied the immigrants to America; Mary King describes it in her memoir of South Dakota in the 1880s: "For coffee we cooked potatoes and mashed them fine, and then mixed in flour, graham, for that was all we had. This was rolled with the rolling pin about as thick as pie crust. Then it was cut into little squares about the size of a coffee kernel, and mixed with a little flour so they didn't stick together. They were then placed in the oven on a big dripping pan to brown. These were ground in the coffee mill, and made what is called 'knup.' "[45]

Porridge

Though coffee is the staple people most readily associate with Norwegians today, it was porridge that deserved that distinction in the nineteenth century, so it comes as no surprise that *grøt* (also spelled *graut*) accompanied the immigrants to America. There it continued to hold its prominent place as both a dietary staple and a festive food.[46] Porridge recipes, like those for so many foods, varied widely throughout the Norwegian countryside according to local custom and available foods. Just as the immigrants encountered Norwegians of diverse origins whom they would never have met in Norway, they also encountered previously unknown foods, not least the varying types of porridge, among their fellow countrymen on the prairie.[47]

Underscoring the dietary prominence of porridge, Great-grandma's 1907 *Minneapolis Tidende's kogebog* not only begins with porridge but supplies instructions for a stunning variety, including *byggrynsgrød* (barley porridge), *risengrød* (rice porridge), *smørgrød* (butter porridge), *fløielsgrød* (velvet porridge), *flødegrød* (cream porridge), *grynevelling* (whole grain porridge), and *havrevelling* (oat porridge), all made from the basic ingredients of barley, rice, wheat (flour, cracked, or whole-grain), or oats and cooked with various combinations of water, butter, milk, or cream.

Norwegian Americans' admiration for and desire to imitate the cooking of their immigrant ancestors applied no less to their porridge, as Norma Sersland Hegg (born 1922) asserts: "I remember one supper meal I wish I could make like Mom did. She used a large black skillet on the stove filled with milk. It would come to a boil and then she would sift into this whole wheat and white flour, and salt, I'm sure, and stirred until thickened. This was milk mush. It was poured on our plates. In the center we put a clump of homemade butter and sprinkled all with brown sugar."[48]

In the 1940s and 1950s we had a variation of this porridge in our St. Paul, Minnesota, home, too, made by my father, who called it "white pudding." Always having suspected him of inventing this dish himself, I was intrigued to learn from several letters received while researching this book that other Norwegian American families enjoyed a dish similar to this "poor man's rømmegrøt."[49]

Christmas, however, demanded the genuine article, and real rømmegrøt (sour cream porridge) or *risengrynsgrøt* (rice porridge) prevailed. The latter almost replaced rømmegrøt as Norway's favored festive dish in the 1880s, but by the late 1890s rømmegrøt had achieved status as a *nasjonalrett,* a national dish.[50] In Norwegian American circles rømmegrøt has always superseded risengrynsgrøt and has by now taken its place alongside lutefisk and

Using a tvare, Hanna Solheim stirred rømmegrøt in 1983 for a fundraiser at Mindekirken, the Norwegian Lutheran Memorial Church in Minneapolis.

lefse as an ethnic identifier; like them it is as much a symbol as a food and frequently serves as a reliable fundraiser for Norwegian American causes.[51]

The dish known in America as rømmegrøt might in Norway sometimes be called *fløtegrøt* (though both the name and the recipe vary in considerably more inscrutable ways than merely whether the porridge has a sour or sweet cream base). By either name, the dish requires high-fat (35 percent butterfat) natural cream, with no stabilizers or gelatin added. Commercial sour cream will not do, since its processing prevents the butter separation that is essential to making the dish. For best results, Astrid Karlsen Scott in *Authentic Norwegian Cooking* recommends making your own "rømme" by stirring 2 tablespoons lemon juice into 2 cups of heavy cream in a saucepan and letting it stand for fifteen minutes. The remaining ingredients are 1 cup flour, ½ teaspoon salt, and 2 cups hot milk (or more, if needed for desired consistency).

> The milk is minimum amount. You could need as much as 1 cup more to achieve proper consistency. Pour cream into saucepan and stir in lemon juice. Let stand for 15 minutes. Bring cream to a boil and simmer gently for 5 minutes. Sprinkle with ½ cup of the flour and blend thoroughly. Continue cooking for 10 minutes or more, or until butter comes to the surface. Beat constantly. According to your taste the butter may stay in the porridge, or you may skim it off and keep hot in a separate pan. When no more butter oozes from the mixture, under constant stirring, sprinkle in the remaining flour. Add hot milk a tablespoon at a time, stirring constantly until porridge is thickened and smooth. Salt mildly to taste. Serve hot, with butter, sugar and cinnamon.[52]

The rømmegrøt-making process conjures up scenes of family togetherness for Martha Elliott (born 1946), whose grandmother emigrated from Stavanger in 1909 to Rugby, North Dakota:

> I remember standing on a chair next to my grandmother, close to the kitchen stove, watching and helping her. She would get the real farm cream cooking so that the butter would surface. We removed the butter for later and added the flour and then the heated milk. Many times at this point I had the assignment of stirring the mixture as grandma added more flour (through her flour sifter) and milk, sometimes using a Norwegian tvare, but most of the time a hand beater. We cooked the

rømmegrøt until grandma had the smoothest, whitest rømmegrøt you could imagine.[53]

Echoing the Norwegian American refrain of ancestral culinary admiration, Elliott concludes: "I have never been able to make rømmegrøt like Grandma Martha. She would make it at a moment's notice, if she had the cream."

In Norway rømmegrøt still appears on festive occasions, though more likely on St. Hans (Midsummer's Eve, June 23) and Olsok (St. Olav's Day, July 29) than on Christmas, when risengrynsgrøt now prevails. Norwegians also serve rømmegrøt when celebrating weddings and baptisms. In some places a somewhat different sour cream dish, though bearing the same name, is served plain (instead of as a sweetened, spiced porridge) as a luncheon or light supper dish accompanied by *fenelår* (cured leg of mutton) and other dried or smoked meats.

Fruit Soup

Though considered by many Norwegian Americans to be as traditional as rømmegrøt, *søtsuppe* or *fruktsuppe* originated far more recently. In fact most Norwegian immigrants probably learned to eat this dish in America rather than Norway. During the nineteenth century Norwegians considered eating berries and fruit to be *finere skikk* (a more refined or *kondisjonert* custom), engaged in by townspeople, farm owners, and *embetsmenn* (civil servants), and therefore shunned by workers, *husmenn* (cotters), and peasants. Even if the lower classes had wanted to cook sweet soup, their cast iron cooking kettles would have discolored the fruit and ruined the dish.[54] Early Norwegian immigrants from less affluent backgrounds probably learned about søtsuppe from Danish and Swedish immigrants, more affluent Norwegian immigrants, or Norwegian American cookbooks. The 1907 *Minneapolis Tidende norsk-amerikansk kogebog* describes three different ways of making "sødsuppe," based on rice, sago, or whole barley.

Though of recent origin, søtsuppe caught on fast, and by the time Mohn published his cookbook in 1924, the dish appeared there in several variants, including one similar to the one Orel Winjum described as simmering all afternoon on the back burner of the wood-burning stove before initiating the Christmas Eve meal. Like Winjum's descendants, Mary Ann Braaten

Snyder (born 1930) continues the custom: "Every Christmas I make a big kettle of søtsuppe, full of fruit, especially prunes. . . . My mother would save "scum" off the top when making jams and jellies in the fall and add it to the søtsuppe, so I do that too—adds rich flavor, especially from wild grape jelly, and it must have stick cinnamon. We have it for dessert for days, then I freeze the remaining for dessert later."[55]

Dumplings (Klubb)

Though far less widely known than grøt or fruktsuppe, *klubb* is still prepared and eaten by a surprising number of rural Norwegian Americans at Christmastime. Klubb probably retains its popularity as an ethnic marker because like grøt, flatbread, and lutefisk, it was a food known all over Norway and could therefore, like those dishes, form a common bond among Norwegians from different areas, even when their other customs diverged. Norwegian Americans make these fist-sized dumplings by mixing grated raw and boiled potatoes, flour, and salt with water or sometimes cream. A very old dish, also known as *kumle,* klubb once consisted mainly of flour, but when crop failures and import embargoes devastated the grain supply in the early 1800s, potatoes increasingly replaced grain as the dietary staple, also becoming the main ingredient in kumle. A new treat was thus invented, which—like a beloved child—has many names, including *kompe, komle, raspeball, krumne, klot, kams,* and *kanotes,* reflecting the differing dialects of the areas in which it was enjoyed.[56] By any name, says Enid Johnson Ringdahl of Fergus Falls, Minnesota (born 1941), they are her "all-time favorite food": "On the 5th of December, my birthday, my husband makes a big kettle of kanotes. We serve them with ham and beet pickles (mom's recipe). Once a year we have to make it the old way by grinding the potatoes—for a quicker method we can use the processor."[57]

The initiated distinguish between two types of klubb: *blodklubb* combines fresh pork blood, sugar, and rye flour, while the—not surprisingly—more popular white klubb omits the blood. For extra flavor some cooks press a piece of sweet or salt pork into the center of each dumpling before cooking. Both types of klubb are then boiled in a pot of water to which a ham hock is added for flavor.

Klubb evokes deep nostalgia in many Norwegian Americans, such as Eldoris Leyse Hustad (born 1931), who has good reason to enjoy klubb with extra verve at Christmastime:

> The recipe we use is an old family recipe. My husband's grandmother brought it with her when she immigrated from Norway in 1886. One of her ancestors introduced potato growing to their area (Hjorundfjord) of Norway. My husband's grandmother, Karoline Aarseth, married Iver Hustad on Christmas Eve the same year they both arrived in Minnesota from Norway. They had eleven children. Potato dumplings were served at least once a week in their home. They were farmers, planted and harvested huge quantities of potatoes. . . . My family always makes a double batch so we have plenty of leftovers for slicing and frying for our Christmas morning breakfast.[58]

Considering blodklubb "a real delicacy," Mary Ann Braaten Snyder has made it often:

> But, of course, it's illegal to sell blood now, so this was in the days when butchering was done on the farms, of beef cattle. The last time we had blodklubb I gathered the blood myself, from a pig that was butchered on a neighboring farm. (The people watching thought it was great sport. After the pig was shot, I cut the pig's throat to reach an artery, gathered the blood in a big wash basin, transferred it to a large cold container, stirred it so it wouldn't clot, then got more blood, etc.) No, I suppose this sounds quite "bloody" to someone unfamiliar with the custom—but that's the way it's done. Keep the container cold, setting it in the snow and it didn't clot—and once again we could enjoy the delicious blodklubb.

Enjoy it they did. Some, such as Arlys Halverson Wiese, even held "Klubb parties." Growing up in the community of Trondheim, Minnesota (named by its immigrant settlers for their home in Norway), Wiese (born 1939) says:

> Every winter when we would butcher a pig—always done in winter 'cause we didn't have freezers to keep meat any other time—we would make Klubb from the pig's blood. It was made of blood, flour, and po-

tatoes with cut-up chunks of pork in the center. You made them in a big
ball like a dumpling and cooked them for hours. We'd always have all
the relatives over to enjoy this special treat. If there were any left we
would warm them up in milk for breakfast the next day.[59]

That not everyone found the dish worth celebrating is clear from the words
of Joyce McCracken, a less ardent fan of blodklubb:

> Dad usually had 2 sows on the farm [in Norman County, Minnesota].
> In the late fall a pig would be butchered. Grandpa was usually in charge
> of "sticking" it and taking care of the blood to prevent it from clumping
> or clotting. Ma made blood Klubb for supper. I had a hard time getting
> that meal down—and how I hated to have to wash up those pots and
> pans—the dish water was all bright red. But I loved potet Klubb.[60]

Cured Meats: Head Cheese and Lamb Roll

As if Christmas preparations did not already require enough work, Norwegians and Norwegian Americans also made special meat delicacies, which
eventually became sandwich toppings (*pålegg*) when *smørbrød* (open-faced
sandwiches) replaced porridge as the Norwegians' dietary staple. Like the
making of blodklubb, the custom of making these home-cured meats originated when slaughter dominated the Christmas preparations. McCracken
recalls her family's experiences with these meats, experiences that also reflect
the eventual transition from self-sufficiency to professional butchering:
"After the pig was butchered, Ma would make head cheese [*sylte*], too. We'd
come home from school to find her picking the meat from the cavities of
the head bones. By the time I was old enough to help in the kitchen a lot,
the locker plant in town took care of butchering and the meat packaging."

Dishes like sylte and *rull* (lamb roll) derived from necessity in the old
peasant society, but more affluent landowners and farmers used them, too.
As a money-based economy began to replace subsistence farming, they
would sell the cuts of meat that brought the best prices, then use the leftovers to make dishes like sylte and rull for home consumption.

Reconnecting with his roots, Norwegian American Judeen Johnson
(born 1925) has recently revived the custom of preparing these meats:

Since retiring over three years ago, I began—with my wife's encouragement—to make *rullepølse* [now more often called *rull*] and *sylte* as our
Christmas season cold meats, to serve guests at other than the main
meal of the day. The rullepølse recipe is traditional. The sylte no longer
begins with freshly butchered hog's head (we now favor the other end
of the hog), but the taste of the sylte is very close to the traditional.[61]

Like Johnson's, the following recipe for sylte includes the possibility of
using either the pig's head or the flank, calling for half a pig's head (or one
and a half to two pounds pork flank).

Scrub the pig's head well and soak it in cold water for 1–2 days. Put the
head in a large kettle, bone side down. Cover with boiling water. Add
1 tsp. salt for every 1 quart water.

    Cook the head until the meat loosens from the bone, approx. 2 hours.
(See instructions below for using the flank.)

    Cut the rind off the head and pick out all meat and fat. Cut the meat
and fat in strips. Remove veins and lymph nodes. Wring a piece of cheesecloth or a kitchen towel out in water and lay it in a mold. Place the rind,
fat side up, on the bottom and sides of the mold. Fill mold with layered
meat and fat, seasoned with the mixed spices [1 teaspoon pepper, 1 teaspoon ground clove, 1 teaspoon allspice, 1 teaspoon ground ginger,
1 tablespoon salt, and 2 teaspoons powdered gelatin].

    Cover with rind, fat side down, and pull the cloth tightly over the
head cheese. Tie a string around the cloth ends, so it is held in place
around the head cheese. Put it back into the cooking liquid and let it
stand, just under the boiling point until it is heated through, about
20 minutes.

    Weight the warm head cheese until it is cold. Remove the cloth and
slice the head cheese thin when serving.

    When using pork flank instead: Rub the flank meat with the mixed
spices, fold it together with the rind out, lash it with string and simmer
in lightly salted water until it is tender, approximately 1–1½ hours.
Weight it and use in the same way as head cheese made from the head.[62]

If this process sounds complicated, consider the plight of the twenty-two-
year-old Elisabeth Koren, daughter of a kondisjonerte Norwegian home,
experiencing the process for the first time out on the Iowa frontier when
even her reliable standby—Hanna Winsnes's classic cookbook—could not

completely put her mind at ease, as this November 13, 1854, diary entry reveals: "That was a job—making head cheese! It was the first time I had tried such a task, and it was really very difficult. Mother Winsnes insists that I sew the head around the edges, but it was no easy job to fasten the soft fragile pork rind. Now the head lies in press and I have a secret fear that it will break in two, and my almonds and other glorious things will be lost in the brine."[63]

The Availability of Norwegian American Ethnic Foods

Given their complexity, it is no wonder that not everyone makes these Norwegian delicacies at home any more. Other resources do exist, however. Ethnic and nonethnic food markets, even locally owned chain grocery stores in the Upper Midwest, cater to Scandinavian customers and stock lutefisk, sylte, lefse, and *geitost* (a peanut-butter-brown, caramelized goat cheese, essential to the Norwegian daily diet).[64] Combination food market–gift shops offer a variety of specialty implements for preparing Scandinavian pastries and sell a wide range of imported and domestic spices, meats, fish, and baked goods.

Lingonberries, almond paste, even *gammelost* ("old cheese," strongly scented and fermented)[65] and reindeer meatballs can be found on the shelves of these stores, some of which also prepare Christmas delicacies normally available only by means of painstaking home preparation, such as fruktsuppe, rullepølse, *spekekjøtt* (cured meat), and *pinnekjøtt* (steamed mutton).[66]

Norwegian Lutheran colleges like Concordia, St. Olaf, and Luther promote awareness and enjoyment of ethnic dishes by offering a Norwegian smorgasbord concurrently with their well-attended annual Christmas concerts. Observing the incipient stages of this growing phenomenon in 1976, Johan Hambro (then president of Nordmanns Forbundet [Norseman's Federation], headquartered in Oslo, Norway) commented:

> Students at St. Olaf College who are not of Norwegian background sometimes complain about all this "heritage stuff" they constantly hear and which they sometimes think can go a bit too far. Particularly the last days before Christmas. They claim that the entire campus reeks of an alien odor which they find disgusting but which draws Norwegian Americans like flies. That's lutefisk reeking out there in Minnesota—in

Lutefisk dinner at Gloria Dei Lutheran Church, St. Paul, Minnesota, 1999

celebration of a several-days-long pre-Christmas festival, complete with
a lutefisk dinner and all the trimmings. This relatively new tradition has
met with great success. . . . St. Olaf boasts that during the last three or
four days before Christmas vacation, they consume several thousand
pounds of the fish.[67]

The role of the Lutheran church in preserving and developing ethnic
cooking goes back much further than these collegiate Christmas dinners,
however. In this regard the American phenomena of the Ladies' Auxiliary
and the church basement kitchen played vital roles. Readily adapted by the
Norwegian immigrants, the shared cooking opportunities these presented
lay at the heart of preserving and developing ethnic cooking (and of teaching the immigrants American foodways).[68] On days when the women of
the "Church Circle" met to sew quilts or do other handwork to raise money
for the church, their efforts consumed the entire day, and together they
would prepare meals for their husbands and children, who would join

That not all clergy accepted with equal readiness the role of ethnic cooking in the life of the church is evident from the cover illustration of the 1920 book *Lutherdom med lutefisk etc.* (Lutheranism with lutefisk, etc.), written and published by Johannes Høifjell of Minneapolis, Minnesota. It shows Christ praying in the posture usually associated with Gethsemane, while being bombarded by the words "socials," "bazaars," "lutefisk suppers." In words enclosed in a cartoon speech balloon, he implores, "Don't you know my father's house is a house of prayer?"

them at the church for supper those evenings. Used for serving meals after funerals and weddings, the church basement kitchen also provided the setting for sharing recipes that had passed down through the generations.[69]

A modern-day outgrowth of this synergy of Lutheran church and Norwegian American foodways occurs each January at the Minneapolis Mindekirken *julebord,* the Norwegian Memorial Lutheran Church Christmas buffet. Unlike its Norwegian counterparts, the Mindekirken julebord concludes rather than initiates the Christmas season, but like them it offers a comprehensive array of traditional dishes, authentically prepared and thoroughly enjoyed.[70] The buffet includes *ribbe* (pork roast), *kjøttkaker* (meatballs), *medisterpølse* (pork sausage), sild (pickled herring) in several different sauces, boiled potatoes, traditional rømmegrøt, *surkål* (Norwegian-style saurkraut with caraway seeds), *fiskecabaret* (fish-based mousse), ham, sylte, rull, a variety of pickles and relishes, cranberries, lingonberries, homemade breads, lefse, and flatbread. At a separate dessert table guests help themselves to pastries—fattigmann, rosetter, sandbakkelse, krumkake, and Berlinerkranser—and *bløtkake* (cake with cream custard between its multiple layers and frosted with whipped cream), *risgrøt* (rice pudding) with raspberry sauce, *karamelpudding* (caramel pudding), and *kransekake* (a tower of baked almond flavored rings decorated with white sugar icing and Norwegian flags). Coffee is served continuously, and—in keeping with the Norwegian aesthetic that food should please the eye as well as the palate—festively folded napkins, butter painstakingly molded into attractive shapes, and glowing candles accompany the beautifully presented foods.

Still exerting a special hold on Norwegian Americans, whether in a group setting or at home, these foods remain the way most Norwegian Americans celebrate their ethnicity—at Christmas and other times. Affirming heritage, stimulating happy memories of family togetherness during Christmases past, and providing continuity from one year to the next, these culinary treats also serve as reminders of the constraints endured by economically challenged ancestors, even as they permit a sense of exhilaration about the distance the family has come since that impoverished past. Partaking in these treats is to celebrate—whether consciously or unconsciously—the values Norwegian Americans associate with their immigrant ancestors, from resourcefulness and tenacity to self-control, precision, and reserve, values that, like the foodways themselves, help to hold families together.

From Stagnation to Revival
Weathering the Twentieth Century

*I still [1997] have a lutefisk and lefse dinner and all the trimmings
every December for the few brothers and sisters that can participate.
I am the youngest (now 66) of a family of 10 so I like to carry on a
few of the traditions we grew up with.*

*We enjoy reminiscing and try to say the Norwegian table prayer
before our meal. I usually serve potatoes, rutabagas, relishes, lingonberries and peas with the meal above. For dessert I use sandbakkels
filled with a cranberry/apricot mixture topped with a dollop of
whipped cream. I also serve a tray of rosettes.*

*This is about all we do now. My mother used to make an ale for
Christmas that was a little like beer, but she didn't leave the recipe.*

*I do attend the Sons of Norway lutefisk dinner every year
and took my grandchildren to the Sons of Norway Christmas party
last year.*

Lorna Conners, Appleton, Wisconsin

Christmastime brewing, slaughter, and language fluency may have faded
with the ancestors who brought them from Norway, but, as we can see in
the epigraph to this chapter, beloved foodways persist, along with cherished childhood memories and a desire to pass this heritage on to succeeding generations. How did this Norwegian American Christmas evolve and
what has lately triggered its revival?

Old Country brewing, slaughtering, and basement-to-attic house cleaning, though no longer the norm, continued through the 1930s to number among the Christmas customs of many Norwegian American families. Those who maintained a strong knowledge of the language, however, were quickly becoming a minority. Judeen Johnson (born 1925) writes: "In my childhood home [rural Waseca, Minnesota] I was one of an already diminishing number of children who were comfortably able to sing in Norwegian, and I distinctly remember being one of those persuaded to kneel around the Christ-child's manger while singing, 'Her kommer dine arme smaa' [Thy little ones, dear Lord, are we]."[1] Use of the Norwegian language had declined sharply with the American nativism that surrounded World War I. The English-only movement had helped dissolve the Norwegian parochial school during the 1920s and significantly diminished the ethnic role of the church, whose services gradually came to be conducted exclusively in English.[2] American radio and cinema competed with Norwegian by giving audiences an intensely communal feeling, along with the seductive sense of being part of something national. Increasingly this national community took the place of the ethnic one, even as it shifted the population's focus from past to future.

Though many had become disillusioned by the worship of business in the wake of the 1929 stock market crash, they nevertheless retained their faith in the American system and shared a remarkable solidarity with their fellow Americans. Norwegian Americans began dispersing among the general population, reducing the number of specifically Norwegian neighborhoods, and fewer new immigrants arrived to counter the neglect that the Norwegian language and customs had suffered.

Compounding the situation of growing American uniformity, the generation who most clearly recalled Old Country ways began falling away during the next three decades. As the American lifestyle grew increasingly standardized during the 1950s, Americans turned to the business of business—as they had in the 1920s—and looked toward the time-honored virtues of home, church, and community. The pressure of the melting pot increased, and the cooking pot, too, came to reflect conformity. A national diet arose based on a host of dazzling new products created by recent advances in food chemistry. Kraft processed cheese, Bisquick easy-baking mix, frozen TV dinners, Minute Rice, Reddi-wip, foolproof cake mixes, along with an onslaught of marshmallow-fruit-gelatin salads and canned-soup-based cas-seroles: these standardized convenience foods competed with what ethnic cooking remained and kept most American consumers in their thrall well into the 1960s.[3]

Then the trend toward assimilation suddenly and unexpectedly reversed itself. More rapid and affordable air travel brought Norwegian Americans face to face with their ancestors' homeland. The increase in travel to Norway was also a response to Alex Haley's epic of black American history, *Roots,* and the enormously popular television miniseries based on it. Meant to engender a sense of ethnic pride in African Americans, Haley's work succeeded in performing that service for all American ethnic groups, and it sparked an unparalleled interest in genealogy that has yet to subside.

As ethnic uniqueness became a source of enrichment rather than embarrassment, many Norwegian Americans focused their newfound family pride on the way they celebrated Christmas. Sampling accounts of Norwegian American Christmas celebrations from the 1930s through the 1970s renaissance and on to the present, even stronger, resurgence of ethnic interest, this chapter considers how the meaning of these celebrations has changed through the years.

Christmas Preparations in the 1930s

Little had apparently changed between the way Joyce McCracken's Norwegian ancestors celebrated Christmas and the northeastern Minnesota holiday of her 1930s childhood. Her paternal grandfather had come to America with his mother and siblings in the late 1880s and homesteaded in Norman County. McCracken (born 1927) grew up on the "home place," which has since been passed on to her brother. When she was a girl, her family slaughtered in the Norwegian way; their other preparations also followed the painstaking patterns of the Old Country Christmas, but added the modern touch of a store-bought Christmas tree: "Preparations for Christmas Eve began many days earlier. The house was scrubbed from top to bottom. A fir tree was purchased from Tommy's General Fairway Store. . . . It remained outside in the cold air until just the day before—December 23rd."[4]

December 23, known as *Lillejulaften,* little Christmas Eve, and in Norway still the day for putting up the tree, looms large in other accounts of

Norwegian American Christmases in the 1930s, as well. Doreen Rentz (born 1927) describes December 23 in Holt, Minnesota:

> Regardless of what day in the week this date came on, it was always the busiest of the year. A common local saying was: "It looks like the day before Christmas around here" whenever the household was busy with a large number of different tasks on the same day.
>
> This was the day the tree was brought in and trimmed, and it was surprising to learn that in the Twin Cities people put up their trees well before Christmas. At home, some of the cooking and cleaning was done a few days in advance, but a lot was left to the last minute to ensure that everything would be nice and fresh for the big evening.[5]

As Rentz notes, rural Norwegian Americans differed from their urban counterparts by more closely following the Old Country ways. Whether rural or urban, most Norwegian Americans continued to observe Christmas Eve, rather than Christmas Day, as "the main event of the Christmas season," one that Rentz emphasizes was "family oriented." Christmas Eve dinner featured Norwegian traditional foods served simply but with elegance, as Joyce McCracken's words reflect:

> Grandpa [who by then lived in town] often walked the two miles from his home to the farm for the Christmas Eve celebration. By the time he arrived, Ma and my older sisters would have the dining room table set with a white linen cloth. A bowl of red delicious apples escorted a pair of glass single tall candle holders, each with white tapers. Supper always consisted of boiled potatoes, lutefisk with drawn butter, lefse and one type of meat, usually spareribs for the benefit of some of the family who did not like lutefisk. Table prayers were in Norwegian.

In both the ingredients and the need to have a lutefisk alternative, the Rentzes' Christmas dinner echoes the McCrackens': "Supper consisted of lutefisk and homemade lefse (a small pork roast was put in the oven for those who refused to eat lutefisk). The meal was simple since time was at a premium that day, and the lutefisk, lefse (or pork roast) was accompanied by boiled potatoes, peas or carrots plus homemade pickles and freshly prepared cranberries." The gift-giving followed, but only after the kitchen had been cleaned, says Rentz: "Our custom was to do the dishes before gifts could be opened—rather hard on the younger ones! After opening gifts (and we didn't get a lot of presents nor very large ones!), Christmas cookies, homemade fruitcake, fattigman and other goodies were served with hot coffee. Dad might even open up a bottle of Mogen David wine—usually not found in the house at all!"

A similar pattern of cleaning up the kitchen before moving on to the gifts characterized the McCracken family celebration, as did special indulgences such as gathering in the rarely used formal parlor, normally left unheated:

> After supper dishes were washed and put away, and the kitchen cleaned up, the arrival of aunts and uncles and cousins was anticipated. As they came, the goodies [they had specially made and brought along] were stacked on the kitchen table and cupboards. . . .
>
> By this time, the parlor was quite warm as Dad had built a fire in the pot-bellied stove in there. All available chairs were lined up around the room. Dad had made additional seating from a length of 2 x 10 plank supported on two large wooden chunks. This was covered with a blanket to improve appearance.

Amid the festivities McCracken's family continued their ancestors' custom of holding family devotionals, often in Norwegian: "The door between parlor and dining room was left open. With all the relatives present and seated about, our Christmas Eve service was about to begin. Cousin Beatrice sat at the piano, Grandpa stood in the doorway. The reading of the Christmas story and singing of hymns was all in the Norwegian language."

All this would soon change, in some families sooner than others. If a core of family members who recalled their immigrant ancestors stayed together, as in McCracken's case, some continuity might be maintained: "In the 1940s after Grandpa died, an older cousin, Berthold Flaaten, was asked to lead the devotions—in the Norwegian language. Family members were older but Beatrice was still at the piano and all who were able because of travel distance, continued to come to the home farm for Christmas Eve. Thus with Grandpa's spirit in our hearts we continued to carry on the tradition through the 1940s." But with increasingly mobile lifestyles and less homogeneous communities and families, traditional customs could not long endure, even in the McCracken family: "I was married in 1950, moved from northwest Minnesota to Sioux City, Iowa, to make a 'home of my own' with my husband. Even though my husband's mother was Norwegian and his father partly Dane, their holiday traditions were vastly different from those with which I had grown up." Marrying into a family with different customs, moving to the city, away from familiar surroundings—such transitions took their toll on Old Country ways.

Decline and Revival of Ethnic Interest

Even in areas largely populated by Norwegians, only bits and pieces remained of the once rich tapestry of intricately woven customs. The Norwegian language—if present—was recited by rote and exerted little fascination upon the American-born generation. Eugene Boe (born 1923 in Fergus Falls, Minnesota) recalls: "I was just starting school and nothing was less enticing than the study of Norwegian. To be able to speak Norwegian, I reasoned, meant you were going to speak English with a Norwegian accent. And that would be fatal. To speak with an accent of any kind was to invite the mockery and abuse of one's peers—a punishment far outweighing all possible benefits."[6] In retrospect many Norwegian Americans who grew up in Norwegian-speaking families deeply regret that their parents did not (often would not) teach them the language. Puzzling over how this could be, they forget the atmosphere of intolerance that Boe describes.

Further evidence of declining ethnic interest (demographics notwithstanding) and loss of the Norwegian language emerges in the experience of Robert D. Bolstad:

> I was born in Lake Mills, Iowa, a community populated by an overwhelming majority of people of Norwegian descent. When I was growing up (1930–1950), the community was even more "Norwegian" than it is today, but there was very little emphasis placed on Norwegian heritage. Christmas was the only time that some elements of Norwegian culture were observed. The school chorus learned "Jeg er så glad hver julekveld" [I am so glad each Christmas Eve] phonetically, mothers made lefse, flatbread, kringle and other traditional foods, and most of us remember eating the dreaded lutefisk at Christmas dinner.[7]

Only at Christmastime did a few ethnic foodways (always the most resilient of ethnic customs) persist, but even many of them had begun to fade away, as Boe points out: "Some of the confections that came from [my grand-

A letter from Einar (Fred) Fretheim (born 1916, the grandson of 1870 emigrants from Flåm and Undredal, Norway) shows how ethnic customs were fading by the 1930s:

Our folks did not carry on many traditional Norwegian ways over the holiday. Our Christmas celebration started on Christmas Eve and was all over the following night. No rituals, but plenty to eat and lots of good will.

Our Christmas meals were about half Norwegian and half American. On Christmas Eve we had lutefisk and lefsa for sure. Mom made the lefsa on top of our wood-burning kitchen stove and my father bought the frozen lutefisk slabs from the local grocery store where they had been displayed in the open in front of the store and had been well spiced by passing dogs. We always ate it in the good old Norwegian way—lutefisk inside of some rolled up lefsa with melted butter poured on top. Sure the butter ran down the arms, but it was Christmas so what the heck! Then came the meat balls and gravy and cooked potatoes. On Christmas Day we had baked chicken, cranberries, mashed potatoes and gravy and corn-starch pudding.

mother's] kitchen—such as the delicate rosettes with their topping of Devonshire-thick cream and lingonberries and krumkage and Berliner Kranser—can't be found anywhere today." The decline of ethnic enthusiasm seemed to be an irreversible trend, as is evident in Boe's 1971 obituary for the *bygdelags* (organizations of Norwegian Americans from the same rural district in Norway): "Today the lags are fading from the scene. Their founders are dead and so are most of their children. Succeeding generations, for the most part, have never bothered to learn the language and simply do not have that much interest in perpetuating their ties to the Old Country."[8] Who could have foreseen that the bygdelags would celebrate their hundredth anniversary in July 1999 (at Luther College) with record attendance?

Bolstad's experience reflected a downward trend in ethnic interest, yet it also gives us an example of its revival: "After military service, college and marriage, three of us who had grown up together during that period [1930–50] happened to live near each other in Illinois. We decided to get together one Christmas to recreate, to the best of our memories, some of the traditional Christmas foods we had experienced as children." The first get-together of Bolstad and his childhood friends occurred in 1974, when they drove some seventy miles out of their way to buy lutefisk:

We drove to Norway, Illinois, in a dangerous ice storm to buy lutefisk, even though I'm sure it could have been purchased in the Chicagoland area.[9] We made lefse, and enjoyed the product of our effort, despite the fact that we completely covered the kitchen with flour! We wrapped the lutefisk in cheesecloth and boiled it in water as our parents and grandparents had done, and found it to be less disagreeable than we remembered. All in all, we reveled in the nostalgia that this simple meal created for us.

The timing of Bolstad's expedition coincides with America's 1970s "ethnic renaissance." Suddenly "being different is no longer a fault, but a virtue," Lloyd Hustvedt could observe in the March 1972 *Norwegian-American Historical Association (NAHA) Newsletter*. This "renaissance" resulted from a sea change in American attitude about many aspects of social relations. Taking place during the decade that started with the Kennedy assassination in 1963 and ended with the Watergate investigation, this attitudinal change culminated in a rejection of cultural conformity, a move that ultimately led to a heightening of ethnic awareness. Books like Nathan Glazer and Daniel Patrick Moynihan's *Beyond the Melting Pot* (1963) and Michael Novak's *Rise of Unmeltable Ethnics* (1973) documented the survival of ethnic groups that had not "melted" and rejected the notion that they should.[10]

It was in this context that Alex Haley's *Roots* appeared, the best-known manifestation and further stimulus of the ethnic renaissance. Another contemporary observer of the renewed ethnic interest, Dorothy Skårdal (author of *The Divided Heart: Scandinavian Immigrant Experience through Literary Sources*) commented in 1976 about its ramifications for groups once rejected as "hyphenated Americans":

> The melting pot has not worked as predicted. . . . Instead Americans today are starting to talk about their "salad bowl." Each vegetable retains its own texture and appearance, but soaked in a common sauce, they all become a blended unit. While the immigrants' special institutions—churches, schools, newspapers, and organizations and festivals—were formerly despised and combated, they are now getting greater support from all sides.[11]

Suddenly the aspects of their existence that hyphenated Americans had endeavored to keep hidden had come into vogue.

Revival of Ethnic Interest on Both Sides of the Atlantic

American ethnic groups had come full circle. While less assimilated groups were being celebrated, those which had dutifully shed their Old Country ways in order to fit American expectations of good citizenship now came under fire for lacking character: "The irony of American opportunity is that it required rootlessness. . . . Shorn of tradition, we have been extremists in materialism [and now find ourselves] without a past to preserve." Thomas Wheeler wrote those words in 1971, surveying the wreckage of ethnic identity just as its renaissance was poised to begin. Increasing numbers of Americans returned from their first trip to Europe "sighing . . . over the cleanliness and grace of its cities and suburbs." To counterbalance what they now saw as the "blandness and massiveness in American life," they launched a "desperate and pathetic" search "for custom, for ceremony, for aesthetics in life," says Wheeler, and they looked to ethnic connection for "an oasis of identity."[12]

In his description of this urgent search, Wheeler echoes the noted Norwegian American author Waldemar Ager. Some fifty years earlier, Ager argued that the best foundation for creating and sustaining a vibrant America lay in preserving individual ethnic cultures.[13] In his five-part essay, "The Great Leveling" (1917–22), Ager bemoaned the dull, bland, mechanized uniformity that was replacing the diversity of American life, and he warned that the liquidation of ethnic heritages would dry up America's only dependable sources of creativity and thus destroy its further cultural development.[14] As if to bear out Ager's warning, Wheeler disparages the resulting void: "The immigrant experience of all Americans has left an American vacancy. The building of an American self needs the rich and diverse sources that made us. . . . If America is a set of paradoxes, we had better use them, each his own, rather than melt individually away into foam rubber. Perhaps America is on the verge of an honest meeting of the old and the new."[15]

Indeed, it was just such a meeting of old and new that had begun, with its "most forceful thrust" (Hustvedt observed in his 1972 editorial) coming "from minority groups who seek dignity and self-identity in terms of their past. One finds pride in being Black, Chicano, Indian, Polish-, Italian-, and German-American."[16] Though the words suggest how novel ethnic pride still seemed at the time, it had in fact already borne fruit for many cultures, including the Norwegian Americans, since the same issue of the NAHA newsletter could announce the establishment of new Scandinavian Studies programs at Luther and Gustavus Adolphus colleges as well as at the University of Wisconsin–Platteville and Moorhead (Minnesota) State University.

Now, too, ethnic interest started migrating across the Atlantic in both directions, as Norwegians themselves began paying attention to the emigrants and their descendants, a group said to approximate the size of their nation's own population. Visiting the United States in the 1970s, then president of Nordmanns Forbundet (the Norseman's Federation) Johan Hambro was surprised by his encounter with "the Norwegian-America":

> Traveling through this immense land and shaking hands of the Norwegian-Americans in Brookings and Seattle, Grand Forks and Decorah, Phoenix and Blue Earth, Devil's Lake and Salt Lake City, one gets the overwhelming impression that Norwegian-America definitely is a living reality that is promoted by a vigorous and vibrant element of the population—not of immigrants but of second, third, and fourth generation who decidedly are—and regard themselves to be—part of the Norwegian-America.

Not only did this ethnic group exist, it was expanding. Observing what has come to be known as the "*Roots* phenomenon," Hambro notes the growing interest and pride in tracing the family tree: "What especially strikes a visitor today is that there is remarkable growth in the Norwegian-America. Among the new generations there is a growing interest in the Norwegian heritage, in the family's history and roots, in emigration and immigration, and attempts at finding living relatives in Norway. One finds a need for belonging, a clear consciousness of Norwegian background—not seldom also a pride in it."[17]

Such ethnic pride lives on in Robert Bolstad's experience, for the spontaneous lutefisk dinner he and his friends enjoyed in 1974 inaugurated "a lasting tradition which has gone on uninterrupted for 22 years." Dubbed the "Uff-Da party" (featuring lutefisk, lefse, and rømmegrøt, preceded by a toast of Linie aquavit, chased with Ringnes beer), this now annual gathering has "nurtured an ethnic awareness in all of us." The broader implications of the seemingly private reunion of a few old friends became evident a few years later when their home community of Lake Mills, Iowa (population 2,300), sponsored the creation of a life-size bronze statue of a Norwegian immigrant family, a development that "pleased and delighted" Bolstad and his dinner group. Christened *The Promise of America,* the monument was dedicated with "gratitude to all immigrants who settled on the prairie so long ago" and is thought to be the first Norwegian American monument erected to honor the immigrant movement itself.[18] Dedication ceremonies took place on Sunday, October 8, 1995, an occasion that also provided an opportunity for Bolstad and his friends to hold their twenty-second annual "Uff-Da" party in their own home town, with meaningful results: "While the date of the dedication was somewhat early for our annual Christmas party, the dedication ceremonies brought our heritage awareness to a new level and made the event the best ever. . . . our cultural observances had come full circle!" Interest in their heritage had broadened from a pleasurable personal nostalgia to more generalized interest in and knowledge of the Norwegian immigrant experience.

Childhood Nostalgia and Travel Abroad

While for Bolstad it was a meal remembered from childhood that led to a renewed interest in ethnicity, for others, following their roots to Norway provided the catalyst. Consider the effect of a month in Norway spent by Eldoris Lyse Hustad (born 1931) and her husband in 1975, when they visited ancestral homes and met a number of distant relatives: "Upon returning home I decided that although we do celebrate our Norwegian heritage in various ways, we could incorporate more traditions into our celebrations. I went to a Scandinavian shop and purchased wooden and straw Christmas tree ornaments and many strings of little Norwegian flags to hang on our tree."[19] Her efforts to incorporate her ethnic interest into the family Christmas celebration did not always delight the younger generation, however:

> When my four young children saw the beautiful "Norwegian" Christmas tree, they didn't like it! They protested that none of their friends put flags on their trees [and] one day when I came into our living room, I discovered all of the flags had been removed from our tree! Not a one of our four children knew what had happened to them or who could

have removed them. One day about a week after Christmas very myste-
riously all the flags were very nicely lying on our buffet. Again, no one
knew who put them there or where they had been.

Hustad never did find out who did it, but every year for the next twenty-
some years she put the flags on the tree, where they remained untouched.
"Now," she says, "they are an important part of my holiday decorations."

Hustad's experience illustrates again the difficulty parents have in passing on their own traditions to their children. As Gail Farris laments, "I am
the only one that listens to Christmas songs sung in Norwegian. It drives
my kids crazy!"[20] This concern also resides at the very heart of the immigrant experience: just as those in the first American-born generation did not
share their parents' native land and could therefore not possibly have the
same memories of it, neither can children share their parents' childhood
memories or personal experiences of Christmas. In this way, the study of
Christmas provides an unexpected insight into the immigrant experience,
for our own regret that we cannot pass along the Christmas of our childhood to the next generation parallels the disappointed hopes of the immigrants who attempted the equally impossible task of handing down to their
children the love of a foreign homeland far across the sea.

Hard as traditions can be to pass along, however, once they are shared
with others who find them equally attractive they can just as quickly attain
meaning. Hustad's children, for example, eventually came to accept the
custom of flags on the tree, contradicting Minnesota author Bill Holm's
contention that "a tradition must be so old that its true origin [is] lost to us
consciously." Rather, it seems that the more accurate insight comes from
his mother, who, Holm says in *Faces of Christmas Past,* "might have defined
tradition as anything you did once that looked good to you, so you practiced it forty or fifty times more—and behold you have invented a 'tradition.' "[21] This more relaxed view of tradition, as exemplified by Hustad's
experience, constitutes an essential facet of today's ethnicity: people choose
their own traditions, whether or not they reflect ancestral practices or even
the practices of their own childhood. Since most Norwegians did not begin displaying the flag on Christmas trees until after their 1905 independence from Sweden, it was probably not a tradition known to Hustad's

Norwegian ancestors nor one she had practiced in her own childhood. It could, nevertheless, within the space of a few years become a meaningful part of her Christmas.

Continuity and Stability

Whether newly adopted or deeply engrained, traditions provide stability. One of the reasons that Norwegian Americans have found their traditions so meaningful is the similarity they often find between their own experiences and those of other Norwegian Americans, despite differences in time and geography. Moving to a new town or city, today's Norwegian Americans might seek out others with the same background, knowing they will soon find something in common.[22] This continuity operated in past generations, too. The Norwegian immigrants' tendency to settle in neighborhoods already inhabited by Norwegians often led to the creation of a generic Norwegian Christmas tradition within the settlement to even out regional differences from the homeland. A. A. Veblen noticed this phenomenon during the 1850s when his family settled in a community consisting mostly of *sambygdinger* (people from the same rural area of Norway, in this case Valdres), with some Vestlendinger (people from western Norway) mixed in: "Their Christmas customs were in many ways different from ours, and in a short time this mixture of *bygdefolk* [people from different rural districts] evened out the differences."[23] A greater consistency among Norwegian American Christmas traditions thereby arose than existed among Christmas traditions in the various areas of Norway.

While the earliest settlers may have experienced this "evening out" of traditions as compromising their purity, for many Norwegian Americans the resulting continuity has provided a welcome sense of connection, as it does for Judeen Johnson: "Since earliest childhood, from mid-December until some undefinable point beyond Epiphany, we always were served lutefisk, lefse, flatbrød, rosettes, fattigmandbakkels, sandbakkels, and sødt-suppe. My wife is skilled in the preparation of all these things, as her own childhood was similar to mine, even though our home communities were 170 miles apart." The shared background not only creates a bond between individuals, its ties extend intergenerationally:

Neither my wife nor I can remember a single Christmas Eve in our parental homes when the main course was other than *risengrynsgrøt med rosiner* [rice porridge with raisins]. Since our marriage over 42 years ago, we have not missed a single year in serving this as our main course. Our daughters continue the tradition today in their homes. Both my wife Marian and I have devout forebears in the Norwegian Lutheran tradition, and eating this traditional food seems to help recall the faith of our immigrant ancestors. (Since our whole family remains solidly in the Lutheran faith-tradition, the bond is real.)

The connection Johnson makes between Christmas traditions and his ancestors' Christian faith bears out the hopes projected by G. M. Bruce in *Jul i Vesterheimen* some sixty-five years earlier. Bruce applauded the Norwegian American pioneers' attempt to celebrate Christmas in their adopted land as it had been observed in the land of their birth, and he especially commended their use of the holiday to "transmit the rich religious legacy of their fathers to their American-born children, endearing it to them":

The hearts of many American-born Norwegians were thereby instilled not only with a love for the land and ancestry of their father and mother, but also with love and devotion to the religion of their parents. The treasures of their parents' religious observance were passed on to them principally through the instrumentality of the Norwegian Christmas celebration and the customs and religious exercises that went with them.[24]

Bruce and Johnson share a view of Christmas as a highly effective conduit of their ancestors' Christian faith, expressed in celebrations that would seem to fulfill the earliest hopes of the church fathers when they instituted Christmas in fourth-century Rome. Parallel as they seem, however, a closer look at Bruce's and Johnson's sentiments shows a fundamental difference in their reasons for honoring the yuletide customs of their forefathers. Ethnicity has revived, but it has also changed, changed in ways that influence how Norwegian Americans celebrate Christmas today.

Christmas Holds the Key

While the pioneers imitated Christmas in Norway as a bond with the Old Country, a way to provide continuity with the past, and a legacy to the next generation, their customs could not remain unchanged forever. Even when the customs themselves did not change, the reasons people had for continuing them did.

Norwegians had emigrated to America in order to pursue a lifestyle unavailable to them in Norway—whether to continue a way of life no longer possible in a changing Norwegian countryside or to find a new way of life in the city. Along with immigrants from other countries, they provided necessary human energy to open the new nation's frontier, establish its homes, and work in its factories. As the population grew increasingly diverse, Americans had to address the problem of how these diffuse elements could be bound together into a cohesive nation. Work, says Peter Salins in *Assimilation American Style,* forged that bond. Nothing, he asserts, has so united immigrants and "native white America" over the years as the world of work and the work ethic.[25] The immigrants gained acceptance and were encouraged to assimilate in direct proportion to their dedication to the work ethic. Hard work and talent could earn respect in America, where money replaced such Old World criteria as breeding, heredity, and education in determining social status.[26]

The process of binding diverse immigrant groups together received an important boost from a surprising source—Santa Claus. Developed during the course of the 1800s, Santa's image served to instill, consolidate, and maintain unifying ideas about the value of work. Detailing this development in her book *Christmas in America,* Penne Restad shows how Santa came to take on a more unified image as an American folk hero. Beginning with Clement C. Moore's 1822 poem "A Visit from St. Nicholas" (more often called " 'Twas the Night before Christmas"), Santa's ever more credible human dimension ultimately came to personify the qualities most valued by the emerging nation.

Reflecting the work-centered lives of many Americans, Santa returned to a warm hearth after a long day of making his Christmas rounds, as would any other Victorian head of household. Santa's workshop turned out a seemingly limitless supply of quality goods that he annually managed to distribute in an innovative, orderly, and timely fashion. Besides personifying the dedicated worker, Santa also shared characteristics of American financiers, manufacturers, and industrial moguls, reigning over a workforce of elves (a fixture of Victorian literature). This workforce offered a highly romanticized view of American capitalism, driven by skilled, reliable laborers who worked hard, long, and unselfishly, dedicated to the maxim that hard work and a cheerful attitude benefited all.[27]

The political cartoonist Thomas Nast was largely responsible for this unified and uplifting image of Santa. Nast began a series of drawings in 1863 that continued to appear in *Harper's Weekly* over the next twenty years. In creating Santa's North Pole workshop in 1866, he chose a location "equidistant from most countries in the Northern Hemisphere so that no single country could claim Santa as their own. Belonging to no one of America's ethnic groups, Santa could bind them all together." (Nast's lesser concern with the Southern Hemisphere is, of course, symptomatic of his times.)[28]

In addition to personifying the ideals of hard work essential to the evolving national mythology, Santa demonstrated a generosity of spirit, love of family, and dedication to the "American Idea" that were also indispensable to it. Brandishing a strap imprinted "US" on his forearm (in Nast's widely circulated 1881 portrait of him), Santa literally wears his patriotism on his sleeve. Though he directs his elf-driven workshop like the consummate "captain of industry," says Restad, Santa also displays qualities distinctly at odds with capitalism, shedding wealth rather than acquiring it, giving gifts away without regard for financial profit, and above all rewarding not the most wily investors, but rather the most innocent and naive of all Americans—the children. Santa's image thus embraced both the material and the spiritual values aspired to by the emerging middle class.[29]

Taken together, the values Santa embodied conform to the very ones Peter Salins identifies as defining the "contract" that nineteenth-century immigrants had with America.[30] These were the values, he says, that would permit them citizenship on an equal footing with already established middle-class Americans: hard work (first and foremost), love of family (Mrs. Santa was created in 1899 by Katherine Lee Bates), and loyalty to America. Flying through the air on a reindeer-drawn sleigh, Santa issued from the realm of dreams, hopes, wishes, and beliefs, says Restad. This supernatural image imparted an air of magic to the quintessentially American qualities he portrayed, cloaking them in power and granting them distinction.

Santa's powerful and unifying image soon joined other middle-class Christmas customs learned in America, such as putting up Christmas trees, hanging Christmas stockings, and exchanging store-bought Christmas gifts.

The Norwegian Americans blended these practices with their native butchering, baking, cleaning, and any other Old Country traditions they had managed to retain by the turn of the twentieth century. These unified practices were increasingly important in helping to emphasize national unity during the subsequent shift away from ethnic communities and growing awareness of the interdependence of all Americans. Consciousness of racial, national, and ethnic differences intensified dramatically as Americans' willingness to live with a divided heritage and ambiguous national identity declined. A demand for consistency swept through American opinion. Santa's image arose in response to this mood and helped create the notion of a homogeneous society.

Expressions of ethnic uniqueness, already growing undesirable, soon came, in the wave of American nativism surrounding World War I, to seem downright threatening. In response to the contemporary mood and rhetoric (such as Theodore Roosevelt's 1915 proclamation that America had no room for hyphenated Americans), Norwegian Americans emphasized their ability to join the American mainstream, pointing out the congruence between Norwegian and American values, both firmly founded in the Protestant work ethic.[31] During the next three decades the prevailing national climate continued to demand conformity to those shared values, and Norwegian Americans felt little call to emphasize their ethnicity.

Then the country was shaken out of its complacency: Watergate shocked the nation by the extent of its leaders' moral turpitude; peace without victory in Vietnam led to an unclarified sense of defeat and moral disaffection. National disillusionment and the gradual integration into the mainstream of the 1960s ideals of equality, diversity, and individual rights urged a rejection of cultural conformity. Encouraged to cultivate their distinctive national and family backgrounds, Norwegian Americans joined other ethnic groups in the ethnic renaissance.

This break with conformity, however, also subverted the immigrant contract with America, says Salins. It redefined family, replaced moral absolutes with situational ethics, supplanted the work ethic with welfare, and questioned the American Idea.[32] How do these issues relate to today's rejuvenation in ethnic interest? Is the current focus on family background and roots merely a continuation of the 1970s renaissance or does it represent something new?

Follow the Lutefisk

Remarkably, the answer to these questions may lie in the much maligned lutefisk. The changing attitude (besides disgust) that celebrants express toward the lye-soaked cod can actually provide insights into the changing nature of Norwegian American ethnicity. During the nineteenth century, for example, immigrants ate lutefisk "as in Valdres" (as C. R. Remme put it), because Christmas should be marked by special foods as a continuation of Old Country ways. During the ebb of ethnic interest in the 1930s to 1950s, "the dreaded lutefisk" constituted one of the few ways of marking Norwegian ethnicity, though little was made of the cultural context of that heritage. By the 1970s and 1980s, Norwegian Americans were going out of their way to find lutefisk and were eating it in conscious remembrance of their humble beginnings, a reminder of the time when "Norwegians didn't always have it so good" and to celebrate the distance traveled from those roots.

In the 1990s, by contrast, informants far more often mention family cohesiveness as the reason they celebrate ethnicity. For many, such as Lorna Conners (whose words opened this chapter), lutefisk brings back memories of her own childhood. Others use lutefisk and other Norwegian Christmas traditions to teach the younger generation "where they come from." Enid Ringdahl (born 1941) writes, "When I grew up and had my own home I knew I wanted Christmas to be a special time *in* the home, and also the time to teach my children about their heritage."[33] Continuing to "put out" *Jul i Vesterheimen* for a family who cannot read Norwegian, Ringdahl makes visible a cherished tie to her ancestors who knew the language.

A similarly meaningful visual ancestral link has recently entered the Christmas celebration of Jean Iverson of Decorah, Iowa, in the form of a notched log from her grandfather's North Dakota homestead house (dismantled in 1990). He had built it in 1883, and Iverson remembers her father telling about

> his mother singing "Jeg er så glad" as she trimmed the tree in the log house and twilight descended over the Dakota prairie. I wonder if a bit of loneliness crept into her song as she remembered her home and going to church in the Gol [Hallingdal] stavechurch. I placed the log under the tree and each year my collection of wooden nisser perch on the

Though the reasons for maintaining traditions may have changed through the years, the experiences of two women, both writing in the 1990s, demonstrate the enormous satisfaction derived from perpetuating the age-old yuletide rituals.

Siri Hustvedt describes the Christmas rituals she learned during the late 1950s and early 1960s in Northfield, Minnesota: "As children my sisters and I cultivated the holiday rituals in our house to a degree that bordered on the fanatical. We still do. . . . The sequence of the celebration is written in stone and never altered. From bringing in of the *jul* log, to the food, the dancing and singing around the Christmas tree, the event unfolds as it always has. Age has made us more flexible in theory but in practice our Christmas is as predictable as the sunrise and we love it whole-heartedly."

Enid Ringdahl of Fergus Falls, Minnesota, writes: "Our Christmas Eve supper is always lutefisk, Norwegian meatballs, boiled potatoes, melted butter, lefsa, julekake and rice pudding with a hidden almond. The birds are always given an extra treat on Christmas Eve day, and a bundle of grain is put out if we are able to find one. We attend the Lutheran Church services which are nearest in time to 4 o'clock. We come home, have our traditional supper which is 'white.' I use my mother's white china, white table cloth, white decorations, etc. Kitchen must be cleaned before opening gifts. Our oldest son would read the Christmas story from the Bible. Our youngest son would pass a two-handled ale bowl which contained a non-alcoholic gløgg. Presents would be opened on Christmas Eve."

Hustvedt (born 1955), quoted in a letter to the author from Lloyd Hustvedt, March 1998;
Ringdahl, letter to the author, March 24, 1997

log—skiing, chopping wood and some standing with red hats pointing the way to Christmas.[34]

The comical nisser no doubt help younger family members share Iverson's historically significant tie to her immigrant past.

Building a tie between younger and older generations may also be accomplished by engaging them in the process of making lefse or serving at the church lutefisk supper. These shared experiences, notes Ruth Halbert (born 1917), pass along much more than just the traditions themselves: "My two girls (both in their fifties) were raised with the old Norwegian traditions. They have passed many of those traditions down to their children and grandchildren . . . especially the fellowship and love of keeping a family together."[35]

Keeping the family together has attained new value in these unstable times. Broken families seem to grow more numerous every year, as do headlines about troubled schools and a general retreat from the work ethic. In the face of this societal meltdown, many Norwegian Americans have sought stability in their Norwegian roots.[36] Turning to their immigrant ancestors, they find role models who knew the value of hard work, a good education, and a closely knit family—the very values that today seem most imperiled. They feel that cultivating the Norwegian heritage can help cure America's ills, as Chester Reiten explains in a 1993 *Aftenposten* interview: "Americans must find their way back to the *grunnverdier* (basic values) the United States was founded on if the country is going to get back on the right track. These are the very same values the Norwegian emigrants brought to the New World . . . moderation, a will to work, dedication to God and country."[37] Rediscovering the values brought by the Norwegian immigrants, says Reiten, can turn America around.

While Reiten regards these values as uniquely Norwegian, it turns out that they are the very same values most Americans mention when asked to identify qualities that make their own particular ethnic group unique.[38] Love of family, hard work, belief in education, loyalty to God and country—regardless of ethnic background, these are the qualities people feel characterize their roots. How can each group claim them as their own when, to Norwegian Americans, they seem so undeniably Norwegian?

What these values have in common is their origin in the immigrant experience: Life was a struggle; the immigrants *had* to be serious and hardworking, seeming to get little joy out of life—as many would certainly characterize their unsmiling Norwegian ancestors. They put a high priority on assuring their children a good education; in America education permitted a social mobility unheard of in the homeland and was therefore well worth the sacrifice. Having left their extended family in the Old Country, many grew more closely attached to their nuclear family; besides conforming to the child-centered ethic that had arisen during the nineteenth century, the growing family attachment provided necessary practical assistance, supplied an essential workforce, and granted comfort amid strange surroundings.

Along with their values, the immigrants shared an attitude of stoicism, summed up here by Norma Sersland Hegg (born 1922): "If we had any unwritten rules on the farm they went like this: Don't complain. Don't make excuses. Just get the job done. I hope all of you have raised your families the same way."[39] These immigrant attitudes, Hegg believed, like many before her, provided a legacy worth preserving. The immigrant legacy is, moreover, what all nonindigenous Americans have in common.

Putting the American in Norwegian American

That valued legacy has drawn unprecedented interest in recent years. Noting the way Americans have rediscovered their immigrant legacy and the revival of customs that during the 1950s appeared slated for certain extinction, students of ethnicity have had to redefine their subject.[40] Once regarded as something static, an inheritance from ancestors that grew weaker with distance from those ancestors, ethnicity is now seen as dynamic, something that changes in response to changing circumstances.[41]

Disproving the once accepted notion that assimilation progressed in a straight line and would soon be completed, many Norwegian Americans feel closer to and possess more accurate knowledge about their Norwegian heritage today than they did thirty or forty years ago.[42] Chester Reiten accounts for this fact by the greater freedom we now have than did his parents to express ethnicity: "My parents' generation was perhaps nervous about making a point of their ethnic origins. My own generation is secure enough in their American belonging to be able to search out our roots in Norwegianness."[43] When people no longer fear that their ethnicity may threaten their life chances, they can express it more freely. With greater time separating them from the Old Country, they can also feel less constraint about the way they choose to express their attachment to it. As a result, individuals and families increasingly create the content of their ethnicity, picking and choosing the items that they themselves find meaningful, as Gail Farris of Arcadia, Florida, has done: "My grandparents lived in a Norwegian-American community, so they kept more traditions. We live far from most who share our heritage and only keep the customs that we really enjoy." With the constraints of the Old Country and of homogeneous ethnic immigrant communities removed, people today no longer follow the whole panoply of once intricately interwoven Norwegian Christmas customs; instead they select and often create items that hold personal meaning.[44] That they do so is significant. So are the reasons why they do.

Choosing Ethnicity

If today's ethnic customs boil down to being a matter of choice and do not greatly affect daily life, why do people cling so tenaciously to them? Mary Waters answers this question in her 1990 book *Ethnic Options* by pointing to the way in which ethnicity fulfills the particularly American need for origins and belonging—the need to be from somewhere. In a highly mobile population of immigrants, a sense of heritage and rootedness provides stability without imposing a complex of required behaviors and ongoing commitments to the group.

Allowing Americans a sense of belonging without sustained constraints, the new ethnicity also provides them a way to express their individuality without standing out as being different from other people. In this way, says Waters, it addresses the dilemma deeply embedded in American culture of how to find social affirmation while remaining unique.[45] By simultaneously being both an individual and part of a community, Americans find in ethnicity an antidote to the isolation that has grown increasingly acute in the wake of the massive suburbanization that began in the 1940s.

Since the modern ethnicity has arisen from uniquely American circumstances and borrows selectively from now distant ancestral cultures, some "Norwegian" practices contain little knowledge of what the ancestors themselves actually did or of the meaning their practices held for them; they express merely a desire to honor the Norwegian ancestry by doing *something* Norwegian. Actual practice in Norway, past or present, matters less than the feeling of connection to Norway.

As a result, Norwegians observing the way Norwegian Americans celebrate their Norwegian ethnicity often feel that these practices "virker noe skjevt" (seem somewhat out of kilter).[46] But while such things as the Norwegian Americans' reverence for lutefisk and lefse may elicit smiles from Norwegians in Norway, the Norwegian American observances have validity in their own right. Serving as reminders of the persistence and self-sacrifice that saw their ancestors through, these foods derive meaning from the symbolic value that Norwegian Americans assign them. Is this a meaning inferior to the one assigned—as an Advent fasting food—by medieval Norwegians in Norway?[47]

How could Norwegian American customs help but differ from those of Norway? They have evolved in a time and place different from the setting in which Norwegian customs developed. Does this entitle them to less respect? Questions of this sort began arising in the minds of Norwegian Americans during the 1940s; for example, in Knute Knutson's comments in the 1941 *Jul i Vesterheimen:* "Also we who grew up in Norwegian settlements here in America have childhood memories that in their own way are Norwegian, though not exactly in the same way as our fathers' were, still *Norwegian.*" Odd Lovoll's book *The Promise Fulfilled* adds depth and weight to Knutson's claim, forcefully answering the posited questions in the affirmative: "The Norwegian-ness of Americans of Norwegian ancestry deserves to be viewed with respect . . . taken seriously and understood on its own premises as a valid and logical outcome of the group's American experience."[48]

As the most stable and explicit expression of Norwegian ethnicity, Norwegian American Christmas customs have derived from the central facts of the Norwegians' American experience. According to Stephen Stern, folklore offers solutions to problems caused by living in a modern world: "Symbols of ethnicity are not merely static products of ethnic culture but are solutions to problematic situations that characterize, project and parody everyday life. . . . Through these symbols, ethnic men and women define their place and position in regard to their ethnic past and present."[49] Thus, Norwegian Americans deliberately and legitimately choose their symbols and endow them with meaning that they find relevant to their own situation rather than observing customs as an accurate imitation of past or current Norwegian practice.

Since Norwegian Americans celebrate not only their Norwegian roots, but also the memory of their American-born forebears, their ethnicity, Lovoll agrees, concerns itself less with modern-day Norway than with the ancestors' American transition: the dramatic leave-taking and journey from Norway, arrival in America, and early struggles of adjustment. Besides honoring these memories, Norwegian Americans use their ethnicity to pass along the specific moral and social values they associate with being Norwegian. "Letting their children know where they come from," parents weave such typically middle-class values as love of family, hard work, and patriotism into the more dramatic family narrative of self-sacrifice and stoic persistence. This glowing ethnic overlay attracts attention to these values; it also makes them seem more appealing and worthy of emulation, in much the same way as the figure of Santa once lent an aura of magic to the work ethic.

In addition to playing a valuable role in socializing the young, Norwegian American ethnicity confers a longed-for sense of family cohesion and fellowship. Whether it be decorating with nisser or going julebukking, displaying heirloom issues of *Jul i Vesterheimen* or eating lutefisk and lefse, "these are the bits and pieces of our past that keep us tied together," says Joyce McCracken. They are, Crystal Lokken declares, "the hidden part that lurks just inside the well-educated, modern Norwegian-American. The side that is part of their identity and which will not go away."[50] Deeply embedded, profoundly meaningful, and the product of two dynamic cultures, the new Norwegian American ethnicity is worth taking seriously—and enjoying for all it's worth.

Incorporating change while retaining everything that makes it so beloved, Christmas holds within its vast and monumental embrace diverse individuals, families, and cultures, allowing each a means of self-expression. Amid the combined pressures of Americanization, modernization, and mobilization into the middle class, Christmas helped mediate the initial strangeness of the New Land. Intensifying Norwegian American sentiment about both their ancestral home and their adopted one, Christmas helped Norwegians assimilate into the American culture of Christmas trees, Santa, and store-bought gifts even as it allowed them to retain the beloved yuletide carols and julebukking, fattigmann, lutefisk, and lefse from home. These customs and foodways provided a touchstone to Christmases past—first those in the Old Country, then those Norwegian American and American Christmastimes that inevitably and ineffably soon grew equally dear.

Though no generation can pass its childhood Christmas on to the next, children of every generation create in glorious anticipation and fond memories their own meaning and an equally strong desire to pass it on. Thus has Christmas linked the ages, as a messenger: communicating Christian doctrine to the newly converted, helping to institute a child-centered concept of family, assisting immigrants in their adjustment to a new land, bringing Norwegians and Norwegian Americans back to their roots, and reminding us all what really matters. Christmas works its magic at the seam of the year when, according to beliefs that long predate it, doors open onto other realms, myriad spirits—the returning dead, goblins, our own generous "Christmas spirit," angels—walk among us, and anything can happen!

Notes

Unless otherwise noted,
all translations are the author's.

NOTES TO THE INTRODUCTION

Epigraph: Dorothy Nelson Helmke (McFarland, Wis.) to her granddaughter Mary Lokken, letter written in the early 1970s and quoted in letters to the author by Dorothy's daughters Crystal Lokken (Berkeley, Calif.) and Corrine Niedenthal (Chicago, Ill.), January 15 and January 27, 1997.

1. Marcus O. Bøckman, "Jul i Vesterheimen," no pagination.

2. Letter to the author from Lloyd Hustvedt, August 18, 1999.

3. Bøckman, "Jul i Vesterheimen."

4. According to G. M. Bruce, "Christmas on the Prairies": "High regard for the church festivals of the year was an important trait inherited from the Norwegians, especially during the Christmas season, and the Norwegians' greatest desire is to celebrate it in the land of their adoption as it was celebrated in distant Norway, because by so doing they feel the bonds of blood and affection which still bind them to the Fatherland will be strengthened and perpetuated. They view Christmas customs, moreover, as a means of transmitting the rich religious legacy of their fathers to their American-born children and endear it to them."

5. April Schultz, *Ethnicity on Parade,* 17–18.

6. From *Fanny Kemble in America* (1835), quoted in Penne Restad, *Christmas in America,* 17.

7. Stephen Nissenbaum, *Battle for Christmas,* 3–8; Restad, *Christmas in America,* 7–8. In a 1712 sermon Cotton Mather asked rhetorically: "Can you in your *Conscience* think, that our Holy *Saviour* is honored, by *Mad Mirth,* by long *Eating,* by hard *Drinking,* by lewd *Gaming,* by rude *Reveling*; by a *Mass* fitt for none but a *Saturn,* or a *Bacchus,* or the Night of a *Mahometan Ramadam*?" (quoted in Leigh Eric Schmidt, *Consumer Rites,* 176).

8. Schmidt, *Consumer Rites,* 110.

9. This description was written by Gabriel Furman about 1830; the manuscript was edited and published as *Winter Amusements in New York in the Early Nineteenth Century* (New York Historical Society, 1930) (quoted in Schmidt, *Consumer Rites,* 110).

10. Schmidt, *Consumer Rites,* 178–81.

11. Nissenbaum, *Battle for Christmas,* 64–66.

12. This more austere version of St. Nicholas was also known in America.

13. Nissenbaum, *Battle for Christmas,* 81–85.

14. Nissenbaum, *Battle for Christmas,* 196–97. Goethe's novel describes a Christmas tree decorated by the heroine with sweets and apples and lighted with wax candles (Henry H. Albers and Ann Kirk Davis, *The Wonderful World of Christmas Trees,* 5).

15. Restad, *Christmas in America,* 59.

16. Restad, *Christmas in America,* 44. Middle-class periodicals from the 1840s and 1850s reflect America's growing fascination with the way Germans observed Christmas. Affectionate articles on the German Christmas tree and gift giving began appearing in periodicals like *Godey's, Sartain's* and

Peterson's. Americans found other sources of inspiration, as well, and gradually patched together a quilt of their own traditions (Schmidt, *Consumer Rites,* 124).

17.   Because of the repression of Christmas by the Puritans and others, Scandinavians traveling in the Upper Midwest regarded the adoption of the Christmas tree as the influence of their own culture, and they wrote of Americans adopting Scandinavian ways of celebrating. Thus, Hugo Nisbeth, a Swedish traveler who visited Minnesota in 1872, commented: "It is not only the Scandinavians who celebrate Christmas here in America in a true ancient northern fashion, but even the Americans themselves have in late years begun to give more and more attention to this festival of children and have as nearly as possible taken our method of celebration as a pattern" (quoted in Bertha L. Heilbron, "Christmas and New Years on the Frontier," 388).

18.   Restad, *Christmas in America,* 125.

19.   This changeover may have also been influenced by immigrants from Northern Europe, where the celebration of Christmas has traditionally overshadowed New Year's observances. Perhaps it is not least this custom, as well, that Hugo Nisbeth is referring to when he refers to Scandinavian customs being adopted in the New World.

20.   Schmidt, *Consumer Rites,* 123–24.

21.   An example is "The Holly Wreath" by Ina Churchill in *Godey's* 1875 issue, extolling the ability of gifts to join people together by creating "invisible chaplets . . . a mystical cordage where with to bind heart to heart" (519). A piece in the 1856 *Harper's* had already asked: "What are gifts but the proof and signs of love?" (265).

22.   Schmidt, *Consumer Rites,* 134. Schmidt insightfully analyzes the sometimes contesting, often complementary commercial and religious aspects of the American Christmas. I am indebted to Professor Todd Nichol of Luther Northwestern Seminary, St. Paul, Minn., for this reference.

23.   Restad, *Christmas in America,* 128.

24.   Restad, *Christmas in America,* 131. Complaints of materialism are even older: Harriet Beecher

Stowe's story "The Christmas Fairy" from 1850 bemoans the problem posed by Christmas shopping: "Oh dear. . . . Christmas is coming in a fortnight, and I have got to think up presents for everybody. Dear me, it is so tedious!" (quoted in Nissenbaum, *Battle for Christmas,* 133–34).

And a *New York Times* editorial from 1880 comments: "It seems the fashion to be extravagant, almost reckless in expenditures, and people of all classes vie with each other in the costliness of their presents until the rivalry in only too many cases becomes nothing more nor less than vulgar ostentation and coarse display of money bags" (quoted in Schmidt, *Consumer Rites,* 183).

25.   Dorothy Skårdal, *The Divided Heart,* 289.

26.   Veblen, "Jul i Manitowac-Skogen," 144.

27.   Jon Gjerde, *From Peasants to Farmers,* 50–51.

28.   Skårdal, *Divided Heart,* 287.

29.   Skårdal, *Divided Heart,* 289.

30.   D. G. Ristad, "Slik holder vi jul."

EPIGRAPH, PART ONE

Quoted in Solberg, "Gamle juleskikkar i Sogn," 126.

NOTES TO CHAPTER 1

1.   My treatment in this chapter of the early Christian church relies on Williston Walker, Richard A. Norris, David W. Lotz, and Robert T. Handy, *A History of the Christian Church,* 122–125. I am indebted to Terry Sparkes, Luther College Department of Religion, for this reference.

2.   Pope Gregory I sanctioned this development in 601. His instructions to missionaries among the pagans read: "Because they have been used to slaughter many oxen in the sacrifices to devils, some solemnity must be exchanged for them on this account . . . to the end that, whilst some gratifications are outwardly permitted them, they may the more easily consent to the inward consolation of the grace of God" (J. A. Giles, *The Venerable Bede's Ecclesiastical History of England,* 56).

3.   A familiar example of this biblical sun imagery is John 8:12: "I am the light of the world; who-

soever follows me shall not walk in darkness, but have the light of life."

4. Snorri Sturluson, *Heimskringla*, 106.

5. Brigit and Peter Sawyer, *Medieval Scandinavia*, 83.

6. Gula is thought to be at the site of the west coast community now known as Eivindvik; two tenth-century stone crosses still stand there.

7. The Gulatingslov is quoted in Per Sveaas Andersen, *Samlingen av Norge og kristningen av landet 800–1150*, 194–95.

8. Andersen points out, however, that a major difference between these two toasts actually did exist, though the difference—reflected in the Gulatingslov—may not always have been understood by the people. While the pagan religion had stipulated that as long as human beings fulfilled their obligations they could *ask favors* of the gods—in this case prosperity and peace in the new year—Christianity turned this relationship upside down. Now it was God who made demands on human beings who were responsible to live up to those demands; they showed their *gratitude* to Christ and the Virgin Mary for peace and prosperity and celebrated Christmas in joy and thanksgiving for the greatest gift of all, Christ's birth (Andersen, *Samlingen*, 194).

9. A twelfth-century painting inscribed *Olavus Rex Norvegiae* (Olav, king of Norway) still graces a pillar in the Church of the Nativity in Bethlehem.

10. Olav Bø, "Madr er manns gaman. Høgtider i livet og året," in *Norrønn kulturhistorie*, ed. Olav Bø and Olav Høyland, 125.

11. The Reformation progressed slowly in Norway. Only faint echoes of the Protestant movement had reached Norway before the new teachings and new order of worship became fixed by law, since the middle class that elsewhere had been the vanguard of the movement was almost nonexistent in Norway, nor did the country have the university or other educational institutions that might have prepared the way. Understanding that the Norwegian situation required special care, King Christian III recommended that the Norwegian clergy be allowed to retain their posts to avoid "fright and consternation"

among the peasants. For the next generation Catholic priests remained in place as leaders of their churches. Some worked zealously to enforce the new church ordinance, while others continued to conduct worship in the Catholic manner. More serious reforms began with the next generation of clergy, but yet another generation would pass before the laity accepted the new worship form, which many perceived as another inconvenience thrust upon the people of Norway by the Danish king.

12. Luther promoted hymn singing as an effective way to get the Word of the Bible into the mouths of the people. The first Norwegian hymnal came in 1569; the words were in Danish and most people learned them by rote.

13. The education of the people also began to increase significantly after the Reformation. A huge step in that regard came with the 1736 law that mandated confirmation in the state church. Because of the requirement to show a confirmation certificate before marrying or emigrating, the overwhelming majority of the population learned to read.

14. The Black Book was a compilation of magical formulas that, it was believed, the knowledgeable could use to conjure up the devil and force him to do their bidding. In attributing to the clergy the power to save or damn their parishioners, the people's view runs contrary to Luther's doctrine. For an exploration of how the popular view of the Lutheran minister contrasted with both Luther's and the official Norwegian view, see the following articles by Kathleen Stokker: "To Catch a Thief," "ML3005—'The Would-Be Ghost': Why Be He a Ghost?," and "Between Sin and Salvation." Some of the Black Book legends reflect an attitude of profound respect for the minister (for example, those about Petter Dass), as the attitude toward the clergy eventually improved.

15. Nils Lagli, *Julspel i Ranen*.

16. Quoted in Bengt Holbek and Iørn Piø, *Fabeldyr og sagnfolk*, 129.

17. Joh. Th. Storaker, in *Tiden i den norske Folketro*, expresses the popular perception of the Christmas period: "At Christmas everything evil is out and

about. At the fall of darkness on Christmas Eve, the doors open up to the underworld and scores of dangerous beings soon come visiting."

18. In western and southwestern Norway, the areas from which most Norwegian immigrants came, the transition from self-sufficiency farming to industrialization did not come until close to the end of the century.

19. Perhaps the most telling example of Norway's realization that its folklore continues to define its uniqueness as a nation came when the Lillehammer Olympic committee ultimately chose to use the *vetter* (supernatural beings that populated pre-industrial folk belief) as the major characters of the opening ceremony during the 1994 Winter Games. This initially controversial decision flew in the face of the Norwegian desire to be identified as a modern, enlightened, and prosperous industrial society. Ultimately the folklore theme not only prevailed, it proved overwhelmingly popular.

NOTES TO CHAPTER 2

1. Purple is growing in popularity and corresponds with the church's designation of Advent as a *bots og bedetid,* time of prayer and penitence.

2. As used in this book the word *peasant* stands for a person living in a rural rather than an urban area. The term *old peasant society* refers to Norway's pre-industrial agrarian society. The time of industrialization varied in different areas of the country. Mechanization began in the mid-1800s but did not reach many rural areas until nearer the end of the 1800s or even the beginning of the 1900s.

Peasants constituted the majority population; the number of *kondisjonerte*—members of the professional, cultured class consisting of doctors, ministers, and civil servants—was much smaller. They tended to live in more urban areas and had a lifestyle more akin to that of contemporary Continental Europeans.

Much of the folklore this book describes derived from the context of self-sufficient farming in a pre-industrial society in which work relied on the phys-

ical labor of humans and horses. The lore promotes the values of conserving these vital resources and using them wisely.

3. According to Jahn Otto Johansen, Engebret's in Oslo serves the most: more than sixteen tons to sixteen thousand guests during 1996. Restaurants in Norway's other major cities have followed suit; Bergen, with its ready access to fresh fish, took longer to get started, but during the mid-1990s began to experience a rapid growth of interest in lutefisk as well (Johansen, *Lutefisk—Tradisjon—Tilberedning— Tilbehør,* 42–43).

4. A version of this legend is quoted by Gary Legwold, who attributes it to Odd Unstad of Minneapolis (Legwold, *The Last Word on Lutefisk,* 52).

5. Astri Riddervold, *Lutefisk, Rakkefisk, and Sild in Norwegian Tradition,* 21–29. Much of the discussion about lutefisk presented here draws upon Riddervold's authoritative book, which appeared in 1990.

6. In *Lutefisk—Tradisjon—Tilberedning—Tilbehør,* Johansen, a Norwegian journalist, identifies Jann Holst as the person responsible for the delicacy's new popularity in Norway today; it was his idea to adopt American marketing methods to the Norwegian context, substituting ethnic identity with a group identity as "lutefisk lovers"—complete with the suggestion of extra potency provided by lutefisk. Had this happened somewhat later, he might have called it "Norwegian Viagra."

7. So far Norwegian American lutefisk humor has no real counterpart in Norway, but the Drøbak authors Tom E. Johansen and Jan Kåre Øien produced in 1996 a *Håndbok for lutefiskelskere* (Handbook for lutefisk lovers), which comes pretty close. In Drøbak there is also a tongue-in-cheek Lutefisk Museum.

8. Before the arrival of plates and forks, each individual's ration of meat and fish doled out by the husmor, the housewife, was placed on the flatbread. The diner used a sheath knife to cut off small pieces and placed them on a portion of the flatbread, which then might be dipped into soup or gravy. With time wooden or pewter plates came into use, followed by

stoneware. Forks and table knives came later still. Each individual had a spoon, however. Originally made from wood or animal horn, spoons hung in a row on the wall by the table. After the meal the diner wiped off the spoon and placed it back in the holder. Not everyone welcomed metal spoons once they became available: "The hired help, especially the older ones, would not use metal spoons. The food wouldn't taste right and then there was the risk of hitting and damaging a tooth, they said" (John Dieseth, *The Life and Times of John Dieseth,* 35).

9. According to P. C. Asbjørnsen in his 1864 book *Fornuftig matstell* (Commonsense cooking), the preservation of this *spekekjøtt* (dried meat) could get out of hand, with the meat stored so long it got rancid. Farmers competed over their supply of *spekemat* (cured meat), staking their reputations on its old age, equating their supply with prosperity and foresight. The meat was most often boiled and served as *sodd* (soup), both an everyday and a festive food all over Norway.

10. Rationing the meat supply was no easy job because the farm had to feed so many: not only the family, but also all those who had their daily work on the farm. Anne-Lise Mellbye gives an example from the traditional estate of Grefsheim (near Hamar) in the 1950s, when the workers included one stable hand, four to five cow and pig tenders, wood cutters, and at least one supervisor who saw to the animal fodder. Working inside the house were a housekeeper and four "girls." Then there were the *kårfolk* (older people who had formerly run the farm and continued to live there), as well as the *husmann* (cotter) families who had to have their quota of meat from the slaughter, which at Grefsheim consisted of several cows, four pigs and a couple of calves and sheep (Anne-Lise Mellbye, *Jul i Norge,* 18).

11. Sylte appears in the well-known 1845 cookbook by Hanna Winsnes, *Lærebog i de forskjellige Grene af Huusholdningen* (Textbook in the various branches of housekeeping), and the dish may not be much older. A pastor's wife, Winsnes belonged to a higher social class (*de kondisjonerte*) than the peasant farmers, but included many of the slaughter-time del-

icacies in her cookbook, alongside urban dishes the peasants would not have known.

12. *Blodpudding* called for one liter of pig's blood mixed with sugar, tallow, crushed rusks, barley porridge, and flour, with cloves, nutmeg flowers, and raisins added for flavoring. The mixture was then heated in a form.

Blodklubb was made by mixing blood with water and/or milk and barley porridge and/or shredded potatoes. Seasoned with salt and pepper, yarrow, allspice, and thyme, a firm mixture was made and boiled in meat juices for one to two hours. To serve it, slices were fried in fat and eaten as a breakfast food (Ambjørnrud et al., eds., *Norsk mat,* 191).

13. Also known as *svinelabber,* pickled pig's feet were made by washing and brushing the slaughtered pig's feet, binding and placing them in water, and cooking them until tender in salt water. They were then cut up and placed in a brine of two parts salt to nine parts water (Henriette Schønberg and Carolina Steen, *Kogebog for skole og hjem,* 376).

14. Dieseth, *Life and Times,* 69–70.

15. The peasants' varied use of horns, hooves, and skins provides further examples of their resourcefulness. They used horns and hooves to make spoons, combs, and sausage horns, and boiled the hooves of sheep and cattle to obtain an oil (*klaufeita*) used in lubricating spinning wheels, clocks, and rifles. Large, intact sheepskins served as bed coverings, while smaller pieces made seagoing flour sacks; turning the wool to the outside made the sacks water resistant.

16. Astrid Karlsen Scott's recipe for rullepølse calls for 2 lbs. lamb flank, $\frac{1}{2}$ tsp. pepper, $\frac{1}{2}$ tsp. ginger, $1\frac{1}{2}$ Tbsp. salt, 1 tsp. sugar, and $2\frac{1}{2}$ Tbsp. unflavored gelatin.

> Carefully remove the thin membrane without cutting into the meat. Trim the meat into a rectangular shape about 8 inches long. Distribute the excess trimmings evenly in the roll. Mix spices and gelatine and sprinkle over the meat. Roll tightly, beginning with the thickest end of the roll to get an even shape. Fasten with toothpicks and tie securely with

cotton thread. Place in a plastic bag in the refrigerator for 24 hours, to help the salt and spices to be absorbed into the meat before cooking. Wrap in a cloth, cheesecloth or cotton towel and tie again with cotton thread. Place in boiling, unsalted water and let simmer approx. 1 and a half hours. (Timing depends on thickness of roll.)

When cooked, remove from water, let rest 10–15 minutes before being placed in press. Place between 2 small trays with a weight on tip, approx. 12 pounds. The roll will keep in refrigerator in a light brine for about 10 days. It may be frozen before being cooked (Scott, *Authentic Norwegian Cooking,* 67–68).

17. *Spekeskinke* is made by taking a ten-to-twelve-pound ham and placing it in a deep enamel container or wooden tub. A sweetened brine is poured over the ham to completely cover it. The ham soaks in this solution for six weeks and is then ready to be smoked, a task usually performed by the local butcher. When the ham comes from the smokehouse, it is hung in an airy storage place, preferably the attic (wrapped in cheesecloth if flies are a problem). After four to five weeks (or, traditionally, when the cuckoo has returned in the spring), the ham is ready to be served. Spekeskinke is served sliced very thin and is popular as a supper dish with scrambled eggs mixed with finely chopped chives, accompanied by cold beer and aquavit.

Fenelår resembles spekeskinke but is made from a leg of lamb. It used to be the traditional fare in those areas of the country richer in sheep than in pigs. Long rows of these "sheep hams" used to hang in the stabbur, frequently not eaten until they were several years old. Known for their durability, these meats were kept in reserve for shortages and emergencies, and did not come into their own as delicacies until the twentieth century.

18. The now outmoded word *bakelse* simply meant "something baked"; it is a singular noun, but since English makes plurals by adding *s,* the word gradually became *bakkels,* which felt like a plural to Norwegian Americans and came to mean "cookies."

19. The practical and pedagogical nature of Winsnes's book makes it stand out among its contemporaries; it was the one women grew to depend on. Women called Winsnes the "husmødrenes orakel" (housewives' oracle) and always kept her book open at their side (Henry Notaker, "Kokebokas nasjonale gjennombrudd. De første norske kokebøkene 1831–46," *Nytt norsk Tidsskrift* 4 [1991]: 325–38).

20. Letter to the author from Shirley Olson Sorensen, January 11, 1997.

21. Winsnes, *Lærebog,* 298.

22. Winsnes, *Lærebog,* 262.

23. The six egg yolks made many Norwegian Americans wonder if the cookie hadn't been misnamed, a thought already current in Norway in 1833, when a cotter's son named Allum wrote a satirical verse about fattigmann, observing from personal experience that a poor man's diet more likely consisted of potatoes, *sild* (herring), and porridge than the six eggs, pot of sweet cream, sugar, glass of French liqueur, cinnamon, wheat flour, and cardamom that fattigmann required.

24. Recipe books that readers may wish to consult include Aase Strømstad, *Eat the Norway. Traditional Dishes and Specialties from Norwegian Cooking*; Kjell Innli, ed., *The Norwegian Kitchen*; George Mohn, *Cook Book of Popular Norse Recipes*; Anne R. Kaplan, Marjorie A. Hoover, and Willard B. Moore, eds., *The Minnesota Ethnic Food Book*; and Dale Brown, *The Cooking of Scandinavia.* See the bibliography for publication information.

25. Until quite recently *brød* (bread) meant flatbread. Raised bread went by other names, usually *kaku* or *stamp.* Oven-baked breads didn't come into everyday use in Norway until the 1920s. Gradually meals went from flatbread with sild or *flesk* (pork) and potatoes to oven-baked bread and *pålegg* (topping), such as most Norwegians today eat for three of their four meals a day—*frokost* (breakfast), either *formiddagsmat* or *lunsj* (lunch), and *aftens* (a late evening snack). Instead of one warm meal a day, as now, Norwegians used to eat two, usually consisting of boiled potatoes served with boiled meat and flatbread. In addition, porridge was served at least

one if not two times a day. Eventually the pattern that exists today prevailed: breakfast, lunch, and the light evening meal, consisting largely of open-faced sandwiches, and only the main meal—*middag*—consisting of warm food (Marit Ekne Ruud, *Hverdagsmat på landsbygda ved århundreskiftet*).

26. In his cookbook P. C. Asbjørnsen said that barley and oats are best employed in flatbread and lefse, staples he termed "Almuens hovednæring i vårt land" (The common man's main nourishment in our country) (quoted in Olga Ambjørnrud et al., eds., *Norsk mat*, 115).

27. Another flatbread dish that was traditionally eaten during the week before Christmas was called *mølje*. Common all over Norway since earliest times, it was made when they cured the holiday meats. A rye or barley flatbread was broken into pieces and placed in a dish; boiling meat juices from the cauldron were poured over it. When the flatbread had soaked up the juices, warm fat was placed on top and the mølje was ready. Some Norwegians continue to enjoy mølje today.

28. Knut Anders Berg, Liv Berit Tessem, and Kjetil Wiedswang, *Julen i norsk og utenlandsk tradisjon*, 146.

29. *Tyristikker* (pine sticks) augmented candles as a source of lighting, but they gave a flickering light and were not suitable for close work.

30. Berg, Tessem, and Wiedswang, *Julen*, 195. Much of the discussion in this section also builds on Olav Bø, *Vår norske jul*, 30–36.

31. The buildings on a Norwegian farm were all constructed of wood and arranged around an open area called a *tun* (farmyard). Their placement was determined by function. The stabbur, the architecturally distinctive storage house often built on pillars, provided a dry place, removed from the dampness of the ground. Other outbuildings included the *låve* (haybarn), *fjøs* (cow barn), *eldhus* (cookhouse, used for washing, baking, brewing, and drying), *stall* (horse stable), *smid* (smithy), and *kvern* (mill).

32. Ambjørnrud et al., *Norsk mat*, 264.

33. The peasants regularly reinterpreted the ecclesiastical symbols on the *primstav*, a medieval cal-

endar stick based on the saints' days, to fit the agricultural year; see chapter 5. For more about the primstav, see Stokker, "A Measure of Time."

34. See also Odd Nordland, *Brewing and Beer Traditions in Norway: The Social Anthropological Background of the Brewing Industry*.

35. Concerning the Christmas bath as renewal, the noted clergyman M. B. Landstad recorded the following custom from his parish: "The custom among Telemark farmers was to take a bath on Christmas Eve—to wash off the dirt of everyday. They all come back in as strangers (new people?) and shake hands around the room, whereupon a bowl is handed to them" (Landstad, *Mytiske sagn fra Telemarken*, 13). The custom of Christmas renewal and treating family members as guests or strangers, or, as Landstad suggests, "new people," continued in America, as Thom Myking's reminiscence in the 1918 issue of *Hallingen* shows: "On Christmas morning Mother served us as though we were strangers. We got coffee, *lefsekling*, and *rømebrød* in bed."

36. Winsnes, *Lærebog*, 6–7.

37. Erik Hetle, "Jul i Nordfjord," 15–19; quote at 16.

38. The memory of these fears persisted in modern times. An anonymous informant born in 1906 in Feios (Sogn) said in an August 1996 interview: "There was a lot of superstition that Mother and Grandmother told about. They painted crosses on the animal barn during Christmas to prevent anything coming in and causing harm. The door to the stabbur would be thick with these tar crosses" (interview with the author and Aud Ross Solberg, curator of Sogn Folkemuseum).

39. Landstad, *Mytiske sagn fra Telemarken*, 13.

40. Both the painting and the poem appeared in the 1932 *Jul i Vesterheimen* to accompany a story by Wilhelm Pettersen titled "Ralph Roemer." Neither the poem nor the painting, however, reflects the actual folk belief about the oskorei, since neither Welhaven nor Arbo had grown up in a milieu where belief in these beings survived. Their oskorei seem more inspired by classical mythology. A painting titled *Jolerei* by Nils Bergslien, owned by the Voss Undom-

slag (and reproduced in Bø, *Vår norske jul,* 81) does a far better job of capturing the actual folk belief about the oskerei.

41. Bø, *Vår norske jul,* 56.

42. Ivar Ulvestad, ed., *Vennlig hilsen: Postkortets historie i Norge,* 76.

43. See Kathleen Stokker, *Folklore Fights the Nazis* and "Anti-Nazi Card Tricks."

44. Norwegian shopping centers set new sales records during the Christmas 1997 season: "Sales volumes at the ten largest shopping centers are expected to reach nearly 9.8 billion *kroner* by the end of the year, an 8.5 percent increase over last year" (*Dagens Næringsliv,* December 1997).

45. Berg, Tessem, and Wiedswang, *Julen,* 92. Much of the material in this section is based on this work, especially 61–62, 88–87, 91–92, and 106–10.

46. E-mail from Thomas Juell, January 12, 1997: "The decorations go up the Sunday closest to the first of December, but long before that Christmas carols have begun playing on the radio and Christmas advertising has begun running in the newspapers." Indicative of Norway's ongoing internationalization, Juell adds that "while we have many beautiful songs of our own, the American carols have crossed over the Atlantic and have now been adopted by the Norwegians, in their original English version, and in the case of some, with Norwegian words to boot."

47. Dieseth, *Life and Times,* 70.

48. The tradition of New Year's gifts in Norway is evident in the well-known Norwegian Christmas carol "Det kimer nu til julefest" (The bells of Christmas are ringing), which refers to the "nyårsgaver, fryd og fred" (New Year's gifts of joy and peace).

49. Berg, Tessem, and Wiedswang, *Julen,* 92.

50. Berg, Tessem, and Wiedswang, *Julen,* 92.

51. Quoted in Berg, Tessem, and Wiedswang, *Julen,* 37.

52. The blessings longed for echo the Old Norse formulation, "til árs ok friðar."

53. Note how this continuing practice goes against the Gulatingslov, which specifically forbade sacrificing to *hauger* (grave mounds) and decreed

that the Christmas toast for peace and prosperity, "til àrs ok friðar," be drunk only to the Virgin Mary and Christ.

54. It was the Danes who first associated the nisse with Christmas. Between 1818 and 1822 the Danish folktale collector J. M. Thiele published some stories about the gardvord, mentioning that many Danes had given this being the nickname "Nis," the diminutive of Niels (J. M. Thiele, *Danske Folkesagn*; Bengt Holbek and Iørn Piø, *Fabeldyr og sagnfolk,* 126).

55. Meanwhile, as the elite were casting about for images to help define Norwegian identity during this period of National Romanticism, which had identified peasant culture as the repository of the true national spirit, the continued prominence of the nisse in peasant folk culture caused it to become a popular emblem for Norwegian nationhood, a goal toward which the cultural elite was striving.

56. Nissenbaum, *Battle for Christmas,* 65.

57. Nissenbaum, *Battle for Christmas,* 70.

58. E-mail to the author from Thomas Juell, Ål, Norway, then stationed as a soldier with the UN Interim Forces in Lebanon, November 22, 1997.

59. Innli, *The Norwegian Kitchen,* 55.

60. Innli, *The Norwegian Kitchen,* 51.

61. Innli, *The Norwegian Kitchen,* 55.

62. Dale Brown, *The Cooking of Scandinavia,* 128.

NOTES TO CHAPTER 3

Epigraph: Letter to the author, March 24, 1997.

1. Clean Christmas curtains replace the regular ones, which need laundering after being inundated with the pungent odors of deep fat and other aromas of Christmas preparation. (Note how this parallels the practice in the old peasant culture of scraping the soot off the walls and decorating them with *kroting* or handwoven tapestries as part of Christmas preparations and after completing the slaughter, candle making, and other messier chores.) Though these curtains may be bought ready-made, some Norwegians still hand embroider their *julegardiner* (Christmas curtains), often making a *juleduk* (Christmas

tablecloth) to match. Handicraft stores sell patterns for these year-round.

2. Knut Anders Berg, Liv Berit Tessem, and Kjetil Wiedswang, *Julen i norsk og utenlandsk tradisjon*, 123.

3. The peasants often refused to adopt the customs of the *kondisjonerte* because of strong peer pressure to *være tro mot ens stand,* that is, to act in accordance with one's station in life. Thus, N. N. Rønning displays his negative view of the Christmas tree: "The first Christmas tree I recall I saw in the parsonage when I was thirteen years old. I'm sure I thought it looked nice, but I thought the young branches covered with snow out in the woods looked nice, too. And I thought, too, that it was good economy to save all the trees that could grow up into valuable timber" (N. N. Rønning, "Gamle juleminner fra Telemark," in *Jul i Vesterheimen,* 1952). After coming to America, many Norwegian Americans, freed from this peer pressure, more readily adopted the Christmas tree and other practices they saw modeled by the clergy, no doubt also regarding them as aids on their own journey into the middle class.

4. Dieseth, *The Life and Times of John Dieseth,* 71. The autobiography of the former Luther College regent includes many details of daily life in both Norway (where he lived until he was seventeen) and America, to which he immigrated in 1912.

5. Henry H. Albers and Ann Kirk Davis, *The Wonderful World of Christmas Trees,* 4.

6. Quoted in Albers and Davis, *Christmas Trees,* 5.

7. Though an 1845 painting by Carl Schwerdgeburth did much to perpetuate the Luther story, Otto Lauffer, the leading German authority on the subject, characterizes Luther's role in inventing the Christmas tree as "pure myth" (Albers and Davis, *Christmas Trees,* 3).

8. Knut Anders Berg, Liv Berit Tessem, and Kjetil Wiedswang, *Julen i norsk og utenlandsk tradisjon*, 123.

9. This custom was mentioned—and forbidden—in the Gulatingslov.

10. The first electric Christmas tree lights were made in America as early as 1892, but did not become usual in Norway until the 1950s.

11. See also chapter 2 about wartime Christmas cards.

12. Growing up in a Norwegian-American household in Minnesota during the 1940s and 1950s, I recall cone-shaped baskets (known in Norwegian as *kremmerhus*) of heavy, shiny paper still used in this traditional way, though no mention was made of their Norwegian origin, which I remained unaware of until writing this book.

13. Residents on the preindustrial, self-sufficiency farm went beyond the immediate family of the landowner (*bonde*) to include owners of smaller subdivisions (*brukere*), tenant farmers, and cotters (*husmenn,* who neither owned nor rented but worked on the farm in exchange for permission to stay in a cottage on the farm's periphery); many emigrants to America belonged to the latter category. Additional farmhands (*gårdsarbeidere*) and young people in service (*tjenestegutter* and *tjenestejenter*) rounded out the farm's population. The farm workers usually slept in the barn, except at Christmas.

14. The idea that everyone in the household should receive equal treatment on Christmas persisted, among the affluent in towns, as well. H. K. Daniels, a houseguest of a merchant family during the early 1900s, writes: "The Herr Grosserer invites his servants to a seat at his family table on Christmas Eve as a matter of course and custom, and 'skaals' them to their heart's content and delight; after dinner (an occasion being exclusively a family one) they enter his *salon,* still in the position of honoured guests. Here they and all the members of the family are presented with their Christmas gifts for that year, and then hand in hand with their master and mistress and the young people of the house, they proceed with full-throated song to dance around and about the resplendent Christmas tree" (Daniels, *Home Life in Norway,* 109).

15. Anne-Lise Mellbye reports a lively version of the custom from Møre and Romsdal and attributes the custom's discontinuation to the danger of fire

with the open hearth and straw on the floor and the introduction of increasingly strict fire regulations after 1850: "When all the other outside work was done, and they were finished with lunch [about 4 o'clock], it was time to carry in the Christmas straw, chopping block, and sheepskin. The straw was spread out on the floor and the sheepskin put over the chopping block. Gigantic and covered with black wool, the sheepskin was round and had a radius of six feet. In the center it had a hole large enough to fit around the chopping block. When the Christmas table was set again at 11 o'clock—and supplied with two large tallow-candles (sized to last all night), then everything was ready for the uninvited 'guests.' Now the farmer and his wife went 'to bed' under the sheepskin with unconfirmed children [those in greatest danger of the *huldrefolk*] between them and confirmed children on either side, the boys beside the father and the girls beside the mother. Then came those who served on the farm and any others who were included in the household—the men on the husband's side and the women on the wife's. The cook then made the rounds with the ale bowl and then she also went to bed, like the others with the chopping block at her feet."

Mellbye's description continues to Christmas morning: "The cook was the first one out from under the sheepskin the next morning. Before she made breakfast, she once again made the rounds with the ale bowl. When everyone had gotten dressed, they received a *juledram* [liquor] from the husband's hand. Then the sheepskin was rolled up and taken outside" (Mellbye, *Jul i Norge*, 76–77).

16. "Katta på Dovre," in Asbjørnsen and Moe, *Samlede eventyr II,* 521–22. The term *trolls* was used by the folk to refer not only to the giants of legend and fairy tale, but also to all manner of hidden beings.

17. You can make four servings of risengrynsgrøt using 1⅔ cups water, 1 cup long grain rice, 1 quart boiling milk, 1½ tablespoons butter, salt, sugar, and cinnamon. Boil the water in a heavy-bottomed pan, sprinkle in the rice, and stir until it returns to a boil. Reduce heat and cover; cook slowly until most of the water has been absorbed. Add the boiling milk, stir, and continue to simmer until the rice is tender and the porridge has thickened (total cooking time is about 1½ hours). Add the butter, and salt to taste. Serve hot with sugar and cinnamon sprinkled on top (Scott, *Authentic Norwegian Cooking,* 89). Norwegians usually serve risengrynsgrøt with a glass of chilled red or black currant juice.

18. Michael Stephenson, *The Christmas Almanac,* 69.

19. Barley (*bygg*) was the most usual grain; until 1900 the generic word for grain (*korn*) signified barley. Other kinds of grain were mentioned by name. Wheat was harder to grow because of Norway's damp climate. Barley and oats were more reliable. Grain used to be ground in hand mills, and it was women's work. Norwegian peasants resisted use of water-run grinding wheels: they worried that while the mill wheel might make it easier for mankind, the nature spirits who dwelled in the water—the *nøkk* and *fossegrim*—might take a different view. What if they didn't like this disruption of their realm? Paying to have grain ground at the water-driven mills also seemed an unnecessary expense, since women had traditionally done the hand milling as part of their regular routine. "Den gamle ordninga har greid seg bra før [The old arrangement has worked fine until now]," they said. Grain from the hand mills was coarse and full of unground grain, and we can only admire the housewives who had to work with it. Sometimes they made *grynegraut* from whole, unground grain (Olga Ambjørnrud et al., eds., *Norsk mat,* 96–99).

During the middle of the eighteenth century Norway experienced a long period of crop failures. In an effort to relieve the peasants' suffering, the clergy introduced new agricultural methods and crops, and it was these clerics who became known as *potetprester* (potato pastors). Their efforts paid off during the famine years of 1807–14, when the potato really came into its own; by the mid-1800s it attained its position as Norway's major dietary staple.

20. Asbjørnsen included in his cookbook a detailed description of porridge cooking, criticizing

the wastefulness of the Norwegian husmor in following this practice. He thereby unleashed a protracted debate with the sociologist Eilert Sundt, who defended the Norwegian housewives' practice. The 1865 dispute, popularly known as *Grøtstriden* (the porridge fight), attained a high profile in the media of the day.

21. The best spoons for porridge were made from animal horns. The spoon maker sat in front of the fire and warmed the horn until it was pliable enough to be shaped by a knife. He then pressed the horn into shape and polished it to a smooth shine.

22. Many insisted on a grøt that was almost hard because the men took along chunks of it (known as *nævegrøt*, fist porridge) as a *niste* (packed lunch) to eat when they worked in the forest, field, or fishing boat.

Because of porridge's long cooking time, up to two or three hours for a large cauldron of it, the husmor often made an extra large portion that could be warmed up or served cold at the next meal. Replacing grøt in the summer with *søll*—crushed flatbread with milk poured over—also saved time.

23. Today's cream may also present a problem in making this dish in that it contains less butterfat than formerly. If sufficient butter does not ooze out while cooking, supplement it with 2 or 3 tablespoons of unsalted butter. Far from cheating, Scott would say, this is simply making the best of available resources (Scott, *Authentic Norwegian Cooking*, 88).

24. For *smørgrøt* they used 2½ lbs. *natur smør* (pure churned butter with nothing added), ½ quart sweet cream, 2½ lbs. flour, 4 quarts whole milk, about 1/10 quart hot water, and ½ cup sugar. Cook up the butter and cream, add sugar. Add flour. Then thin with milk and finally with water. Add the sugar last. The porridge should be *krotet* (not smooth) and should float in butter.

25. Asbjørnsen and Moe, "En gammeldags julaften," in *Samlede eventyr I*, 23–36.

26. Letter to the author from Eirik Eid Olsson, January 6, 1997.

27. Letter to the author from Kjersti Pettersvold (born 1956), January 3, 1997.

28. Letter to the author from Cecilie Sanden, January 6, 1997.

29. See also chapter 1 about the discontinuation of this mass after the Lutheran Reformation. The tradition of celebrating the eve of a saint's day (even more than the saint's day itself) lies behind the continued prominence of Christmas Eve over Christmas Day in Norway; the custom is even more pronounced at Midsummer, when only the eve is celebrated.

30. Berg, Tessem, and Wiedswang, *Julen*, 145.

31. According to a 1991 survey conducted by the Nielsen rating system, 95 percent of the Norwegian population follows a prescribed Christmas Eve menu.

32. Berg, Tessem, and Wiedswang, *Julen*, 104. In Norway's increasingly mobile society, households that have two different traditions alternate, each enjoying the meal learned from home every other Christmas Eve.

33. "Clean, wash, and parboil the meat in a covered kettle in a little lightly salted water, then remove the meat from the juice, replacing it with a generous dab of butter. Dredge the meat in a mixture of the crushed rusks, salt and pepper, add a little light syrup and brown the meat lightly in the butter, and finally add the rømme. Cook under a tight cover over low heat until tender, stirring occasionally" (Ambjørnrud et al., eds., *Norsk mat*, 177).

Recent years have witnessed a revival of interest among Norwegians in their culinary traditions. The dishes their grandmothers made are reappearing, and a great pride is being taken in Norwegian raw materials and historically authentic cooking methods. Several recent books reflect this trend: Velle Espeland, *Tippoldemors oppskrifter* (Great-grandmother's recipes); Harald Osa and Gudrun Alltveit, *Norsk mat gjennom tidene* (Norwegian food through time); Ardis Kaspersen, *Husmenn og husmannskost fra hele landet* (Cotters and their food from all over Norway); and Else Rønnevig, *Mat og hus: kulturhistorisk kokebok* (Food and home: cultural historical cookbook).

34. This popular recipe appears in several sources, including a Scandinavian American cookbook published in Chicago in 1884, *Skandinavisk-amerikansk kogebog, af en husmoder,* 217. It also appears in Ambjørnrud et al., eds., *Norsk mat,* 198.

Winsnes's cookbook contains it as well (118–119), even as it demonstrates a dramatically different attitude toward fat than exists today: "If you want the sausages really fat, it is best to knead them with boiled cold milk and also have a tablespoon of fine white flour or potato starch in a portion of ca. 30 sausages—it keeps the fat from flowing out so easily when the sausages are fried" (119).

35. Even cabbage and turnips rarely appeared, despite their long history in Norway. Discovered by the Vikings on their raids of England (where Roman conquerors had first introduced them), these vegetables also appeared in the monastery gardens of Norway, brought by monks from southern Europe after Christianity was introduced to Norway (ca. 1000), though they used the herbs and vegetables they grew more as medicines than food. During the late 1700s progressive Norwegian clergymen attempted to introduce vegetables into the diet, but despite their efforts vegetable eating remained largely restricted to those living in cities and towns. Written for these more affluent urban dwellers, the first cookbooks included vegetable dishes unknown to most Norwegians.

36. Reflective of the negative attitude toward vegetables, a work hand who was offered *får-i-kål* (mutton and cabbage stew, now something of a *nasjonalrett,* [national dish] and extremely popular all over Norway) turned it down, saying he didn't eat *grismat* (pig fodder) (Harald Osa and Gudrun Ulltvedt, *Norsk mat gjennom tidene,* 89). Nor was the negative view of vegetables limited to Norway; an 1879 cookbook admonished Americans "to realize the wealth of green food abounding in their gardens and fields, which they have too long abandoned to their beasts of burden" (quoted in Harvey A. Levenstein, *Revolution at the Table: The Transformation of the American Diet,* 5).

37. Osa and Ulltvedt, *Norsk mat gjennom tidene,* 89.

38. For surkål, use 1½ lbs. cabbage, 1–2 apples, 2 Tbsp. salt, 1 tsp. caraway seeds, 1 cup water, ½–1 cup water, ½–1 Tbsp. vinegar, ½–1 Tbsp. sugar. "Finely shred cabbage with a sharp knife or *ostehøvel* (Norwegian cheese plane) and cut apples into wedges. Place cabbage, apples and seasonings in layers in a pan. Pour water over. Simmer cabbage, covered, until tender, 30–45 minutes. Add more water during cooking if necessary to keep cabbage from sticking to bottom of pan. Season to taste with vinegar and sugar. The cabbage should have a tangy sweet-sour taste" (Strømstad, *Eat the Norway, 65*).

39. Strømstad's recipe for *kålrot stappe* calls for 1 ½ lbs. rutabaga or yellow turnip, 1 large potato, 1 tsp. salt, pepper, and 3–4 Tbsp. milk. "Peel the rutabaga and potato. Slice rutabaga and cook with the whole potato in as little water as possible. Pour off water and steam off moisture. Mash potato and rutabaga together. Season to taste with salt and pepper and add milk until the mixture has the desired consistency. Reheat and serve piping hot" (Strømstad, *Eat the Norway, 65*).

40. Today's two-career Norwegian households leave little time for preparing food on a daily basis, when Norwegians must usually settle for *snarretter* (prepared foods) and store-bought bread and cookies. This, too, strengthens the desire for special foods that require extra care and special ingredients at Christmastime.

41. Letter to the author, March 24, 1997; author's translation.

42. E-mail to the author, December 31, 1996.

43. On the American carols, see Schmidt, *Consumer Rites,* 181–82.

44. Reflective of the Norwegian Americans' high regard for this song, Irma Chamberlain (born 1932) writes: "A very special memory comes from when I was in high school. Our small church had a small choir and as a surprise for our very Norwegian, very strict pastor, we learned *Jeg er så glad* in Norwegian and sang it to him. It was the only time I ever saw

him emotionally moved. What joy this little gesture gave us—and to this day, Christmas only comes alive for me when I first hear or sing *Jeg er så glad!*" (Letter to the author, January 29, 1997).

45. Bø, *Vår norske jul,* 170.

46. E-mail to the author November 22, 1997. Juell, then stationed with UN forces in Lebanon, is "now the happy grandfather of a little boy of one and a half years so next year [on returning to Norway] I'll be taking out the old suit that has not been used for many years."

47. Bø, *Vår norske jul,* 171.

NOTES TO CHAPTER 4

Epigraph: Quoted in Bø, *Vår norske jul,* 184.

1. Eilert Sundt, the founder of sociology and ethnology in Norway, traveled in Norway from 1848 to 1869, supported by a grant from the Norwegian Storting (parliament) to study people's ways and conditions of life. The results of his studies were published in several books about folk life, discussing customs of marriage, handicrafts, Christmas, and so on. Ahead of his time, Sundt developed reliable analytical and statistical methods that are still in use.

2. Quoted in Bø, *Vår norske jul,* 99; compare Norman Reitan's description of a Norwegian American Christmas Day breakfast in chapter 6. Henry Notaker in *Ganens makt* quotes Sundt's description of the Christmas morning *skjenk på sengen* (breakfast in bed) in Trøndelag as consisting of a quarter home-baked pastry, a large *goderåd* (goro), *sirupskake* (gingersnap), *vaffelkake* (waffle), and a *kringle,* along with *brennevin* and *øl* (237).

3. Bø and Ørnulf Hodne, *Norsk natur i folketru og segn,* 54.

4. Letter to the author from Erna Skarsbø, Undredal, December 3, 1997.

5. According to Old Norse mythology, the conditions for entertaining were laid down by the god Odin in the poem "Håvamål" ("Words of the High One," in *The Elder Edda: A Selection,* trans. Paul B. Taylor and W. H. Auden [New York: Vintage Books, 1970], 38):

Fire is needed by the newcomer
Whose knees are frozen numb;
Meat and clean linen a man needs
Who has fared across the fells.

Water, too, that he may wash before eating,
Handcloths and a hearty welcome,
Courteous words, then courteous silence
That he may tell his tale.

6. Quoted in Bø, *Vår norske jul,* 122.

7. Knut Hermundstad, *I manns minne. Gamal Valdres-kultur III,* 130.

8. Troels Lund, *Dagligt liv i Norden i det 16de Aarhundrede,* vol. 7: *Aarlige Fester,* 49–50.

9. According to the memoirs of Hans Øen, the belief in the julegeit as a supervisor of Christmas preparations may have come to be personified by an individual playing the role of julegeit on Christmas Eve, and this practice may in some places eventually have given rise to "going julebukk": "Uncle Hans [born 1870] said that in the old days they used to threaten children with the julegeit when they misbehaved before Christmas. They said that the julegeit got as far as Trollesteinen eight days before Christmas. In the summer she stayed farther up in the mountains, but by 'Lillejulaften' [December 23] she had gotten as far as the farm's blacksmith shanty; after that they were afraid to go out after it was dark. My understanding is that the julegeit originally went around here on Christmas Eve. One person seems to have taken the initiative in getting the custom started here. She came about the time she could smell the food cooking and they treated her to a dram, but it was difficult for her to drink it [because of the disguise] and it ran down on the floor. Afterward the julegeit procession came later on in the Christmas season, and by then the custom had come to include julebukker, too. Eventually the custom changed and the julegeit disappeared, leaving only the bukker, and this they called 'going julebukk'" (quoted in Bø, *Vår norske jul,* 186). Julebukking is also discussed in chapters seven and nine.

10. Bjarne Hodne and Anna-Marie Wiersholm, *Glædelig jul,* 37–38.

11. Letter to the author from Cecilie Sanden, January 3, 1997; the English is from the original.

12. *Familiens julebok,* 169.

13. Erlend Sande, *Bergens Tidende,* January 2, 1997.

14. Letter to the author from Kjersti Pettersvold (born 1956), January 3, 1997. The English is from the original.

15. Sonja Innselsæt (in "Julebukk," an unpublished report in the Valdres Folkemuseum files, provided to the author by museum director Monika Paasche, August 1996), described the custom, which featured both a male and female goat:

> The *bukk* [male goat] and *geit* [female goat] heads used by julebukkers in the past were artificially made with horns nailed to a goat's head. These heads could have mouths lined with red cloth that could be opened by pulling on a string fastened under the chin. The one carrying the head on a pole had wrapped himself in a horse blanket or sheepskin so his body joined seamlessly with the head. When he opened the goat's mouth, he bleated.
>
> The one carrying the bukk went through the door first, while the one carrying the geit followed the rest of the group. On most farms they were served beer from a large ale bowl that went from mouth to mouth. At the last place they visited, usually by prearrangement, they'd stay until the wee hours of the morning, accompanied by a *spelemann* [fiddler], for dancing and other entertainment.

Bringing the custom up to the present, Innselsæt continues:

> While the bukk and geit heads propped on poles disappeared in the 1950s, people still make special masks, including goat likenesses, although goat imagery has ceased being an indispensable part of the custom. Otherwise the old pattern persists. Conversation continues to be an important part, and the julebukkers must be served a treat, so they

don't—as the saying goes—"bære julen ut" [carry Christmas away].

16. Letter to the author, December 30, 1996.

17. Letter to the author, January 1997.

18. The traditional day for *juletrefester* was Fourth Christmas Day, December 28, a day known as *Barnemesse* (children's mass) and observed in Norway during the Middle Ages in memory of all the male infants in Bethlehem ordered killed by King Herod, who feared the truth of the prophecy that the newborn child named Jesus would someday usurp his power. According to folk tradition, therefore, the children were permitted to "rule" that day (Birger Sivertsen, *Mari Vassause og den hellige Margareta,* 1998).

NOTES TO CHAPTER 5

Epigraph: E-mail from Lorentzen to the author, January 3, 1998.

1. Knut Anders Berg, Liv Berit Tessem, and Kjetil Wiedswang, *Julen i norsk og utenlandsk tradisjon,* 156.

2. Anne-Lise Mellbye, *Jul i Norge,* 28–29.

3. These may be found (in English and Norwegian) on the World Wide Web. Search Yahoo for "Norge," then select "Yahoo! Norge," then search for "juleleker." Choose the "smak" (taste) alternative and you will find a lively description of a Norwegian Christmas.

4. Mellbye, *Jul i Norge,* 29.

5. Bø, *Vår norske jul,* 133.

6. Berg, Tessem, and Wiedswang, *Julen,* 120–21.

7. E-mails from Jeanine Lorentzen, January 3, 1998, and February 11, 2000.

8. E-mail from Øyvind and Jeanine Lorentzen, February 11, 2000. They mention that during these first two weeks of the New Year some secondary schools hold dress balls resembling American junior and senior proms.

9. Memories of these customs did come to America, however. Both are mentioned in Thom Myking's memoir, "Juleminder" (Christmas memories).

10. Knut Hermundstad, *Samversskikkar i Valdres,* 97–144.; Ørnulf Hodne, *Jul i Norge. Gamle og nye tradisjoner,* 139–41. Thanks also to Carol Hasvold of Vesterheim Museum, who co-curated an exhibit with Jennifer Johnston on these and other betrothal gifts in 1995.

11. The custom also went by the name of *sidde i julestuen*—sitting in the Christmas chamber. Myking described it as follows: "He or she who wanted to *sidde i julestuen* had to fast on Christmas Eve and not talk to anyone after sundown. This person was blindfolded and led into a dark place, from which comes the expression, 'dark as a *julestue.*' The awful thing about it was that this all occurred in the name of the devil, and that it was he who showed the person his or her future mate. On a table stood a bowl each of water and beer and a bottle of hard liquor. If the future spouse drank the water, it meant poverty; if beer, prosperity; and if the liquor, riches. If the future mate appeared immediately, the person would be married soon; if time passed before he or she appeared, marriage would be delayed, and if no one came, the person would never marry. It was said that when the spouse came, light radiated from every corner of the room" (Thom Myking, "Juleminder," 70).

12. When the Santa Lucia procession gained popularity in Norway during the 1950s, the Star Boys began to reappear, dressed in white robes and cone-shaped hats, accompanying Lucia and her court.

13. All three examples are cited in Olav Bø, *Vår norske jul,* 152–54.

14. In popular speech, *sankt* (saint) became *sant* (true); with Catholicism outlawed since 1537, the term *sankt* had lost its meaning and people substituted a word they understood.

15. The influence may have gone both ways, since some descriptions of julebukking include sweeping, such as an illustration of julebukkers that appeared in the 1869 issue of *Norsk Familieblad.* It is also attested on this side of the Atlantic. In 1905 Troy Gordon (then eight years old) went julebukking in Nelsonville (Portage County), Wis.; he recalls: "One julebuk in the party would bring a broom. He would

be the last to leave. As he took leave he would sweep out the old year and all its evil spirits to welcome in the new" (Patricia Lalim Falcone, " 'Julebuk'—Lively Old Norse Yule Custom").

16. Adding to the confusion, early Swedish almanacs indicate that St. Knut's Day was moved from January 7 to January 13 at the end of the 1600s and the beginning of the 1700s, a circumstance that seems to have obtained in eastern Norway as well.

17. Mellbye, *Jul i Norge,* 153.

18. Mellbye, *Jul i Norge,* 28–29.

19. Collected by Lonnie Morken, a student in Stokker's 1993 folklore class.

20. *Den store fest- og høytidsboka* (Big book of celebrations), edited by Jo Tenfjord and Toril Bang Lancelot, gives today's Norwegian children clear instructions for making a *trekongerslys.*

21. Caroline Mathilde Koren Næseth, "Memoirs from Little Iowa Parsonage," NAHA *Studies and Records* 13 (1943): 68.

22. For more on the primstav, see Stokker, "A Measure of Time."

23. Bø, *Vår norske jul,* 161–64.

NOTES TO CHAPTER 6

1. By 1850, 18,200 Norwegians had left their homeland for America. Nearly 70,000 had done so by the outbreak of the Civil War (Odd Lovoll, *The Promise Fulfilled,* 10). At first those who emigrated were largely farmers of moderate means—"those who were poorer couldn't afford to, those who were better off didn't need to," as Laur. Larsen commented in the 1913 *Symra* ("Nogle gamle Minder," 169). Farmers who had sold their smallholdings to finance their trip, younger sons of independent farmers unable to continue in familiar pursuits, and gradually, especially in the 1850s and later, cotters and members of the lower classes in rural society all joined the movement overseas (Lovoll, *The Promise Fulfilled,* 10).

2. I. F. Grose, "A Pioneer Boy's Experiences in a Corner of Goodhue County," n.p.

3. Jon Gjerde, *From Peasants to Farmers,* 9.

4. A. A. Veblen, "Jul i Manitowoc-Skogen," 134–48. Veblen was a professor of physics at the University of Iowa and became the first president of the Valdres Samband.

5. Knute Olson Løkensgaard, "Jul i gamle dage," 4–7. Løkensgaard also authored several readers, textbooks, and handbooks for the Norwegian American parochial schools. The vital role played by these lengthy Christmas preparations in helping the immigrants overcome their homesickness (and the ways in which they began to adjust time-honored practices to fit their new surroundings) may be seen from this January 1858 letter from Caja Munch, a pastor's wife living in Wiota, Wis.: "I had a lot of butchering done for Christmas, which I enjoyed doing—I seemed to live over again the old days in my home. Everything turned out well. I made almost all the things you prepare, dear Mother, although I did make some kind of meat sausage which I marvel that we never thought of cooking at home. I had to make black pudding for Munch, he likes it so well, and I had the pleasure of treating my dear Emil and Munch to delicious things for a long time." The same letter also shows that her baking included new American treats (apple pie) among the old Norwegian favorites: "My baking for Christmas consisted of wort-cake, Christmas bread, flead cakes, hartshorn pastry, and apple pie" (Munch, *The Strange American Way,* 131).

6. Knut Teigen, *Ligt og uligt* (A bit of everything), 162–77. Teigen's book first appeared in 1899; it includes his account of Christmas customs as practiced in rural Wisconsin during the 1860s and 1870s. Quotations in this chapter are from the second revised edition, which appeared in 1907. Pioneer slaughter and brewing processes appear prominently in two early Norwegian American cookbooks: *Skandinavisk-Amerikansk kogebog af en husmoder* and *Ny norsk-dansk og amerikansk kogebog.* The latter assumes less prior knowledge and gives clear details of preparation methods and ingredients as well as useful advice.

7. The slaughter may have been done several different ways, depending on each family's tradi-tions. Lloyd Hustvedt comments in a letter to the author (August 18, 1999): "Teigen's claim that a hog's heart was pierced at butchering time is nonsense. A pig was first stunned by a blow to the head with a sledge hammer or shot with a rifle. The jugular vein was then cut and the blood collected."

8. Similar resourcefulness emerges as Teigen describes the by-products of slaughtering a cow: "The horns were sawed off at their base and used for gunpowder horns or *hornkopper* (cups for the then popular medical treatment of bleeding patients), and from the skin over the hocks, the pioneer sewed hide shoes for winter" (166).

9. Teigen, *Ligt og uligt,* 165. The folklore enforced the ethic expressed in nineteenth-century cookbook directions, which admonish, "Det er af stor vigtighed at dyret bliver pent slagtet" (It is of great importance that the animal is humanely slaughtered) (Henriette Schønberg and Caroline Steen, *Kogebog for skole og hjem* [Kra: Aschehoug, 1899], 369).

10. Thurine Oleson, born in Winchester, Wis., in 1866, the daughter of parents from Telemark, Norway, also remembers the Christmas ale. The process closely resembles that described in chapter 2, except that molasses replaced juniper as a flavoring agent.

11. Teigen may again be speaking figuratively, as it seems doubtful that one could transfer the beer to its permanent barrel in the evening of the day brewing began. In the Norwegian process described in chapter 2, a couple of days of fermentation passed before the brew was tapped into the barrels.

12. Grose, "A Pioneer Boy's Experiences."

13. The saying was well known and widely circulated. Here it is quoted from the memories of Elias Aas, *The Pioneer Pastor,* 28.

14. Not all observers agree that the pioneers followed the julenek custom. C. R. Remme (Luverne, Minn.), who emphasized the pioneers' break with the Old Country's arduous customs, writes, "Nor did we raise *fugleband,* but allowed birds to eat at the pig trough and chicken coops throughout the year" ("Jul blandt nybyggerne").

Some observers suggest that the Swedes, rather

than the Norwegians, may have been the first to use the julenek on the prairie; Veblen says he knew nothing of the custom, which he calls *juleband,* until a recently arrived Swedish neighbor erected one. Meanwhile Hugo Nisbeth, a Swedish traveler visiting Minnesota in 1872, tells of spending a rural Christmas with a Swedish family near Litchfield. Though they lived in a sod house, they nevertheless set out "a small sheaf of unthreshed wheat for the birds" (Nisbeth, quoted in Bertha Heilbron, "Christmas and New Year's on the Frontier," 389).

15. Modern Norwegians call the living room *stue,* the word once applied to the dwelling-house on the preindustrial farm. The word "levingsrom" is an example of the immigrants' application of an American term to an American phenomenon—in this case, a separate room quite different from what they had known in Norway, where the main room of the peasant home served as kitchen, bedroom, and workroom, as well as living room.

16. Jon Gjerde explains the persistence of Old World patterns in America. Norwegian American communities were based on Old World affinities, and this pattern of Norwegian American settlement in the New World resulted in strongly defined communities centered on the church as a focal point of interaction. Letters underscore the influence of kinship ties in emigration. The nuclear family was the principal unit of emigration among the earliest emigrants, but Norwegian neighborhood ties also played an important role (see Gjerde, *From Peasants to Farmers,* 132, 166–67).

17. Elisabeth Koren, *The Diary of Elisabeth Koren, 1853–1855,* 101. The cabin that the Egges and the Korens shared has been preserved by Decorah's Vesterheim Museum and is open to the public. Elisabeth describes it more thoroughly in a March 8, 1854, diary entry: "The whole house is 15 feet wide and 16 feet long and consists of one room and the loft. About a third of one room is partitioned off by a shining chintz curtain with large, variegated flowers, which win universal admiration from those who visit Helene; this curtained space is again divided by another, which thus forms two sleeping chambers

with half a window for each; actually each has just room for a bed."

18. Koren, *Diary,* 369. She added this memory in 1914 when her children decided to publish her diary.

19. Vilhelm Koren's words are quoted in Lovoll, *The Promise of America,* 66–67. Remarkably open to her new experiences, Elisabeth wrote in a letter to her father dated May 4, 1855: "Would you believe that the services in the small houses here make a stronger and more satisfying impression on me than those at home? I do not know why it should be. I think it is the ardent singing of the hymns and the crowded room, whereby the pastor and the congregation come into a much closer and more intimate relationship to each other." In her diaries Elisabeth confided that neither she nor Vilhelm had any plans of staying permanently in America: "Sunday, June 18, 1854 . . . It is beautiful outside, but so quiet and monotonous, green upon green, almost no color variation. Oh, for a mountain with a view of forest and sea! . . . It is something new for me to be completely alone and not see a soul. . . . I do not for a moment wish that we had not come here. . . . But to stay here forever—I cannot think of such a thing, nor can Vilhelm either. . . . Never to gaze again on what I left behind—that would be too heavy a burden." Yet they returned to Norway only once for a brief visit in May 1870. They made the journey with their seven children and returned to America shortly before Christmas that same year. They are buried in the cemetery at Washington Prairie Church.

20. Lulla Preus, "Minder fra den gamle Paint Creek pæstegaard," 8.

21. Dikka Hjort Koren, "Minner fra Paint Creek prestegård," 18–20.

22. Another Luther College student who enjoyed these outings was Pastor George Taylor Rygh (born in Chicago in 1860, graduated from Luther College in 1881). He recalled their delights in his short story "The Dominie" in the 1930 *Jul i Vesterheimen:* "A college boy's Christmas vacation in the country a few decades ago was an experience to be remembered. . . . There were skiing parties, coasting groups along the bluffs that lined the river, skaters

on the glittering surface of the river itself; jolly sleigh-rides in the moonlight along wintry roads through the frosted woods and groves; social doings at the parsonage and in the farm homes round about, and the festive days passed all too quickly."

23. O. E. Brandt (born in 1862 to Nils and Diderikke Brandt; Nils Brandt was the first Lutheran pastor west of the Mississippi and later Luther College pastor and faculty member) gives this taste of the unparalleled excitement evoked by the revelation of the Christmas tree: "As children we waited for nothing with such excitement as the great moment when the door to the parlor, which had been locked while the adults decorated the tree, should be opened. So enthralled by joy when we finally got inside and the Christmas tree shone in all its radiant splendor, we stood spellbound, unable to speak a word. It was like peering into Paradise itself" (Brandt, "Juletréts historie").

24. Other memoirs, too, tell of parents interpreting the Christmas tree symbolically to teach children Christian doctrine, such as Doreen Rentz, who writes in a February 10, 1997, letter to the author: "The tree stand was homemade from equal length pieces of 2 x 4 board. It formed a tan cross. One year, I recall, Dad was carefully trimming the lower end of the trunk to fit the hole in the center. He explained [that] the star to be placed on top was the Bethlehem Star, the green of the fir tree was everlasting life, and the cross of the tree stand was the reminder of Calvary."

25. "At Christmastime a large tree was put up that we children decorated as best we could. The decorations consisted of Christmas baskets of colored paper and walnuts that we gilded. The candles were put on pins stuck in the stem. This last was the Decorah boys' work: they were supposed to learn that the items' expense was not the issue, my parents said" (Koren, "Minner fra Paint Creek prestegård").

26. That this was their goal may be seen in their father's efforts to organize a lending library for the congregation in one of the parsonage's outbuildings. The books were for the most part Norwegian literary works, but also religious and other learned treatises that he brought back from his visit to Norway in 1873. After the Sunday service the assistant to the minister, or *klokker* (literally, "bell ringer"), Ingebret Johnson, would guide interested members of the congregation in choosing a book (Koren, "Minner fra Paint Creek prestegård").

The fact that upper-class city people had the Christmas tree first reflects the dichotomy that existed in Norway between conservative peasants and cosmopolitan city and coastal folk more open to new ways. Gjerde explains the reason for the divergent customs of these two groups: "For hundreds of years migrants had moved from the inner communities toward the coast and into the cities. It was in these more cosmopolitan areas where pressure to give up old folk ways was strongest, that much of the regional folk culture was abandoned. Accordingly a barrier developed between the conservative traditional inland communities and the areas on the coast and especially in the cities" (Gjerde, *From Peasants to Farmers,* 134–35).

27. Another early Norwegian American Christmas tree appeared at Luther College in 1862 at the home of the college's first president, Laur. Larsen: "On Christmas Eve that year we had a Christmas tree on a table in the president's parlor, where those students who had not gone home joined him and his family, and where everybody received small Christmas presents. This was the first of a series of Christmas Eves at which we thereafter each year gathered the students and teachers with their families around a Christmas tree which soon became larger and more splendid than the poor, little one we had that first Christmas in Decorah." (The passage appeared originally in "Nogle gamle Minder," *Symra,* 1913, 169–70, and is translated here by Professor John Christianson, for a paper shared with Decorah's Symra Society.) The affectionately known "mother of Luther College," Diderikke Brandt, also began putting up a Christmas tree for the students in 1865. Recalling her activities during his student days, Pastor Knut Seehuus (class of 1881) later wrote: "Especially at Christmastime she went into action. Since very few of the students could travel home for Christmas, she had a Christmas tree

put up in the college dining room and decorated it herself with the help of her two daughters. . . . She did all that she could so the poor students shouldn't be homesick. I always went home for Christmas, but when I got back, I always heard how much fun they had had, the ones who hadn't gone home" (quoted in Inga Bredesen Norstog, "Til Diderikke Brandts minne"). These early Luther College Christmas trees probably played an instrumental role in introducing the custom to the larger Norwegian American community; the students, having experienced the practice, no doubt encouraged their parents to adopt the practice in their own homes.

28. Though the Norwegians in Løkensgaard's Lake Prairie, Minn., settlement had not yet heard of a Christmas tree, other contemporary Minnesotans recognized it as a German import; the Red Wing *Republican* reported on December 28, 1869: "One of the most pleasant of all our Christmas festivals was that of the German Methodist Church in the City. The Germans have transplanted the beautiful tree of their fatherland. All its emblems are as significant here as across the waters."

29. On the lack of a Christmas tree, Hugo Nisbeth commented from Litchfield, Minn., in 1872, "There is no Christmas tree, for fir trees are not yet planted in this part of Minnesota" (quoted in Heilbron, "Christmas and New Year's on the Frontier," 389). Some immigrants did not let the absence of evergreens stop them from having a Christmas tree, as the following account shows: "Mother was bound to have a tree, so she got the hired boy to find a nice black oak tree that was the right size. Those trees keep their leaves in winter, but turned brown so mother twined green tissue paper among the branches until there was as much green as brown. Then she made stars, chains, cornucopias and flowers out of paper and trimmed the tree, so that when the candles were lit, it was perfect in our eyes. . . . When Christmas Eve day arrived, . . . we were not allowed to see the tree until supper was over. Then the door to the living room was opened and there in the middle of the floor stood the lighted tree in all its glory. There were oh's and ah's from the older

children; the younger ones were struck dumb by all this splendor" (Christmas in Freeborn County, Minn., in the 1870s, from "The Wulfsberg Family in America," by Wulfsberg family members, 1985, NAHA archives, Northfield, Minn.). G. M. Bruce's romanticized description "Christmas on the Prairies" also noted the lack of evergreens and of Christmas gifts among the immigrants during the first poverty-stricken years: "Of presents and goodies we saw but very little, but as we gathered about the little box-elder tree, which served the purpose of the evergreen as a Christmas tree, and joined in the singing of our Christmas songs and partook of the few things which mother's loving hands had prepared for that occasion and listened to the stories told of the Christ child and of Christmas across the sea, we felt rich and happy even in our poverty."

30. "The Christmas Tree Festival at the School House," in *Viking Early Settlement Days, 1886–1934* (privately published, n.p.).

31. Eugene Boe, "Pioneers to Eternity," 71.

32. Grose, "A Pioneer Boy's Experiences."

33. In his memoir of pioneer childhood in Goodhue County, Grose says about the immigrants' reading habits: "Books were few among the pioneers. The Catechism, Kingo [hymns] or Guldberg [a *postill*] and the Bible frequently made up their entire library." Among the books of my own immigrant great-grandparents (Martin Gulbrandson of Skedsmo, born 1845, and Gjertrud Knudsen Fjelbroten, born 1847 in Aadalen) was the postill by Heinrich Muller, *Aandelige hviletimer, 296 Betraktninger til Huus og Bord Andakt* (Sessions of spiritual rest: 296 meditations for home and table devotions), translated from the German and published in Stavanger in 1855.

34. Of the solemnity that characterizes the first part of Christmas, Teigen says, "Few were so irredeemable as to play the fiddle or cards, dance, or go julebukking until after the third day, but then the merriment really broke loose" (*Ligt og uligt,* 174).

35. This custom derives from Barnemesse (children's Mass), December 28, which became the traditional day for children's Christmas tree parties.

36. Thurine Oleson, *Wisconsin My Home,* 102.

37. Helgeson's book appeared in 1923 under the title *Folkesagn og folketro. Fortalt af de første Nybyggere paa Indilandet, Wisconsin* (Folk legends and folk belief told by the first settlers in the Indian lands of Wisconsin). Helgeson was an itinerant parochial schoolteacher and talented raconteur. He had earlier (1916) published a book called *Fra indianernes lande* (From the Indian lands), followed by a second volume by the same title about two years later. The latter volume is entirely devoted to stories told to Helgeson by local Norwegian immigrants. Malcolm Rosholt has translated these first two books as *From the Indian Land: First-hand Accounts of Central Wisconsin Pioneer Life* (1985), which also contains Rosholt's own thorough research of the area. Helgeson's 1923 collection appears to be an additional collection rather than a revision of the first two. I am grateful to Professor Pat Williams of the University of Wisconsin at Stevens Point for the Rosholt reference.

38. Rosholt, *From the Indian Land,* 257.

39. Helgeson identifies the source of this story as Hans Halvorsen Pladsen, an immigrant from Lund in Telemark (Helgeson, *Folkesagn og folketro,* 16–17).

40. The story "The Jutul and Johannes Blessom" may be found in Reidar Christiansen, *Folktales of Norway.* Asbjørnsen's version of the story originated the phrase, "Du lytt tåle det, Blessomen" (You'll just have to put up with it, Blessom; similar to the English "just grin and bear it"), still current in Norway today. During Blessom's wild ride through the air on the jutul's sled, he loses a mitten. Being in no position to go back and fetch it, his driver tersely makes the now familiar remark.

41. Helgeson names his source for this story as Thorstein Kvie, originally of Hurum in Valdres (Helgeson, *Folkesagn og folketro,* 3–4).

42. Helgeson attributes his version to Per Torgerson Vestlie, an immigrant from Vestre Gausdal in Gudbrandsdal (Helgeson, *Folkesagn og folketro,* 22–23).

43. Jerome P. Field, "Folktales from North Dakota, 1910."

44. The coexistence of pre-Christian and Christian beliefs may also be observed in the way Norwegians persisted in venerating the *tuntre* (the farm's ancestral burial mound tree) and *gardvord* long after the Gulatingslov and other Christian laws specifically forbade these practices. Though the customs did usually coexist peacefully, the deep-seated conflict between Christian and folk views emerges in Thom Myking's 1918 description of "å sidde i julestuen" (see chapter five, note 11). By some, at least, the folk practices were thought to proceed at the devil's behest, a notion that probably grew out of the church's efforts to eradicate them.

45. Rosholt, *From the Indian Land,* 257.

46. The goat's head that Teigen describes closely resembles the goat's head discussed in chapter 9, note 1.

47. L. DeAne Lagerquist reflects this sexual division in the title and body of her 1991 book, *In America the Men Milk the Cows.* So strong was the sexual division of labor in preindustrial Norway that it was unthinkable for the husband to tend to the animals even when his wife was in childbed—as she often was. A man simply did not do women's work, and to avoid that happening a neighbor's wife would be summoned instead. But when necessary, women did all kinds of men's work, both inside and out. This was especially true in the districts along the coast, where the men left for extended periods of fishing while women remained behind and ran the farm alone (Gunvor Øverland Bergan and Trinelise Dysthe, *Hjemme i Norge. Tradisjon og fornyelse,* 61). Though women once had the role of overseeing all the farm's most vital resources, proudly wearing the keys to the stabbur as a visible symbol of their status in the household as they had done for centuries, the situation changed after industrialization.

48. Gjerde traces the profound changes in family structure, division of labor, and fertility that occurred among immigrants from Balestrand, showing how roles within the family came more to resemble urban conditions in terms of furnishings and cultural refinements in *From Peasants to Farmers,* 167–69. The changes observed in Christmas customs demonstrate the same pattern of upward mobility.

Helping Midwestern women become knowledgeable consumers ("queens" of their households, as the book puts it), *Buckeye Cookery and Practical Housekeeping* joined a spate of other practical advice books, American counterparts of Hanna Winsnes's Norwegian "Textbook in the various aspects of housekeeping." *Buckeye Cookery,* originally published in Minneapolis, was reissued in 1988 by Minnesota Historical Society Press and provides a wealth of insights into Midwestern conditions, especially foodways and home life during the last half of the nineteenth century.

49. Veblen comments that the customs in Norway were also changing: "Something similar is happening in Norway, too, since newly arriving immigrants know nothing more about the old Christmas customs than the youngsters who have grown up here" (Veblen, "Jul i Manitowoc-Skogen"). Besides reflecting a change in customs, Veblen's perception of the newcomers' lack of familiarity with peasant traditions may also be ascribed to the greater portion of post-1900 immigrants who came from urban areas of Norway, where those practices had died out much earlier.

50. Munch, *The Strange American Way,* 30, 59.

51. The letter, dated February 8, 1883, appeared in the March 13, 1883, issue of *Vestlands-Posten*; the source of this quotation is Frederick Hale, ed., *Their Own Saga: Letters from the Norwegian Global Migration,* 27. Elisabeth Koren complains of the lacking Easter celebration in America and explains the importance of such rituals in this 1854 diary entry: "It is the eve of Easter, but no indication of it in my surroundings—nothing to distinguish this evening from an ordinary Saturday evening. And yet it is so pleasant when one can notice everywhere that it is a festal eve, when everything is polished and tidied and the daily work is laid aside—and thus it all had to be at home before the church bells began to ring. . . . I remember as a child how often I hurried in order to be ready before the holy day was rung in—here there is nothing like that."

52. N. N. Rønning, "Some Experiences of a Newcomer."

53. O. A. Miller, "Julen i Norge og julen i Amerika," 6. Other observers missed church bells, too.

Elisabeth Koren wrote on Maundy Thursday Eve in April 1854: "How I miss the church bells! I should so much like to hear them on Sunday mornings and when they call people to work in the summer." L. J. Njus wrote in 1946 about a long-ago visit with his relative Nils Henjum, the klokker of a newly established church and congregation in South Dakota: "It was a Saturday evening. We were both walking toward the house with a milk pail in each hand. Then we suddenly and unexpectedly heard the sound of bells. Nils, who was walking ahead, stopped and set the milk pails on the ground. He turned toward the church which stands on a rising. He doffed his cap and held it in folded hands for a long time until the tones had completely died away. For me it was the first time I heard a church bell in America and this episode fixed itself permanently in my memory" (Njus, "Fra Midtvestens saga," *Jul i Vesterheimen,* 45). Lloyd Hustvedt (born 1922) offers this vignette from his time as a ringer of these bells in Goodhue County, Minn.: "We lived near the church. For years I and two brothers took over the bell ringing on Christmas Eve. This took energy and stamina that the old custodian lacked. We went into the bell tower and hand operated a heavy hammer or clapper. This was done as rapidly as our strength permitted. This was called chiming as opposed to the ringing that came with tilting the bell back and forth. When you chimed, the bell stood still, but the ringing had an enduring quality. We worked in three minute shifts until we were exhausted. We know the meaning of 'ringing in Christmas.' Those who heard it, loved the ritual" (letter to the author, August 18, 1999).

54. Klaveness's book, whose full title was *Blandt udvandrede Nordmænd. Vore landsmænds liv og vilkaar i den nye verden* (Among emigrated Norwegians: Our compatriots' lives and conditions in the New World) met with severe criticism (unfairly so, in Andreas Ueland's view). Klaveness was the first Norwegian to use the Norwegian government writer's stipend (*digtergasje*) to go to America rather than Rome or Paris. Although opposed to emigration, Klaveness expressed high regard for what the Norwegian immigrants had achieved in America: "Norwegians

have played a role not only in the cultivation, politics, and business life of America, but to just as great a degree participated in the creation of American cultural and social life. There are Norwegian schools, churches, and hospitals over there in a number that no other nation in relation to the size of its population can match. In American wars, especially the Civil War, Norwegians have participated with honor." But he thought they should make their achievements better known and called for someone to write a history of the Norwegian role in making America: "We as a people have played a part in morally establishing the strongest nation of the world, we as a nation in peace and through hard work and knowledge have won new land for our culture" (32–34).

55. Klaveness, *Blandt udvandrede Nordmænd,* 60–61. Similar sentiments about the contrast between affluence and happiness are voiced by a friend of Klaveness who had lived in America for about fifteen years: "I live well. I earn money easily, more than I need to live. And I live in beautiful surroundings; the scenery on the West Coast is lovely and the climate comfortable. But I don't feel happy. I was too old when I left and cannot forget Norway. Homesickness sits in my blood and will always make me homeless." He concludes, "We can attain everything over here, but never full and complete human happiness" (59–69).

56. Harriet Beecher Stowe, "Christmas; or, The Good Fairy," *National Era* 4 (December 26, 1850); Stephen Nissenbaum, *Battle for Christmas,* 133–34, 338.

57. Axel Smith Papers, Vesterheim Museum Archives. I am indebted to Laurann Gilbertson, curator of textiles, for alerting me to this source.

58. Letter to the author from Fred Fretheim, Bloomington, Minn., August 19, 1996.

NOTES TO CHAPTER 7

1. Emigration most often originated from the very districts that possessed Norway's most traditional folk cultures, namely the inner fjord districts of western Norway and the central mountain districts.

2. Jon Gjerde, *From Peasants to Farmers,* 10, 115. Gjerde points out how the commercial character of America worked at cross-purposes with the immigrants' desire to preserve traditions: "They were trying to preserve their social fabric in an environment that was more conducive to economic growth."

3. Borghild Estness, *Josie Rykken's Family,* 165.

4. Ethel Odegard, *A Norwegian Family Transplanted,* 130–32.

5. Norman Reitan, *Bright Patches: Growing Up Norwegian in Shawano County, Wisconsin,* 33. Leavened bread would not have been part of the traditional Norwegian meal; Reitan must mean that the flatbread replaced the leavened bread of everyday meals in America.

6. The custom of repeating the hymn three times also appears in the memoirs of Reverend Elias Aas, there describing Christmas in Norway in the mid-1800s: "Early Christmas morning we were awakened by Father's beautiful singing. The hymn 'To us is born a blessed child' (Et lidet barn saa lystelig / Er født os paa jorden) was sung three times" (Aas, *The Pioneer Pastor,* 29). I am indebted to Professor Todd Nichol of Luther Seminary for this reference.

7. In some homes special fruit wines were used (quite sparingly among teetotalers, who on such special occasions allowed their temperance views to be outweighed by their desire to observe tradition): "According to an old Christmas custom in Norway, the lady of the house gave wine to each member of the family Christmas morning while everyone was still in bed. For this ceremony my grandmother used chokecherry wine made from berries gathered on the farm. The amount of wine received was . . . hardly enough to relax the central nervous system of an ant" (Eugene Boe, "Pioneers to Eternity," 75).

8. C. R. Remme, "Jul blandt nybyggerne," 71–74.

9. The prominent Norwegian immigrant judge, Andreas Ueland, speculates that it may in fact have been the need to make Christmas special, in a way that food no longer could, that made the Christmas tree and presents such an important part of the American celebration. In letters to his daughters, he muses: "[December 5, 1920] I am wondering whether [the

tree and presents] did not come into use after eating became so good all the year around that something had to be found to make Christmas different from other holidays.... [December 18, 1921] There can never be such Christmas in this country as there was in the old because there the enjoyment came largely from the Christmas food and drink, and here the food at least is that way every day of the year" (*Recollections of an Immigrant*, 166–67).

10. Remme's remarks accord well with the second of the three-stage process that folklorist Robert Klymasz has proposed for the evolution of immigrant folklore: (1) Resistance (to change), which is "best exemplified by an effort to retain and amplify that segment of the Old Country narrative that serves to promote and maintain a tight and cohesive framework for group continuity in the new and ostensibly hostile social and natural environment." In chapter 6 we saw the great care with which the Norwegian immigrants followed their forefathers' traditional Christmas preparations—brewing, butchering, cleaning, and baking in time-honored ways. This chapter, too, shows how their socializing, often using Norwegian language and Old Country reminiscences, helped to retain and promote group identity. (2) Breakdown (due to change), which "signals the crucial attempt on the part of certain segments of the community to scrutinize and evaluate its traditions and to detach itself from what appear to be meaningless and dysfunctional survivals, while asserting the need for a continuity of the folklore heritage in some form or another." Remme rejects as old-fashioned and unnecessary the practices associated with the belief in the supernatural, but maintains the foodways as a continuity with practices in Valdres. (3) Reconstitution (adjustment to change), which "acts to resolve the ongoing tensions between the old and the new by meeting the challenge of acculturation on its own terms, as it were, and by reformulating the folklore legacy in keeping with the demands and pressures of modern and materialistic civilization." Both this chapter and chapter eleven demonstrate how Norwegian Americans began combining elements from the American Christmas with their traditional practices and more

recently began self-consciously choosing and reshaping those elements of their ethnicity that continue to have meaning in their own lives. See Robert B. Klymasz, "From Immigrant to Ethnic Folklore," 134–35. I am indebted to Professor James P. Leary of the University of Wisconsin Folklore Program for this reference.

11. The relationship Norwegian Americans had with the supernatural varied with the individual; some rejected it entirely, while others maintained a few of the practices and beliefs, and still a few were "true believers." Teigen's mention in chapter 6 of the brewer rapping the beer barrel with a knife to rid the brewing process of "djevelskap" and the stories collected by Helgeson show that supernatural beings and beliefs remained present in some pioneer minds and practices.

The long memory of certain folk customs is also evident in the following statements collected by Brad Rost, a student in the author's 1983 Norwegian folklore class: Francis Ronning (born 1915) was told by her grandmother, who had heard from her mother: "After finishing chores on Christmas Eve, the people would put a cross on the stable door while saying 'In Jesus' Name.' This was to protect the animals from the evil spirits which flew at Christmastime." Francis's husband, James Ronning (born 1915), says that his grandfather, who grew up in America, learned from his Norwegian immigrant parents about "a custom in the old days that by running steel over a colt, the animal would be protected from various spirits. In this way one could protect the colt and ensure its safekeeping."

12. D. G. Ristad, "Slik holder vi jul."

13. Winjum's typewritten account may be found in the Minnesota Historical Society library under the title "Farm Stories." It has been slightly edited here for language usage and style. I am indebted to Deborah Miller, research supervisor at the Minnesota Historical Society, for this reference.

14. Chrystene Nordness Weedman (born 1911) notes a similar time period for the shift to English-language services: "Coming from Norwegian parents (though they both were born in the USA), I knew very little English when I started school. We

had Norwegian services only in our church until about the mid-20s" (letter to the author, February 27, 1997).

15. The process for making sylte is described by Bertha O'Crowley (born in 1917 of Norwegian immigrant parents), who grew up in northern Minnesota: "After long boiling of the pig's head, the meat was picked off the bones, seasoned and tied in a gauze bag and chilled in the cold air (during late fall and winter season). I still savor the taste of it, as it is unobtainable now." She adds, "We lived on a farm [in a predominantly Norwegian area] and did all our own slaughtering. My mother would can meatballs and stew meat as we had no refrigeration. Our neighbor would cure our bacon and ham" (letter to the author, January 30, 1997).

16. Knut Takla, *Det norske folk i de forenede stater,* 275.

17. Collected by Heidi Sundet, a student in the author's 1983 Luther College folklore class.

18. Collected by Dirk Torkelson, a student in the author's 1983 Luther College folklore class.

19. Collected by Angela Jacobsen, a student in the author's 1983 Luther College folklore class.

20. Letter to the author from Leif Lie (born 1915), January 1997.

21. Young people in Decorah, Iowa, still grow up learning tales (often told tongue in cheek) about the nisser. They also see them in their neighbors' windows and hear about them on "troll walks" conducted during Nordic Fest, the annual Scandinavian festival (the last weekend in July). Janee Eckheart (born 1961 in Decorah) says: "The older generation believes there are trolls and nisses living in the hills of Decorah. They were here before people. It is believed that during the day the nisses are out and watch over us and at night the trolls come out and look after the people in the community." Eckheart herself just thinks it's fun to tell others about nisser (collected by Judy Finanger, a student in the author's 1983 Luther College folklore class).

22. O. E. Brandt, "Juletreets historie." Brandt was born in Rock River, Wis., in 1862. His father was the first Norwegian pastor to visit the state of

Iowa and the first pastor of Luther College. His mother, Diderikke Brandt, fondly known as the Mother of Luther College, played an influential role in acquainting the students with the Christmas tree custom.

23. Winjum says: "Before they had enough room for a genuine tree, they had on at least one occasion erected a bare poplar branch, festooned with pink roses homemade from crepe tissue paper, showing that the idea and desire for a home Christmas tree had been present before space allowed." The Winjums' action resembles a custom once practiced in some parts of Norway of forcing branches of mountain ash brought into the house at Christmastime to leaf out. They would then study the process in order to predict the coming growing season. The practice has by no means died out, but today's Norwegians follow it during Lent, when charitable organizations earn money by selling feather-festooned branches (known as *fastelavnsriser,* Lenten whips) on street corners. Put into a water-filled vase at home, these branches make a colorful decoration and a happy harbinger of spring, leafing out long before the trees outdoors.

Both customs resemble a Central European Christmas custom Brandt mentions in his article on the history of the Christmas tree: "Some weeks before Christmas they took cherry or pear tree branches and potted them in the living room so they could leaf and flower out by Christmas. During the Middle Ages they usually picked these branches around midnight on November 30. Later it became common to begin this greenhouse work on St. Barbara's day, November 4, and for that reason such branches today are called 'St. Barbara's branches' in those areas where the custom continues" (Brandt, "Juletrets historie"). Brandt says the custom probably came as a first step toward eventually using the evergreen for a Christmas tree, and that is, of course, just the way it also functioned centuries later for the Winjum family on the northern Minnesota prairie.

24. We can see the deep meaning those childhood trees held—along with the great vigilance they

required—in the following accounts: "I only had one Christmas tree growing up. I gave my children some of the candle holders and I still put a few on my tree with little candles in them. My dad had pails of water by the tree. He was so scared of fire. Our church burned down from a candle that must have still been burning" (letter to the author from Alice Olson, [born 1914], McFarland, Wis., April 30, 1997). Tina Olson (born ca. 1910), Prairie View Township, Minn., recalls: "Our Christmas tree was generally a fir, oak, or scrub from our wood lot in Norway Grove near Olaf Lake. Dad brought the tree home when he hauled our wood for winter fuel. We trimmed the tree the night before Christmas with popcorn strings, paper chains, some tinsel, bells, candy canes and lastly candles of many colors. These candles could be lit only by two people when all others sat still to be sure no fire got started in the dry tree. 'Silent Night' was sung as all watched the candles burn to small stumps before they were blown out and removed" (*Seasons to Remember: Barnesville, the First Hundred Years*).

25. While Americans of other ethnic groups—for example, English, Irish, French, or Italian—opened their presents on Christmas Day, Norwegian Americans continued the Scandinavian custom of opening them on Christmas Eve. Winjum says: "It seems that from the very first, the family celebration of Christmas was on Christmas Eve. Because we had the family Christmas celebration on Christmas Eve this early, it probably was also the practice in Dad's and Mother's families, and became a tradition in our own family."

26. "Home-made Santa and a Christmas Tree," *Ladies' Home Journal* 25 (December 1907): 35.

27. Written by Alida Johnson (born 1922 in Hendricks, Minn.) in December 1993, sent in a letter to the author, February 3, 1997.

28. In his book *The Joys of Christmas Past,* Phillip Snyder credits James Edgar, who owned the Boston Store in Brockton, Mass., as being the father of the department store Santa. A Scottish immigrant, he was tall and roly-poly, with a white beard and a hearty laugh. He also loved children. For the Christ-

mas of 1890, he had a Santa Claus suit made and wore it to the store during children's after-school hours. In just a few days the idea had proven so popular that there were long lines waiting outside the store. By the turn of the century, department stores in large cities all around the country had added a throne for Santa (252).

29. Quoted in Leigh Eric Schmidt, *Consumer Rites: The Buying and Selling of American Holidays,* 140–41. Street corner Santas were well received by the public, and the demand for their services rose steadily during the early twentieth century; the first Santa training school was founded in 1937. A debate accompanied this development during the first four decades of the twentieth century: Should Santa be perpetuated, what were the long-term consequences for the nation's children?

30. Letter to the author from Alida Johnson, February 3, 1997.

31. Letter to the author from Chrystene Nordness Weedman (born 1911), February 27, 1997.

32. Letter to the author from Ruth Halbert (born 1917), May 15, 1997. Halbert's parents were both born in Norway.

33. Letter to the author from Lois Bjelland, January 15, 1997.

34. Letter to the author from Irma Chamberlain, January 29, 1997.

35. Speaking in 1915, Woodrow Wilson said: "You cannot dedicate yourself to America unless you become in every respect and with every purpose of your will a thorough American and you can't become a thorough American if you think of yourselves in groups." Quoted (p. 35) by Carl Chrislock in the introduction to *Cultural Pluralism versus Assimilation,* ed. Odd Lovoll, 3–37. My discussion in this section draws extensively on Chrislock's essay.

36. The phrase appears in the title of a book edited by Thomas Wheeler, *The Immigrant Experience: The Anguish of Becoming American.*

37. This emphasis on public performance may have been unknown in Norway at the time (though it has since become part of their Christmas programs, too).

38. Written by Alida Johnson in December 1993, sent in a letter to the author, February 3, 1997.

39. William B. Waits, *The Modern Christmas in America: A Cultural History of Gift Giving,* 132.

40. Schmidt, *Consumer Rites,* 187–88.

41. *Seasons to Remember,* 71.

42. "People always looked forward to julebukking, even more than Christmas!" (anonymous informant, born ca. 1910, living near Harvey, N.D.; collected in 1985 by Percy Steichen of Ulen, Minn., for an English course taught by John Serman, Moorhead State University). Two additional collections of oral histories of julebukking have also contributed insights to this chapter, one submitted by James P. Leary, professor of folklore at the University of Wisconsin–Madison, and the other by Gerald Anderson, professor of history at North Dakota State University. Julebukking is discussed in detail in chapter nine.

43. Winjum defines "julebrukking" as "night callers," a term that more commonly refers to a Norwegian custom usually practiced at the mountain *seter* (dairy farm) during the summer, when young men would visit the young women staying there to tend the livestock. In Norwegian the custom is known as *nattefrieri* (night courting). At first I assumed that Winjum had simply applied the wrong term, but other sources, too, describe a julebukking practice followed in the United States that seems to combine the two practices, such that Norwegian American julebukking, at least in some areas, came to include the features of courting associated with nattefrieri. Perhaps there was, at least in some areas, a Norwegian American variant of julebukking that combined both customs.

44. *Seasons to Remember,* 134–35.

45. The article comes from the *Clinton [Wis.] Times Observer,* January 30, 1930. Given the dearth of contemporary descriptions of the custom, I include the rest of the article here:

Norwegian Custom of "Yuleboking"
Observed by Young Folks

The crowd of masked young people in town Monday evening had come in from Bergen after making the rounds of their neighborhood in observance of the old Norwegian custom of "Yuleboking." On some evening between Christmas and New Year's day every year since Bergen young folks can remember they have carried out this holiday celebration feature from the land of their fathers and mothers.

Dressed in the most comical costumes they can produce, and masked, the party goes from house to house with holiday greetings. Everywhere they are cordially received by the older folks. Even if they have retired for the night they will good-naturedly arise to welcome the "Yulebokers." They will try to guess who their guests are, and will provide something to eat and drink if possible.

I am indebted to Ruth Crane of the Norwegian-American Historical Association for this reference.

46. Klaveness, *Blandt udvandrede nordmaend,* 62.

47. B. F. Bergesen, "Julemindet—Barnesindet," n.p.

48. Knute Løkensgaard, "Jul i gamle dage."

49. Marcus O. Bøckman "Jul i Vesterheimen," n.p.

50. Stephen Nissenbaum, *Battle for Christmas,* 133–34.

51. Klaveness, *Blandt udvandrede nordmaend,* 159. The Norwegian American novelists Ole Rølvaag and Waldemar Ager shared Klaveness's view that Norwegians could contribute most to American society by retaining and cultivating their Norwegian heritage.

52. Carl M. Roan, "Amerika og Norskdommen" in *Paa tur hit og dit: Reiseskildringer og litt til* (Journeys here and there: Stories of travel and a little more) (Minneapolis: *Folkebladet* 1921), 129.

53. Andreas Ueland, in an October 27, 1918, letter to his daughter, quoted in his *Recollections of an Immigrant,* 136–37.

NOTES TO CHAPTER 8

1. Though often thought of as a Scandinavian tradition, these yearbooks, which possibly began as

New Year's gifts, became fixtures of the holiday season in both Europe and America during the nineteenth century.

2. Letter to the author from Enid Ringdahl (born 1947), March 24, 1997.

3. J. A. Holvik, "Et glimt av vaart virke," n.p.

4. Ueland was born in Norway in 1852, the son of the prominent Norwegian statesman Ole Gabriel Ueland. When his father died, Andreas, then eighteen, became possessed by "America fever." Immigrating to Rushford, Minnesota, he subsequently settled in Minneapolis and became the first Scandinavian American to practice law, eventually achieving a reputation as the most eminent jurist in the Northwest. His wife Clara Hampson Ueland—"Mother," in the epigraph—was of Yankee stock, and she had a distinguished career in Minnesota as a progressive reformer, leading the Minnesota Woman Suffrage Association. No wonder she had little time to butcher, bake, and brew.

5. For a lively portrayal of the entire Norwegian American literary scene, see Orm Øverland's 1996 book, *The Western Home: A Literary History of Norwegian America.*

6. An English translation of this story appears in *Jul i Vesterheimen*'s 1920 issue.

7. Quoted in Carl Chrislock's introductory essay in *Cultural Pluralism versus Assimilation,* ed. Odd Lovoll, 25.

8. *Lutheraneren,* May 17, 1917.

9. The early Norwegian clergy was critical of the common school in America, and during the 1850s controversy over religious versus public schools raged in the Norwegian settlements and became a favorite topic of the Norwegian American press. The debate caused irreversible schisms in many congregations. By the 1870s the controversy had subsided and most Norwegian settlers no longer opposed the free public school, but they were not ready to give up religious school, either, continuing for a long time to view the common school as "not Christian." Many chose the compromise of holding religious school during the summer when the public school was not in session. The schools not only taught the immigrants and their descendants religion, but helped preserve their culture and heritage. Well into the twentieth century, Norwegian school curriculum in the settlements contained stories and poems depicting Norway's heroes, writers, and artists, accounts of Norwegian settlements in America, and other material relating to conditions among Norwegians on both sides of the Atlantic.

10. B. F. Bergesen, "Julemindet-Barnesindet," n.p.

NOTES TO CHAPTER 9

Epigraph: Pearson, "I Remember, I Remember," 171.

1. The julebukk head was bought at a Rochester, Minn., antique store in the spring of 1973 by Luis Torres, then a resident of Decorah. He learned that the object had originally come from Whitehall, Wis. That summer he traveled to Whitehall, where he interviewed several residents about the head. He and his quest were featured in an article in the local newspaper that asked readers for more information about the artifact, but there was no response. Further inquiries by the author in the 1980s also brought no response. The Vesterheim Norwegian-American Museum owns a copy of the head. Julebukking is also discussed in chapters four and seven.

2. Though one informant from Rothsay, Minn. (born in the 1880s, emigrated from Norway at age twenty-eight), remembered the custom from Norway and could correctly identify the meaning of *julebukk* as "Christmas goat," most informants give answers more like the one from this informant (born in Norway in 1892, emigrated at age seventeen): "I think juleboeking means to dress up like something else." The informants were interviewed by students of John Sherman, professor of English at Moorhead State University, in response to Sherman's 1985 assignment that they learn about julebukking from local residents. One student, Perry C. Steicher of Ulen, Minn., turned in a particularly impressive collection of interviews from his hometown and from a rest home in Moorhead. Several more will be quoted below. All informants requested anonymity.

3. Even as recently as 1985, Norwegian Americans born around the turn of this century were reluctant to be interviewed about the practice and requested anonymity. Steicher attributed the informants' reluctance to the custom's association with alcohol. Given the strong position of the church and the clergy's rejection of the practice because of the drinking involved, this explanation makes sense, but embarrassment about participating in a custom ridiculed by the majority Yankee society may have also played a role.

4. Elaine Olson (born 1935) mentions that her Coon Valley, Wis., family used to save a goat's head from the fall slaughter for use in their julebukking (interview with author, February 16, 1991).

5. Elaine Olson, interviewed by the author, February 16, 1991.

6. Though other ethnic groups (notably the British and Germans) practiced Christmas masquerading, it seems to have become associated with Norwegians when it moved farther west. John Baur, in his *Christmas on the American Frontier, 1800–1900,* describes Christmas in the Rockies (Montana), saying, "Already by the seventies it had become a melting pot, a cross section of the America that was 'becoming.'" Butte was populated by, among others, Albanians, Montenegrins, Serbs, Bulgarians, Ukrainians, Russians, and Norwegians, all attracted by mining. Singling out the Norwegians, Baur specifically characterizes them by their custom of going julebukking: "Norwegians were also in the copper camp, and on December 25 they went about in fantastic costumes, garbed as 'Christmas fools,' invading the homes of their friends and entertaining the surprised residents" (193).

7. My thanks to Brian O'Connell of VOCM Radio Newfoundland for supplying the text of the song made popular by a duo known as Simani (Bud Davidge and Sim Savory): Here's a sample:

Come in, lovely mummers, don't bother the snow,
We can wipe up the water sure after you go.
Sit if you can or on some mummer's knee.
Let's see if we know who you be.

Chorus:
There's big ones and small ones and tall ones and thin.
Boys dressed as women and girls dressed as men.
With humps on their backs and mitts on their feet,
My Blessed, we'll die with the heat.

Written in 1983, the song immediately became popular and part of Newfoundland's Christmas repertory. In 1991 it was also published in children's book format, illustrated by Ian Wallace.

8. For Newfoundland *mummering* or *janneying,* see Halpert and Story, *Christmas Mumming in Newfoundland,* and Robertson, *The Newfoundland Mummers' Christmas House Visit.* For "a-sernatin'" as practiced in Rock Springs, Ga., and Randolph County, Ala., see White, "Sernatin': A Traditional Christmas Custom in Northeast Georgia." For "belsnickles" as practiced in southern Pennsylvania and the Shenandoah Valley of Virginia, see Cline, "Belsnickles and Shanghais," and Shoemaker, *Christmas in Pennsylvania,* 73–85. For mumming in Philadelphia, see Welch, "Oh Dem Golden Slippers," and Shoemaker, *Christmas in Pennsylvania.*

9. Some informants admitted to being less than thrilled with the custom in earlier times, as well, such as this Swedish American woman (born 1902) living near Hawley, Minn.: "A gang of them would dress up and put a sack over their heads and you'd have to treat them. We'd just give them candy and then they'd go. My husband would say, 'I hope we don't get any more,' because it was sometimes late and we were in bed" (collected by students of John Sherman, Moorhead State University).

10. Reported to the author in January 1996 by Georgia Rosendahl and Geneva Tweeten (who, it turns out, is the housewife who got her husband out of bed to identify those in our 1985 julebukking group). A related story was sent to the author by Alice A. Olson (born 1914), of McFarland, Wis.: "One of our neighbors who grew up here married a nurse from Chicago. The first year they were married, about 1950 or 1951, Julebukkers came and rapped on

the front door. It was between Christmas and New Years. She opened the door and they walked in. A couple of them were pretty bad looking and sat down, and she went screaming to the kitchen, 'Roger, call the cops!' He walked in and started laughing and she was almost hysterical. He told her to get some cookies and he got the wine. She didn't, he had to, and she ran into the bedroom and locked the door."

11. An anonymous informant from Ulen, Minn. (born 1898), confirms this: "But you only went to places where they knew what julebukking was or you would scare the life out of the kids and newcomers. If you did a thing like that now, they'd shoot you." In some isolated areas, though, the custom apparently became more inclusive, as this anonymous informant living near Harvey, N.D., indicates: "I think it started with the Norwegians, but when they all found out, they all came, even the Germans." Another woman (born ca. 1910 and a lifelong resident of Ulen, Minn.) said: "It was a must to go out, and you didn't have to be Norwegian or Swedish." All of the above observations were collected by Perry C. Steicher for a class taught by John Sherman, Moorhead State University, 1985.

12. In addition to allowing a release from rigid social control, the pattern of reversal is consistent with the preindustrial Norwegian Christmas itself, being an upside-down time when food was not spared, work remained undone, and servants became the guests of the house. Coming at the seam of the year, Christmas is a ritual time of transition or liminality during which such deviance is sanctioned without jeopardizing social values and relationships, but also when social mores are upheld (Robertson, *Newfoundland Mummer's Christmas House Visit*, 139–40).

13. Letter to the author from Elaine Nelson (born 1930), Holmen, Wis., January 22, 1997.

14. Letter to the author from Marion Oman (born 1917), Waseca, Minn., April 7, 1997.

15. Donna Bergan (born 1940), Decorah, Iowa. Interviewed by Luther College folklore student and Vesterheim intern, Heidi Sundet, March 7, 1985.

16. Henry Glassie identified the two-part struc-

ture of the process in Irish mumming; see *All Silver and No Brass,* 93.

17. Clifford Dopson, Coon Valley, Wis., recounting a julebukking outing initiated by Lee Grippen of Caledonia, Minn., and including friends from Norskedalen near Coon Valley; interviewed by the author, February 16, 1991.

18. Orville Bakken (born 1910), Northwood, N.D., interviewed by the author, February 19, 1991.

19. I am indebted to Willard B. Moore for this reference. Though Spring Grove didn't go so far as to ban julebukking, authorities have banned Christmas masquerading in other places and times, probably most notably in late-nineteenth-century Philadelphia, where the 1808 banning of mumming eventually led to the development of the more formal, orderly, and now well known Mummers' Parade on New Year's Day (Halpert and Story, *Christmas Mumming in Newfoundland,* 54).

20. Willard Moore has pointed out the interesting similarity between the anecdotes mentioned in this nineteenth-century article and the stories about julebukking told today, such as the account above of the Spring Grove woman who was punched by her intended host. During our 1985 julebukking foray we heard other colorful anecdotes of near tragedy, households upset by julebukkers' irreverent behavior, and violence ranging from bloodied noses to shotguns discharged in the night to drive off Christmas Fools mistaken for thieves. No longer intended to condemn, the stories told now highlight the boldness and high-spirited nature of the community that features such a colorful custom (Moore, "Ritual and Remembrance in Minnesota Folk Celebrations").

21. Quoted in Solveig Zempel, ed., *In Their Own Words,* 65.

22. Todd Charles interviewed his mother in January 1987.

23. Letter to the author from Elaine Nelson, January 22, 1997.

24. Clifford Dopson, interviewed by the author at Norskedalen near Coon Valley, Wis., February 16, 1911; Inez Rude (born 1920), quoted on a tape describing julebukking in Blair, Wis., prepared for the

author by Søren Urberg, formerly a pastor there, January 1990.

25. Orville Bakken, interviewed by the author, February 19, 1991.

26. Letter to the author from Lloyd Hustvedt, December 20, 1990.

27. Arnold Elvestrom (born 1907), quoted by Todd Charles, December 21, 1987.

28. "Nowadays coming to someone's house in a mask would probably get you shot" (Steve Ringlien, a student in the author's 1989 Luther College folklore class). "It was something people made themselves. People didn't have money . . . and they made their own fun" (Elaine Olson, Coon Valley, Wis., interviewed by the author).

29. Orville Bakken, interviewed by the author, February 19, 1991.

30. Director of volunteers, Doris Barnaal, coordinates the activity at Vesterheim Museum. The Sons of Norway in Hastings, Minn., and the town of Elbow Lake, Minn., are among those who have revived the julebukking custom in recent years.

NOTES TO CHAPTER 10

1. Elisabeth Koren, *The Diary of Elisabeth Koren, 1853–1855*, 156, 239, 234.

2. Mary King, "Memoirs of a Prairie Girlhood," recording in 1928 memories of her childhood in the 1870s and 1880s (typed manuscript, Minnesota Historical Society, St. Paul). By modern nutritional standards the immigrants' diet was heavy, and it was deficient in key vitamins and minerals. Fatty meat, potatoes, and white bread constituted the essential table. Nor is it only a modern eye that looks askance at the pioneer meals. Writing in his diary on December 4, 1843, Søren Bache observes: "Food here is not the right sort for the new-comers, since the usual food here is pork, beef and wheat bread, whereas in Norway they were accustomed to coarse rye bread, milk and cheese" (Søren Bache, *A Chronicle of Old Muskego: The Diary of Søren Bache, 1839–1847*, 99).

3. Reidar Bakken, *Lat ingen sladdrelystne læse mine brever*, 202–3. Rakefisk, like the other Norwe-

gian delicacies described elsewhere in this book, derived from the necessity of managing quantities of food over time. Fishermen caught more than the family could consume at once; what could not be eaten had to be preserved. Any freshwater fish may be used to make rakefisk, but most agree that fermented trout, *rakørret*, tastes best. Reaching its peak at Christmastime, it often appears at Christmas parties, especially in eastern Norway. Norwegians serve rakørret with boiled potatoes, flatbread or lefse, and butter (Aase Strømstad, *Eat the Norway*, 24–25).

4. Letter to the author from Crystal Lokken (born in McFarland, Wis.), Berkeley, Calif., January 27, 1997.

5. "My father [who immigrated from Harstad, Norway, in 1903] would send for lutefisk for the Christmas holidays—it would arrive by mail in a small wooden crate"; letter to the author from Bertha O'Crowley (born 1917), January 30, 1997.

6. George Mohn's 1924 *Cook Book of Popular Norse Recipes* mentions that prepared lutefisk could be purchased, but he also includes recipes for those who wished to prepare the dish from dried stockfish.

7. Gary Legwold, *The Last Word on Lutefisk*, 97.

8. Andreas Ueland, *Recollections of an Immigrant*, 211.

9. Letter to the author from Avis Holmgreen Ruhnke (born 1926 in Black River Falls, Wis.), March 19, 1997. She adds, "But everyone likes the lefse."

10. Letter to the author from Joyce McCracken (born in Norman County, Minn.), March 28, 1997). Like Ruhnke, she adds, "We did have lefse though."

11. Legwold, *Lutefisk*, 84.

12. Letter to the author from Chrystene Weedman, February 27, 1997.

13. Legwold points out that since the early 1980s another kind of fish, ling, has replaced cod. Ling tastes like cod, but requires less handling, cures whiter, and has a texture that holds up better; it therefore provides a more appealing product less expensively (45).

14. Lise-Lunge Larsen, "Legalizing Lutefisk"

(master's degree thesis, College of St. Catherine, St. Paul, Minn.), quoted in Astri Riddervold, *Lutefisk, Rakefisk, and Herring in Norwegian Tradition,* 42.

15. Roger L. Welsch, "Lutefisk: Food as Symbol—The Mysterious Ritual of the Norwegian-American Christmas Dinner," *The World and I* 2 (December 1987): 462–68.

16. Legwold, *Lutefisk,* 51–53.

17. This may in part account for the continuing appeal of lutefisk to Torskeklubben, a group of successful Norwegian American businessmen who regularly meet over a sumptuous meal of the fish. Organized in 1933 as a social club in Minneapolis during the Great Depression, the group originally offered fellowship and mutual support in the harsh commercial climate of that decade.

18. The verse is from "Uncle Torvald's Christmas Carol" as performed December 18, 1998, at the Decorah Sons of Norway Lodge. Originally by E. C. "Red" Stangeland, who during the 1970s and 1980s regularly appeared in stand-up comic acts with "Uncle Torvald" (alias Robert Johnson), the verse has by now become part of oral tradition and exists in many variants.

19. "Some People Hold Lutefisk in Esteem; Others Hold Noses," *Wall Street Journal,* December 14, 1982.

20. Letter to the author from Joyce McCracken, March 28, 1997.

21. Letter to the author from Avis Holmgreen Ruhnke, March 19, 1997.

22. Quoted in Francie Berg, *Ethnic Heritage in North Dakota,* 49.

23. Jo Ann Kana, quoted in Legwold, *Lutefisk,* 148–49.

24. Some now use potato flakes to avoid this look, while others object that the more uniform appearance comes at the expense of flavor.

25. Letter to the author from Crystal Lokken, January 27, 1997.

26. The recipe was published in 1924 in Mohn's *Cook Book of Popular Norse Recipes.*

27. Letter to the author from Marion Oman, Waseca, Minn., April 7, 1997.

28. Gary Legwold, *The Last Word on Lefse,* 112.

29. Legwold, *Lefse,* 29.

30. Letter to the author from Avis Holmgreen Ruhnke, March 19, 1997.

31. Letter to the author from Chrystene Weedman, February 27, 1997.

32. Between 1809 and 1835, the Norwegian potato crop increased tenfold. The potato's sturdiness far outstripped that of grain. A field yielding a bushel of grain would yield four bushels of potatoes, a crop less vulnerable than grain to weather and wind. Potatoes would grow in less rich soil and could be more easily planted; after burning away the juniper and heather, one could set potatoes in the ashes, fertilize with manure, cover with seaweed, and watch them grow. The new crop improved the nation's health dramatically. Child mortality sank noticeably and scurvy decreased, as potatoes provided a steady supply of vitamin C. Military records show that average height also increased, especially among *husmannsgutter* (cotters' sons), who became a large component of the immigrant population. By the mid-1800s the potato had become one of Norway's most important foods. It continued to benefit the population and even save lives, keeping Norwegians from starving to death (Harald Osa and Gudrun Ulltveit, *Norsk mat gjennom tidene,* 85). As the potato benefited the Norwegians in Norway, lefse and flatbread helped the pioneers survive on the prairie. Mary King, in her memoir "Memories of a Prairie Girlhood," recalls her family's trek west by covered wagon from Fillmore County, Minn., to Canby, S.D., in the mid-1870s. After many other preparations, she says, her mother "then baked lefse or flatbread, an awful lot of it [and put it into] an immense box at the very back end of the wagon" (14–15).

33. "Just a Little Lefse Will Go a Long Way" is by Stan Boreson and Doug Setterberg. The entire text and much more lefse humor can be found in Legwold, *Lefse.*

34. Norwegian cookbooks traditionally distinguish three types of julekaker: those fried in lard, for which a kettle is needed, such as fattigmann and rosetter; those with patterns baked in an iron, such

as goro and krumkake; and those made with yeast and baking powder and baked in an oven. The first two types have a far longer history in Norway than the last, which did not become widespread until after the turn of the twentieth century.

35. Henry Notaker, *Ganens makt*, 237.

36. Recipes for additional types of cookies may be found in Strømstad, *Eat the Norway*; Kjell Innli, ed., *The Norwegian Kitchen*; Mohn, *Cook Book of Popular Norse Recipes*; Anne R. Kaplan, Marjorie A. Hoover, and Willard B. Moore, eds., *The Minnesota Ethnic Food Book*; and Dale Brown, *The Cooking of Scandinavia*.

37. Barbara Levorsen, "Our Bread and Meat."

38. Koren, *Diary*, 102, 104.

39. Letter to the author from Mary Ann Braaten Snyder, Nisswa, Minn., April 7, 1997.

40. Hartshorn and its mixed reviews have a long history in American kitchens. Harriet Beecher Stowe and her sister Catharine referred to it as "Volatile alkali" and marveled over its former preparation from harts' horns in their 1869 book *American Woman's Home*. Twelve years earlier another popular cookbook writer, Eliza Leslie, had taken an even dimmer view. She decried the use of hartshorn, saying that its presence in bread and cake rendered the articles "equally unpalatable as unwholesome." To underscore her revulsion, she implored, "Can not the use of hartshorn in food be put down? Which of our *American* doctors will write a book on culinary poisons?" (Marjorie Kreidberg, *Food on the Frontier*, 53–54). Despite such mixed reviews, hartshorn saw much use during the nineteenth century because baking powder—a combination of baking soda and an acid salt such as cream of tartar—was not marketed until the middle of the century; it was still too new to be widely accepted, too suspect because of its questionable purity, and condemned for high cost and poor performance. As a result, baking powder remained conspicuously absent from lists of recommended ingredients until late in the nineteenth century (Kreidberg, *Food on the Frontier*, 54).

41. Sugar was one of the few items that had to be bought on the self-subsistence farm. Its high cost and the difficulty in obtaining and transporting it dictated sparing use.

42. Kriedberg, *Food on the Frontier*, 169.

43. Kreidberg, *Food on the Frontier*, 169–70.

44. Daniels, *Home Life in Norway*, 252.

45. Mary King, "Memories of a Prairie Girlhood," 28.

46. Both spellings remain common in Norway. Elisabeth Koren mentions three types of porridge in her diary: flødegrød, melkevælling, and risgrød.

47. Koren comments about meeting people from a variety of classes and locations whom she would not have known in Norway: "It pleases and interests me to see and talk to all these different people, our Norwegian farm folk, with whom I have had so little acquaintance up to this time" (December 25, 1853); "I am now meeting a great many people from all districts of Norway" (December 31, 1853).

48. Unpublished memoir, printed for Hegg's family. I am grateful to Joan Jurs of the Luther College Treasurer's Office for this reference.

49. "I periodically made 'modified rømmegrøt' like a thick white sauce, with lots of melted butter—and eaten covered with melted butter, sugar and cinnamon" (letter to the author from Mary Ann Braaten Snyder, Nisswa, Minn., April 7, 1997). Odd Lovoll mentions the difficulty of distinguishing ethnic from family idiosyncrasies in *The Promise Fulfilled*. Such confusion arises when ethnic identity is individually rather than communally practiced.

50. According to Henry Notaker, N. R. Østgaard wrote a book in 1858 saying risengrynsgrøt was pushing out rømmegrøt, but by 1897 Olaug Løken was characterizing rømmegrøt as a national dish (Notaker, *Ganens makt*, 236); Englishman H. K. Daniels also characterizes the dish this way in his 1911 book on Norwegian daily life: "Now, this *rømmegrøt* or sour cream porridge is a national dish, a very satisfying dish, and a rich one, withal" (277–78).

51. A sign of rømmegrøt's status as an ethnic emblem is the emerging humor about it, such as the version of the "food pyramid" that identifies the "five Norwegian food groups" as rømmegrøt, lefse, flatbrød, coffee, and lutefisk. Actually, rømmegrøt

has a long history of standing for something beyond its nutritional content: in the preindustrial peasant society women brought this porridge to a new mother as a token of her fruitfulness, a custom that continued among the early immigrants in America, as well.

52. Scott, *Authentic Norwegian Cooking,* 88.

53. Letter to the author from Martha Elliott, April 23, 1998.

54. Enameled cookware represented a huge step forward; a form of it known as Granite Ware was first exhibited at the Philadelphia Centennial in 1876. Though it immediately became popular, enameled cookware did not become truly widespread among peasants in the Norwegian countryside until after the turn of the century (Carol McD. Wallace, *Victorian Treasures,* 114).

55. Letter to the author from Mary Ann Braaten Snyder, Nisswa, Minn., April 7, 1997.

56. The reference is to the common Norwegian expression "Kjært barn har mange navn" (a beloved child has many names).

57. Letter to the author from Enid Ringdahl (born 1942) of Fergus Falls, Minn., March 24, 1997. The modern, high-tech method of producing klubb contrasts with the peasant origins of the dish. Hanna Winsnes includes klubb in her 1845 cookbook, but adds: "It's used for the *tjenestefolkene* [farm workers], who either heat it in water or fry it in fat. Some like it cut in thin slices, fried in butter and topped with a couple of spoonfuls of syrup in the pan." Her last comment suggests better means among some of those who enjoyed klubb (Winsnes, *Lærebog,* 114).

58. Letter to the author from Eldoris Leyse Hustad (born 1931), Granite Falls, Minn., January 21, 1997.

59. Collected by Jennifer Gehler, a student in the author's 1991 Luther College folklore class. Gehler notes that Wiese's mother was very conscious of her Norwegian background and kept many of her mother's traditions. As paraphrased by Gehler, Wiese, too, joined in the "Norwegian-American lament," saying that while she attempts to reproduce her mother's recipes for many of the Norwegian foods, klubb included, she is unable to get them to turn out as she remembers them.

60. Letter to the author from Joyce McCracken, Macomb, Ill., March 28, 1997.

61. Letter to the author from Judeen Johnson, Brookings, S.D., January 10, 1997.

62. Aase Strømstad, *Eat the Norway,* 43.

63. Koren's role as *husmor,* the female head of household, on the prairie differed substantially from what it would have been in her kondisjonerte circle back in Norway.

64. Though considered by many to be the most typically Norwegian cheese, geitost is not really a cheese at all, since it is made by cooking down the whey after the curds have separated out. Gudbrandsdalsost, the most popular type, was invented around the middle of the 1800s and is made with a mixture of goat's and cow's milk. Geitost always appears on the Norwegian breakfast table and in most packed lunches.

65. Gammelost is made from a centuries-old recipe and is indigenous to Norway. It is a low-fat cheese made with soured skim milk and has a characteristic tangy flavor, an unusual brownish color, and a dry, soft, granular consistency. It is eaten on dark bread or flatbrød with butter spread both over and under the cheese.

66. Kaplan et al., eds., *Minnesota Ethnic Food Book,* 107.

67. Johan Hambro, "Mitt møte med det norske Amerika," in *Møte med Amerika,* ed. Bjørn Jensen, 216–17.

68. Kaplan et al., eds., *Minnesota Ethnic Food Book,* 111–12. The church became a focal point of community activity, though parish life developed along different lines than in Norway. There the pastor was part of the state administrative system, while in Norwegian America the ministers were employed by the community and therefore had to relate directly to the community, dealing, among other things, with the indelible linkage of the church with ethnic expression. The Minneapolis Mindekirken, with a pastor from Norway and some services still

conducted in Norwegian, constitutes a lasting legacy of this linkage.

69. Krin Poppe, 1997 Luther College Scandinavian Studies graduate from Rushford, Minn., provided this perspective in her senior paper.

70. Kaplan et al., eds., *Minnesota Ethnic Food Book,* 114–15.

NOTES TO CHAPTER 11

Epigraph: Letter to the author, January 1997.

1. Letter to the author from Judeen O. Johnson, January, 10, 1997. Johnson is president of Fjordland Sons of Norway Lodge, Brookings, S.D.

2. Until the 1920s the church had been the "biggest and most important factor working for the preservation of the Norwegian language" (Carl Chrislock, introduction to *Cultural Pluralism versus Assimilation,* ed. Odd Lovoll, 34).

3. Karal Ann Marling, *As Seen on TV,* 209–31.

4. Letter to the author from Joyce McCracken, March 28, 1997. She adds: "The parlor room in which the tree would be the center of attention was unheated until the early eve of Christmas Eve. After the tree was in place, my sister and I would decorate it with tinsel, fragile glass balls, candles in clip-on holders. A previous evening had been spent stringing pop corn on white thread; this was now added to the decorations." McCracken's family also maintained the Old Country custom of giving animals, both wild and domestic, a special Christmas treat: "At the completion of the evening farm chores, Dad would attach a sheaf of grain to a tall pole by the side of the barn. This sheaf of wheat had been set aside from the falltime harvest as a treat for the birds. The cattle and horses would get an extra helping of feed on Christmas Eve."

5. Letter to the author from Doreen Rentz, February 10, 1997.

6. Eugene Boe, "Pioneers to Eternity," 81–82.

7. Letter to the author from Robert Bolstad (Itasca, Ill.), editor, historian, and librarian of Skjold Sons of Norway Lodge, December 20, 1996.

8. Boe, "Pioneers to Eternity," 77.

9. Norway, Ill., seventy miles southwest of Chicago, is officially designated by the state of Illinois as the site of the first Norwegian settlement in the Midwest, in 1834.

10. Peter Salins, *Assimilation American Style,* 8–11.

11. Dorothy Burton Skårdal, "Et samfunn av innvandrere," 48.

12. Thomas Wheeler, ed., *The Immigrant Experience,* 11.

13. Ole Rølvaag similarly argued for preserving "Fædrearven" (the heritage of the fatherland). In his novel *Peder Victorious,* the character Pastor Kaldahl disabuses the title character of the notion that America was a new foundation where "the whole structure must be new," with the reminder that many of the timbers in that structure had been brought from far away, some even from Norway.

14. Waldemar Ager's essay is quoted in Carl Chrislock's introduction to *Cultural Pluralism versus Assimilation,* ed. Lovoll, 33.

15. Wheeler, ed., *The Immigrant Experience,* 14–15.

16. *Norwegian-American Historical Association Newsletter,* March 1972.

17. Johan Hambro, "Mitt møte med det norske Amerika," 212–13.

18. Lloyd Hustvedt, editorial, *NAHA Newsletter,* January 1996. An additional indication of the Norwegians' recently aroused interest in emigration was the rededication of the Norwegian American immigrant church moved to Sletta, Norway, near Bergen, from Brampton, N.D. These ceremonies took place July 4–6, 1997, and featured a seminar on emigration, focusing on special events of the emigration to the United States, as well as a gathering "in memory of our mutual past" to "reunite ties and contacts between descendants of the emigrants and the descendants of those who remained in the Old Country, and building a bridge for the future." Three more buildings from the "Norwegian pioneer time in America" will later be moved to Sletta, adding to an emigration archive already established there.

19. Letter to the author from Eldoris Lyse Hustad, January 21, 1997.

20. Letter to the author from Gail Farris, Arcadia, Fla., January 13, 1997.

21. Bill Holm, *Faces of Christmas Past*, 24–25.

22. According to Herbert J. Gans, ethnicity gives America's various groups something in common. In a mobile society in which people often find themselves living in communities of strangers, they tend to look for commonalities that make strangers become neighbors; shared ethnicity may provide mobile people with at least an initial excuse to get together. Herbert Gans, "Symbolic Ethnicity: The Future of Ethnic Groups and Cultures in America."

23. A. A. Veblen, "Jul i Manitowoc-Skogen," 144.

24. G. M. Bruce, "Christmas on the Prairies," n.p.

25. Salins, *Assimilation American Style*, 121–23.

26. The Protestant merchant class of post-Reformation Europe considered personal economic success a sign of God's grace. Work contributed to the common good. While in Europe old traditions fought against capitalism, in the United States these ancient anticapitalist traditions never gained a foothold, making America the one country in the world where the Protestant work ethic and capitalism could prevail unchecked (Salins, *Assimilation American Style*, 127).

27. Penee L. Restad, *Christmas in America: A History*, 147–49.

28. Restad, *Christmas in America*, 148. Restad cites Nast's grandson as her source for this information.

29. Restad, *Christmas in America*, 56, 147–48.

30. Salins, *Assimilation American Style*, 124–25.

31. The pageant presented for the 1925 Centennial Celebration of Norwegian immigration to America at the state fairgrounds in St. Paul, Minn., showed a Norwegian consciousness of their values as those which helped build America. In one tableau representing the ease of Norwegian assimilation into the American mainstream red, white, and blue clad schoolchildren stood first in the form of a Norwegian flag, then smoothly reconfigured themselves into an American flag. The pageant contained a subtext that subverted this message, however, saying that Norwegians had centuries earlier laid the groundwork for the very values that now were considered uniquely American. In contrast to most pageants of the Progressive Era, the Norwegian American 1925 effort thus became a celebration not of American progress, but of Norwegian American progress (April Schultz, *Ethnicity on Parade*, 114–15, 128).

32. Salins, *Assimilation American Style*, 9.

33. Letter to the author from Enid Ringdahl, Fergus Falls, Minn., March 24, 1997.

34. E-mail to the author from Jean Iverson, December 17, 1998. The homestead farm of Iverson's grandfather, Ole Lovdokken, stood in Garborg Township, Richland County, N.D.

35. Letter to the author from Ruth Halbert, May 15, 1997.

36. Sons of Norway revitalized its emphasis on the family in 1998. According to a statement in the January issue of *Viking* magazine: "At Sons of Norway we have resolved to make 1998 the year of the Nordic family. We are committed to introducing members to practical ways to add some 'Nordicness' to their daily lives. We hope that you will join us in our efforts and follow us throughout the year as we suggest ways to live a Nordic Family Lifestyle with your family." That month they also inaugurated a new monthly department called "Nordic Family Traditions," "designed to give readers practical ideas to blend elements of their Norwegian heritage into today's busy lifestyles."

37. "Patriotenes fest med Chester og Sputnik," *Aftenposten*, October 20, 1993. Reiten is the founder of *Høstfest*, the fall Scandinavian festival held annually in Minot, N.D. His ancestors emigrated from Norway in the late 1800s. In *The Promise Fulfilled*, Odd Lovoll notes that when Norwegian Americans talk about heritage, "what they frequently mean and what they wish to transmit to their children is more a sense of where ancestors came from, family memories, origin, rather than being an ethnic identity or

being a part of a contemporary ethnic group." They speak glowingly of a broad Norwegian cultural heritage that they wish to pass on, frequently in terms of specific moral and social values they associate with being Norwegian American (190).

38. Identifying values with one's ethnic group gives them an emotional and social resonance that would not be engendered by simply connecting them with the middle class or even one's own family (Mary Waters, *Ethnic Options,* 138–39).

39. Norma Sersland Hegg, unpublished memoir of life near Decorah, Iowa, during the 1920s and 1930s.

40. Schultz gives an overview of some of this literature, and says, "Ethnicity is not inherent, but constructed as a dialogue between immigrants and the dominant society, a process of identification at a particular moment to cope with historical realities" (Schultz, *Ethnicity on Parade,* 11–12). Folklorists have also grappled with the concept of created ethnicity, such as Stephen Stern in his introduction to *Creative Ethnicity* and in his "Ethnic Folklore and the Folklore of Ethnicity" in *Western Folklore,* and Robert Klymasz's "From Immigrant to Ethnic Folklore" in the *Journal of the Folklore Institute.* (I am indebted to James P. Leary, Folklore Department, University of Wisconsin–Madison, for these references.)

41. The evolving view of ethnicity is dramatically illustrated by the changed views seen within the work of a single scholar, Richard Alba. While in "The Twilight of Ethnicity" he dismisses the 1970s resurgence of ethnicity as perception rather than reality, in the 1990s his work has emphasized the significance of ethnicity in American society and its dynamic reshaping within relatively brief periods of historical time (Lovoll, *The Promise Fulfilled,* 182).

42. How new this idea of nonlinear assimilation seemed in the 1970s emerges in the words of James A. Crispino, *The Assimilation of Ethnic Groups: The Italian Case,* where he sounds quite tentative as he redefines assimilation: "Assimilation must be understood as a process, perhaps one that cannot be described as ever being completed. It may be that ethnicity will always matter to some degree" (164).

The idea was still so new in the 1970s that he felt compelled to modify his statement with a "perhaps" that observers today would feel more comfortable deleting.

43. "Patriotenes fest med Chester og Sputnik."

44. Schultz, *Ethnicity on Parade,* 18. The term *symbolic ethnicity* was coined by Herbert J. Gans in 1979 to refer to a pride in the culture that can be felt without its having to be incorporated into everyday behavior (Gans, "Symbolic Ethnicity").

45. The dilemma was, as Waters notes, already noted by de Tocqueville: while American individualism caused individuals to find their own beliefs within themselves, they also constantly sought affirmation of those beliefs in the people around them (Waters, *Ethnic Options,* 148).

46. "Patriotenes fest med Chester og Sputnik."

47. Lovoll cites other examples, such as the unique blend of foods at the traditional church lutefisk dinner, which in the name of celebrating Norwegian heritage features lefse, flatbrød, rømmegrøt, kjøttkaker, rutabagas, boiled potatoes, sweet soup, cranberries, rolls, and krumkake—a combination of foods hardly acceptable to taste in Norway. Perhaps even more striking is his observation about the disregard for accuracy in Norwegian language usage: "In Norwegian-American settings in the 1990s, the use of any kind of Norwegian at all, rather than its accuracy, is obviously the paramount concern" (Lovoll, *The Promise Fulfilled,* 90, 220).

48. Lovoll, *The Promise Fulfilled,* 37.

49. Stephen Stern and John Allan Cicala, eds., *Creative Ethnicity: Symbols and Strategies of Contemporary Ethnic Life,* xiii. In this volume various folklorists analyze the way ethnic group members living in the United States have adapted and modified their folklore in response to living in a pluralistic society. Stern emphasizes the authenticity of the very ethnic expressions that Old Country Norwegians would question, arguing: "The uncertainties of life in a multicultural society have been reflected in the folklore of ethnic groups, and these groups have found the power . . . to adapt traditional folklore genres to new settings. . . . This creative flexibility in

many forms of cultural expression suggests that ethnicity is a dynamic and evolving force in American life rather than a conservative grouping of old and outmoded ways" (xi). The adaptations that ethnic Americans have made come about, says Stern, because the "precarious" nature of ethnicity in a multicultural setting presents modern ethnics with a "constant need to balance available resources with the demands of relevance." (I am indebted to James P. Leary of the University of Wisconsin Folklore Program for this reference.)

50. Letters to the author from Joyce McCracken, March 28, 1998, and Crystal Lokken, January 27, 1997.

Bibliography

Aanrud, Mona. "Glade jul" (Merry Christmas). *Jul i Vesterheimen* (Christmas in the Western Home), 1948, 28–32.

Aas, Elias. *The Pioneer Pastor: Highlights from the Life and Work of Rev. Elias Aas.* Trans. Leif H. Awes. Minneapolis: Free Church Press, [1970?].

Ager, Waldemar. "Bare mor" (Only mother). *Jul i Vesterheimen,* 1928 (no pagination).

Albers, Henry H., and Ann Kirk Davis. *The Wonderful World of Christmas Trees.* Parkersburg, Iowa: Mid-Prairie Books, [1997].

Ambjørnrud, Olga, Ingunn Børke, Johanne Jansen, and Elisabeth Moe, eds. *Norsk mat* (Norwegian food). Oslo: Cappelen, 1965.

Andersen, Arlow. *The Norwegian Americans.* Boston: Twayne, [1975].

Andersen, Per Sveaas. *Samlingen av Norge og kristningen av landet 800–1130* (The unification and Christianization of Norway, 800–1130). Oslo: Universitetsforlaget, 1977.

Andrews, Clarence. *Christmas in Iowa.* Iowa City: Midwest Heritage, 1979.

Asbjørnsen, P. C. [Clemens Bonifacius, pseud.] *Fornuftigt Madstel. En tidsmæssig Koge- og Husholdningsbog* (Commonsense cooking: A timely cooking and housekeeping book). Christiania, 1864.

Asbjørnsen, P. C., and Jørgen Moe. *Samlede eventyr* (Collected folktales). 2 vols. Oslo: Den norske Bokklubb, 1982, 1983.

Bache, Søren. *A Chronicle of Old Muskego: The Diary of Søren Bache, 1839–1847.* Trans. and ed. Clarence A. Clausen and Andreas Elviken. Northfield, Minn.: Norwegian-American Historical Association, 1951.

Bakken, Reidar. *Lad ingen sladdrelystne læse mine brever: Nordmenn blir amerikanarar. Brev hjemsendt frå norske emigranter frå 1844–1930* (Let no gossip-mongers read my letters: Norwegians become Americans. Letters sent home from Norwegian emigrants, 1844–1930). Fagernes: Valdres, 1995.

Baur, John E. *Christmas on the American Frontier, 1800–1900.* Caldwell, Idaho: Caxton, 1961.

Beeman, William O. "Freedom to Choose." In *Symbolizing America,* ed. Herve Varenne, 52–65. Lincoln: University of Nebraska Press, 1986.

Berg, Francie. *Ethnic Heritage in North Dakota.* Washington, D.C.: Attiyeh Foundation, 1983.

Berg, Knut Anders, Liv Berit Tessem, and Kjetil Wiedswang. *Julen i norsk og utenlandsk tradisjon* (Christmas in Norwegian and foreign tradition). Oslo: Gyldendal, [1994].

Bergan, Gunvor Øverland, and Trinelise Dysthe. *Hjemme i Norge. Tradisjon og fornyelse* (At home in Norway: Tradition and renewal). Oslo: Cappelen, 1994.

Bergesen, B. F. "Julemindet-Barnesindet" (The memory of Christmas—the mind of a child). *Jul i Vesterheimen,* 1914 (no pagination).

Bergmann, Leola Nelson. *Americans from Norway.* New York: Lippincott, 1950.

Bergstøl, Tore. *Atterljom: Folkeminne fraa smaadalene kring Lindesnes II* (Echoes: Folklore from the small valleys around Lindesness II). Norsk

Folkeminnelag (NFL) 22. Oslo: Universitets-forlaget, 1930.

Birkeli, Fridtjov. *Norge møter kristendommen. Fra vikingtiden til ca. 1050* (Norway meets Christianity: From the Viking age until about 1050). Oslo: Aschehoug, 1979.

Blegen, Theodore. *Norwegian Migration to America: The American Transition*. New York: Arno Press, 1969.

Bø, Olav. *Høgtider og minnedagar* (Holidays and days of remembrance). Oslo: Det Norske Samlaget, 1985.

——. "Madr er manns gaman. Høgtider i livet og året" (Annual holidays and rites of passage). In *Norrønn kulturhistorie* (Old Norse cultural history), ed. Olav Bø and Olav Høyland, 107–28. Oslo: Det Norske Samlaget, 1974.

——. *Norske årshøgtider* (Norwegian annual holidays). Oslo: Universitetsforlaget, 1980.

——. *Vår norske jul* (Our Norwegian Christmas). Oslo: Det Norske Samlaget, 1986.

Bø, Olav, and Ørnulf Hodne. *Norsk natur i folketru og segn* (Norwegian nature in folk belief and legend). Oslo: Det Norske Samlaget, 1974.

Bøckman, Marcus O. "Jul i Vesterheimen" (Christmas in the Western Home). *Jul i Vesterheimen,* 1936 (no pagination).

Boe, Eugene, "Pioneers to Eternity." In *The Immigrant Experience: The Anguish of Becoming American,* ed. Thomas C. Wheeler, 51–83. New York: Dial Press, 1971.

Borgen, H. H. "Jul." *Nord-Norge,* 1941–46, 15–16.

Borgstrom, Greta, and Birgit Danfors. *Scandinavian Cookbook: A Culinary Guide to Denmark, Finland, Norway, and Sweden.* Oslo: Gyldendal, 1965.

Brandt, O. E. "Juletréts historie" (The history of the Christmas tree). *Jul i Vesterheimen,* 1918 (no pagination).

Brimi, Arne. *A Taste of Norway: A Cookbook Based on Nature's Own Ingredients.* Oslo: Norwegian University Press, 1987.

Brown, Dale. *The Cooking of Scandinavia.* New York: Time-Life Books, 1968.

Bruce, G. M. "Christmas on the Prairies." *Jul i Vesterheimen,* 1912 (no pagination).

Brunvand, Jan Harold. *Norwegian Settlers in Alberta.* Canadian Centre for Folk Culture Studies, paper no. 8. Ottawa: National Museum of Man, 1974.

Buckeye Cookery and Practical Housekeeping. Ed. Estelle Woods Wilcox. St. Paul: Minnesota Historical Society Press, 1988.

Charles, Todd. "Art of Julebukking Is Lost on Younger Generation." *Blue Earth (Minn.) Post/ Ambassador,* December 21, 1987.

Christiansen, Reidar. *Folktales of Norway.* Chicago: University of Chicago Press, 1964.

Christianson, John. "Christmas in Iowa, 1862 and 1853." Paper presented at the Decorah (Iowa) Symra Society, 1980.

Crispino, James A. *The Assimilation of Ethnic Groups: The Italian Case.* Staten Island, N.Y.: Center for Migration Studies, 1980.

Dahl, Dorothea. "The Beckoning Distance." *Jul i Vesterheimen,* 1926 (no pagination).

——. "Det gamle bokskap" (The old bookcase). *Jul i Vesterheimen,* 1919 (no pagination).

Daniels, H. K. *Home Life in Norway.* New York: Macmillan, 1911.

Dieseth, John. *The Life and Times of John Dieseth: Norwegian Boyhood, Immigrant, Engineer, and Road Builder.* Self-published, n.d.

Espeland, Velle. *Tippoldemors oppskrifter* (Great-grandmother's recipes). NFL 133. Oslo: Norsk Folkeminnelag, 1990.

Estness, Borghild. *Josie Rykken's Family: A Story about the Immigrants from Hardanger, Norway.* [Minneapolis, Minn.]: Estness, 1983.

Falcone, Patricia. "'Julebuk'—Lively Old Norse Yule Custom." *Madison (Wis.) Capital Times,* December 24, 1965.

Familiens julebok (The family Christmas book). Oslo: Mortensen, 1962.

Field, Jerome P. "Folktales from North Dakota, 1910." *Western Folklore* 17 (1958): 29–33.

Fuhr, Anna Dahl. "Severini & Co." *Jul i Vesterheimen,* 1935 (no pagination).

Gans, Herbert. "Symbolic Ethnicity: The Future of Ethnic Groups and Cultures in America." *Ethnic and Racial Studies* 2 (1979): 1–20.

Gesme, Ann Urness. *Between Rocks and Hard Places.* Cedar Rapids, Iowa: Gesme Enterprises, 1993.

Giles, J. A. *The Venerable Bede's Ecclesiastical History of England.* London: Bell, 1900.

Gjerde, Jon. *From Peasants to Farmers: The Migration from Balestrand, Norway, to the Upper Middle West.* New York: Cambridge University Press, 1985.

Glassie, Henry. *All Silver and No Brass: An Irish Christmas Mumming.* Philadelphia: University of Pennsylvania Press, 1983.

Grose, I. F. "A Pioneer Boy's Experiences in a Corner of Goodhue County." *Jul i Vesterheimen,* 1919 (no pagination).

Gulbranssen, Trygve. *Beyond Sing the Woods.* Trans. Naomi Walford. New York: Literary Guild, 1936. Originally published as *Og bakom synger skogene.* Oslo: Aschehoug, 1933.

Guterman, Stanley S. "The Americanization of Norwegian Immigrants: A Study in Historical Sociology." *Sociology and Social Research* 52 (1968): 252–70.

Hale, Frederick, ed. *Their Own Saga: Letters from the Norwegian Global Migration.* Minneapolis: Minnesota Press, 1986.

Hambro, Johan. "Mitt møte med det norske Amerika" (My meeting with the Norwegian-America). In *Møte med Amerika. 25 nordmenn oppfatter amerikansk historie og nåtid,* ed. Bjørn Jensen. Oslo: Aschehoug, 1976.

Heilborn, Bertha L. "Christmas and New Year's on the Frontier." *Minnesota History* 16 (1935): 373–90.

Helgeson, Thor. *Folkesagn og folketro. Fortalt af de første Nybyggere paa Indilandet, Wisconsin* (Folk legends and belief: Told by the first settlers on the Indian Land). Eau Claire, Wis.: Fremad, 1923.

Helland, Amund. *Topografisk-statistisk beskrivelse over Nordre Bergenshus Amt.* Kristiania: Aschehoug, 1901.

Henriksen, Vera. *Christmas in Norway: Past and Present.* Oslo: Aschehoug, 1970.

Hermundstad, Knut. *I manns minne. Gamal Valdreskultur III* (In living memory: Old Valdres culture). NFL 55. Oslo: Universitetsforlaget, 1944.

——. *Samversskikkar i Valdres.* Gjøvik, 1975.

Hetle, Erik. "Det ble jul lell" (Christmas came after all). *Jul i Vesterheimen,* 1951, 42–43.

——. "Jul i Nordfjord" (Christmas in Nordfjord). *Nordfjordlagets Aarbok 1920,* 15–19.

Hildahl, Hild Næss. "Vi i Trollstua. Et norsk dukkeeventyr fra Minnesota-skogen" (We in the trollhouse: A Norwegian doll-fairy tale from the Minnesota woods). *Jul i Vesterheimen,* 1945, 8–12.

Hodne, Bjarne, and Anna-Marie Wiersholm. *Glædelig jul! Glimt fra julefeiringens historie* (Merry Christmas! Glimpses from the history of celebrating Christmas). Oslo: Universitetsforlaget, 1982.

Hodne, Ørnulf. *Jul i Norge. Gamle og nye tradisjoner* (Christmas in Norway. Old and new traditions). Oslo: Cappelen, 1997.

Høifjell, Johannes. *Lutherdom med lutefisk, etc.* (Lutheranism with lutefisk, etc.). Minneapolis: Self-published, [1920].

Holbek, Bengt, and Iørn Piø. *Fabeldyr og sagnfolk* (Animals and people of legend and fable). Copenhagen: Politikken, 1979.

Holm, Bill. *Faces of Christmas Past.* Afton, Minn.: Afton Historical Society Press, 1998.

Holvik, J. A. "Et glimt av vaart virke" (A glimpse at our work). *Jul i Vesterheimen,* 1938.

Innli, Kjell E., ed. *The Norwegian Kitchen.* Kristiansund: KOM, 1993.

Jacobson, Clara. "Childhood Memories." Unpublished memoir. Publication rights held by Norwegian-American Historical Association, St. Olaf College, Northfield, Minn.

Jensen, Bjørn, ed. *Møte med Amerika. 25 Nordmenn oppfatter amerikansk historie og nåtid* (Meeting with America: Twenty-five Norwegian perceptions of the American past and present). Oslo: Aschehoug, 1976.

Jensvold, John R. "In Search of a Norwegian-American Working Class." *Minnesota History* 50, no. 2 (1986): 63–70.

Johansen, Jahn Otto. *Lutefisk—Tradisjon—Tilbered-ning—Tilbehør* (Lutefisk—tradition—prepara-tion—accompaniments). Oslo: Teknologisk For-lag, 1997.

Johansen, Tom B., and Jan-Kåre Øien. *Håndbok for lutefiskelskere* (Handbook for lutefisk lovers). Oslo: Teknologisk Forlag, 1996.

Johnson, Eivind. "Den sterkeste vant" (The strongest won). *Jul i Vesterheimen*, 1953.

Johnson, O. S. *Nybyggerhistorie fra Spring Grove og omegn, Minnesota* (Settlement history from Spring Grove and the surrounding area). Min-neapolis: Forfatterens forlag; Folkebladet, 1920.

Johnson, Simon. "Blaa øine" (Blue eyes). *Jul i Vester-heimen*, 1914 (no pagination).

Kaplan, Anne R., Marjorie A. Hoover, and Willard B. Moore, eds. *The Minnesota Ethnic Food Book.* St. Paul: Minnesota Historical Society Press, 1986.

King, Mary. "Memoirs of a Prairie Girlhood." Typed manuscript, Minnesota Historical Society, 1928.

Klaveness, Thoralv. *Blandt udvandrede nordmænd. Vore landsmænds liv og vilkaar i den nye verden* (Among emigrated Norwegians: Lives and liv-ing conditions of our compatriots in the New World). Kristiania: Cammermeyer, 1904.

Klymasz, Robert B. "From Immigrant to Ethnic Folklore." *Journal of the Folklore Institute* 10 (1973): 131–39.

Knaplund, Paul. *Moorings Old and New: Entries in an Immigrant Log.* Madison, Wis.: State Histor-ical Society, 1963.

Knutson, Knute. "Minner fra en norsk bygd i Minne-sota" (Memories from a Norwegian community in rural Minnesota). *Jul i Vesterheimen*, 1941, 54–56.

Koren, Dikka Hjort, "Minner fra Paint Creek pres-tegård" (Memories from Paint Creek parsonage). *Jul i Vesterheimen*, 1941, 18–21.

Koren, Elisabeth. *The Diary of Elisabeth Koren, 1853–1855.* Trans. and ed. David T. Nelson. Northfield, Minn.: Norwegian-American Historical Associ-ation, 1955.

Kreidberg, Marjorie. *Food on the Frontier: Minnesota Cooking from 1850 to 1900.* St. Paul: Minnesota His-torical Society Press, 1975.

Lagerquist, L. DeAne. *In America the Men Milk the Cows: Factors of Gender, Ethnicity, and Religion in the Americanization of Norwegian-American Women.* Brooklyn, N.Y.: Carlson, 1990.

Lagli, Nils. *Julspel i Ranen* (Christmas games in Ranen). NFL 139. Oslo: Norsk Folkeminnelag, 1994.

Landstad, M. B. *Mytiske sagn fra Telemarken* (Myth-ical legends from Telemark). Oslo: Norske Fol-keminnelag, 1926.

Landsverk, Halvor, ed. *Gilde og gjestebod.* (Celebra-tions and banquets). Oslo: Det Norske Samlaget, 1967.

Larsen, Dina, and Dorthea Rabbe. *Norsk mat. Upp-skrifter på najsonale retter fra eldre og nyare tid* (Norwegian food: Recipes for national dishes from the past and present). Oslo: Cappelens, 1932.

Larson, Laurence M. *The Log Book of a Young Immi-grant.* Northfield, Minn.: Norwegian-American Historical Association, 1939.

Legwold, Gary. *The Last Word on Lefse: Heartwarm-ing Stories—and Recipes Too.* Cambridge, Minn.: Adventure, 1992.

———. *The Last Word on Lutefisk: True Tales of Cod and Tradition.* Minneapolis: Conrad Henry Press, 1996.

Levenstein, Harvey A. *Paradox of Plenty: A Social History of Eating in Modern America.* New York: Oxford, 1993.

———. *Revolution at the Table: The Transformation of the American Diet.* New York: Oxford University Press, 1988.

Levorsen, Barbara. "Our Bread and Meat." *NAHA Studies and Records* 22 (1965): 178–97.

Løkensgaard, K. "Jul i gamle dage" (Christmas in the old days). *Hallingen*, 1919/20, 4–7.

Lovoll, Odd. *The Promise Fulfilled: A Portrait of Norwegian-Americans Today.* Minneapolis: Uni-versity of Minnesota Press, 1998.

———. *The Promise of America: A History of the Norwegian-American People.* Minneapolis: Uni-versity of Minnesota Press, 1984.

———, ed. *Cultural Pluralism versus Assimilation: The Views of Waldemar Ager.* Northfield, Minn.:

Norwegian-American Historical Association, 1977.

Lund, Einar. "Solstraalen i nybygget" (The sunbeam of the settlement). *Jul i Vesterheimen,* 1945, 25–29.

Lund Troels. *Dagligt liv i Norden i det 16de Aarhundrede* (Daily life in Scandinavia in the sixteenth century). Vol. 7, *Aarlige Fester* (Annual celebrations). Copenhagen: Gyldendal, 1903.

Marling, Karal Ann. *As Seen on TV: The Visual Culture of Everyday Life in the 1950s.* Cambridge: Harvard University Press, 1994.

Martinsen, Haakon. "Naar hjertet begynner aa banke" (When the heart starts beating). *Jul i Vesterheimen,* 1955, 12–15.

Mellbye, Anne-Lise. *Den store juleboken for hele familien* (The big Christmas book for the entire family). Oslo: Gyldendal, 1988.

———. *Jul i Norge* (Christmas in Norway). Oslo: Gyldendal, 1995.

Midtlien, J. N. "En jul i Coon Valley gamle prestegaard" (A Christmas at the old Coon Valley parsonage). *Jul i Vesterheimen,* 1946, 27–30.

Miller, O. A. "Julen i Norge og julen i Amerika" (Christmas in Norway and Christmas in America). *Nord-Norge* 1941–46, 6.

Minneapolis Tidende's norsk-amerikanske kogebog. En samling af opskrifter paa gamle og nye retter (Minnesota Tidende's Norwegian-American cookbook: A collection of recipes for old and new dishes). Minneapolis, Minn.: Guldbrandsen, 1907.

Moberg, John. *Graut* (Porridge). Oslo: Det Norske Samlaget, 1989.

Mohn, George. *Cook Book of Popular Norse Recipes.* Northfield, Minn.: Mohn Printing Co. [1924].

Moore, Willard B. "Ritual and Remembrance in Minnesota Folk Celebrations." *Humanities Education* 3 (September 1986): 43–52.

Munch, Caja. *The Strange American Way: The Letters of Caja Munch from Wiota, Wisconsin, 1855–1859.* Carbondale: Southern Illinois University Press, [1970].

Myking, Thom. "Juleminder" (Christmas memories). *Hallingen,* 1918, 68–71.

Nelson, Hilda. "Jul hjemme hos mor" (Christmas at Mom's). *Jul i Vesterheimen,* 1954, 30–34.

Nergaard, Sigurd. *Gard og grend. Folkeminne fraa Østerdalen* (Farm and neighborhood: Folklore from Østerdalen). NFL 3. Oslo: Norsk Folkeminnelag, 1921.

———. *Hulder og trollskap. Folkeminne fraa Østerdalen IV* (Hidden folk and magic: Folklore from Østerdalen). NFL 11. Oslo: Norsk Folkeminnelag, 1925.

Nilsen, Frida. *Growing Up in the Old Parsonage.* Lake Mills: Graphic Publishing Co., 1975.

Nissenbaum, Stephen. *The Battle for Christmas.* New York: Knopf, 1996.

Nordland, Odd. *Brewing and Beer Traditions in Norway: The Social Anthropological Background of the Brewing Industry.* Oslo: Universitetsforlaget, 1969.

Norstog, Inga Bredesen, "Til Diderikke Brandts minne" (To the memory of Diderikke Brandt). *Jul i Vesterheimen,* 1950, 10–15.

Notaker, Henry. *Ganens makt. Norsk kokekunst og matkultur gjennom tusen år* (The power of the palate: A thousand years of Norwegian cooking and food culture). Oslo: Aschehoug, 1993.

———. "Kokebokas nasjonale gjennombrudd. De første norske kokebøkene 1831–46" (The international breakthrough of the cookbook: The first Norwegian cookbooks, 1831–46). *Nytt norsk tidsskrift* 8 (1991): 325–38.

Ny norsk-dansk og amerikansk kogebog. Samlet og bearbeidet af en husmoder (New Norwegian-Danish cookbook: Collected and edited by a housewife). Chicago: Anderson, 1905

Odegard, Ethel J. *A Norwegian Family Transplanted.* Decorah, Iowa: Anundsen, 1974.

Oleson, Thurine. *Wisconsin My Home,* by Erna Oleson Xan as told by her mother Thurine Oleson. Madison: University of Wisconsin Press, 1950.

Olson, Ernst W. "Loyalty under fire." *Jul i Vesterheimen,* 1924 (no pagination).

Osa, Harald, and Gudrun Ulltveit. *Norsk mat gjennom tidene. Tradisjonsmat fra naturens spiskammer* (Norwegian food through the ages: Traditional foods from nature's pantry). Oslo: Teknologisk Forlag, 1993.

Osland, Birger. *A Long Pull from Stavanger: The Reminiscences of a Norwegian Emigrant.* Northfield, Minn.: Norwegian-American Historical Association, 1945.

Øverland, Orm. *The Western Home: A Literary History of Norwegian America.* Northfield, Minn.: Norwegian-American Historical Association, 1996.

"Patriotenes fest med Chester og Sputnik" (The patriots' party with Chester and Sputnik). *Aftenposten,* October 20, 1993.

Pearson, Eva. *I Remember, I Remember! Your Viking Heritage: The Ancestors and Descendants of Otto Alfred Pearson, 1887–1973, and Ingeborg Nornes, 1892–1985, Olav Marius Mykleby, 1885–1956, and Minnie Boukind, 1890–1985.* St. Paul, Minn.: E. M. M. Pearson, 1989.

Peterson, Otis S. "Vegen tilbake" (The way back). *Jul i Vesterheimen,* 1949, 9–15.

Preus, Lulla. "Minder fra den gamle Paint Creek præstegaard" (Memories from the old Paint Creek parsonage). *Symra. En aarbog for norske paa begge sider af havet* (Symra: A yearbook for Norwegians on both sides of the sea) 7 (1911): 1–15.

Raaen, Aagot. *Grass of the Earth.* Northfield: Norwegian-American Historical Association, 1950; St. Paul: Minnesota Historical Society Press, 1994.

Reese, Lisa M. "Julebokking . . . A look at the tradition." *The Hancock (Minn.) Record,* December 1986.

Reitan, Norman. *Bright Patches: Growing Up Norwegian in Shawano County, Wisconsin.* Ed. Rolf H. Erickson and Wilbert Peterson. Chicago: Self-published, 1991.

Remme, C. R. "Jul blandt nybyggerne" (Christmas among the settlers). *Samband,* December 1914, 71–74.

Restad, Penne L. *Christmas in America: A History.* New York: Oxford University Press, 1995.

Riddervold, Astri. *Lutefisk, Rakefisk, and Herring in Norwegian Tradition.* Oslo: Novus Press, 1990.

Ristad, D. G. "Slik holder vi jul" (This is how we keep Christmas). *Jul i Vesterheimen,* 1923 (no pagination).

Rønnevik, Hans. "Det gaar saa underlig til" (Things turn out so strangely). *Jul i Vesterheimen,* 1932 (no pagination).

Rønning, N. N. "Når et folk mister sitt morsmål" (When a people lose their native language). *Jul i Vesterheimen,* 1943, 35–37.

———. "Some Experiences of a Newcomer," *Jul i Vesterheimen,* 1912 (no pagination).

Rosholt, Malcolm. *From the Indian Land: First-hand Accounts of Central Wisconsin Pioneer Life.* Iola, Wis.: Krause, 1985.

Ruud, Marit Ekne. *Hverdagsmat på landsbygda ved århundreskiftet. Fra svarene på NEG's spørrelister* (Everyday food in rural areas around the turn of the century: From the answers to Norwegian Ethnological Institute's questionnaire). Oslo: Norges etnografiske institutt, 1990.

Rygh, George Taylor, "The Dominie." *Jul i Vesterheimen,* 1930 (no pagination).

Salins, Peter. *Assimilation American Style.* New York: Basic Books, 1997.

Sawyer, Birgit, and Peter Sawyer. *Medieval Scandinavia: From Conversion to Reformation, circa 800–1500.* Minneapolis: University of Minnesota Press, 1993.

Schmidt, Leigh Eric. *Consumer Rites: The Buying and Selling of American Holidays.* Princeton, N.J.: Princeton University Press, 1995.

Schultz, April. *Ethnicity on Parade: Inventing the Norwegian-American through Celebration.* Amherst: University of Massachusetts Press, 1994.

———. "A Peculiar People: Celebration, Historical Memory and the Creation of Ethnic Identity among Norwegian-Americans in the 1920s." Ph.D. dissertation, University of Minnesota, 1991.

Scott, Astrid Karlsen. *Authentic Norwegian Cooking.* Olympia, Wash.: Nordic Adventures, 1995.

———. *Ekte norsk jul: Traditional Norwegian Christmas.* Vol 1. Olympia, Wash.: Nordic Adventures Press, 1992

——. *Ekte norsk jul: Traditional Norwegian Christmas Foods.* Vol 2. Olympia, Wash.: Nordic Adventures Press, 1993.

Seasons to Remember: Barnesville, the First Hundred Years. Barnesville, Minn.: Barnesville Centennial Corporation, 1982.

Sivertsen, Birgir. *Mari Vassause og den hellige Margareta: Gamle Norske merkedager* (Mari ladle and St. Margaret: Old Norwegian calendar days). [Oslo]: Andresen og Butenschøn, 1998.

Skandinavisk-amerikansk kogebog, af en husmoder (Scandinavian-American cookbook, by a housewife). Chicago, 1884.

Skårdal, Dorothy Burton. *The Divided Heart: Scandinavian Immigrant Experience through Literary Sources.* Lincoln: University of Nebraska Press, 1974.

——. "Et samfunn av innvandrerer" (A society of immigrants). In *Møte med Amerika. 25 Nordmenn oppfatter amerikansk historie og nåtid,* ed. Bjørn Jensen. Oslo: Aschehoug, 1976.

Snorri Sturluson. *Heimskringla: The Sagas of the Viking Kings of Norway.* Trans. Lee Hollander. Oslo: Stenersen, 1987.

Snyder, Phillip. *The Joys of Christmas Past: A Social History.* New York: Dodd, Mead, 1985.

Solberg, Aud Ross. "Gamle juleskikkar i Sogn— deira opphav og utvikling" (Old Christmas customs in Sogn—their origin and development). In *Årbok for Sogn 1999.* Kaupanger: Historielaget for Sogn, Sogn Folkemuseum, 111–31.

"Some People Hold Lutefisk in Esteem; Others Hold Noses." *Wall Street Journal,* December 14, 1982.

Stangland, Red. *Norwegian Home Companion.* New York: Dorset Press, 1990.

——. *O Lutefisk: A Nostalgic Look Back to the "Good Old Days" of the 1920s and 30s Growing Up in a Small Town in a Norwegian Family.* Sioux Falls, S.D.: Norse Press, 1985.

Stephenson, Michael. *The Christmas Almanac.* New York: Oxford University Press, 1992.

Stern, Stephen. "Ethnic Folklore and the Folklore of Ethnicity." *Western Folklore* 36 (1977): 7–32.

——. "Untangling Complexities of Ethnic Sources, Representations, and Meanings." In *Creative Ethnicity: Symbols and Strategies of Contemporary Ethnic Life,* ed. Stephen Stern and John Allan Cicala. Logan: Utah State University Press, 1991.

Stokker, Kathleen. "Anti-Nazi Card Tricks: Underground Christmas Cards in Occupied Norway." *Journal of Popular Culture* 31, no. 1 (1997): 189–97.

——. "Between Sin and Salvation: The Human Condition in Legends of the Black Book Minister." *Scandinavian Studies* 67 (1995): 91–108.

——. *Folklore Fights the Nazis: Humor in Occupied Norway, 1940–1945.* Madison: University of Wisconsin Press, 1996.

——. "*Julebukk:* Christmas Masquerading in Norwegian America." In *Norwegian-American Essays,* ed. Knut Djupedal et al., 28–39. Oslo, Hamar, Stavanger: Norwegian-American Historical Association, 1993.

——. "*Julebukk:* The Norwegian Art of Christmas Fooling." *Sons of Norway Viking,* December 1990.

——. "A Measure of Time." *Sons of Norway Viking,* April 1999, 12–13, 28.

——. "ML3005 'The Would-Be Ghost': Why Be He a Ghost? Lutheran Views of Confession and Salvation in Legends of the Black Book Minister." *Arv: Scandinavian Yearbook of Folklore* 47 (1991): 143–52.

——. "To Catch a Thief: Binding and Loosing and the Black Book Minister." *Scandinavian Studies* 61(1989): 353–74.

Storaker, Joh. Th. *Tiden i den norske Folketro* (Time in Norwegian folk belief). NFL 2. Oslo: Norsk Folkeminnelag, 1921.

Strandvold, Georg. "Maleriet" (The painting). *Jul i Vesterheimen,* 1938 (no pagination).

Strømstad, Aase. *Eat the Norway: Traditional Dishes and Specialties from Norwegian Cooking.* Trans. Mary Lee Nielsen. Oslo: Aschehoug, 1984.

Sundt, Eilert. *Om Rensligheds-Stellet i Norge* (About cleanliness in Norway). Christiania, 1869.

Svendsen, Gro. *Frontier Mother: The Letters of Gro Svendsen.* Trans. and ed. Pauline Farseth and Theodore Blegen. Northfield, Minn.: Norwegian-American Historical Association, 1950.

Takla, Knut. *Det norske folk i de forenede stater. Deres daglige liv og økonomiske stilling, historik over Amerika—landets fremtidsmuligheter for en indvandrer* (The Norwegian people in the United States: Their daily life and economic postion, the historical background of America—the country's future possibilities for an immigrant). Kristiania [Oslo]: Stenersen, 1913.

Teigen, Knut. *Ligt og uligt. Skisser, humoresker, eventyr og pennebilleder fra livet blandt vestens vikinger* (A little bit of everything: Sketches, humoresques, fairy tales, and drawings from life among the Vikings of the West). Minneapolis, Minn.: Kreidt, 1907.

Tenfjord, Jo, and Toril Bang Lancelot, eds. *Den store fest- og høytidsboka* (The big book of celebrations and holidays). Oslo: Aschehoug, n.d.

Touchet, Alexis. "The Norwegian Christmas Kaffebord." *Gourmet,* December 1990.

Tunheim, John R. *A Scandinavian Saga: Pioneering in New Folden Township, Marshall County, Minnesota, 1882–1905.* Newfolden, Minn.: Self-published, 1984.

Ueland, Andreas. *The Recollections of an Immigrant.* New York: Minton Balch, 1929.

Ulvestad, Ivar, ed. *Vennlig hilsen: Postkortets historie i Norge* (Best regards: The history of the postcard in Norway). Oslo: Aventura, n.d.

Vangsnes, O. P. "Jeg glemmer aldrig den første jul" (I'll never forget the first Christmas). *Jul i Vesterheimen,* 1914 (no pagination).

Vasvik, Stian. "Aqua Vita—fra medisin til juledrikk" (Aquavit—from medicine to Christmas drink). *The Norseman,* November 1994, 36–37.

Veblen, A. A. "Jul i Manitowoc-Skogen" (Christmas in the Manitowoc woods). *Sambandet Maanedskrift* 93 (January 1916): 134–48.

Waits, William B. *The Modern Christmas in America: A Cultural History of Gift Giving.* New York: NYU Press, 1993.

Walker, Williston, Richard A. Norris, David W. Lotz, and Robert T. Handy. *A History of the Christian Church.* New York: Scribner, 1918; reprint, 1985.

Wallace, Carol McD. *Victorian Treasures.* New York: Abrams, 1996.

Waters, Mary. *Ethnic Options: Choosing Identities in America.* Berkeley: University of California Press, 1990.

Welsch, Roger L. "Lutefisk: Food as Symbol—The Mysterious Ritual of the Norwegian-American Christmas Dinner." *The World and I* 2 (December 1987): 462–68.

Wheeler, Thomas, ed. *The Immigrant Experience: The Anguish of Becoming American.* New York: Dial Press, 1971.

Williams, Mary Wilhelmina. "Scandinavian Qualities and American Ideals." *Jul i Vesterheimen,* 1921 (no pagination).

Wilson, Aaste. "Live blant nybyggjarane." *Telesoga* 33 (September 1917): 30–32.

Winjum, Orel R. "Christmas on the Farm." In "Farm Stories, Deer Township, Roseau Co., Minnesota." St. Paul, Minnesota Historical Society, February 1973, 1–19.

Winsnes, Hanna. *Lærebog i de forskjellige Grene af Husholdningen* (Textbook in the various branches of housekeeping). 11th ed. Christiania: Cappelen, 1880.

[Wisness, Hilda, and Levard Quarre]. *Viking Early Settlement Days, 1886–1936.* Viking, N.D.: Self-published, 1936.

Zempel, Solveig, ed. *In Their Own Words: Letters from Norwegian Immigrants.* Minneapolis: University of Minnesota Press, 1991.

Index

Illustration Credits

Vesterheim Norwegian-American Museum, Decorah, Iowa: 14, 129, 186 and 188 (prints by Darrell Henning), 221 (courtesy Luis Torres), 225, 237

Courtesy of the author: 22, 53, 182

Anne-Lise Mellbye, Den store juleboken for hele familien: 36, 88

Nasjonalgalleriet, Oslo: 44 (photo J. Lathion, © Nasjonalgalleriet)

Norsk Folkemuseum: 49, 84, 93

Oslo Bymuseum: 63, 98

Luther College Archives, Decorah, Iowa: 131

St. Olaf College Archives, Northfield, Minnesota: 135

Minnesota Historical Society: 159, 163, 185, 199, 203, 209, 214, 235, 241, 265 (Liza Fourré)

Gary Legwold: 245

St. Paul Pioneer Press: 246 (Sully)

Darrell Henning: 249

Irene Small: 273

Kathleen Stokker is a professor of Norwegian at Luther College in Decorah, Iowa. She is the author of *Folklore Fights the Nazis: Humor in Occupied Norway, 1940–1945* and the forthcoming *Remedies and Rituals: Folk Medicine in Norway and the New Land* (Minnesota Historical Society Press, 2007). She has coauthored a widely used Norwegian-language textbook and written many articles on folklore and humor, which have appeared in *The Journal of American Folklore; Humor, the International Journal of Humor Research; The Journal of Popular Culture; Arv, the Scandinavian Yearbook of Folklore;* and *Scandinavian Studies.* In 2005 Ms. Stokker received Norway's prestigious St. Olav Medal for service and achievements in strengthening the bonds between Norway and Norwegian Americans. She travels to Norway every summer to hike in the mountains and eat Freia chocolate.

Keeping Christmas was designed at the Minnesota Historical Society Press by Will Powers. The book was set in type by Allan S. Johnson, Phoenix Type, Milan, Minnesota, and was printed by Malloy Lithographing, Ann Arbor. The typefaces are Galliard, designed by Matthew Carter in 1978, and Amerigo, designed by Gerard Unger in 1987.